The Rise and Fall of State-Owned Enterprise in the Western World

This book examines the rise and fall in the twentieth-century Western world of state-owned enterprises, a chief instrument of state intervention in the economy. It offers historical perspectives on the origins and purpose of state-owned enterprises, their performance, and the reasons for their precipitate decline from their heyday in the 1960s to the waves of privatization in the 1980s and 1990s. Looking to the future as well as the past of state business, this book explores the concept of state-owned enterprise and its context in Western political economy, as well as the permutations and future prospects of the institution in practice. The contributors present studies of the development of state-owned enterprises in seven Western European countries and the United States.

Pier Angelo Toninelli is Professor of Economic History at the University of Milan–Bicocca.

COMPARATIVE PERSPECTIVES IN BUSINESS HISTORY

At the dawn of the twenty-first century the world economy is in the midst of the most profound transformation since the industrial revolution. Firms, communications systems, and markets for products, services, labor, and currencies are all breaking out of national boundaries. Business enterprises today must negotiate a global environment in order to innovate and to compete in ways that will protect or enhance their market shares. At the same time, they are finding it essential to understand the different perspectives growing out of local, regional, and national experiences with business and economic development. This has become a crucial competitive advantage to companies and a vital skill for those who study them. *Comparative Perspectives in Business History* explores these developments in a series of volumes that draw upon the best work of scholars from a variety of nations writing on the history of enterprise, public and private. The series encourages the use of new styles of analysis and seeks to enhance understanding of modern enterprise and its social and political relations, leaders, cultures, economic strategies, accomplishments, and failures.

Series Editors

Franco Amatori, *Bocconi University*
Louis Galambos, *The Johns Hopkins University*

Managing Editor

Madeleine Adams

Sponsors

Associazione per gli Studi Storici sull'Impresa (ASSI), Milan
Istituto di Storia Economica, Bocconi University, Milan
The Institute for Applied Economics and Study of Business Enterprise,
The Johns Hopkins University

The Rise and Fall of
State-Owned Enterprise in the
Western World

Edited by

PIER ANGELO TONINELLI

University of Milan-Bicocca

CAMBRIDGE
UNIVERSITY PRESS

PUBLISHED BY THE PRESS SYNDICATE OF THE UNIVERSITY OF CAMBRIDGE
The Pitt Building, Trumpington Street, Cambridge, United Kingdom

CAMBRIDGE UNIVERSITY PRESS
The Edinburgh Building, Cambridge CB2 2RU, UK
http://www.cup.cam.ac.uk
40 West 20th Street, New York, NY 10011-4211, USA
http://www.cup.org
10 Stamford Road, Oakleigh, Melbourne 3166, Australia
Ruiz de Alarcón 13, 28014 Madrid, Spain

First published 2000

Printed in the United States of America

Typeface ITC Garamond Book 10.25/13 pt.   *System* QuarkXPress [BTS]

A catalog record for this book is available from the British Library.

Library of Congress Cataloging in Publication Data
The rise and fall of state-owned enterprise in the western world /
edited by Pier Angelo Toninelli.
p. cm. – (Comparative perspectives in business history)
Revised papers from a conference held in Milan.
Includes bibliographical references and index.
ISBN 0-521-78081-0 (hb)
1. Government business enterprises – History.
I. Toninelli, Pierangelo Maria. II. Series.
HD3850.R49 2000 338.6'2'09–dc21 99-087918

ISBN 0 521 78081 0 hardback

Contents

Preface   *page* ix

Contributors   xii

PART I: SETTING THE STAGE

1 The Rise and Fall of Public Enterprise: The Framework   3
   Pier Angelo Toninelli

2 The Decline of State-Owned Enterprise and the New
   Foundations of the State–Industry Relationship   25
   Nicola Bellini

3 The Performance of State-Owned Enterprises   49
   Yair Aharoni

4 The Role of the State in Economic Growth   73
   Erik S. Reinert

PART II: NATIONAL CASES

5 The Rise and Fall of State-Owned Enterprise in Germany   103
   Ulrich Wengenroth

6 Beyond State and Market: Italy's Futile Search for
   a Third Way   128
   Franco Amatori

7 State Enterprise in Britain in the Twentieth Century   157
   Robert Millward

8 The Rise and Decline of State-Owned Industry in
   Twentieth-Century France   185
   Emmanuel Chadeau

9 The Rise and Decline of Spanish State-Owned Firms   208
   Albert Carreras, Xavier Tafunell, and Eugenio Torres

10 Fifty Years of State-Owned Industry in Austria, 1946–1996   237
   Dieter Stiefel

11 A Reluctant State and Its Enterprises: State-Owned
   Enterprises in the Netherlands in the "Long"
   Twentieth Century   253
   M. Davids and Jan L. van Zanden

12 State-Owned Enterprises in a Hostile Environment:
   The U.S. Experience   273
   Louis Galambos

   Conclusion: Schumpeter Revisited   303
   Louis Galambos and William Baumol

Index   311

Preface

State-owned enterprises (SOEs) have long stirred up intense debates and political struggles throughout the world. In recent years, public sentiment and academic reasoning about the role of the state in the economy have fluctuated sharply. During the 1980s and early 1990s, a major wave of disenchantment with state intervention swept through the industrial nations. In those years the fortunes of SOEs reached their nadir, and countries, such as Italy, that had previously resisted privatization started a massive dismantling of public undertakings. This movement resulted from the convergence of long-term forces and country-specific events, all of which are discussed in this book. The pro-market and anti-state climate of those years was reinforced by the sudden collapse of the socialist regimes of Eastern Europe and by the severe fiscal and monetary measures required of the members of the European Economic Community in order to meet the conditions of the Maastricht agreement.

In the second half of the 1990s, however, a new climate developed. In Eastern Europe the initial euphoria over the liberalization of the planned economies began to wane as the hard, grinding work of reconstruction continued. In Western Europe the recent success of center–left coalitions in France, Britain, Italy, and Germany brought the social price of economic change back into consideration. Judging from the Vienna Conference of December 1998, the emphasis now promises to be on

ix

growth, employment, and human capital formation rather than on fiscal and monetary issues. The pace of privatization and deregulation seems to have slowed. This does not mean that we will witness a massive return of the state to the economic stage or that the past experience of SOE will be repeated. What it does suggest is that Western countries will continue to debate and alter the role of the state, processes that will be influenced in important ways by global competition and increasing immigration. Perhaps the challenge for the market economies of the twenty-first century will be to invent some new public–private mixture, one that could well include SOEs as well as private, market-oriented organizations.

These experiences take us back to the fundamental question Albert Hirschman (1982, 3–4) has already asked: "whether our societies are in some way predisposed toward oscillations between periods of intense preoccupation with public issue[s] and of almost total concentration on individual improvement and private welfare goals." We may thus be living through either a recurrent cycle or a permanent secular trend in society's employment of SOEs. Several of the contributors to this volume – including myself – believe that the future may hold new cycles of increased dependence on SOEs. But other authors – including Louis Galambos and William Baumol, who wrote our Conclusion – think the evidence more strongly supports a secular decline in SOEs that will continue far into the future.

We leave our readers to decide which prophecy is most compelling. In any case, we will need to understand the rise and fall of SOEs in the past, the subject of this collection of essays. Our main purpose is to offer historical perspectives on the parabolic paths of SOEs in Western countries in the twentieth century: their origins, the motivations of their leaders, their performance, and the reasons for their decline. Our readers will then be able to judge for themselves whether the turn away from the state will be permanent.

It was these concerns that brought us to Milan, to a conference sponsored jointly by Bocconi University's Istituto di Storia Economica and Fondazione ASSI di Storia e Studie sul'Impresa. There we presented and discussed early drafts of the essays presented in this volume. In the months that followed, we revised and re-revised our papers with help from a number of colleagues, editors, and referees. The publication of this collection would not have been possible without their collaboration, and I am deeply indebted to all of them. I would like to thank the participants at the Milan Colloquium, and in particular Dieter Bös, Takeo

Kikkawa, Corrado Molteni, William Baumol, Vera Zamagni, Giovanni Federico, Alfredo Macchiati, and Renato Giannetti. Their comments have been helpful in preparing the final version of this volume, as have the suggestions of our three anonymous referees. Madeleine Adams did a superb job of editing our essays. Many thanks to our copy editor, Helen Greenberg, and our indexer, Shirley Kessel. Louise Calabro and the staff of Cambridge University Press shepherded this book through production with professionalism, grace, and unflagging good humor. Andrea Colli acted as a factotum without peer throughout the process. Special thanks go to my friends Lou Galambos and Franco Amatori, who have constantly taken a strong interest in this endeavor, never stinting with their good advice and stimulating ideas. None of them should be held responsible for any errors still present in the book.

P.A.T
Milan, January 2000

REFERENCE

Hirschman, A. O. 1982. *Shifting involvements: Private interest and public action.* Princeton, N.J.

Contributors

Yair Aharoni is Rector of the College of Management and Professor Emeritus at Tel-Aviv University.

Franco Amatori is Professor of Economic History at Bocconi University in Milan. He has written extensively on Italian business history. Together with Alfred Chandler and Takashi Hikino, he edited *Big Business and the Wealth of Nations*.

William Baumol is Professor of Economics and Director of the C. V. Starr Center for Applied Economics at New York University and Professor Emeritus at Princeton University.

Nicola Bellini is Associate Professor of Business Economics at the Scuola Superiore Sant'Anna in Pisa and author of books and essays on industrial policies and industry–state relationships.

Albert Carreras is Professor of Economic History at the University Pompeu Fabra, Barcelona.

Emmanuel Chadeau is Professor Emeritus of Contemporary History at the University Charles de Gaulle–Lille III.

M. Davids is Research Associate at the Technical University Eindhoven in the Netherlands. She is the author of *The Road to Independence:*

History of the Denationalization of the State Enterprise for Postal, Telegraph and Telephone Services (PTT) in 1989.

Louis Galambos is Professor of History at the Johns Hopkins University in Baltimore.

Robert Millward is Professor of Economic History at the University of Manchester. He has recently published two books on the British public sector, *The Political Economy of Nationalisation in Britain, 1920-1950* (edited with John Singleton) and *Public and Private Ownership of British Industry, 1820-1990* (with J. Foreman-Peck).

Erik S. Reinert is Senior Research Associate at SUM–The Centre for Development and the Environment, University of Oslo, and Head of Research at Norsk Investorforum, Oslo. He is the editor of *Evolutionary Economics and Income Inequalities*. Mail to the author may be addressed to esr@nifo.no.

Dieter Stiefel is Professor of Economic History at the University of Vienna and Director of the Schumpeter Society at the University for Economics and Business Administration in Vienna.

Xavier Tafunell is Professor of Economic History at the University Pompeu Fabra, Barcelona.

Pier Angelo Toninelli is Professor of Economic History at the University of Milan–Bicocca and Professor of Business History at the IULM of Milan. He is currently Scientific Secretary of ASSI, the Italian Association for the History of Enterprise.

Eugenio Torres is Professor of Applied Economics at the Complutense University of Madrid.

Jan L. van Zanden is Professor of Economic History at Utrecht University and Secretary General of the International Economic History Association. Among his publications is *The Economic History of the Netherlands in the Twentieth Century, 1914-1995*.

Ulrich Wengenroth is Professor of the History of Technology at the University of Technology, Munich, and Chairman of the Academic Council of the German Society for Business History.

PART I

Setting the Stage

1

The Rise and Fall of Public Enterprise

The Framework

PIER ANGELO TONINELLI

In recent times, the role and even the existence of public enterprise have been subjected to strong, often devastating criticism, both in economic-political literature and in sociopolitical debate. At the same time, the term and the concept of "nationalization," the main process by which state-owned enterprises (SOEs) are created, has been assuming a negative value. It is increasingly used in close connection with its opposite term, "privatization": this emphasizes the dramatic change that has taken place in the economic policies of most Western economies.

The declining fortune of public enterprise has to be explained primarily by its increasing economic, financial, and managerial difficulties, as the essays in this volume show. These difficulties derive from the public and political nature of SOE activities. A comprehensive survey of SOE history has to take into consideration changes in the social, economic, and political environments that have profoundly influenced the course of the twentieth century. The move to autarkic and state-controlled policies in many Southern and Central European countries, the diffusion of collectivism and socialism in Eastern European countries, and the progressive growth of mixed economies in Western European countries all should be considered reactions - albeit profoundly different ones - to the same issue: the deep crisis that struck liberal capitalism in the period between the two world wars. Different though they

3

were, these reactions shared at least two common features. First, there was a more or less explicit recognition that the free market economy had grown progressively weaker. Its very nature and viability were menaced by increasing failures and by the belief that the state could and should play a greater (or, for some, a total) role in overcoming these failures. Second, the enlargement of the public sector, mainly through the nationalization of a few strategic activities and/or industries, became a significant part of the new economic policies even where democracy remained intact.

The poor performance of mixed economies in the 1970s and 1980s, as well as the collapse of collectivist regimes in the early 1990s, contributed to a reappraisal of the economic role of the state in the West as well as elsewhere. It also challenged what in previous decades had been perceived as a necessary outcome of the evolution of capitalism: the notion of SOE and nationalization policy lost much of the thaumaturgic valence attributed to it by even progressive elites.

This essay introduces the theme of public enterprise in its historical perspective. The first section is devoted to a brief description of the motives and fields of activity of public enterprise; the middle three sections deal with SOE origins and evolution; and the last section introduces the issue of SOE decline.

Before proceeding, some terminological and conceptual issues need clarification. These concern the levels at which public authorities decide to intervene directly in the economy, as well as the forms that such intervention may assume. Generally speaking, and for the sake of simplicity, there are two levels of public enterprise: a central level (at which SOEs are created) and a local level (at which municipal companies usually operate). In the case of federal states such as Germany and the United States, however, the picture must be completed by introducing a third level, above that of the state, to which national/federal enterprises belong. In Germany, for example, national/federal companies are to be found in the railway and postal sectors and in industrial activities; state-owned (*Länder*) enterprises are to be found in infrastructure (and, before the Weimar Republic, in the railway sector) and industrial activities; and municipal companies are to be found in public utilities and savings banks.[1]

At the state level, the term "state-owned enterprise" provides only an approximate description of the complexity of forms and organizations

[1] See Wengenroth's essay.

that state companies may assume. This reaches an apogee of fantasy and ingenuity in the terminology and legal forms used in Italy, where state companies, state shareholding companies, state concerns, and so on have coexisted throughout the twentieth century.[2] Finally, considerable differences are to be found in the ways public enterprises are managed, as "state-owned enterprise" does not automatically mean "state-managed enterprise."[3] In this respect, the outcomes concerning economic performance can vary greatly, as shown in several essays in this volume.[4]

MOTIVES AND FIELDS OF ACTIVITY OF PUBLIC ENTERPRISE

Many factors explain the choice of nationalizing previously private activities or establishing state-owned and state-managed enterprises. Sometimes the motives for that choice are multiple, and sometimes they are not clearly defined or are even contradictory (Zamagni 1987, 122). In a few cases, the origin of a public enterprise cannot be fully explained in terms of deliberate choice; elements of chance must be introduced. Examples of this have been adduced in the cases of the nationalization of Volkswagen in Germany and in the 1937 transformation of the Institute per la Ricostrugione Industriale (IRI) into a permanent public agency in Italy.[5]

At some risk of overgeneralization, the motives for nationalization can, however, be grouped into three main categories. First, there are political and ideological reasons for nationalization. These, of course, were fundamental in the policies that led to collectivist economies in Communist countries. They also played an important role in the nationalization programs of Western countries in the post–World War II period. Such nationalization programs were based on the belief that enlarging public properties and activities could open the way to a fundamental change in the distribution of power within society, thus engendering a

[2] See, for instance, Bianchi 1994; Posner and Woolf 1967; Saraceno 1975; and Amatori's essay.

[3] Nor can we exclude from consideration private companies managed as state companies (e.g., where the state appoints CEOs and other managers), as Chadeau argues in his essay.

[4] See the essays by Aharoni, Davids and van Zanden, and Millward.

[5] On Volkswagen, Wengenroth (this volume) speaks of nationalization by default, as the state was forced to intervene in the sale by the default of other possible buyers. The transformation of IRI has been seen as "more the result of historical accident than of deliberate political decision" (Shonfield 1965, 178), but on this point see the discussion in Amatori's essay.

new socioeconomic equilibrium based on the diminished power of private capital and the increased power of labor. Further, SOE executives are accountable to the whole community for their decisions, not just to private shareholders. "At the base of the pyramid, in the enterprise, the essential self-government function should be assigned to workers and management to extend the idea of community life"; the nationalization process can be considered "as an instrument for achieving 'genuine' industrial democracy" (J. Delors as quoted in Bös 1986, 26). This ideological and political belief was shared mainly by the progressive – Labour, Socialist, and Social Democratic – parties. It was not by chance that the main waves of nationalization occurred in France, Austria, Great Britain, and the Netherlands when these parties were in control.[6] A strong ideological bias also characterized the nationalization policies of the fascist regimes in Italy, Spain, and Germany. SOEs in these countries were conceived as instruments for achieving autarky and for forcing the economy and society toward their "superior" destiny – that is, the power policy of the nation-state. Sometimes the reasons for nationalization were more strictly political. According to Stiefel, postwar nationalization in Austria is to be explained primarily by the desire of both of the main parties not to leave former German properties in foreign (that is, Allied) hands. Chadeau shows that France's nationalization wave of the early 1980s was perceived as a way of protecting France from the globalization of the economy and from competition among European Economic Community (EEC) firms.[7] Millward stresses a "distinctly national focus" in Britain's nationalization wave of the 1940s linked to the postwar reconstruction program.

Second, there are social motives for nationalization, such as the desire to guarantee full employment, to offer better working conditions to the labor force, and to improve industrial relations. This social component

---

[6] The growth of public ownership in these countries cannot be explained simply as a manifestation of socialism, however. See, for example, Millward's essay.

[7] See Chadeau's essay. France and Italy shared a clear political intent in choosing to create SOEs for the production and distribution of oil and, in general, in their "oil nationalism" policies against the excessive power of the Seven Sisters (see Sapelli et al. 1993). In the case of Italy, it has been shown that the growth and enlargement of the two main public holdings, IRI and ENI, in the 1950s and 1960s should be interpreted as a more or less conscious attempt to transform them into autonomous agents of economic policy to replace the weakness and inconsistency of the central government in pursuing a coherent strategy of development. As a consequence, these holdings eventually became an arena for continuous political compromise, struggle, and occupation by political parties (Balconi et al. 1995; Barca 1997).

can be found in the post–World War II nationalization by France and Italy, "which acted as pioneers in the field of social innovations" (Fridenson 1987, 149). In Austria, SOEs stubbornly resisted pressure to reduce employment in the 1960s and 1970s; Stiefel reminds us of Kreisky's famous statement that he preferred a budget deficit of a few billion to unemployment of a few thousand.[8] Sometimes the creation of public enterprises can be directed to the development of national entrepreneurship, as in the case of the Meiji administration in Japan in the late nineteenth century. This gave rise to several state activities in a few strategic sectors (railways, iron and steel, shipyards, and so on). In some cases, nationalization is intended to overcome the weakness and provincialism of large private enterprises and their inability to deal with trade unions, as discussed in the essay on France by Chadeau.

Finally, there are a number of economic reasons for nationalization. The one most commonly discussed in economic theory is market failure. According to this theory, nationalization is not only justified but necessary when there is a lack of information or when economic and social externalities are strong enough to make management by the invisible hand of the market and private profits unsatisfactory (Nove 1973). Natural monopoly is the typical case. This can be found in the public utilities sector, where "it is cheaper to produce goods by a monopoly than by many firms, and where potential market entrants can be held off without predatory measures. In such cases unregulated private enterprise would exploit the market" (Bös 1986, 27). Such exploitation would lead to diseconomies for consumers, mainly in the form of increased prices and tariffs, as well as to an unreliability of supply. Ownership and management by the state or other public agencies of industries and services operating in the field of natural monopolies should guarantee fair tariffs and prices under both the economic and political profiles. In fact, up to the 1980s this was the path followed by most Western countries. When the choice was made to leave these activities to private enterprise, as in the United States, severe regulation of prices, tariffs, the quality of supply, and the level of profits was introduced, although close regulation was partially removed by the conservative governments of the 1980s.[9] The establishment of special American-type regulatory agencies and authorities appears to be the necessary prerequisite for the privatization of wide sectors of public activities, which has been gaining

---

[8] See Stiefel's essay.
[9] On the problems arising from excessive bureaucratic regulation see Galambos's essay.

favor in Europe. This favor arises from both a change of mind about the role of SOEs because of their recent poor performance and the progressive erosion of natural monopolies caused by technological progress, particularly in the communications sector.[10]

A second category of economic motives may underlie nationalization policies: those linked to the promotion of economic growth and social transformation in underdeveloped countries or regions (Jones 1982; Vernon and Aharoni 1981). In these cases, the argument in favor of SOEs can be summarized thus: public enterprise "makes its decisions on the basis of long-term considerations, and these are not or cannot be profit-minded" (Kaldor 1980, 5). Further, the state can foster modernization in the neglected sections of otherwise developed economies or stimulate growth in strategic sectors of the economy by initiating public activities.[11] History shows that the range of possible initiatives is very wide. It embraces the exploitation of natural resources – for example, the nationalization of oil companies or the foundation of public agencies for the exploitation and supply of energy resources, as in the state mines in the Netherlands, the Italian General Oil Company (AGIP) and the National Hydrocarbon Concern (ENI) in Italy, and Elf-Aquitaine in France. It also includes the construction of infrastructures such as railways in Germany, turnpikes in the United States, and highways in Germany and postwar Italy. Finally, state intervention may be intended to ensure the cheap supply of raw materials necessary for the growth of the national economy in basic industries such as iron and steel. This was a policy followed in several European countries, notably Italy, Spain, and France.

A third economic motive that can explain state ownership is to be found in industrial bailouts, where the state decides to rescue private businesses affected by deep, sometimes irreversible, economic and financial crises. These rescues have often been aimed at large-scale units in strategic activities where a social concern – anxiety about employment – influences the decision. This form of nationalization has often occurred in Italy, and such decisions frequently had perverse political effects, as Amatori's essay shows. The same motivation, however, led to the 1931 nationalization of the Vereinigte Stahlworke in Germany and

---

[10] See, for instance, the essay by Davids and van Zanden.

[11] Among the reasons explaining the early-twentieth-century disintegration of the consensus in favor of a laissez-faire economy in the Netherlands, Davids and van Zanden (this volume) point to the failure of the market to develop strategic new industries.

to the temporary nationalization of Rolls Royce, Jaguar, and Rover in Great Britain in the 1970s. The strategy of rescuing private firms from failure has become more frequent in Spain since the 1950s.[12]

Further economic reasons for nationalization are attributable to the distributory argument and to the stabilizing effects of nationalization policies. The distributory argument is related not only to the possible change in property ownership and to the form of compensation to which it can give rise, but also to the fact that "contrary to private firms, public enterprises are often instructed to reduce the prices of goods which are mainly demanded by lower income earners, thereby influencing the personal distribution of real income" (Bös 1986, 29). As far as stabilizing effects are concerned, it has been maintained that "the existence of a public sector of some size is a favorable basis for anticyclic policies in the field of investment" (Tinbergen, quoted in Bös 1986, 29).

Brief though it is, the preceding review of motives makes it clear that although public enterprises are commonly assumed to operate only in a limited number of natural monopolies, their range of activity is potentially limitless, as the following essays show. R. P. Short has argued that during the early 1980s public enterprise accounted for 10–25 percent of manufacturing output in industrial countries such as Italy and developing countries such as Korea. In many less developed countries (LDCs), however, more – often considerably more – than 25 percent of manufacturing output came from SOEs (excluding the public utilities, communications, and natural resources sectors). The list of industries covered by public enterprises was indeed impressive. It ranged from textiles and clothing (Italy and Denmark among the industrialized countries and almost every non–Latin American LDC) to food, drink, and tobacco (France, Italy, Australia, Germany, Ireland, Japan, and the Scandinavian countries being totally or partially involved in them among the developed countries – DCs – and again the great majority of LDCs), from pottery and cement (Austria and Germany in pottery and Italy in cement among the DCs, and the majority of Asian and African LDCs in both) to transport equipment – motor vehicles, ships, and aircraft (all three being present in Italy and the United Kingdom, on the one hand, and the first two in Indonesia, Colombia, India, Nigeria, and Pakistan, on the other) – and the list could go much further (Short 1984, 124–42).

---

[12] See Wengenroth's essay; Hannah 1994, 187–8; and Table 9.2 in the essay by Carreras, Tafunell, and Torres.

For the sake of clarity, and following the suggestion of Dieter Bös, all these activities can be classified into four categories: (1) public utilities, communications, and transportation; (2) basic goods industries (coal, oil, atomic energy, steel); (3) banks, insurance, social security; and (4) education (public universities) and health (public hospitals) (Bös 1986, 16–19). These represent the main fields of state entrepreneurship.

HISTORICAL BACKGROUND: THE ORIGINS OF SOES

The increased role of the state in the economy as the manager-entrepreneur of scarce resources is a phenomenon with deep roots in the modern age. As the essay by Reinert shows, there are a number of significant historical antecedents for the direct economic activities of the visible hand of governments. The historical evolution of the phenomenon can be divided into three main periods. The first phase begins in the Renaissance and continues until the end of the nineteenth century. It seems more important to emphasize the maturing of a dynamic approach by the state to the economy and society during this period rather than the depth of intervention. The second phase covers the first forty years of the twentieth century, when the traditional mechanisms that had worked so well in the market economy encountered turbulence caused by World War I and the disastrous recession following the 1929 crisis.[13] The third phase, the period from World War II to the present, covers the apogee and then the decline of nationalization policies, both in developed Western countries and in less developed ones elsewhere.

During the first phase prior to the first Industrial Revolution, nationalization experiences were essentially occasional and sporadic. They occurred mainly in sectors such as metals and mining that were considered strategic in terms of national defense. Major exceptions were the French *manifactures royales*, first developed by Henri IV and later strengthened by Jean Baptiste Colbert, as well as the more or less successful imitations in Russia by Peter the Great, in Prussia by Frederick II, in Austria by Maria Theresa, and in Spain by Felipe V.

It is especially in the nineteenth century that the economic, political, and ideological premises of the changing relations between the state and the market and between the state and society – in other words,

---

[13] The fallout from World War I affected even neutral countries like the Netherlands. See the essay by Davids and van Zanden.

between public and private – should be sought. Those premises would become concrete policies only in the twentieth century. They were mostly nurtured in countries that could be regarded as second comers to industrialization: Belgium, France, Germany, and, initially, the United States. In different periods of the nineteenth century, all these countries shared the belief that the state could and should perform a primary role in catching up with the nation that led world industrialization: Great Britain. Great Britain itself had long been attached to limited state intervention and free trade policies. The first champion of this approach was Alexander Hamilton, George Washington's secretary of state, who prompted the program of the Federalist Party in the United States, even if this program was launched in a somewhat hostile environment and opposed by the Democratic Party.[14] An outstanding contribution was also made by Friedrich List, who had been in contact with Federalist circles during his American exile. Once back in his own country, List strove successfully for the *Zollverein* (Customs Union). Further, in newly created nations such as the United States, Belgium, Germany, and Italy, "bigger government," at least in the first decades after independence and unification, was likely to facilitate the sociopolitical unification of the nation.

In the late nineteenth century, it was already obvious that the same premises had given rise to two different patterns of state behavior with regard to the economy. The continental pattern leaned toward more and more massive government intervention in the economy, such as the direct takeover of production activities. The American pattern was characterized by a limited involvement in production but a greater reliance on state regulation of the market through the ad hoc establishment of special authorities. In other words, in the first case the entrepreneurial state took priority over the regulative state, and in the second the reverse was true.

The "strong" model – that is, bigger government – was applied first in the state control policies that reached their climax in the nationalization policies of several continental countries on the eve of World War II and, after the war, in the establishment of the mixed economies of Western Europe. This was the outcome of various traditions and currents of thought, at least four of which should be mentioned: (1) the French tradition supporting a strongly centralizing and authoritative bureaucracy, which since the seventeenth century had given the public

---

[14] On the hostile environment, see Galambos's essay.

administration "manifold and heterogeneous powers over, among other things, public order, public works, taxation policy and the law" (D'Alberti 1992, 15); (2) the new vision of the state, either under the economic profile or the legal-administrative one, that matured in Germany in the second half of the nineteenth century and developed within the idealist philosophy. This vision can be synthesized in Adolf Wagner's belief that individual actions could not solve problems concerning the public interest, and that there was an irresistible tendency to the gradual replacement of private enterprise, which was unable to keep pace with the rhythm of technical and organizational progress (Wagner 1891). This "Academic Theoretical Socialism," propounded by one of the champions of the Young Historical School, was only apparently convergent with (3) the current of scientific socialism inspired by Marx, which advocated the socialization of the means of production; and (4) the influence of Keynesian economics in the twentieth century, which undoubtedly supplied the most important contribution to the theoretical foundation of the mixed economy.

The American model of the regulatory state emerged in the last quarter of the nineteenth century, after the establishment of the Interstate Commerce Commission (ICC) in 1887 and the subsequent independent federal agencies for the control and regulation of economic activity. It was the first outcome of a legal-administrative system in which British common-law tradition and French political, cultural, and juridical influences converged. It must be said that in the period prior to the American Civil War, the French tradition seemed almost to fare better than the Anglo-Saxon one. At that time, both federal and state authorities were the prime movers of initiatives in turnpike, waterway, and canal construction, as well as in the establishment of the First and Second Banks of the United States.[15] After the unhappy financial outcome of some of these initiatives in the late 1830s, however, state ownership declined, opening the way to the unique regulatory state of the nineteenth century. Since the establishment of the ICC in 1887,

---

[15] See Goodrich 1960; North 1972; Scheiber 1969; Toninelli 1993; and the discussion in the first paragraph of Galambos's essay. Further, in the following period, when regulatory activity would have prevailed, the activity of state-entrepreneurs did not completely cease, as shown by the formation of federal government corporations – such as the Panama Canal Company (1903), the Alaska Railroad (1923, later passed to the state of Alaska), and the Tennessee Valley Authority (1935). It is also shown by the nationalization of public services such as the mail (U.S. Postal Service, 1970) and railroads (Amtrak, 1970, which subsequently become a private–public mixed corporation) (Scheiber 1987).

forty-seven federal agencies having social and economic regulatory functions have been created (forty-three still survive).[16] Twenty-three of these were "purely regulatory" – that is, having the sole mission "to change market outcomes such as price, service, and number of firms in the industry, or to moderate the broader impact that private production and marketing decisions may have on society" (Du Boff 1996, 164). Seven agencies were already in operation in 1914. In the 1930s and early 1940s there was a great wave of regulatory legislation associated with the New Deal. Finally, a new surge occurred in the 1960s and early 1970s, when the "new social regulation" came along as a response to the environmental, consumer, and civil rights movements of those years. This was regulation strongly supported by the electorate but fiercely opposed by the business community (Herman 1981; Litan and Nordhaus 1983). In the late 1970s and early 1980s, this opposition increased as more and more sectors of society faced growing administrative and regulatory costs.[17] It also increased as a result of clashes among special interest groups trying "to protect themselves by obtaining various forms of government relief from competition" (North 1985, 389). A phase of cautious deregulation began.

The dimension of public enterprise in the majority of mixed economies, both within and outside Europe, was much larger than in the United States, especially during its peak in the mid-1970s. According to a survey of more than seventy mixed economies outside the United States, the many initiatives that were classifiable as public enterprise (nationalized enterprises and industries, state-controlled and state-partnership firms, public-run concerns, and so on, but excluding municipal enterprises) produced on average 10 percent of the gross national product and contributed 16.5 percent of gross capital formation (Short 1984, 115). But disaggregating the latter value for industrialized countries (including the United States) and developing countries, it emerges that gross annual investment of the public sector averaged 27 percent of overall investment in developing countries and was still increasing, whereas in the industrialized countries public investment averaged no more than 11 percent of the total. This supports the view

---

[16] The distinction between social and economic regulation is that the former deals with market failures or externalities, where the full social costs of production and marketing, as well as disposal of wastes, are not reflected in prices. The latter, designed to be implemented on an industry-specific basis, addresses market structure and restrains various types of anticompetitive behavior (Du Boff 1996, 163).

[17] On this issue see the essay by Galambos.

that direct government involvement in the productive sectors was, until recently, a strategic component of the growth and catching-up policies of LDCs.

PUBLIC ENTERPRISE AND NATIONALIZATION POLICIES
UP TO WORLD WAR I

Except in France, no major change in the size of the public sector occurred between the late 1960s and the early 1980s. In most Western countries, mainly in Europe, the great age of nationalization and successful public enterprise was the three decades following the Great Depression. However, several significant direct state interventions in the economy had already occurred in the early twentieth century – particularly during World War I and immediately afterward. These concerned both the nationalization of existing activities and the establishment of new ones. They assumed the form of special agencies or public and mixed corporations.

The outstanding example was Germany during the Weimar Republic. Until World War I the activities owned or controlled by the Reich were quite scattered (mail, telegraph and telephone, railroads in the Alsace-Lorraine region, arsenals, the Reichbank, and a few others). Individual states (*Länder*) were involved in mining and salt, in construction, and in railways. In the Weimar period, both the Reich and individual states greatly enlarged their properties. The Reich first took control of large sections of the public utilities sector (postal services and power distribution), and reorganized the railway system into the *Reichbahn* (1920). Both the Reich and the states were involved in industrial production (power generation, chemicals, food, metals, coal and iron mining, construction and municipal building, insurance, finance and banking, agriculture, forestry, and so on). In 1925 almost 1.2 million workers were employed in the Reich's productive activities, and a further quarter million were employed in *Länder* enterprises. These activities were usually in the form of public shareholdings, such as the Reich's Vereinigte Industrieunternenmungen AG (VIAG) or the Prussian Vereinigte Elektrizitäs- und Bergwerks-Aktiengesellschaft (VEBA).[18] This growth of public activities in Germany after World War I can be explained both by

[18] See Ambrosius 1994 and Wengenroth's essay, which also underlines the relevance of the third level of public intervention in the Weimar Republic. In 1930, 84 percent of German gas and 45 percent of German electricity were produced by municipal companies.

the problem of industrial reconstruction and by the need to rationalize the production system. Rationalization was similar to socialization. According to Walter Rathenau – the president of Allgemeine Electrizitäts-Gesellschaft (AEG), who coordinated the 1920 Committee for Socialization and later acted as minister for reconstruction – postwar Germany needed a radical change in economic policy in order to create *die neue Wirtschaft*, the New Economy. In *die neue Wirtschaft* the *Socialisierung* would lead to social regeneration and productive renewal of the capitalist system. For Rathenau the New Economy did not mean a state-run economy, but rather "a private economy which has to pass the examination of the public powers" (Rathenau 1976, 62).

Aside from the war phase, a few remarkable but isolated initiatives marked the growth experience of a number of Western European economies in the period before the 1929 crisis. In England there was the partial nationalization of British Petroleum (BP, 1914) and the establishment of the Port of London Authority (1908), the British Broadcasting Corporation (BBC, 1926), and the Central Electricity Board (1926).[19] In Italy there was the nationalization of the railway system (which from 1905 on was managed by the Azienda Autonoma delle Ferrovie dello Stato) and the establishment of the National Insurance Institute (INA, 1912) and the Italian General Oil Company (AGIP, 1926). In France there was the foundation of Potasses d'Alsace (1919), the Office National Industriel de l'Azote (1922), the Compagnie Française de Raffinage (1924), and the Compagnie Française de Petroles (1928). In the Netherlands the state financed the establishment of the first blast furnace (N.V. Hoogovens, 1917) and the salt industry (Nederlande Zoutinustrie, 1917), as well as acquiring a large majority interest in the railway (1920) and the airline (1927). Finally, in Spain there were some initiatives in the banking and financial sectors (such as the establishment of the Banco di Credito Industrial, 1920) and the establishment of a state monopoly in the trade and distribution of oil products (CAMPSA, 1927) – although these did not prevent mixed-ownership enterprises from retaining private management (Comin and Martin Aceña 1991).

Although government and other public agencies had increased their participation in the economy during the 1914–18 war period, a real

---

[19] Winston Churchill explained the partial nationalization of BP by referring to the wish to secure naval fuel supplies in wartime. BP was controlled by the state between 1914 and 1979, although for most of that time the British government was a passive shareholder (Hannah 1994, 173).

change in climate and approach occurred in the following fifteen years.
This was the result, first, of the social and political tensions of the
postwar period and, later, of the disastrous aftermath of the 1929 crisis.
The working pattern of the capitalist system itself underwent profound
criticism, opening the way to doubt about the soundness of market-
economy mechanisms. Increasingly, liberal democratic and Catholic
forces (the latter inspired by Pope Pius XI's 1931 encyclical *Quadra-
gesimo Anno*) moved toward the conclusions reached by social reformers and conservative reactionaries. They recognized that stronger
government intervention in the form of state control of crucial sectors
of the economy could resolve the problems of market failures and the
excessive power of giant private corporations.

As a consequence, in the 1930s an impressive first wave of nationalization began, particularly in those Western European countries most
affected by the depression. The principal aim was to rescue firms or
whole sectors of the economy. The origin of the IRI (1933) is a good
example of this. IRI was first conceived as a temporary agency to release
the three leading banks (Banca Commerciale, Credito Italiano, and
Banco di Roma) from their excessive industrial holdings. IRI eventually
came to control about 42 percent of the overall capital of Italian corporations. In 1937 it was transformed into a permanent public corporation and became the main public agent in the Italian mixed economy,
a role it maintained until after World War II (Amatori 1987 and this
volume). In pre-Nazi Germany the Reich was directly involved in the
restructuring of the banking and financial system; in 1931 it became a
large shareholder in *Grossbanken*. Because of the close ties between
banking and industry, these holdings gave it effective power over most
of the leading industrial firms, while those in very poor condition were
taken over by the state. The autarkic phase that followed, characterized
by coercive measures such as compulsory trade unions and *Konzern*,
brought about a strong centralization that de facto put the entire
economy under state control (Landes 1979, 490–7, 524–36).[20] In Spain,
however, the establishment of the Instituto Nacional de Industria (INI)
in 1941, inspired by the Italian IRI, was motivated by the twin desires
to stimulate national industry and to reduce imports and dependence
on other countries (Martin Aceña and Comin 1991).

---

[20] According to Wengenroth, the Nazi state controlled 50 percent of all German stock before
the end of the war.

Among the democratic nations, France undoubtedly moved furthest toward nationalization under the government of the Popular Front (1936–7). A mixed-property corporation was created that gave the state a controlling share in the railway sector Société Nationale des Chemins de Fer Français, SNCF). At the same time, the process of nationalizing the Bank of France was begun; this was completed in 1945. Further, government intervention was predominant in arms production and in aircraft construction (air transport had already been partially placed under state control in 1933 through the creation of Air France). However, the realization that the government could effectively act to improve and rationalize the economy was probably more important than the nationalization itself (Chadeau 1987 and this volume). The same can be said of England. In the 1930s a few public enterprises were created – including the transport system in the London region (London Passenger Transport Board, 1933) and several airlines (with the establishment of the British Overseas Airways Corporation, BOAC, 1939) – but, more important, in that period Labour Party plans for state intervention were taking shape. These were to be fully realized a few years later, in 1945, when the Labour Party assumed power (Grassini and Yamey 1979; Hannah 1994). Millward (this volume) shows that proposals to reform and rationalize the economy were advanced, particularly in the 1930s, to counter economic depression and industrial decline. This was especially true of the infrastructure sector, which was then dominated by a plethora of small local private or municipal productive units. The failure of these arm's-length attempts opened the way to postwar nationalization.

In countries where political conditions might have been favorable to the growth of public enterprise but where the effects of the depression had been milder, such as Sweden, Norway, and the Netherlands, there was no real nationalization process. In the Netherlands, however, a number of declining, mostly small, activities (such as canals and tramways) were taken over by the state.[21] Finally, beyond Europe – in Japan, in Latin America, and to a lesser extent in the United States – indirect state intervention to stimulate economic recovery was fostered.

---

[21] See the essay by Davids and van Zanden.

PUBLIC ENTERPRISE AFTER WORLD WAR II

The great age of public enterprise and nationalization policies began after World War II, when governments took over property and control of large sectors of economic activity, both directly and through government agencies. This, together with increasing efforts at economic planning – such as the 1942 Beveridge Report entitled *Full Employment in a Free Society* in England and Jean Monnet's 1945 *Plan de Modernisation e d'Equipment* in France – became the keystone of reconstruction and development policies in the mixed economies. The policies aimed, on the one hand, at "the removal of sectoral imbalance and the catching-up with full employment" and, on the other, at "the enlargement of the public sector in order to down-size monopolistic and rent positions as well as to build infrastructures and strengthen the interest and welfare of the community." Moreover, "if in Europe economic planning and nationalization policies assumed a previously unknown scale, this was the result mostly of efforts to overcome the scarcity of raw materials, to rationalise productive structures and to ensure the functioning of absolutely necessary services" (Castronovo 1989, 4-5).

At the political level, the predominance of the Left was of very little importance, as was the fact that nationalization and economic planning were the central issues of their political programs. It is true that in Great Britain the public sector was enlarged during the Labour administrations of Clement Attlee (1945-51), Harold Wilson (1964-9), and John Callaghan (1974-9), when the state took over the Bank of England, the coal industry (1946), the railway system, inland waterways, civil airlines, the electricity industry (1947), the gas industry (1948), the iron and steel sector (1949), the postal services (1969), and the automobile, shipbuilding, and aerospace industries (1974-7). The nationalization of Rolls-Royce in 1971, however, occurred during a Tory administration and was intended to rescue the prestigious auto company.[22]

In France the most intense phases of public enterprise enlargement occurred between 1944 and 1948 and, later, in 1982. In the first phase, when both the Communist and Socialist parties were in government, the complete nationalization of the Bank of France, as well as of four leading credit banks, took place. In addition, all of air transport, a large

---

[22] See Grassini and Yamey 1979; Hannah 1994; Kelf-Cohen 1973; Robson 1962; and Table 7.1 in Millward's essay.

part of the insurance sector, and about 20 percent of the industry of the country passed into public hands – including the entire energy sector (coal, gas, and electricity), as well as firms such as Renault and Gnome & Rhône (which was charged with wartime collaboration).[23] After a long interval of negligible enlargement of public activities, nationalization resumed during Pierre Mauroy's Socialist government, when almost 53 percent of the corporate capital of the country was taken over by the state. A February 1982 law placed the iron and steel industry, almost the entire banking system, the telecommunications sector, and five primary industrial concerns (Rhône-Poulenc, Cie Gale d'Electricité [CGE], Pechiney-Ugine Kuhlman [PUK], Saint-Gobain, and Thompson-Brandt) under state control. This measure was temporary. The center–right government that assumed office in 1986 immediately reprivatized most of the activities and began to dismantle the system of public enterprise that had been set up in the 1930s and 1940s.

After World War II the Social Democrats assumed power in the Scandinavian countries, in Belgium, and in the Netherlands, prompting a policy of profound structural reformation and growth of public enterprises, particularly in the transportation, communication, and natural resources sectors. In Austria the state took control of former German properties in the country, which led to the nationalization of 20 percent of the industrial sector, 85 percent of the electric companies, and the three leading banks, so that Austria had one of the largest public sectors in the West (see Stiefel's essay). Finally, in Italy, as the progressive-Catholic forces and the secular Left converged on a policy supporting nationalization, there was considerable expansion of the public enterprise sector. In 1975 the state-entrepreneur supplied about a fifth of the added value of the manufacturing sector (Grassini and Scognamiglio 1979, 80). The most significant stages of this process were the following: the establishment of ENI (1953), which was granted a monopoly on the research and production of hydrocarbons in the Po Valley; the establishment of the Ministero delle Partecipazioni Statali (State Shareholding, 1956); and, following the rise to power of the center–left coalition, the nationalization of almost all the electricity sector in the National Agency for Electric Power (ENEL, 1962).

The creation of the state shareholding system was probably the most original feature of the history of Italian public enterprise. The system had a pyramid-shaped structure. At the base were the operative units,

---

[23] On this point see Chadeau's essay.

which had the legal status of joint-stock companies subject to private law. These were responsible for economic management and performance. In the middle were the *enti di gestione* (state super–holding companies) (IRI, ENI, and, since 1963, EFIM, the Autonomous Concern for Financing the Machinery Industry), which were subject to public law. These controlled the capital of the operating companies and provided them with financial and technical support (while themselves receiving financial aid from the state). Finally, there was a top level, the minister of state shareholdings, charged with planning and implementing long-term strategies and coordinating the sectoral planning of the intermediate concerns. This top level was accountable for the political responsibility of the overall behavior of the entire public sector (Saraceno 1975). Although this structure seemed rational and viable in theory, the recent history of Italian public enterprise has shown how its practical application ran into increasing financial and managerial difficulties, and how it was easily influenced by political lobbies and conflicting parties.

The growth of public enterprise after World War II was not limited to European countries. Australia and Canada stand out among the industrialized countries, as large sections of the internal transportation system and the energy sector were taken over by the federal and state powers. As mentioned previously, however, it is in the less developed world that the phenomenon has been most evident. The Bombay Plan in India, initiated in the mid-1950s by Jawaharal Nehru's reformist government, resulted in that country's being "the largest non-market economy outside the Communist world" (Berend 1994, 191). Nationalization strategies in many developing countries included the expropriation of foreign firms operating on national territory. These expropriations were the outcome of autarkic or even dictatorial policies in a number of Latin American countries, Egypt, Indonesia, South Korea, and several other Asian and African countries.

Two important exceptions to the general trend, apart from the United States, need to be identified: Germany and Japan. In the case of Germany, defined as "the neo-liberal variation" of the mixed economy (Van der Wee 1989), the drive to postwar reconstruction involved the partial dismantling of the huge public structure established under the Nazi regime. As Wengenroth shows (in this volume), this was a controversial process. In 1980 almost 11 percent of German output was still produced by SOEs.[24] In Japan the state also played an important role

---

[24] See table 6.1 in Hannah 1994, 169.

Table 1.1. The Economic Weight of Public Enterprise
(Percent of Total Enterprise)[a]

	1963	1979	1985	1990
Italy	12	20	20	19
France	19	18	24	18
Spain	12	10	12	10
Germany	11	13	12	10
UK	10	19	13	4

[a] Average of the shares of employment, gross investment, and
value added.
Source: Macchiati 1996, 27.

in the growth of the nation's economy. Intervention was mostly
indirect, however, and took the form of economic planning under the
direction of the very dynamic Ministry of International Trade and Industry (MITI).

THE DECLINE: TEMPORARY OR PERMANENT?

Since the late 1970s the fortune of public enterprise has been in steady
decline. In most Western countries (as well as formerly socialist countries), waves of privatization have led to the progressive erosion of the
public sector. During the first ten years of the Thatcher administration
in Great Britain (before the privatization of the energy sector began),
the shares of value added to total gross national product and of total
employment of the nationalized industries and public corporations fell
by more than 50 percent of their 1978 values (11.1 and 8.2 percent,
respectively). The trend is emphasized in Table 1.1, which measures the
weight of public enterprise in five Western European economies
between 1963 and 1990. Italy is the only one to show no clear change
in trend.

Only in 1992 was it possible to glimpse a real change in public-sector
policy in Italy. Thereafter the pace of privatization was fast. Between
1992 and 1994, public activities amounting to 29,000 billion liras
were given back to the market. This was not a bad performance over
such a short period. In England the government raised the equivalent
of about 48,000 billion liras from the sale of public enterprises in the
period 1985-7. French dismantling of the public sector yielded the
equivalent of 35,000 billion liras in the period 1992-5 (Macchiati 1996,
42-4). In 1996-7 the privatization process accelerated, leading to the

total or partial denationalization of industrial giants such as Telecom and ENI.

Since the mid-1980s, denationalization policies have characterized several LDC economies, too, particularly in Latin America. Under the influence of the Chicago school of economics, Chile began the trend as early as the mid-1970s.

Bellini (this volume) discusses the issue of the decline of public enterprise and the problems linked to the changing role of the state in the economy. Here it is enough to say that the decline of public enterprise now seems irreversible. It should be borne in mind, however, that nationalization policies slowed down in several countries, such as Chile, in the mid-1980s and in Argentina, Mexico, and Brazil a few years later. Most of the reasons for the expansion of the public sector in the past grew weaker as the aims of public enterprise were at least partly achieved. At the same time, increasing budgetary constraints necessarily reduced efforts to achieve social and economic goals. Moreover, innovations in technology, management, and information made the heavy bureaucratic structure and inefficiency of public enterprise obsolete and uncompetitive. On the one hand, public enterprise was unable to achieve the flexibility required by market internalization and globalization. On the other hand, it was increasingly exposed to political pressure and constraints.

In economic theory also, the development of a positive approach has shown that government failure is as frequent as market failure. A search has begun for the causes of this phenomenon (Bös 1989; Stiglitz 1989). Before declaring the end of the age of the active presence of the state in the economy, however, one should consider Arnold Heertje's caveat that history has always been characterized by the alternation of phases of extreme state activity and reactions in the opposite direction (Heertje 1989). Reinert's essay and most of the following contributions discuss how the role of the state has changed from a historical perspective. Bellini suggests that the problem before us is to find new foundations, after the experience of the state-entrepreneur, for the state–industry relationship and the role of the state in economic development.

REFERENCES

Amatori, F. 1987. IRI: From industrial saviour to industrial group. In *Annali di storia dell'impresa*, ed. V. Zamagni, pp. 213–19. Milan.

Ambrosius, G. 1994. *Lo stato come imprenditore: Economia pubblica e capitalismo in Germania nel XIX e XX secolo*. Milan.

Balconi, M., L. Orsenigo, and P. A. Toninelli. 1995. Tra gerarchie politiche e mercati: Il caso delle imprese pubbliche in Italia (acciaio e petrolio). In *Potere, mercati, gerarchie*, ed. M. Magatti, pp. 299-338. Bologna.

Barca, F., ed. 1997. *Storia del capitalismo italiano dal dopoguerra a oggi*. Rome.

Berend, I. T. 1994. Toward a new world system: Problems of transition to a market economy. In *Debates and controversies in economic history. A-sessions: Eleventh International Economic History Congress*, pp. 169-236. Milan.

Bianchi, P. 1994. Impresa pubblica. In *Enciclopedia delle scienze sociali*, 4: 587-96. Rome.

Bös, D. 1986. *Public enterprise economics: Theory and application*. Amsterdam. 1989. Comment. In *The economic role of the state*, by J. E. Stiglitz. Oxford.

Castronovo, V., ed. 1989. *La nazionalizzazione dell'energia elettrica*. Bari.

Chadeau, E. 1987. French early nationalizations in a long-term perspective. In *Annali di storia dell'impresa*, ed. V. Zamagni, pp. 156-72. Milan.

Comin, F., and P. Martin Aceña, eds. 1991. *Historia de la empresa publica en España*. Madrid.

D'Alberti, M. 1992. *Diritto amministrativo comparato*. Bologna.

Du Boff, R. B. 1996. The growth of the federal regulatory sector in the United States: A brief economic history. *Research in Economic History* 16: 157-84.

Fridenson, P. 1987. Les entreprises publiques en France de 1944 à 1986. In *Annali di storia dell'impresa*, ed. V. Zamagni, pp. 144-55. Milan.

Goodrich, C. 1960. *Government promotions of American canals and railroads*. New York.

Grassini, F. A., and C. Scognamiglio, eds. 1979. *Stato e industria in Europa: L'Italia*. Bologna.

Grassini, F. A., and B. S. Yamey, eds. 1979. *Stato e industria in Europa: Il Regno Unito*. Bologna.

Hannah, L. 1994. The economic consequences of the state ownership of industry, 1945-1990. In *The economic history of Britain since 1700*, vol. 3, *1939-1992*, ed. R. Floud and D. McCloskey, pp. 168-94. Cambridge, Eng.

Heertje, A. 1989. Introduction. In *The economic role of the state*, by J. E. Stiglitz. Oxford.

Herman, E. S. 1981. *Corporate control, corporate power*. New York.

Jones, L. P., ed. 1982. *Public enterprises in less developed countries*. Cambridge.

Kaldor, N. 1980. Public or private enterprises: The issues to be considered. In *Public and private enterprises in a mixed economy*, ed. W. J. Baumol, pp. 1-12. London.

Kelf-Cohen, R. 1973. *British nationalisation, 1945-1973*. London.

Landes, D. 1979. *Prometeo liberato*. Torino.

Litan, R. E., and W. Nordhaus. 1983. *Reforming federal regulation*. New Haven, Conn.

Macchiati, A. 1996. *Privatizzazioni tra econia e politica*. Rome.

Martin Aceña, P., and F. Comin. 1991. *INI: 50 años de industrialización en España*. Madrid.

North, D. C. 1972. Government and the American economy. In *American economic growth: An economist's history of the U.S.*, ed. L. Davis, R. Easterlin, and W. N. Parker, pp. 636–64. New York.

1985. The growth of government in the United States: An economic historian's perspective. *Journal of Public Economics* 28: 383–99.

Nove, A. 1973. *Efficiency criteria for nationalized industries: A study of the misapplication of micro-economic theory.* Toronto.

Posner, M. V., and S. J. Woolf. 1967. *Italian public enterprise.* London.

Rathenau, W. 1976; originally published 1918. *L'economia nuova.* Turin.

Robson, W. A. 1962. *L'industria nazionalizzata e la proprietà pubblica.* Milan.

Sapelli, G., L. Osenigo, P. A. Toninelli, and C. Corduas. 1993. *Nascita e trasformazione d'impresa: Storia dell'Agip Petroli.* Bologna.

Saraceno, P. 1975. *Il sistema della imprese a partecipazione statale nell'esperienza italiana.* Milan.

Scheiber, H. N. 1969. *Ohio Canal era: A case study of government and the economy.* Athens, Ohio.

1987. Patterns of public enterprise: Government intervention and the American economy, 1790 to the present. In *Annali di storia dell'impresa*, ed. V. Zamagni, pp. 254–69. Milan.

Shonfield, A. 1965. *Modern capitalism.* London.

Short, R. P. 1984. The role of public enterprises: An international statistical comparison. In *Public enterprises in mixed economies: Some macroeconomic aspects*, ed. R. H. Floyd, C. S. Gray, and R. P. Short, pp. 110–81. Washington, D.C.

Stiglitz, J. E. 1989. *The economic role of the state.* Oxford.

Tinbergen, J. 1969. *Principi e metodi della politica economica.* Milan.

Toninelli, P. A. 1993. *Nascita di una nazione: Lo sviluppo economico degli Stati Uniti (1780–1914).* Bologna.

Van der Wee, H. 1989. *L'economia mondiale tra crisi e benessere (1945–1980).* Milan.

Vernon, R., and Y. Aharoni. 1981. *State-owned enterprises in western economies.* London.

Wagner, A. 1891. La scienza delle finanze. *Biblioteca dell'economista*, series III, no. 10. Turin.

Zamagni, V. 1987. L'impresa pubblica. In *Annali di storia dell'impresa*, ed. V. Zamagni, pp. 119–26. Milan.

2

∞

The Decline of State-Owned Enterprise and the New Foundations of the State–Industry Relationship

NICOLA BELLINI

This essay deals with the decline in the role of the state as the owner of enterprises. This decline has come about through privatization policies in most industrialized countries as well as in many less advanced countries.[1] This essay does not intend to provide a comprehensive account of such a wide and complex phenomenon. Rather, it attempts to identify and discuss the key issues in the historical analysis of privatization.

The historical record of privatization is impressive by any standard. The importance of the state's retreat from ownership and management of business activities in certain fields can hardly be underestimated. Undoubtedly this retreat implies an unprecedented opportunity for the private sector. It redrafts national political economics and injects profit-oriented and competition-minded entrepreneurship into the mix.

The quantitative dimension of the phenomenon can be only approximately estimated. The most authoritative source, the World Bank, presented figures indicating a clear escalation in the number of transactions. These reached 2,655 in 1988–93, significantly (but not solely)

---

[1] This essay deals with the problems of privatization in advanced industrial countries. On the (positive) relationship between privatization policies and economic growth in less advanced countries, see Plane 1997 and World Bank 1995.

Table 2.1. Divestiture in Industrial and Developing Countries, 1980–93

Region	1980–7 Number of Transactions	1988–93 Number of Transactions	1988–93 Value of Transactions ($ billions)
World	696	2655	270.9
Industrial countries	240	376	174.9
Developing countries	456	2279	96.0
Eastern Europe and Central Asia	2	1097	17.9

Source: World Bank 1995.

affected by the "transition economies" of formerly Communist countries. In terms of value, divestitures in industrial countries represent the largest share (about 65 percent) of the worldwide phenomenon (Table 2.1). More recent data confirm the growing trend. According to press sources, 240 privatization operations were accomplished worldwide in 1996 alone, with a value of almost $90 billion.

Privatization has been the result of an unprecedented convergence of domestic and international causes.[2] Domestically, the need to balance the budget deficit created by overburdened systems of the welfare state has played a major role. Equally important has been the perception of the sales of government assets as a great opportunity to revitalize and develop economies. Internationally, the decline of state ownership has been sustained by pressures on domestic decision makers. These pressures have come from other privatizing governments, worried about unfair competition from foreign state-owned and government-protected companies, and from international and supranational organizations concerned with limiting the disruptive effects on the process of international integration of national aid to state-owned enterprises (SOEs). Most noticeably, the European Union has progressively worked out a set of rules. These have translated the general references of the Treaty of Rome

---

[2] This essay deals principally with the issues of industrial privatization, i.e., the sale of assets of state companies to private individuals. These issues raise specific questions and involve specific sets of actors and policy communities. Nonetheless, it is worth remembering that privatization encompasses a much wider range of actions aimed at limiting the state's role and encouraging private involvement. These actions as a whole define "the general drive in certain countries to retrace the public–private boundary" (Vickers and Wright 1988, 3).

into a strategy aimed at constraining the antimarket effects of state ownership by delegitimizing it. Not only has any special treatment of SOEs been banned, but normal shareholder behavior such as increasing company capital has been investigated for the presence of concealed state subsidies (Cohen 1996, 272ff).

Finally, structural changes have taken place in several industries. These have often been related to the availability of technological innovations, and they have contributed to the trend by eliminating the standard justifications for direct state involvement (especially the "natural monopoly" and "dependency" arguments).

Most remarkable of all has been the radical change in the opinion of both the public and elites toward the role of the state in the economy. This change has played a fundamental role in the development of the neoliberal consensus that has dominated economic policy since the 1980s (Müller and Wright 1994). Part of this consensus has included a belief in the structural inability of SOEs to avoid distorting political interference, and consequently in the long-term superiority of private businesses, no matter how great the efforts made to improve public-sector efficiency.[3]

The rapid spread of intellectual and popular disenchantment with the effectiveness and sustainability of the welfare state and the diffusion of the neoliberal agenda have assumed global dimensions. The main inspiration, source, and benchmarking reference has been Margaret Thatcher's Britain, with its consistent and impressive record of divestiture. The share of SOEs in the British economy (that is, the share of the gross domestic product) declined spectacularly: from 6.1 percent in 1978 to 1.9 percent in 1991. The share of SOE investment in gross domestic investment fell from 15 percent to 4.2 percent in the same period (World Bank 1995).

To this should be added the consequences of the end of the Communist regimes of the former Soviet Union and Eastern Europe, as well as liberalization trends elsewhere. The link between privatization and successful performance in some of those economies, such as China and Poland, has provided "dramatic evidence of the benefits of shrinking the

---

[3] "The performance of state enterprises can improve. The sad reality is that, although some committed governments have reformed their state enterprises in the short term, making these reforms stick is much harder. World Development Report 1983 spotlighted a number of well-performing state enterprises around the world; by 1993 a majority of these had sunk into decline" (World Bank 1997, 64).

state in former centrally planned economies."[4] The massive privatization of the industrial holdings of the German Democratic Republic, initiated by the last Communist government and developed after unification, has been frequently cited in debates in Western countries. Such debates have disregarded the special circumstances of that process and the serious problems that have been transferred from the Treuhandanstalt to much less well known successor companies (Bös 1997). Yet the belief that we have been witnessing a historic turning point of huge significance cannot easily be dismissed.

Not surprisingly, privatization has aroused strong views. Packaged into catchwords and slogans of rare political effectiveness, privatization has appeared to many as the key policy, a political panacea for all, or most, of the fundamental problems of contemporary political economies.

Some have sought evidence in the apparently inevitable sequence of events for an irreversible trend, and this has encouraged an "end-of-history" syndrome. Some have disregarded the role of SOEs in the history of economic development, seeing it as nothing more than a disturbing and temporary deviation from a "natural" laissez-faire condition. Others, with greater wisdom but equal ideological bias, have warned against any attempt to revert or even slow down the trend, arguing that this would be an unacceptable, retrograde step against the flow of history as well as an unforgivable loss of a unique opportunity for development. The ideological dimension has been extraordinarily successful in fostering the international spread of the privatization agenda and the new popular stereotype of the public-private relationship.

The history and ideology of the decline of SOE are closely related to the history and ideology of the supposed decline or retreat of the state itself. Privatization has seemed the potential final blow to a state in irreversible crisis, overloaded by ever-increasing tasks and unresolved complexities (Poggi 1991).

The state has not only survived, however, but has overrun the boundaries set by economic orthodoxy through the theory of "market failures." Neoliberal dogma is less dominant now than in the past. One assessment claims that "in the West progress towards smaller government has been more apparent than real. . . . [T]he demand for collective solutions

---

[4] World Bank 1997. On the Polish and Chinese cases, see Jasinski 1997 and Krug 1997.

to economic and social problems seems, if anything, stronger than before" (*Economist* 1997, 57).

Privatization has been the most complete expression of the neoliberal ambition to establish the "market failure" approach as the only accepted paradigm justifying the role of the state (Stiglitz 1989). With regard to privatization, this conceptual approach is extremely useful and appropriate in normative terms. It suggests when, how, and where state ownership has a sufficient rationale and a reasonable expectation of decent performance. It is, however, unable to explain in a historically meaningful way why state ownership increases or decreases. This is because the market failure paradigm essentially reflects an ideological attitude, evaluating policies in terms of their distance from the ideal of the free market.

History must look at changes in state ownership as a fundamental part of the reshaping of the polity, not by reference to abstract ideology but to the perceived compatibility between the structure of the economy and the collective interests interpreted by the political system. The mercantilist seeds of economic policy (the equation between wealth and power that has always provided, and still provides, more than enough justification for state involvement in the economy) are doubtless still present. In mercantilist terms, privatization is part of the never-ending play of power and plenty. Privatization is simply one more step in the search for better ways to build the wealth of the nation as a function of political ambition.

Leaving aside the neoliberal question of how much state and how much market – which implies that there is too much state and not enough market – we must move to a consideration of the quality of the state's role. From this perspective, privatization is not so much a trend to reduce state involvement as an essential element in reshaping the state into possibly more effective (even if modest, lighter) structures and policy styles (Crozier 1987). In this view, the privatization process appears to be (and actually has been) a great opportunity not for the absolute retreat of the state, but for a substantial increase in its effectiveness, the result of policy refocusing and modernization, which have substituted new forms of control and guidance for the direct management of economic activities.

The decline of SOE is analyzed in the next two sections. It is analyzed first in terms of negative change, that is, decreasing state ownership. It is argued that significant parallels and analogies exist with the opposite process of positively changing the weight of the state in the economy.

Second, the new shape of state policies in a privatized economy is described. The concluding section outlines possible evolutionary paths for state ownership.

THE PROCESS OF DECREASING STATE OWNERSHIP

Privatization is the process of decreasing the level of state ownership. Three sets of variables influence this process of change. The first refers to the starting situation:

1. The extent of previous state ownership;
2. The significance of state ownership within the production apparatus, in terms of both the size of state holdings and the industrial sectors concerned;
3. The linkages with industrial policies, that is, the extent to which holdings have been considered an industrial policy tool;
4. The historical origin of state ownership, that is, whether it derives from policy-conscious nationalization, company establishment, or inheritance from previous regimes or is the unintended result of historic contingencies and is thus "ownership by default";[5]
5. The patterns of previous evolution and performance of SOEs.

The second set of variables concerns the opportunities for privatization. These derive from:

1. Capital markets and their rules and procedures;
2. The existence or introduction of appropriate economic institutions, especially concerning corporate government;
3. The availability of sufficient financial resources to acquire the shares of privatized companies. This availability is based on domestically available resources and also on the international orientation of the privatization process. The latter can be limited by simultaneous privatization operations in other countries that compete for the same financial resources;
4. The salability of state assets, which depends on the present com-

---

[5] "Ownership by default" is probably the best description of the origin of the state role in cases such as Volkswagen after World War II, when the Federal Republic and the Land Niedersachsen came in after the failure of the sale by the British military authorities. Similarly, the state-owned sector in Austria originated as the only alternative, in the absence of Austrian private capital, to foreign ownership of formerly German assets. See Wengenroth's and Steifel's essays in this volume.

petitiveness and profitability of the companies for sale; alternatively, the need for restructuring prior to sale may emerge;

5. The nature and extent of actual and prospective changes in technology and markets.

The third set of variables concerns general political conditions that can work as either opportunities or constraints in the change process:

1. The weight of the "pro-privatization constituency," that is, the role and power of the neoliberal (or otherwise pro-privatization) parties and interest groups;
2. The strength of pro-privatization pressures, such as those deriving from state budgetary requirements, from international commitments, or from politically independent and/or internationally oriented managers in SOEs;
3. The diffusion of neoliberal ideology throughout society, the political elite, the media, and among opinion leaders;
4. The traditional relationships between economic and political interests and power centers; perceptions and expectations regarding change in these relationships as a result of privatization, the increased weight of the private sector, and individual entrepreneurs or industrial and financial groups within the private sector.

These different sets of variables affect three features of the privatization process: speed, reversibility, and outcome. Together they also define different national routes to reduced state ownership.

Variations in speed and reversibility (even if only temporary) have proved to be important features of the privatization process. Rather than maintaining their own pace following the decision to privatize, national divestiture operations have proved to be extremely sensitive to changing conditions and perceptions, undergoing accelerations and slow-downs. The first years of Mitterrand's presidency of France at the beginning of the 1980s provided the most dramatic case of an attempt to reverse privatization policies with a new, outdated wave of nationalization. This was the result of a different ideological approach and was an attempt by the new government of the Left to compensate for the loss of control over the traditional levers of economic growth.

Instances of less extensive, sometimes even tacit, reconsideration of privatization strategies have also occurred elsewhere. The struggle over Enimont, the short-lived public–private joint venture in the Italian chemical industry at the end of the 1980s, can be cited as a deprivatization process that countered the dominance of an aggressive entrepreneur, Raul Gardini. Privatization processes must exploit windows of political and financial opportunity, accelerating the implementation of decisions in favorable circumstances rather than implementing them at a steady pace over longer periods. Even advocates of reducing government's hold on the economy suggest that "although the over-extended State needs to own less, and although there is no good economic reason for State ownership to persist in tradable-goods industries, there is no single 'correct' stage in the reform program to start privatizing. The appropriate timing will depend on the dynamics of reform in each country" (World Bank 1997, 64).

Privatization outcomes may vary. Incomplete privatizations have been frequent. In fact, it is rare for privatization to affect 100 percent of the shares. Partial privatization may just be a temporary stage in a gradual process leading to complete private ownership, but this is not always the case. The sale of a minority share of company ownership helps to raise new funds and adds market discipline to the company's behavior, with the state still retaining control.

The outcome of privatization depends particularly on the extent to which the decrease of state ownership has coincided with a process of "market awareness," embracing both the liberalization of a market and its reinstitutionalization (Jasinski 1997, 160). Assuming some degree of competition as a policy objective, the relationship between competitiveness and state ownership is not something that can be taken for granted. Historically (as in Italy after World War II), state ownership was thought to increase competitiveness in markets governed by private oligopolies because it guaranteed the viability of alternative entrepreneurial projects (Bianchi 1987). Privatization as such does not create a market; "bad" privatizations, on the contrary, simply transfer the ownership of uncompetitive firms or create private national monopolies or stronger oligopolies.

This may happen behind the smoke screen of industrial policy arguments aimed at strengthening, defending or building "national champions." The Alfa Romeo privatization in Italy, when Fiat successfully countered Ford's attempt to acquire the Institute for Industrial Reconstruction (IRI) group car manufacturer, is a good example of how the conflict between reasonable business plans can be resolved by reference to nationalist arguments, even if the latter are mere instruments for protectionism.

Privatization, like nationalization, can be a powerful tool for a better redefinition of the role of state ownership in the economy and the weight and identity of private partners in the state–industry relationship. In some cases, privatization has been seen as an opportunity to democratize economic power through the diffusion of ownership. The flotation of Volksaktien was an integral part of the first wave of privatization in West Germany in the late 1950s and early 1960s. American-style public companies were a feature of the short-lived but important debate in the early stages of privatization in Italy: they were used to overcome the family capitalism model.

In the British case, which is clearly the most radical privatization experience, an attempt was made to create a mass entrepreneurial culture by widening ownership structure into a "people's capitalism." This was an attempt to rejuvenate the capitalist spirit of the nation and to stabilize popular consensus around Thatcherite radicalism. It was also, however, behind the rhetoric of "share-owning democracy," an integral part of a post-Fordist, anti-industrialist vision of the future of the British economy, implying "total dedication to the exchange value of capitalism" and a shift of economic power and political influence to the service sector of the economy (Overbeek 1990, 194).

The French case is equally instructive of how ideological contradictions and practical and historical consistencies work together to bring state ownership to an end. Although state ownership might seem an integral part of the traditionally protectionist culture, whose roots date back to Jean-Baptiste Colbert, targeted privatization can equally be made to serve "high-tech Colbertism." This is an appropriate label for the postwar state intervention that was carried out in the name of the public interest and focused on *de pointe* (strategic) industries and on major projects as the policy method (*grand projet*). The *grand projet* itself defines an ideal evolutionary path: it starts from a *logique d'arsenal*, which implies the suspension of the market and straightforward state intervention, but it ends by delivering the new enterprises and services that have been created and nurtured within the *projet* to the market, so that they find new legitimization on the battlefield of international competition. This, briefly, is the history of ventures such as Elf-Aquitaine, Arianespace, Alcatel Alsthom, France Telecom, Electricité de France (EDF), Airbus Industrie, Snecma, and Aérospatiale (Cohen 1992).

It has been pointed out that

wide-scale privatisation and stepped-up deregulation, with supply-side measures focused on decreasing government spending, cutting the size and funding of government agencies, lowering taxes, eliminating restrictions on business, and further opening the financial markets, were the neoliberals' responses to what they saw as the excessive dirigisme of the Socialists. However, they did not themselves completely abandon dirigisme, which was apparent in their policy style, if not in the policies themselves. Privatization was as heroic an affair for the neoliberals as nationalization was for the Socialists: it was centrally controlled and highly regulated, with government picking the hard core of investors, limiting the amount of foreign investment, and marginalizing small shareholders. (Schmidt 1996, 438-9)

Privatization responded to the same rationale as nationalization once did: the state's building of a new phase of indigenous capitalism (Cohen 1996). Of course, the rhetoric was different. The conservative revolution of Margaret Thatcher and Ronald Reagan inspired the words and programs of politicians such as the ultraliberal Alain Madelin and Jacques Chirac himself, but it is the French model that has permeated the practice of privatization. It is managed by bureaucrats and their political representatives (such as Edouard Balladur), who rely on established networks of political friends and members of the *grands corps* (higher civil service). Expressions such as *privatisations administrées* (administrative privatizations) and *liberalisme d'Etat* (state liberalism) summarize what has happened. Afterward, state disengagement was to be framed in an unheroic, everyday attitude, rejecting radical overtones and mixing the pursuit of privatization opportunities with a more moderate but always present dirigiste instinct.

At the other extreme, Germany represents a case of ownership without political profile. Despite several significant cases of federal participation in enterprises (including Salzgitter, VIAG, Saarbergwerke, VEBA, and Volkswagenwerk), German governments failed to solve structural problems through nationalization and refrained from using those assets to play a guiding role in the economy or specific industrial sectors. They were administered as federal assets (*Bundesvermögen*), and this also explains the absence of special emphasis on privatization later. Despite this, there were some Thatcherite advocates in the Bonner Wende of October 1982 who argued that privatization would restore the *Soziale Marktwirtschaft* (social market economy), the infallible German recipe for economic success, which had been threatened by Social Democratic interventionism. But these voices have remained politically marginal.

The Italian case throws further light on the complex interplay between privatization and political systems. The Italian route to modern capitalism has been a compromise between French guided capitalism and German self-regulated capitalism. The cumbersome presence of state ownership in the economy, in both quantitative and qualitative terms, was never accompanied by consistent guidance of economic development, but only by a complex pattern of bargaining between political and economic powers. Unlike the situation in other countries where they have been significant, collusion and "political exchange" have monopolized industry–state relations in Italy. The state has rarely been anything but a counterpart of business interests, exchanging subsidies and protection for political consensus and the illegal financing of party activities. Dominant ideologies (Catholic and Marxist) were aloof from, when not openly hostile to, the logic of capitalism and the market economy (Amato 1992).

From such a starting point, it is not surprising that privatization in Italy has rarely been an important factor in the redefinition of state–industry relations aimed at improving the competitive position of specific industries or the country's economy. Apart from the sale of Alfa Romeo to Fiat in 1986, all early attempts to divest state-controlled holdings in the interests of efficiency and clarity of business mission were stopped because of the links between business and party politics. Veto power disappeared with the political and moral collapse of the First Republic, and this broke the convergence of private and public interests that had sustained the Italian route to modern capitalism.

Even when the privatization issue was able to gain momentum, there was evidence that its speed was subject to the uncertain evolution of political transition and that sales were subject to calculations of their effect on the balance of power in both the political and business arenas. Progress has been made possible by forcing situations and isolating the process from obstructing influences. Thus, in the summer of 1992, Prime Minister Giuliano Amato was able to restart the privatization process through a decree that drastically and unexpectedly reduced the transition period for state holdings and swept away their boards. The recent crucial privatization of Stet-Telecom was made possible by the de facto confiscation of company shares from the IRI state holdings by the Treasury.

THE STATE IN THE PRIVATIZED ECONOMY

A privatization process is not just a sale of assets as a consequence of the state's divestiture decision; it also implies a process of institutional building (Macchiati 1996). Institutional building is a theme of special significance in countries like the formerly Communist ones of Eastern Europe, where privatization represented a fundamental occasion for the design of new capitalist ownership structures. Industrially advanced countries also carried out more or less thorough reforms in order to manage the process of privatization and give the state the powers and tools needed in the postprivatization situation.

An interesting feature has been the emergence of independent authorities. Clearly inspired by well-known North American models, these regulatory authorities help to define postprivatization political economies in new terms. They have at least two significant features:

1. They are often significantly more powerful and effective, more intrusive and interfering, than the former direct intervention by governments and their agencies. The regulatory state can be as cumbersome a presence in the economy as the previous owner state. This underscores the risk of useless, if not bad, privatizations resulting from inefficient regulations and regulators. It can be argued that the regulatory framework may be such that ownership becomes irrelevant from the point of view of the ability of companies to pursue efficiency and profit maximization.
2. These authorities are often subject to political influence through nomination procedures and guarantees of independence. Impermeability to political pressure can be welcome, especially in countries with a structural propensity to corruption, but there is a potential problem of diminished democratic control over possibly sensitive issues.

The problematic role of independent authorities is only one aspect of the decline of SOE in a more general phenomenon: the reshaping of the role of the state and its policy styles.[6] This phenomenon can be described as a shift away from patterns of policy making that assumed, at least in abstract terms, a capacity to control (if not command) private business on the basis of explicit and formalized powers. Policy styles then emerge that are characterized by informality, flexibility, the search for consensus, and market conformity (that is, policy additionality with minimum interference in the market mechanism, not mere subsidiar-

---

[6] A more detailed discussion of these issues can be found in Bellini 1996.

ity).[7] The apparatus of the state is progressively shaped with declining attention to guaranteeing close coordination and unitary command of significant policy tools (Japan's Ministry of International Trade and Industry model). Governments thus focus on guaranteeing the learning process ("intelligent governments"), the continuous adaptation of policies in response to feedback from the economy, and the capacity to build and manage policy networks for the design and implementation of complex policies.

The concept of policy network best describes a pattern of policy making that responds to territorial and functional fragmentation and provides problem-solving opportunities in the governing of contemporary political economies. Within a wider "policy community," networks identify governance structures that derive from

the interaction of many separate but interdependent organizations, which coordinate their action through interdependencies of resources and interests. Actors, who take an interest in the making of a certain policy and who dispose of resources (material and immaterial) required for the formulation, decision and implementation of the policy, form linkages to exchange these resources.... [Networks] are characterized by predominantly informal interactions between public and private actors with distinctive, but interdependent interests, who strive to solve problems of collective action on a central, non-hierarchical level.[8]

From this perspective, the usual contrast between direct state involvement in the form of ownership and control of companies and a regulatory state role loses much of its explanatory power. It contrasts policy options in order to measure their relative efficiency in responding to market failures. In a mercantilist framework, however, policy networks are a much more obvious and meaningful alternative to direct

---

[7] "Additionality" (a central concept in industrial policy analysis) refers to the ability of a policy to cause behavior in an individual (the company) different from what it would have been in the absence of the policy. Additionality may be absolute (a decision is made that would not have been made otherwise), or relative to the scale (a costlier, riskier decision is made as a consequence of the enactment of the policy), or relative to the timing (the decision is made earlier). Additionality does not occur if the company would have taken the same decision anyway, on the same scale and with the same timing. Policies in that case do not have more than an ex-post, confirmatory significance with regard to company decisions, besides providing a framework to mere transfers of financial resources between the state and industry. Further, additionality evaluations should take into account the distorting effect created by diverting resources from other, nonsubsidized projects.

[8] Börzel 1997, 5. See also Atkinson and Coleman 1989 and Wilks and Wright 1987.

ownership. The objectives of state action are unchanged, but the cost of both design and implementation is shared among a wider group of interested parties.

These general trends do not lead to simple convergence around emerging best practices. Best practices have to be reinterpreted according to the different evolutionary patterns that characterize national institutions and political economies (Berger and Dore 1996). National variations can be described by starting from three main ideal types:[9]

1. The "expert state" has a monopoly on legitimacy in identifying and achieving collective interests. This legitimacy is based on political and social factors as well as technical ones because a specific expertise in this respect is recognized by state bodies. Because of this legitimacy, the state can openly and effectively pursue collective objectives and obtain substantial compliance with its aims from business. Policy networks carry out governmental strategies, and they may be consciously engineered by the state itself.

2. The "referee state" provides the economy with a framework to mediate and control relations between social actors. The state relies on a stable and widespread structure provided by established networks both in society and in the economy. These networks are politically significant and effective because of the high propensity for self-regulation and self-administration of private actors and their social legitimacy in identifying and pursuing collective interests. Further, a number of specialized collective actors are entrusted with specific regulatory and policy implementation tasks: these are semipublic agencies or chartered associations and professional unions.

3. The "bargaining state" is based on a political body whose relationship with economic actors is aimed at preserving power structures and guaranteeing the survival of the groups controlling them. Protection and subsidies are typically exchanged for the support and financing of party activities. In doing this, the political powers may alternate between cooperative and hostile attitudes, between

[9] Although these three ideal types are brief descriptions of three national cases (France, Germany, and Italy), they reflect basic attitudes that are detectable, to a greater or lesser extent, in all other countries, including the three just mentioned. "Bargaining" patterns, including their pathologies, are far from absent in countries like Germany or France; on specific policy issues the German and Italian states have played the "expert" role, and so on.

Table 2.2. National Cases of State–Industry Relationships

Country	Decision Making of the State: Degree of		Degree of Organization of Industrial Interests	Industry–State Relationship: Prevailing Features
	Centralization	Autonomy		
Japan	H	H	H	Expert state integrated into well-structured policy network
France	H	H	L	Expert state with subordinated policy networks
Italy	L	H	H	Bargaining state
Germany	L	L	H	Referee state integrated into well-structured policy network
U.S.	L	L	L	Referee state

Note: H = high; L = low.
Source: Adapted from Bellini 1996.

incentives and blackmail. Networks are shaped by more or less stable alliances and bargains.

Table 2.2 is the result of refining these ideal types by means of information about the degree of centralization of state decision making, the degree of its autonomy (from other power centers in the society), and the degree of structured organization of industrial interests. Table 2.2 includes the least ambiguous and most stable national cases. Centralization of state decision making is shown as a characteristic of what used to be termed "strong" states. These states also show a high level of autonomy from other power centers, a characteristic they share with "weak" states but highly structured political consortia (for example, Italy). The degree of organization of industrial interests thus makes industry a more or less powerful counterpart of both strong and weak states in managing policy networks and extracting advantages from their work.

Policy networks add complexity to policy making compared to traditional hierarchical patterns. Their efficiency is based on their relative ability to "reduce the costs of information and transaction and create mutual trust among the actors, diminishing uncertainty and thus the risk of defection. Due to these functions, networks serve as an ideal institutional framework for horizontal co-ordination between public and private actors. Policy-making occurs in an increasingly complex, dynamic and diversified environment where hierarchical co-ordination is rendered dysfunctional" (Börzel 1997, 1).

Policy networks may well become policy bottlenecks, pushing governments back to more authority-based, hierarchical styles. A fundamental condition for the effective operation of policy networks is sharing values, ideas, identities, and symbols that facilitate communication and strengthen mutual trust. Policy networks are the result of a path-dependent learning process developed from the past. States adapt new policy styles by recycling accumulated knowledge and experience. Some may find themselves better adapted to the new rules of policy making as a result of being accustomed either to relying on societal networks or to referring to the circuits of state-created elites. In these cases, because of the reliability of policy networks and confidence in the ability to manage them effectively, the retreat of the state will not be seen as a loss of power over and guidance of the collective destiny of society.

Within these possible configurations of the industry–state relationship, a distinction can be drawn between state ownership and state entrepreneurship. "State ownership" merely refers to the control of financial and industrial assets. "State entrepreneurship" refers to state intervention in the evolution of the economy, not through regulation or incentives to shape individual behavior, but through the direct assumption of some of the risks involved in structural change or, better, through sharing some of the risks of individual entrepreneurs, giving them the status of collectively significant behavior. This rationale is best described in Alexander Hamilton's discussion of the attitude toward entrepreneurs' risk aversion, their "apprehension of failing in new attempts":

There are dispositions apt to be attracted by the mere novelty of an undertaking; but these are not always the best calculated to give it success. To this it is of importance that the confidence of cautious, sagacious capitalists, both citizens and foreigners, should be excited. And to inspire this description of persons with confidence, it is essential that they should be made to see in any project which is new – and for that reason alone, if for no other, precarious – the prospect of such a degree of countenance and support from governments, as may be capable of overcoming the obstacles inseparable from first experiments. (Hamilton 1957, 204)

The entrepreneur state does not necessarily need to own something, although, under certain conditions, a preference for straightforward control of policy "agents" is likely. The owner state may even lose any reference to an entrepreneurial objective. The state then plays a rentier role, extracting financial and political returns from its assets.

The decline of the owner state does not involve the decline of the entrepreneur state. State entrepreneurship is a basic feature of the state–industry relationship that can be called "state persuasion." One consequence of the absence of the power to command individual entrepreneurs in market economies has been a concentration on the ability to persuade them. A good deal of industrial policy is based on the assumption that individual entrepreneurs can be persuaded to behave in ways that are (or are perceived to be) at least partially distinct from short-term individual interests, but that realize medium and long-term collective interests as these are interpreted by the state. This may concern decisions to innovate, to invest, or to locate beyond the risk margins that individual entrepreneurs would consider acceptable.

This ambition to persuade is, of course, subject to conditions and technical limitations. Although specific areas of the economy are sensitive to this kind of guidance (as in the case of effective moral persuasion by central banks over credit institutions), industry requires possibly less subtle but also more complex and varied means of persuasion. The ambition to persuade, therefore, easily causes skepticism about its effectiveness and importance.

A fundamental means of persuasion consists of the direct entrepreneurial intervention of the state along the lines of Hamilton's argument. The case of France in the immediate postwar period is probably the best example. Planning required state enterprises: state ownership was a function of state entrepreneurship. As the state began to renounce its power to command the private sector, planning policies required a hard core of reliable companies. Especially in operations requiring high levels of investment and innovative solutions, they would have been readier to follow the planners' indications, thus creating a bandwagon effect in the rest of the economy, both because of their market power and because of their ability to trigger imitative behavior (Cohen 1977).

The entrepreneur state does not command; it persuades through example as much as through market power. Its role is based on a combination of political and technical legitimacy. Political legitimacy guarantees that its behavior is focused on collectively significant objectives. Technical legitimacy lends credibility to the solutions proposed to the economy. The decline of state ownership is also the result of its failure as a function of state entrepreneurship: managerial inefficiency and neoliberal attitudes erode legitimacy. State ownership is increasingly perceived as an excessively costly way to bring economic actors together, especially compared with public–private policy networks. This is particularly the case since privatization itself provides the opportunity to build or redesign such networks.

TRENDS: SURVIVAL AND PROSPECTS OF THE STATE AS ENTREPRENEUR

The entrepreneurial state survives, even without (or with reduced) ownership, as a fundamental actor in economic development and responds to the two challenges posed to the nation-state by the contemporary political economy: (1) the need to reidentify the national identities of companies, verifying the consistency of private and collective interests and strategies in a globalized economy, and (2) the need to manage the territorial fragmentation of policy making into a number of overlapping and uncoordinated policy levels (typically, supranational, national, regional, and local).

Common sense suggests that state ownership is at odds with globalization. Although state-owned companies have sometimes demonstrated a remarkable ability to manage complex internationalization strategies, their nationalist imprint has been a serious handicap in their participation in the global economy. Managers have often been among the first to point out the extent to which their domestic structure limited international operations and made them suspect and unwelcome in foreign eyes. Privatization is a frequent credibility condition for international investors. Privatization guarantees the absence of an unfavorable public sector within the economy and the commitment of political institutions to respect the basic rules of the market economy. The process of privatization is also clear evidence of a country's openness to international investors, both in terms of proactive, promotional attitudes of government bodies and agencies and in terms of the avoidance of discriminatory behavior or arbitrary means of control of the "golden share" kind. The state's ability to disregard the rules of the global economy is severely limited by competition from other countries and regions in attracting investment. The need to comply with the requirements of international capital is an expression of limited sovereignty characterizing present-day nation-states.

An even more important consequence follows from the decline of state ownership. This decline furthers the trend toward company "denationalization." Denationalization does not mean the full loss of national reference of an imaginary "Cosmocorp" (Ball 1967). Rather, the "who are we?" syndrome shows that it is impossible to define the nationality of companies within the global economy in terms of the location of headquarters or plants or the nationality of owners or workers (Reich 1991). There is no obvious relationship between the company and collective interests in the global economy.

Privatization implies that nation-states give up those remaining companies that are unambiguously identifiable as national, and underscores the real dilemmas and trauma associated with the "who are we?" syndrome. This happens especially where privatized companies are located in strategic sectors. Dependency rhetoric then rehearses the well-known and usually dubious or instrumental mix of economic and security arguments, with the addition of updated arguments related to the linkage between development and the localization of cumulative, path-dependent learning processes, especially regarding innovation. State-owned companies can be seen as a stronghold resisting the "hollowing out" of industrial corporations and its negative impact on localized (national) systems of innovation.

Here again a change of analytical perspective is appropriate: "the question is not whether or not the Nation State is compatible with international firms, but what functions the Nation State is likely to continue to perform, in an era of international capital, whether all Nation States will be similarly affected, and how 'international' will international institutions be" (Murray 1971, 286). From this perspective, privatization contributes to shifting the role of the state to that of the provider of "club goods" – public goods whose fruition is limited to a limited number of subjects: "national" companies. The companies are national only because their strategies are seen as compatible with and functional for the interests of national communities, irrespective of the legal nationality of the companies.

Club goods are by no means irrelevant to global companies. Some of them are quantitatively significant in terms of the financial resources provided to companies in the form of subsidies or tax breaks. Some of them are still monopolized by the state, as in the case of domestic and international security, enforceable regulations, and so on. Some, although in the private domain, are still managed by state bodies with legitimacy and know-how, such as diplomacy, unattainable in the private sector. Further, the state maintains a pivotal role as the main actor in the strategic positioning of the country's economic apparatus in global networks as well as in engineering country-specific competitive advantages, both in terms of the propensity to innovate (by contributing decisively to the establishment of innovation systems) and in terms of providing a "global platform" to global companies (Lundvall 1993; Porter 1990). What is crucial is the relationship between the interest of the company in the "goods" provided by the state and the ability of the latter to provide them not only within its own territory but even beyond, through political and economic diplomacy and influence in international or supranational organizations.

In conclusion, privatization pushes the state even further away from the inertia of considering nationally owned companies as the depository of the industrial future of the country and toward dynamic participation in globalization.

Still, ownership is not meaningless. Nation-states, and increasingly regional and local levels of government, consider it an appropriate lever for guaranteeing benefits from economic activities. Ownership, then, does not so much reflect the desire for absolute control and the subjection of company decisions to political imperatives as it allows formal participation in the decision-making processes of companies. As shareholders, governments feel better able to receive and convey reliable information. When necessary, they can "vote" for strategies that are consistent with local development policies; alternatively, they can use veto powers to prevent or slow down strategies that involve delocalization of plants, decreased R&D activities, decreased local content of manufactured goods, and so on.

The German *Länder* have always combined direct and indirect ownership with political aims. This case shows the need for the addition of a multilevel dimension to the privatization process. This attitude has clear historical roots: state ownership in nineteenth- and twentieth-century Germany was an expression of the defense of other German states' remaining sovereignty in the face of Prussian dominance.[10] The *Länder* have interfered in the privatization policies of the federal government, especially in the identification of the new ownership structure, or have themselves strengthened regional champions by selling their own assets. *Länder* representatives, often top-level representatives (such as the *Ministerpräsidenten*), regularly appear as major players in

[10] See Wengenroth's essay.

the corporate governance of major German companies. Their role is most important when changes in companies threaten to affect industrial activities within *Länder* territories. A good example is provided by the Daimler Benz–Messerschmitt Boelkow Blohm (MBB) merger in 1989. The city-states of Hamburg and Bremen, which were both shareholders in MBB, led what the press described as a "revolt" of the northern *Länder* (Hamburg, Bremen, Niedersachsen, and Schleswig-Holstein) against the merger. Thanks to their veto power, they managed to postpone the merger for several weeks, and eventually obtained assurances that the operation would not involve the much-feared relocation southward of some of the most important military and aerospace industry plants and research centers, such as those at Bayern and Baden-Württemberg.

Multilevel state ownership implies that different sensitivities toward privatization coexist within the same country. The difference in the level of government (and thus sensitivity to the territorial consequences of industrial adjustments) is nearly always a more powerful variable than government ideology. Adding levels of government increases the likelihood of different sensitivities. In the new eastern *Länder* of Germany at an earlier stage privatization policies were formulated in a vacuum, as the newly established regional governments were an absolute, scarcely rooted novelty. Later on, the strengthening of the new political bodies, which faced the territorial costs of structural adjustment, led to a more diversified range of privatization procedures, allowing for some kinds of direct support by the *Länder* to potentially competitive companies (Seibel 1994).

Decentralization processes seem to provide an irresistible temptation to regional governments to opt for the direct ownership of strategic ventures, even when central governments are engaged in privatization. A good example is provided by the case of Spain. In 1996 the Autonomías held shares in 298 companies, including the industrial holding of the Catalan government, Eplicsa (established 1985); the telecommunications company of the Basque country, Euskaltel; and the Instituto de Fomento de Andalucía.[11]

Moving to subnational levels of government does not imply merely lower-level duplication of traditional patterns of state ownership. In most industrially advanced and less advanced countries, a plurality of semipublic, quasi-nongovernmental entities bears witness to the

---

[11] Data from the Ministry of Economics, as reported by the press.

effectiveness of state ownership as a way of supporting the state as entrepreneur. These entities range from regional development agencies to semipublic organizations providing services to companies (Bianchi and Bellini 1991; Halkier, Danson, and Damborg 1998). They introduce new actors whose function is to guide or support the evolution of the industrial apparatus through the provision of innovative (and mostly intangible) assets. In most cases these new actors are designed and organized as companies, partly out of respect for the neoliberal stereotype and partly out of a genuine search for policy market conformity. Managerial attitudes are required of their governing bodies, which are rewarded or punished on the basis of performance. The markets provide the final assessment of their work by occasional formal reference to self-financing ratios, although this assessment is somewhat inefficient because of the nature of their products. The option to privatize is open as soon as their mission is completed and the services they provide can be sufficiently produced and efficiently sold through market mechanisms.

Once again, the state enters the field to share the risks of "cautious, sagacious capitalists, both citizens and foreigners": ownership is just one of the means the state has of serving an essential and historically lasting function in economic development.

REFERENCES

Amato, G. 1992. Il mercato nella costituzione. *Quaderni Costituzionali* 1(April): 7–20.

Atkinson, M. M., and W. D. Coleman. 1989. Strong states and weak states: Sectoral policy networks in advanced capitalist economies. *British Journal of Political Science* 19: 47–67.

Ball, G. W. 1967. Cosmocorp: The importance of being stateless. *Columbia Journal of World Business* (November–December). Reprinted in *International political economy: Perspectives on global power and wealth*, ed. J. A. Frieden and D. A. Lake, pp. 187–92. New York, 1987.

Bellini, N. 1996. *Stato e industria nelle economie contemporanee*. Rome.

Berger, S., and R. Dore, eds. 1996. *National diversity and global capitalism*. Ithaca, N.Y.

Bianchi, P. 1987. The IRI in Italy: Strategic role and political constraints. *West European Politics* 2(April): 269–90.

Bianchi, P., and N. Bellini. 1991. Public policies for local networks of innovators. *Research Policy* 20: 487–97.

Börzel, T. A. 1997. What's so special about policy networks? An exploration of the concept and its usefuless in studying European governance. *European Integration Online Papers* 1997-016.

Bös, D. 1997. Privatisation in Eastern Germany: The never-ending story of the Treuhand. In *Privatisation at the end of the century*, ed. H. Giersch, pp. 175–98. Berlin.

Cohen, É. 1992. *Le colbertisme "high tech": Économie des telecom et du grand projet*. Paris.

——— 1996. *La tentation hexagonale: La souveraineté à l'épreuve de la mondialisation*. Paris.

Cohen, S. 1977. *Modern capitalist planning: The French model*. Berkeley.

Crozier, M. 1987. *État modeste, état moderne: Strategie pour un autre changement*. Paris.

Economist, The. 1997. The future of the state: A survey of the world economy. *The Economist* (September 20).

Giersch, H., ed. 1997. *Privatisation at the end of the century*. Berlin.

Halkier, H., M. Danson, and C. Damborg, eds. 1998. *Regional development agencies in Europe*. London.

Hamilton, A. 1957. Report on manufactures. In *Alexander Hamilton's papers on public credit and finance*. New York.

Jasinski, P. 1997. Privatisation in the United Kingdom and Poland: The model and its transformation. In *Privatisation at the end of the century*, ed. H. Giersch, pp. 147–74. Berlin.

Krug, B. 1997. Privatisation in China: Something to learn from? In *Privatisation at the end of the century*, ed. H. Giersch, pp. 269–93. Berlin.

Lundvall, B.-Å. 1993. User–producer relationship: National systems of innovation and internationalization. In *Technology and the wealth of nations: The dynamics of constructed advantage*, ed. D. Foray and C. Freeman, pp. 277–300. London.

Macchiati, A. 1996. *Privatizzazioni tra economia e politica*. Rome.

Müller, W. C., and V. Wright, eds. 1994. The state in Western Europe: Retreat or redefinition? *West European Politics* 17(3).

Murray, R. 1971. The internationalization of capital and the nation state. In *The multinational enterprise*, ed. J. H. Dunning, PP. 265–88. London.

Overbeek, H. 1990. *Global capitalism and national decline: The Thatcher decade in perspective*. London.

Plane, P. 1997. Privatisation and economic growth: Reflections and observations. In *Privatisation at the end of the century*, ed. H. Giersch, 29–52. Berlin.

Poggi, G. 1991. *The state: Its nature, development, and prospects*. Stanford, Calif.

Porter, M. 1990. *The competitive advantage of nations*. London.

Reich, R. B. 1991. *The work of nations: Preparing ourselves for twenty-first century capitalism*. New York.

Schmidt, V. 1996. *From state to market? The transformation of French business and government*. Cambridge.

Seibel, W. 1994. Strategische Fehler oder erfolgreiches Scheitern? Zur Entwicklungslogik der Treuhandanstalt 1990–1993. *Politische Vierteljahresschrift* 35(1): 3–39.

Stiglitz, J. E. 1989. On the economic role of the state. In *The economic role of the state*, by J. E. Stiglitz et al., pp. 9–85. Oxford.

Vickers, J., and V. Wright. 1988. The politics of industrial privatisation in Western Europe: An overview. *West European Politics* 4(October): 1-30.

Wilks, S., and M. Wright. 1987. Comparing government-industry relations: States, sectors, and networks. In *Comparative government-industry relations: Western Europe, the United States, and Japan*, ed. S. Wilks and M. Wright, pp. 274-313. Oxford.

World Bank. 1995. *Beaureaucrats in business: The economics and politics of government ownership*. Oxford.

1997. *The state in a changing world:World development report 1997*. Oxford.

3

The Performance of State-Owned Enterprises

YAIR AHARONI

Since the beginning of the 1980s, the World Bank and the International Monetary Fund (IMF) have made great efforts to cajole the governments of developing countries into privatizing state-owned enterprises (SOEs) (Babai 1988, 260–7). This policy has been the result of growing skepticism about the ability of SOEs to achieve optimal economic results (Galal 1991; Kikeri et al. 1992). The performance of SOEs is viewed as abysmal and as having a pernicious effect on the economy as a whole. SOEs have been seen as absorbing government funds because of their huge losses (Short 1984). Policy prescriptions have been to privatize, to deregulate, and to increase and invigorate the role of the private sector. It is often said that history has amply illustrated the limitations and shortcomings of SOEs, which can be a "significant impediment to economic growth" (World Bank 1995, 257). History is also said to have demonstrated the capacity of private enterprises to overcome many of these shortcomings. In fact, however, the empirical evidence is more ambiguous. It lends only limited support to the hypothesis that SOEs are *inherently* less efficient than private enterprises. Moreover, studies rarely take into account issues such as security of supply or environmental constraints (Fells and Lucas 1992). Further, profit maximization by private-sector enterprises may also lead the managers of these enterprises to "shift their battleground from the level of the firm to the political level.

49

Control of the government may then become the means for establishing 'control' of the firm" (Papandreou 1952, 203). The rents granted to private enterprise may exert a drag on growth.

This essay summarizes the evidence on performance. It shows that state ownership is often correlated with politicization, inefficiency, and waste of resources. Yet it is too early to conclude, as the World Bank does, that "state-owned enterprises remain an important obstacle to better economic performance" (World Bank 1995, 175). The assumption that ownership per se creates an environment that is conducive to high or low performance is not proven, and empirical research on this point has yielded conflicting results. Although private firms are not necessarily disciplined by the market or by the threat of bankruptcy, governments do seem to be more willing to use the disciplinary forces of competition when firms are privately owned. In other words, if ownership per se matters, it is because of its impact on the state rather than because of the discipline imposed on the managers of firms or its direct effects on managerial incentives.

In judging the performance of SOEs, one has to consider the following. First, how is performance defined and measured? Second, what is the historical evidence about the performance of SOEs? Third, what variables other than ownership should be analyzed and assessed in explaining performance? Fourth, if the performance of SOEs is so bad, why are reforms and privatization so difficult? This essay analyses the first three issues, and its structure follows the same sequence. In the first section, issues of performance definitions and measurement are discussed. The second section surveys theoretical and empirical studies of the performance of SOEs. The historical evidence shows that most SOEs perform less well than private enterprises on most but not all measures of performance. The possible determinants of this dismal performance, that is, the major variables that may explain differences in performance, are analyzed in the third section.

MEASURING PERFORMANCE

Before performance is gauged, it is important to define it precisely. Economists focus mainly on efficiency as a criterion for performance, but there are different definitions of efficiency. First, efficiency may be defined as the ratio of outputs (products or services) to inputs (the resources used in production). In neoclassical economics, the concern is with allocative efficiency. Allocative efficiency requires that the social costs of producing a given level of output desired by consumers be kept to a minimum.

A second type of efficiency is dynamic efficiency: the rate of change of output per unit of input. Thus, an economy is production-efficient if the supply of any good or service cannot be increased without reducing the supply of some other good or service, including all possibilities of foreign trade. Allocative efficiency also requires that it is impossible to make anyone better off without making someone else worse off; in addition to production efficiency, all final consumers must have exhausted all possibilities of mutually beneficial exchange.

Leibenstein (1966) pointed out that as a result of motivational factors within the firm, motivational factors from external sources, and non-market input efficiency, firms may be what he termed "x-inefficient." The degree of "x-inefficiency" may be defined as the difference between maximum and actual effectiveness in the utilization of inputs. The theory of x-efficiency is akin to managerial theories because it assumes that the effort of individuals is a discretionary variable, that no identity of interests exists between the firm and individuals, that rationality is selective, and that individual motivation is a significant variable. Most observers believe that x-inefficiency is more prevalent in SOEs than in private firms. SOEs are held to be less efficient than they could have been if all possible variations in individual and collective motivational structures had been eliminated.

SOEs have been established to maximize social welfare rather than profits. Therefore, one has to define welfare and the ways in which the behavior of the enterprise must be determined and its performance assessed. This behavior is defined operationally by economists in terms of the prices to be charged by the enterprise and the guidelines for investment decisions. As Bös (1981, 1) argues, "pricing of publicly supplied goods is the primary vehicle for embedding public enterprises adequately into a market economy." Welfare is defined, in cost–benefit analysis, as the difference between social benefits and social costs. Social benefits are equal to the benefit to the SOE, measured by its revenues, plus the consumer surplus, gauged by consumers' willingness to pay. It is not easy to make an empirical calculation of willingness to pay and therefore of consumer surplus. Although it is important to estimate the size of welfare losses, any analysis is fraught with difficult theoretical issues, such as the empirical estimates of external effects, intangibles, and the choice of the optional rate of time preference or the rate of opportunity costs. Technically, the issue is the quantitative importance of allocative efficiency, measured by the difference between marginal cost pricing and profit maximization.

Financial profitability cannot be the sole criterion for judging performance because SOEs were created to achieve social or strategic objectives, and reported profits often depend critically on the prices of both inputs and outputs set by the government. Because economies are riddled with market imperfections and distortions, financial profitability is not necessarily consistent with positive social surplus. Firms in oligopolistic industries control prices and are sometimes protected by high tariff barriers, and market prices for imports do not reflect their opportunity costs. The state has used SOEs as a policy instrument to achieve all sorts of goals – not only economic development, but also political goals and relief of distribution pressures. SOEs have been required to employ individuals with certain political affiliations or to confer largess on certain interest groups. SOEs have also received preferential treatment in purchases from the government, and have been granted below-market-rate loans and easier access to funds. The multitude of goals, the contradictory directions from government, and the perverse incentives make a measurement of performance by financial results inadequate. Further, like any other business enterprise, SOEs have to be managed. Where enterprise management is concerned, performance may have to be gauged by different criteria. Constraints stemming from social role (for example, employment), ill-defined authority relations, or political imperatives, as well as the multiple objectives imposed by administrative or political masters, must all be taken into account (Aharoni 1982). Of course, private enterprises are not immune to social and political pressures or the glare of public scrutiny (Lenway and Murtha 1994). However, state ownership raises the possibility of invoking sovereign prerogatives (Murtha and Lenway 1994, 117). All of this means that it is not enough to measure performance in strict economic terms. One has to measure the stimulus provided to other socioeconomic activities and other externalities. The high cost of such a study makes it expensive to carry out regularly and allows management to use social costs as an excuse for business inefficiency.

Theoretically, a better solution is to measure and assess performance in terms of enterprise effectiveness in achieving various objectives. One approach is a social audit – assessing performance in terms of morale and satisfaction, standard of living, distribution factors, contribution to externalities, and other attributes (Aharoni 1983). An enterprise can be compared to other enterprises (benchmarking), or its past and present achievements can be compared. Another method is to assess internal organizational dynamics, not just the market structure and the regulatory environment.

Thus, measures of performance range from "hard" measures such as profitability, productivity, or growth rate to "softer" behavioral measures such as employee satisfaction, legitimacy, or managerial incentive or adaptability. Financial measures are misleading for those who see an SOE as a government instrument that should strive to achieve objectives such as a more egalitarian distribution of income, regional development, technological self-sufficiency, poverty reduction, or development. For others, the social role of SOEs is seen as an excuse for mismanagement. As we shall see, much of the debate about the comparative efficiency of privately owned firms and SOEs is waged on ideological grounds, generating much heat but very little light. In practice, empirical studies measure performance in terms of accounting profits, and policy makers rely heavily on reported profits. Ramamurti (1987, 891) found that senior bureaucrats and selected journalists who were employed as external evaluators of Indian SOEs espouse one set of standards for judging performance but use a different set of standards (in which profitability plays a very important role) for actually judging performance. His study shows that, in practice, profits are a more important criterion for the performance evaluation of SOEs than they should be, according to official policy or economic theory. Perhaps because of this emphasis on profits, despite its well-known shortcomings, SOEs are judged to be less efficient than private enterprises (Likierman 1983).

Other studies compare cost per unit, capacity utilization, productivity, or growth rates. In doing so, they encounter a difficulty of a different sort. It is not easy to find two firms operating in the same country that are exactly equal. Differences in performance can always be ascribed to differences in size, cost of capital, services rendered, and so on. Some studies have attempted to adjust for differences in size or market structure, but very few have been successful in adjusting for differences in enterprise objectives. More recently, studies have been carried out comparing the performance of SOEs before and after divestiture. Yet here, improved performance may have been achieved by a one-time reduction in staff, a correction of underpricing, or other actions.

To a large extent, much of the belief in the superiority of private ownership has been a reaction to the dramatic collapse of the centrally planned economies. In an earlier book on the topic, I surveyed different studies of the comparative efficiency of socialist and capitalist countries (Aharoni 1986, 172–4; for more recent analyses see De Castro and Uhlenbruck 1997; Laban and Wolf 1993). Clearly, central planning and excessive regulation failed. Whether privatization per se would increase gross national product (GNP) without a change in economic regime (as claimed by Galal et al. 1994), and whether this increase would be achieved in a socially desirable way, is less certain.

COMPARING PRIVATE FIRMS AND SOEs

Financial Performance of SOEs

Most studies of the performance of SOEs measure their accounting profits. If we use such a measure, SOEs show a dismal picture of losses and ill-conceived investments (Ahmed 1982; Gantt and Dutto 1968; Shirley 1983; Short, 1984). In India, when pretax profits were compared with those of private firms in the same industry (but not necessarily in the same product line), SOEs showed much worse profit performance (Sri Ram et al. 1976, 40–1). State-owned banks showed losses, whereas the lean, newly created, privately owned banks were profitable (Rao 1996). SOE losses as a percentage of gross domestic product (GDP) reached 9 percent in Argentina and Poland in 1989 (Kikeri et al. 1992, 2). This financial performance means that SOEs tend to cause serious financial burdens and a drain on resources. More recent studies show a better picture for many countries in the period after 1985 in terms of both pretax profits as a percentage of sales revenues and net operating surplus to sales. It seems that, faced with a heavy financial burden, many countries insisted on improved performance in their SOE sector. It is also possible that price rises were allowed and government restrictions reduced. Alternatively, it may have been the end of a gestation period or a learning curve.

Aggregate figures do not give a very meaningful picture. Thus, most of the profits of the SOE sector in Ghana stem from its Cocoa Board. Mexico's figures are dramatically influenced by the performance of its oil firm. When Pemex is excluded, Mexico's SOEs moved from a deficit of 19 percent in 1978–85 to a surplus of 10 percent in 1986–91. When Pemex is included, the operating surplus as a percentage of sales is almost 60 percent in the first period and about 50 percent in the second period, when oil prices deteriorated (World Bank 1995, 58–9).

The SI deficit can be defined as the difference between current

surplus and investment for the SOE sector. When the SI deficit is a result
of the price of SOE products being too low and/or the SOE being less
productive, this indicates poor performance. One measure of performance is the aggregate financial needs of SOEs. A World Bank study of
forty-six developing countries shows that the annual average SI deficit
declined from 2.2 percent in 1978–85 to 0.8 percent in 1986–91. This
was the result partly of increased savings and partly of decreased investment. In the seventeen poorest countries, however, the SI deficit fell to
an average of 1.7 percent of GDP in 1986–91, despite a reduction in
investment.

Lower profits or losses may point to an indirect subsidy through low,
controlled prices of an SOE's output. At the same time, the government
determines many of the firm's costs. The government may set wage ceilings, fix raw material costs, subsidize interest rates, or give SOEs investment funds at preferential rates. Thus, company profits are the outcome
of policies regulating input and output prices, which the company itself
does not set (Aharoni 1981b). Obviously the degree of profitability of
such a firm cannot be used to indicate how efficiently it exploits its
inputs. Thus, if a subsidy given to farmers is paid directly, an SOE making
fertilizers may be profitable. If the same subsidy is given in the form of
a price reduction for fertilizers, the firm would show losses that are not
necessarily a reflection of its efficiency. Further, certain private firms
(and SOEs) have been profitable because state ownership guaranteed a
supply of raw materials and "virtually ensured the profitability of the
recipient" (Hill 1982, 1019). SOEs may be unprofitable because they are
expected to assist the poor or to create jobs. Whether or not they should
be asked to do so is a different issue. SOEs also subsidize private individuals and firms through low prices for energy, electricity, or water.
When the Mexican electricity firm received real price increases of 7.7
percent in 1990, the financial performance of the SOE sector looked
much better.

Finally, SOE managers may hide profits or at least attempt to smooth
them. Grayson (1981, 254) notes that in the case of national oil companies (NOCs), "the moment that ROI [return on investment] seems
more than 'reasonable,' governments and the news media begin to talk
about 'excess' or 'windfall' profits. A very profitable NOC would lose
some of its managerial independence should the government ask it
to undertake a new nonfinancial project, for instance." The burden of
social welfare programs is often used as an excuse for inefficiency. In
fact, the main reason most economists insist on the separation of the

economic and social tasks of these enterprises is to allow a better assessment of their performance. Today, unfortunately, it is impossible to relate SOE profitability or the rate of self-financing to the ownership factor or to bad management. If the restrictions imposed by government on cost levels or prices are waived as a result of privatization, the privatized firm's profits will increase. This bolstered performance is often erroneously ascribed to the ownership change rather than to a policy shift.

The financial results of SOEs are not the only performance indicator. However, they do have an impact on resource utilization since they create a budgetary burden. They may also produce reduced incentives for cost controls, resulting in greater losses and higher indebtedness. Many developing countries also face acute shortages of trained managers and may choose to bolster their exchange reserves by selling firms to foreign investors.

The major reason for losses, however, is the political milieu in which SOEs operate. According to Dharam Ghai, SOEs in Africa are frequently used as a means of patronage and a source of wealth and power for political and administrative leaders. "The role of the State has therefore been to enable groups which have acquired control over the State apparatus to establish an economic basis for themselves. . . . [T]he government has often a vested interest in hiding the inefficiency of enterprises" (in Reddy 1983, 182).

On the other hand, in countries where SOEs operate with less governmental interference, the financial results are much better (UNIDO 1983). In Brazil, Chile, Peru, Thailand, and Uruguay, more SOEs showed positive accounting profits than losses. The German and Austrian SOEs fared as well as private enterprises. Finally, many SOEs showed poor performance because they were acquired in the first place as a safety net for employment after they had already failed in private hands. Economists would not recommend the continuation of a safety net for enterprises, whatever their ownership; politicians often have a different point of view on this issue.

In summary, there is no doubt of the staggering losses of SOEs in some countries, or that SOEs protected by government subsidies have absorbed a large percentage of banking credit. Inefficient public enterprises have also increased the costs of doing business for those firms acquiring their products or using their services, while lower prices for the output of SOEs have been used as a major subsidy to the users of these outputs. This performance has been a result of government policy – not of ownership per se.

Efficiency

It is extremely difficult to compare efficiency in private enterprises and SOEs because it is not easy to find two exactly comparable firms operating in the same country. Electricity utilities in the United States provide one exception. They have been described as being "as close to perfection in public–private comparability as any other imaginable real world case" (Yunker 1975, 66). Private electricity utilities in California have conceded that their costs are higher than those of state-owned electricity firms but have argued that their territories are more difficult to serve (Neuberg 1977, 310n.). Different electricity firms also have different input costs because one uses hydroelectric power and another coal, or because the cost of capital is lower for the SOE: municipal firms in the United States can raise funds by issuing tax-exempt bonds. At the same time, it may be argued that differences in input costs are a result of the lack of pressure on management to bargain.

Despite these difficulties, a number of studies have contrasted similarly situated private enterprises and SOEs, that is, cases in which both operate in the same country and in the same environment, such as electric power and refuse collection in the United States. These studies are summarized in Aharoni (1986, 196–201). Several showed that municipal electricity firms in the United States were more efficient even when size and the use of hydroelectric power were controlled for (Hellman 1972; Yunker 1975). Overall, the studies of electricity utilities in the United States do not provide support for the assumed superiority of private ownership, although several of the researchers clearly had an ideological bias and tried to substantiate this superiority (see, for example, De Alessi 1980). Gordon (1981) did not find any performance differences when she compared investor-owned and state-owned telephone firms.

Other studies, such as those of fire departments, have found private enterprises to be more efficient (Ahlbrandt 1973; Poole 1983). Most studies in North America have also pointed out that private refuse collection is cheaper. Blankart (1979) reached similar conclusions in a comparison of private and public bus systems.

Caves and Christensen (1980) studied one of the few cases in which the effects of property rights can be isolated from those of non-competitive markets and regulation. They studied the Canadian railroad industry, in which there are two large railroads of roughly the same size. One is the privately owned Canadian Pacific and the other is the state-owned Canadian National. Both compete nationally. They reported that

contrary to what is predicted in the property rights literature, we find no evidence of inferior efficiency performance by the government-owned rail-road. In fact, our evidence indicates that the CN [Canadian National] has achieved larger gains in productivity than the CP [Canadian Pacific] since 1956. In the late 1950s and early 1960s the CN had a level of productivity approximately 90 percent as high as the CP, but this gap has been closed. We conclude that in the case of Canadian railroads the beneficial effects of competition have been sufficient to overcome any tendency toward in-efficiency resulting from public ownership. (Caves and Christensen 1980, 960-1)

They concluded that "public ownership is not inherently less efficient than private ownership – that the oft-noted inefficiency of government enterprises stems from their isolation from effective competition rather than their public ownership per se" (p. 974).

In a later publication, Caves and Christensen continued their inves-tigation with two other authors, this time comparing the economic performance of U.S. and Canadian railroads. They concluded that the degree of economic regulation had a strong influence on the economic performance of North American railroads. "When one controls for the influence of regulation, there is little indication that ownership form influences performance" (in Stanbury and Thompson 1982, 146-7). The substantially less regulated Canadian railroads performed significantly better than the more regulated U.S. railroads in terms of productivity growth rates. The productivity levels of the two Canadian railroads and their growth rates exceeded those of all U.S. railroads except three small ones. The authors concluded that the "specific explanation for the supe-rior economic performance of the two Canadian railroads must ulti-mately lie in the area of organizational design and control" (Stanbury and Thompson 1982, 147).

On the other hand, Davies (1971) compared the performance of the two domestic regulated Australian air carriers for the sixteen-year period from 1958-9 to 1973-4. He concluded: "The evidence indicates that the private firm [Ansett Airlines], operating under the rules and customs associated with exchangeable private property rights, is more productive than the public enterprise [Trans-Australia Airlines]" (Davies 1977, 226). William A. Jordan (in Stanbury and Thompson 1982, 161–99) claimed that Davies used consolidated figures for Ansett and its four subsidiaries, but only one of these subsidiaries was similar to the state-owned Trans-Australia Airlines in providing interstate trunk operations. Based on a more detailed breakdown of the figures, Jordan claimed: "Ownership is not a relevant factor in airline performance where regulatory monopolies exist." Davies (1981) also compared Australian private and state-owned banks.

Finsinger (1983a, 1983b) studied the performance of insurance markets in the Federal Republic of Germany, and concluded that SOEs and mutual companies outperformed privately owned joint-stock companies.

A number of other studies, mostly of developing countries, concluded that private enterprises perform better than SOEs (Bennet and Johnson 1979; Boardman and Vining 1989). Borcherding et al. (1982) summarized the findings of more than fifty studies, forty of which attributed superior results to private firms. Millward (1982, 83), on the other hand, found "no broad support for private enterprise superiority. . . . [T]here seems no general grounds for believing managerial efficiency is less in public firms."

All in all, the empirical evidence on the issue of private versus public efficiency has been somewhat ambiguous, and the conclusions reached may have been based more on ideological beliefs than on clear statistical tests. The early studies of this issue attempted to contrast comparable firms in terms of economic activities carried out, size of firms, and enterprise objectives. Finding pairs that differ only in ownership has turned out to be an arduous task (for a summary, see, for example, Aharoni 1986; Borcherding et al. 1982; Millward 1982; Millward and Parker 1983).

The most obvious gaps in results may be related to the country or level of development (more studies pointing to superior SOE performance were carried out in North America or Europe) and to the level of competition. Thus, Vickers and Yarrow (1988, 426) conclude: "Theoretical analysis and empirical evidence support the view that private ownership is most efficient and hence privatization is most suitable in markets where effective (actual and potential) competition prevails." Where SOEs operate in noncompetitive markets, the results and interpretations are less clear. To Kikeri et al. (1992, 21), however, privatization is "the outcome most likely to produce positive gains. At the very least, the burden of proof is on those who espouse the creation and maintenance of SOEs. *The evidence in this book repeatedly points to the conclusion that ownership itself matters*" (emphasis in original).

The difference in the tone of the conclusions may be ascribed in part to the ideological beliefs of the researchers. It may also be ascribed to political factors. Any enterprise is nestled within a socioeconomic system whose institutions and rules of play are crucial to understanding its performance. There seems to be growing evidence that although ownership does not matter in theory, governments behave differently when they deal with private investors than when they control SOEs. Perhaps subsidies to private firms are harder to sustain than SOE losses (Boycko et al. 1996).

In the last decade or two, there has been an increasing tendency to measure performance by comparing performance before and after privatization. Different studies, however, use different criteria for performance and therefore are not strictly comparable. Most studies emphasize policy variables (Cook and Kirkpatrick 1988; Franks 1993; Galiani and Petrecolla 1996; Goodman and Loveman 1991; Hutchinson 1991; Lieberman 1993; Luders 1993; McDonald 1993; Milman and Lundstedt 1994; Parker and Martin 1993; Perry and Rainey 1988; Pouder 1996; Ramamurti 1996; Ramanadham 1993). Several studies, such as those in Great Britain, have shown that many of the efficiency gains of SOEs were achieved before privatization took place but after it was declared (Bishop and Kay 1988; Megginson et al. 1994). This does not support the hypothesis that the reason for improved performance was a change of ownership. Moreover, changes in organizational status do not appear to guarantee improved performance (Parker and Hartley 1991). Increased levels of performance came from short-term causes, such as higher prices and reductions in the size of the work force, and from longer-term effects, such as more aggressive cost control and a deliberate effort to increase productivity. It seems too early to predict the long-term impact of privatization. There are, however, growing signs that privatization has reduced the opportunistic behavior of government (Levy and Spiller 1994). Theoretically, these changes could have come about without privatization. Unfortunately they did not, except when ownership was maintained and a management contract was used.

Experience seems to indicate that promises and threats between state organs and SOEs are seen as less credible than those between the state and private investors. Governments are also less disciplined in using their sovereign rights vis-à-vis SOEs. Despite theoretical arguments, the relations between governments and SOEs tend to be much less transparent than the relations with private enterprises. Galal et al. (1994) analyzed twelve divestiture cases from Chile, Malaysia, Mexico, and the United Kingdom (three telecommunications firms, four airlines, two electricity companies, a container terminal, a truck transport company, and a lottery). Their study measured the effects of divestiture on the producers, consumers, workers, government, and competitors over time to capture dynamic effects. It isolated the effects of ownership from other factors by asking: What would have happened without divestiture? The study claimed that divestiture improved world and domestic welfare in eleven of the twelve cases. The gains came primarily from improved productivity, increased investment, and better pricing, and they occurred in both competitive and monopoly markets. It is too early to predict whether these results are sustainable. Again, more often than not, increases in the efficiency of privatized enterprises could be traced to one-time adjustments caused by sharp increases in sales prices or a drastic reduction of the labor force. It is possible that managers, freed from government restrictions, reduced the payroll and raised prices, so the positive results were the consequence of a shakeup rather than a change of ownership. Moreover, to ask what would have happened without divestiture is to assume that institutional and regulatory changes were possible only because of the change of ownership. The World Bank carried out a detailed study showing that the retention of state ownership together with contracting management to a global private firm was successful when the government gave the private management the freedom to run the business. Conversely, "all but one of the borderline or unsuccessful contracts limited management authority over labor" (World Bank 1995, 143). There may also have been some neglect of long-term needs (Fells and Lucas 1992).

The studies cited, therefore, seem to call for a conclusion of a different sort. The success of an enterprise and its economic (or social) performance depend more on the quality of its management and on its discretion to adapt strategy to a changing environment than on ownership (see Aharoni 1981a; Ogden and Watson 1996). Moreover, the transformation of social and economic systems depends on the institutions operating in each society and on the way they operate. It may also depend on the social and moral habits that differentiate institutions, such as the degree of social solidarity of the culture (Fukuyama 1995).

The ineluctable fact is that most SOEs in developing countries have had a dismal economic performance, at least in strict economic terms, and that most electorates and civil servants have lost faith in the capacity of SOEs to achieve superior economic results. The failure of the Soviet Union taught the world quite chilling lessons about the limitations of a centralized economic system in a globally interdependent world. Proponents of SOEs found themselves very much on the defensive. Yet those who rightly attacked government intervention and dirigiste policies seem to have reached much too sweeping conclusions. The performance of SOEs has been disconcerting, but much of the success after privatization seems to be a result of the freedom from restraints regarding the labor force, investment, and prices. In other words, performance improved because the environment and the rules of the game changed, not because ownership changed.

DETERMINANTS OF SUPERIOR PERFORMANCE

There are many stereotypes of the impact of ownership. Economists see structure (competitive environment) and the regulatory environment, as well as ownership, as predictors of performance (high competition entails better performance). For organizational scientists, performance is a function of the context (environment, size, technology), the effectiveness of management's strategic response, and the appropriateness of the organization's structure and systems to both context and strategic actions. Further, differences in culture in different countries may affect performance. So does the country's level of development. Culture may have an impact on the autonomy of managers and on the use of political directives to siphon funds from the enterprise to certain interest groups.

In its recent publications the World Bank has argued that private enterprise is more efficient than SOEs even when it exercises a strong monopoly power, and that reform would allow "increased availability of resources for health, education, and other social spending" (World Bank 1995, 35, 23, 257). The World Bank even claimed that private enterprise achieves social goals such as pollution abatement more efficiently "since state-owned plants tend to be more polluting than their private sector counterparts" (World Bank 1995, 38).

Economists at the World Bank trumpet the virtues of private enterprise as the major vehicle for economic development. In doing so, they may confuse ownership and other variables such as competition, culture, and political milieu that may better explain performance. Thus, the quality and style of top management are crucial determinants of performance. Irrespective of ownership, organizations operating in the same environment may show great differences in performance due to differences in managerial quality, style, strategies, systems, or structures. Moreover, when a private enterprise operates in a noncompetitive environment, or when the institutional environment does not guarantee property rights, or when a private firm is heavily subsidized in return for its commitment to achieve employment goals, ownership per se would not make the firm a superior performer.

There are two major theoretical reasons for assuming that ownership is a direct determinant of performance. One is the idea espoused by the property rights school of thought: patterns of incentives at any time are influenced by the property rights structure. Individual owners enjoy the right to change the form, place, substance, or use of any property they own, subject only to minimal government restrictions such as zoning laws.

In an SOE it is virtually impossible to transfer the ownership rights belonging to the state from one individual or group to another. Taxpayers who wish to change their investment portfolios cannot sell their shares in an SOE. In theory, at least, they can change citizenship and move to another country in which the portfolio of assets held by the state is more to their liking. Taxpayers can, of course, vote in elections, thereby attempting to change the preferences of the state and its policies. They do not, however, have an easy or direct way to transfer their share of the property rights in any SOE. The inability to transfer ownership rights is said to result in state ownership being inherently less efficient than private ownership.

Owners of private firms have an incentive to monitor management's behavior to ensure efficiency. By contrast, a taxpayer owner of an SOE, being part of a diffused ownership, does not have a similar incentive to scrutinize management. The greater the personal financial investment, the greater the interest in the operations of the firm. Owner-managers have the highest stake and therefore care more. If ownership is diffused and separated from management, the additional monitoring costs may make the firm less efficient. Owners can still motivate managers, however, by linking their compensation to the firm's profits, allowing managers to capture part of any monetary gains through stock options, for example. In an SOE, neither the manager nor the government bureaucrat has personal wealth invested in the firm, and they have no right to share in profits. The lack of a connection between the firm's economic performance and the manager's personal pecuniary gains, it is claimed, reduces efficiency.

Further, transferability of shares encourages specialization of ownership. According to Armen Alchian (1965, 1977), the fact that a private firm's shareholders can sell their shares in the capital market means that shareholders are the ones who find their highest valued use as an input. Others simply exercise their exit right and sell the shares. Ownership, Peltzman (1971) argues, can be viewed as a productive input that organizes managerial inputs and fulfills the functions of risk bearing. If a market for these rights is not available, as in the case of an SOE, the distribution of taxpayer-owners, or even of government bureaucrats acting as their agents, will not reflect their highest valued use as an input, at least not as frequently as in an investor-owned private enterprise.

The studies surveyed here do not seem to corroborate the property rights point of view. The stereotype that managers of SOEs are less capable than their counterparts in the private sector, and therefore that SOEs are destined to perform poorly, is not necessarily true (Aharoni and Lachman 1982). Unfortunately, there are very few studies of the inner workings of SOEs and their reaction to the environment in which they operate. However, the survey of performance here shows that if both private firms and SOEs operate in a competitive environment and abide by the same rules and the same set of incentives, SOEs are not necessarily less efficient. Competitive market pressures may be sufficient to yield productive efficiency even when shares are nontransferable. Competition can be stimulated by institutional means, too. On the other hand, a large private enterprise may be led to assume that the government would not allow it to go bankrupt. These arguments clearly show that SOEs and private firms are not competing on the same playing field, and thus their performance cannot be strictly compared.

The other possible reason to prefer private ownership is that politicians and bureaucrats find it difficult to refrain from intervening in the operations of SOEs but behave differently when private investors control the firm. Studies of privatized telecommunications firms in Latin America clearly document striking gains in productivity and a rapid expansion of the telephone network. In the first three or four years after privatization, the network grew by 13 percent per year in Argentina and Mexico, 15 percent in Venezuela, and 18 percent in Jamaica. Labor productivity, measured by lines in service per employee, also increased dramatically – from 13 percent per year in Mexico to 19 percent in

Argentina. These enviable achievements came about because capital investment increased and the work force was trimmed (Ramamurti 1996). These changes can be ascribed to privatization, but they could not have been achieved except by a major shift in government policy and regulations. These changes allowed a sharp increase in prices prior to privatization. Clearly, the firms were not allowed to invest the funds needed to expand their services before privatization. Freed from these constraints, the firms were guided by a more focused pursuit of profits and were managed by a clear line of command.

In the real world, therefore, privatization triggered other changes. Large-scale privatization yielded large sums of cash to the government, particularly when large state monopolies were sold. Telmex alone raised four times as much money for the Mexican government as the 723 firms that had been privatized previously (Ramamurti 1996, 24).

In return for their investment, private investors received changes in the regulatory regime that allowed them to pursue profit and efficiency. These changes, however, were also allowed when ownership remained in the hands of the government and the firm was managed under contract. In some countries, buyers of privatized firms were required to guarantee that workers would not be laid off or paid less in the future (Leeds 1989). In other countries, private enterprise encountered a furious chorus of invectives against avarice and cupidity, and government tended to control business through an antagonistic system of regulations. When private investors faced a multitude of restrictions of this sort, performance was less than great. Thus, these efficiency differentials are as much the result of market structure, government policies, and institutional controls as of ownership type. Labor productivity in airlines seems to be related to industrial policies more than to ownership (Ramamurti and Sarathy 1997). SOEs operating in a competitive environment and not impeded by government-imposed constraints may be as efficient as privately owned firms similarly situated. If the government severely restricts a private enterprise's freedom of action, it too becomes inefficient and unprofitable. To be sure, private investors facing such restrictions may simply exit. The unanswered question is: Can government create a regime allowing SOEs the same operational rules as those of private enterprise?

The determinants of performance, therefore, are not rooted in ownership. They may be found in the relationship between country characteristics, government policies, and firm strategies (De Castro and Uhlenbruck 1997; Lenway and Murtha 1994). More precisely, there are four interrelated sets of determinants: (1) objective factors such as level of available infrastructure or market structure; (2) the way managers are recruited; (3) decisions made outside the enterprise concerning rules about investment, pricing, labor policies, or funding; and (4) the internal organization of the firm.

The first determinant of performance does not need to be elaborated here. Clearly, the performance of any firm depends on the availability of a certain infrastructure and on the existence of institutions, for example those protecting property rights. Thus, Iheduru (1994) argues that the privatization of maritime SOEs in West Africa is unlikely to result in increased efficiency because of structural constraints in the world maritime industry and domestic policy contexts.

Major determinants of performance are the way managers are recruited and the incentive structure they face. If managers are recruited for political reasons and abide by political rules rather than by market discipline, or if government ownership of the enterprise means that the managers of the enterprise are accountable to ruling political parties rather than to the dictates of the marketplace, then performance will be harmed. If the external controllers impose managers who are not necessarily the most competent, or if management suffers from cynicism, resentment, low morale, or apathy as a result of external influence, then performance will deteriorate. Resource allocation decisions are influenced by the structure of tasks and authority and by the reward and punishment structure. Performance, in the sense of efficiency, depends on the design of the state system, including the rules of interaction within the internal and external coalitions and between them. It also depends on the credibility of different regulations. Thus, if managers believe that the SOE (or private firm) cannot go bankrupt, they might take more risks. Different rules of the game may reform SOEs and make them more efficient. Because efficiency depends on the rules of interaction of both the internal and external parts of the organization, a change of ownership will change performance only if these rules are changed as well.

Experience shows that governments tend to use SOEs to achieve external objectives when the additional costs can be hidden from the public. One dubious advantage of subsidies through the price mechanism of an SOE is that the subsidies are not transparent. If government controllers behave as if the SOE were an autonomous entity comparable to a private firm, and use the same set of rewards and punishments, the performance of the enterprise will be enhanced. The internal organization of the firm is related to the degree of autonomy enjoyed by management. What I have elsewhere called "an agent without a principal" causes many performance problems (Aharoni 1982, 89). In many cases, privatization has triggered other changes, including a major increase in the level of management autonomy, the creation of a clear line of command, and a more focused pursuit of narrowly defined goals.

Several things seem clear. First, poor monitoring, excessive intervention, and attempts by civil servants to minimize managerial discretion lead to risk aversion, lack of initiative, and waste. Second, the persistent tendency of government to use SOEs as conduits for dispensing subsidies or political patronage has been a major cause of losses and inefficiency. Third, a new managerial class has evolved in some countries, which is attempting to acquire more autonomy for independent action. Finally, in some cases, private entrepreneurs have found it more profitable to extract commitments, subsidies, and other largess from government than to manage the business in the marketplace. It is important to remember that in judging performance, one is engaged in comparing statistics rather than comparing an actual situation to some ideal. Finally, the major determinant of performance is the institutional system within which managers operate. This, in turn, has an impact on managerial incentives and on the structure of the economic system.

Several studies have shown that when the government allows greater autonomy, either through privatization or through management contracts, performance is enhanced. The problem, therefore, is to install mechanisms allowing higher performance, not simply to change ownership. It may be that in a particular society there is a built-in conflict between growth imperatives and distributive pressures. When the latter win and when distributive conflicts impinge on government behavior, the pressures on SOEs become high and they are destined to perform poorly. SOE managers do not have enough incentives to run efficient operations, and their operational monitoring systems suffer from the same weaknesses.

A one-time adjustment when a country faces an economic crisis, as happened in Mexico when its national debt escalated, may allow the government to carry out a reform. Such a reform "must be politically desirable . . . [and] politically feasible, and the government must be able to promise credibly to stick to the reform in the future" (World Bank 1995, 233).

CONCLUSION

Since the end of World War II, SOEs have become ever more important in both developed and developing countries. In the last decade or two, it has been gradually noticed that SOEs perform much worse than large multinational firms in the private sector. Further, governments have found it increasingly difficult to carry the deficit burden of SOEs. Both the World Bank and the IMF have taken steps to cajole governments into reducing trade barriers and increasing the role of the private sector. Around the world, governments have been attempting to privatize SOEs because of the generally held beliefs that their performance has been disappointing, that the results of previous efforts to reform them have been temporary or unsuccessful, and that privatization is necessary to reduce poverty, foster efficiency, and free public resources for social programs and for the creation of infrastructure. Privatization was also initiated to reduce the burden on hard-pressed public budgets. This burden was partly the result of SOEs' heavy losses and could be allevi-ated through the proceeds of sales.

Despite the debate and the pressures, very little has changed. The World Bank (1995, 25) noted that "the SOE sector has remained stub-bornly large." The share of SOEs in GDP has remained at around 11 percent – about the same as two decades ago. In the least developed countries, the share is even higher (around 14 percent). Governments continue to use SOEs for all sorts of political purposes and to placate all sorts of interest groups. Therefore, the means by which improved performance can be achieved are of crucial importance.

We have analyzed the performance of SOEs and found it to have been dismal under some definitions of performance. We have also compared the performance of SOEs and private firms. Finally, based on this analy-sis, we have discussed the more important questions of the determi-nants of performance and the political rules allowing for change. All in all, the performance of any enterprise depends on the incentives man-agers face, the structure of competition, and the environment within which managers operate. The history of the last two decades shows that all of these variables changed simultaneously with the advent of priva-tization. A major theoretical question is the degree to which these changes would have been possible without the change of ownership. It is also essential to choose performance measures carefully. In many cases, performance is equated with profitability.

REFERENCES

Aharoni, Y. 1981a. Managerial discretion in state-owned enterprises. In *State-owned enterprise in the western economies*, ed. R. Vernon and Y. Aharoni, pp. 184–92. London.

1981b. Performance evaluation of state-owned enterprises: A process perspective. *Management Science* 27(11): 1340–7.

1982. State-owned enterprise: An agent without a principal. In *Public enterprise in less-developed countries*, ed. L. P. Jones, pp. 67–76. New York.

1983. Comprehensive audit of management performance in U.S. state-owned enterprises. *Annals of Public and Co-operative Economy* 54(1): 73–92.

1986. *The evolution and management of state-owned enterprises*. Cambridge, Mass.

Aharoni, Y., and R. Lachman. 1982. Can the manager's mind be nationalized? *Organization Studies* 3(1): 33–46.

Ahlbrandt, R. S., Jr. 1973. Efficiency in the provision of fire services. *Public Choice* 16(Fall): 1–15.

Ahmed, Z., ed. 1982. *Financial profitability and losses in public enterprises of developing countries*. Ljubljana, Slovenia.

Alchian, A. A. 1965. Some economics of property rights. *Politico* (December 30): 816–29.

1977. *Economic forces at work*. Indianapolis.

Babai, D. 1988. The World Bank and the IMF: Rolling back the state or backing its role? In *The promise of privatization*, ed. R. Vernon, pp. 254–85. New York.

Bennet, J. T., and M. H. Johnson. 1979. Public versus private provision of collective goods and services: Garbage collection revisited. *Public Choice* 34: 55–63.

Bishop, M., and J. Kay. 1988. *Does privatization work? Lessons from the U.K.* London.

Blankart, C. B. 1979. Bureaucratic problems in public choice: Why do public goods still remain public? In *Public finance and public choice*, ed. R. W. Roskamp, pp. 155–67. Paris.

Boardman, A. E., and A. R. Vining. 1989. Ownership and performance in competitive environments: A comparison of the performance of private, mixed, and state-owned enterprises. *Journal of Law and Economics* 32: 1–33.

Borcherding, T. E., W. W. Pommerehne, and F. Schneider. 1982. Comparing the efficiency of private and public production: The evidence from five countries. *Zeitschrift für Nationalekonomie* suppl. 2: 127–56.

Bös, D. 1981. *Economic theory of public enterprise*. Berlin.

Boycko, M., A. Shleifer, and R. W. Vishny. 1996. A theory of privatization. *Economic Journal* 106(435): 309–19.

Caves, D. W., and L. R. Christensen. 1980. The relative efficiency of public and private firms in a competitive environment: The case of the Canadian railroads. *Journal of Political Economy* 88: 958–76.

Cook, P., and C. Kirkpatrick. 1988. Privatization in less-developed countries:

An overview. In *Privatization in less-developed countries*, ed. P. Cook and
C. Kirkpatrick, pp. 3–44. New York.

Davies, D. G. 1971. The efficiency of public versus private firms: The case of
Australia's two airlines. *Journal of Law and Economics* 14(1): 149–65.

1977. Property rights and economic efficiency: The Australian airlines revisited.
Journal of Law and Economics 20(1): 223–6.

1981. Property rights and economic behavior in private and government enterprises: The case of Australia's banking system. *Research in Law and Economics* 3: 111–42.

De Alessi, L. 1980. The economics of property rights: A review of the evidence.
Research in Law and Economics 2: 1–47.

De Castro, J., and N. Uhlenbruck. 1997. Characteristics of privatization: Evidence
from developed, less-developed, and former communist countries. *Journal
of International Business Studies* 28(1): 123–43.

Fells, I., and N. Lucas. 1992. U.K. energy policy post-privatization. *Energy Policy*
20(5): 386–9.

Finsinger, J. 1983a. Competition, ownership and control in markets with impefect
information. In *Public sector economics*, ed. J. Finsinger, pp. 111–33. Berlin.
1983b. *Economic analysis of regulated markets*. London.

Franks, S. 1993. Rigorous privatization: The New Zealand experience. *Columbia
Journal of World Business* 28(1): 84–96.

Fukuyama, F. 1995. *Trust: The social virtues and the creation of prosperity*. New
York.

Galal, A. 1991. Public enterprise reform: Lessons from the past and issues for the
future. World Bank Discussion Paper 119. Washington, D.C.

Galal, A., L. Jones, P. Tandon, and I. Vogelsand. 1994. *Welfare consequences of
selling public enterprises: An empirical analysis*. New York.

Galiani, S., and D. Petrecolla. 1996. The changing role of the public sector: An
ex-post view of the privatization process in Argentina. *Quarterly Review of
Economics and Finance* 26(2): 131–52.

Gantt, A. H., and G. Dutto. 1968. Financial performance of governmentowned
corporations in less developed countries. *IMF Staff Papers* 15(1): 102–48.

Goodman, J. B., and G. W. Loveman. 1991. Does privatization serve the public
interest? *Harvard Business Review* 69(6): 26–38.

Gordon, M. 1981. *Government in business*. Montreal.

Grayson, L. E. 1981. *National oil companies*. New York.

Hellman, R. 1972. *Government competition in the electric utility industry*. New
York.

Hill, H. 1982. State enterprises in competitive industry: An Indonesian case study.
World Development 10(11): 1015–23.

Hutchinson, G. 1991. Efficiency gains through privatization of UK industries. In
Privatization and economic efficiency, ed. A. F. Ott and K. Hartley, pp.
87–107. Hants, U.K.

Iheduru, O. C. 1994. The limits of public sector reforms: Evidence from the
maritime sector. *Journal of Developing Areas* 28(3): 393–424.

Kikeri, S., J. Nellis, and M. Shirley. 1992. *Privatization: The lessons of experience*.
Washington, D.C.

Laban, R., and H. C. Wolf. 1993. Large-scale privatization in transition economies. *American Economic Review* 83: 1199-1210.

Leeds, R. 1989. Malaysia: Genesis of a privatization transaction. *World Development* 17(5): 741-56.

Leibenstein, H. 1966. Allocative efficiency vs. x-efficiency. *American Economic Review* 56(3): 392-415.

Lenway, S. A., and T. P. Murtha. 1994. The state as strategist in international business research. *Journal of International Business Studies* 25(3): 513-36.

Levy, B., and P. T. Spiller. 1994. Regulation, institutions and commitment in telecommunications: A comparative analysis of five country studies. In *1993 Proceedings of the World Bank annual conference on development economics*, pp. 215-52. Washington, D.C.

Lieberman, I. W. 1993. Privatization: The theme of the 1990's – An overview. *Columbia Journal of World Business* 28(1): 8-17.

Likierman, A. 1983. The use of profitability in assessing the performance of public enterprises. In *Public enterprise and the developing countries*, ed. V. V. Ramanadham, pp. 71-86. London.

Luders, R. J. 1993. The success and failure of state-owned enterprise divestitures in a developing country: The case of Chile. *Columbia Journal of World Business* 28(1): 98-121.

McDonald, K. R. 1993. Why privatization is not enough. *Harvard Business Review* 71(3): 49-59.

Megginson, W., R. Nash, and M. van Randenborgh. 1994. The financial and operating performance of newly-privatized firms: An international empirical analysis. *Journal of Finance* 49(2): 403-52.

Millward, R. 1982. The comparative performance of public and private ownership. In *The mixed economy*, ed. E. Roll, pp. 58-93. New York.

Millward, R., and D. M. Parker. 1983. Public and private enterprise: Comparative behavior and relative efficiency. In *Public sector economics*, ed. R. Millward, D. M. Parker, L. Rosenthal, M. T. Summer, and N. Topman, pp. 199-274. London.

Milman, C., and S. B. Lundstedt. 1994. "Privatizing state owned enterprises in Latin America: A research agenda." *International Journal of Public Administration* 17(9): 1663-77.

Murtha, T. P., and S. A. Lenway. 1994. Country capabilities and the strategic state: How national political institutions affect multinational corporations' strategies. *Strategic Management Journal* 15 (Summer): 113-30.

Neuberg, L. G. 1977. Two issues in the municipal ownership of electric power distribution systems. *Bell Journal of Economics* 8(1): 303-23.

Ogden, S., and R. Watson. 1996. The relationships between changes in incentive structures, executive pay and corporate performance: Some evidence from the privatised water industry in England and Wales. *Journal of Business Finance and Accounting* 23(5/6): 721-51.

Papandreou, A. G. 1952. Some basic problems in the theory of the firm. In *Survey of Contemporary Economics*, ed. B. F. Haley, 2, pp. 183-219. Homewood, Ill.

Parker, D., and K. Hartley. 1991. Do changes in organizational status affect financial performance? *Strategic Management Journal* 12(8): 631–41.

Parker, D., and S. Martin. 1993. Testing time for privatisation. *Management Today* (August): 44–7.

Peltzman, S. 1971. Pricing in public and private enterprises: Electric utilities in the United States. *Journal of Law and Economics* 14(1): 109–47.

Perry, J. L., and H. G. Rainey. 1988. The public–private distinction in organization theory: A critique and research strategy. *Academy of Management Review* 13: 182–201.

Poole, R. W., Jr. 1983. Objections to privatization. *Policy Review* 24(Spring): 105–19.

Pouder, R. W. 1996. Privatizing services in local government: An empirical assessment of efficiency and institutional explanations. *Public Administration Quarterly* 20(1): 103–26.

Ramamurti, R. 1987. Performance evaluation of state-owned enterprises in theory and practice. *Management Science* 33(7): 876–93.

ed. 1996. *Privatizing monopolies: Lessons from the telecommunications and transport sectors in Latin America*. Baltimore.

Ramamurti, R., and R. Sarathy. 1997. Deregulation and globalization of airlines. *International Trade Journal* 9(3): 389–432.

Ramanadham V. V. 1993. Concluding review. In *Privatization: A global perspective*, ed. V. V. Ramanadham, pp. 526–91. London.

Rao, K. 1996. Red faces for state banks. *Banker* 146(850): 60–4.

Reddy, R. G., ed. 1983. *Government and public enterprise: Essays in honour of V. V. Ramandham*. London.

Shirley, M. M. 1983. Managing state-owned enterprises. World Bank Staff Working Paper 577. Washington, D.C.

Short, R. P. 1984. The role of public enterprises: An international statistical comparison. In *Public enterprises in mixed economies: Some macroeconomic aspects*, ed. R. Floyd, C. S. Gray, and R. P. Short, pp. 110–94. Washington, D.C.

Sri Ram, V., N. Sharma, and K. K. P. Nair. 1976. *Performance of public sector undertakings*. New Delhi.

Stanbury, W. T., and F. Thompson, eds. 1982. *Managing public enterprises*. New York.

United Nations Industrial Development Organization (UNIDO). 1983. *The changing role of the public industrial sector in development*. V 83-56863. Vienna.

Vickers, J., and G. Yarrow. 1988. *Privatization: An economic analysis*. Cambridge, Mass.

World Bank. 1995. *Bureaucrats in business: The economics and politics of government ownership*. A World Bank Policy Research Report. New York.

Yunker, J. A. 1975. Economic performance of public and private enterprise: The case of U.S. electric utilities. *Journal of Economics and Business* 28(1): 60–7.

4

The Role of the State in Economic Growth

ERIK S. REINERT

THE RENAISSANCE STATE VERSUS NATURAL HARMONY

In 1338 Ambrogio Lorenzetti finished his frescoes *Allegory of Good and Bad Government* in Sienna's town hall.[1] The fresco symbolizing good government shows thriving shops, fine buildings, and dancing citizens; that symbolizing bad government shows ruin, rape, robbery, and murder. The *Allegory of Good and Bad Government* represents the optimistic Renaissance view of humanity's potential to improve its own situation. In this view, history is the record of "man's wit and will" applied to harnessing the forces of nature to improve his lot through the ongoing acquisition of new knowledge.

The starting point for Renaissance economics and the birth of the modern state was an acute awareness of how far short of an imagined ideal humanity's current lot fell, and how much it could be continuously improved through a learning process that resembles today's evolutionary economics at its best.[2]

[1] The author gratefully acknowledges the comments and suggestions of Moses Abramowitz, Arno Daastøl, and two anonymous referees. The usual disclaimer applies. A much enlarged version of this essay was published under the same title in *Journal of Economic Issues* 26, nos. 4/5 (1999): 268–326.
[2] See, for example, Lundvall 1994. Dynamic optimization is discussed in Nelson 1995, 58–9.

The state's role in this process grows out of the Renaissance concept of the commonweal – the common good or the general welfare – a systemic dimension that is lost in the atomistic and static structure of today's mainstream economics. I use the term "Renaissance state" to denote a type of activist and idealistic state that has been an obligatory stage in the process of creating a modern industrial nation, bringing the nation into economic activities that create a commonweal through increasing returns and self-enforcing feedback mechanisms. I shall argue that the growth of complex economies has important similarities to the growth of complex technological systems, and that in both cases increasing returns are at the core of positive feedback mechanisms that promote the general welfare. Such systemic synergies are further based on diversity and specialization. A commonweal, then, is systemic and synergy-based; it is a dynamic concept in a process that increases the size of the economic pie.[3]

State involvement in the Renaissance economy was both immensely activist and idealistic. Albert Hirschman (1991) discusses the arguments that have been used since the late eighteenth century against this type of interference with the market's "natural harmony" and in favor of passivity as a strategy. In this essay I shall discuss two fundamentally different economic views of the state's role in economic growth and in the history of economic thought: the production-centered Renaissance tradition and the barter-centered, passive-materialistic tradition of Adam Smith, David Ricardo, and neoclassical economics.

The synergies and scale of the highly specialized economic network are essential to the production of systemic effects, the common good of the Renaissance economists. These economists observed the stark contrast between the wealth of populous, economically diversified cities such as Venice and the poverty of the undiversified economic base in the countryside and in agricultural/administrative cities such as Naples. Today, however, systemic effects, and consequently the state's role in the economy, are marginalized by the dominant economic theory. This is all the more harmful because the experiences of the industrialized countries indicate that the poorer a country is, the stronger its need for state

---

[3] My analysis is based on the role of positive and dynamic systemic effects influencing the size of the economic pie. This is a very different argument from that which shows that distributional conflicts over the sharing of the pie – both statically and over time – may very well reduce its size, as in the antisocial collective actions described, for example, in the works of Mancur Olson.

intervention. Those who produce economic theory all live in nations where a strong state is taken for granted, where the obligatory passage point of a Renaissance-type state is ancient history.

Neoclassical economics has kept Adam Smith's myth alive by failing to recognize and account for the systemic synergies among multitudes of industries, each with a minimum efficient size of operation, which, in turn, cause societies to have a minimum efficient size. This minimum efficient size of societies grows as more knowledge is added and more industries are formed, increasing the standard of living and forming the fundamental connection between geography and economics.[4] These same factors led to the creation first of the medieval city economies, then of national economies, and finally of globalization. The need for a state arises from the same synergies and interdependencies, and from the differing abilities of economic activities to provide the increasing returns that are at the core of this system. An important task ahead for economic theory is to recognize and account for the externalities that promote the general welfare: the systemic synergies of scale and scope, which have their origin in the creation and implementation of new knowledge, in those production processes that are subject to increasing returns.

In this essay I attempt to open the field of vision in order to show that from a five-hundred-year perspective the active role of the state in the East Asian "miracle," as described by authors such as Amsden (1989) and Wade (1990), is business as usual: an obligatory passage point in the transition from underdevelopment to development. In the second section, I provide a set of assumptions different from that of mainstream economics about how economic welfare is created and distributed. In the third section I inventory the roles historically played by the state in promoting the commonweal. The fourth section takes a closer look at the role of knowledge and of systemic effects in the policy measures of Schumpeterian mercantilism. In the fifth section I show that while making little sense in a limited neoclassical framework, these policies of Schumpeterian mercantilism are fully compatible with a variety of recent new approaches to economic theory. The sixth section comments on the role of state-owned enterprises (SOEs) in this system, and the seventh section states my conclusions.

---

[4] This relationship between technical change, scale, and geography is very well explained in Bücher 1918–19. The only work in English with a similar scope is Polanyi 1957. Polanyi frequently quotes Bücher.

MECHANISMS CAUSING GROWTH AND DISTRIBUTING
ECONOMIC WELFARE: THE PRODUCTION-BASED
RENAISSANCE TRADITION

The most remarkable of all economic treatises before that of Adam
Smith, in my opinion, is Antonio Serra's (1613) *A brief treatise on the
causes which can make gold and silver plentiful in kingdoms where
there are no mines*, in which Serra produces a sophisticated
model explaining both systemic economic development and
underdevelopment.

Serra writes that the purpose of his work is (1) to understand why
some nations, even though they have no mines, are very rich, and (2)
based on this understanding, to explain the paradox that his own nation,
the kingdom of Naples, although abounding in natural resources, has
reached such an abysmal level of poverty that "it does not leave us to
breathe nor to enjoy what nature has given us." Serra was the first
economist to describe increasing returns.[5] With increasing returns as
his starting point, he describes positive feedback mechanisms that lead
to virtuous circles of development in an economic system.

Serra describes two types of factors that cause the wealth of nations:
(1) specific factors, which can occur only in one nation and not in
others, and (2) general factors, which may occur in any nation.

Specific Factors. The first specific factor in Serra's system is a surplus
of products for export (reminiscent of Smith's "vent for surplus"). Serra
explains why he lists this as a specific factor by pointing out that a surplus
– or a positive balance of trade – cannot apply to all nations. His second
specific factor is the geographical position of the nation relative to other
nations, which can enhance trade.

General Factors. Serra lists four general factors that bring wealth and
shows how they interact with each other and with the specific factor of
the nation's geographical position:

1. *The number and variety of industrial professions.* The "number
   of professions" is fundamentally the same concept as the "division
   of labor." The number of industrial professions in a nation is a
   symptom of – and a proxy for – a variety of economic factors: technological sophistication, a sophisticated pattern of demand, a large
   diversity of skills, and – because of the minimum efficient scale of

---

[5] Both Roscher (1882) and Schumpeter (1954, 258-9) recognize this.

production in each profession – a large market. Serra rates this factor higher than the vent for surplus because he believed that industrial professions behave differently than agriculture.

2. *The quality of the population.* The quality of a population is good when the people are "by nature industrious, or diligent and ingenious in building up trade not only in their own industry, but outside, and on the watch for opportunities to apply their industry."

3. *The presence of great commerce.* Serra describes how the various factors creating wealth interact and mutually reinforce each other in creating positive feedback mechanisms for development.

4. *The regulations of the state.* Serra emphasizes the role of government policy in creating wealth. This is a most difficult task, he says, because one policy measure can have very different effects in different industries. In spite of these difficulties, Serra makes it clear that economic policy is the most important factor causing the wealth of nations.

Assumptions about the Causes of Economic Growth

Bearing Serra's analysis in mind, what can we conclude about the forces creating economic welfare? I would argue that the following factors should be seen as "reactants," factors that, when they are all present – and only then – produce economic welfare:

The Causes of Increased Economic Welfare

1. Markets
2. Capital
3. Technology (the *techno-* part: new hardware and tools)
4. Technology (the *-logy* part: new human skills and new knowledge)
5. Attitudes toward new knowledge (individuals' and nations')
6. Systemic effects that give rise to positive feedback mechanisms (increasing returns; scale and scope)
7. Humankind's rational will ("wit and will")

Today's mainstream economic theory basically limits itself to the first two factors. Markets and capital are necessary but far from sufficient building blocks for a theory of economic growth. New research under the heading of "evolutionary economics" (as sponsored by the Organization for Economic Cooperation and Development [OECD] under the Technology and Economy Programme) also includes factor 3 and, increasingly, factor 4. Another striking feature of Adam Smith's economics is his long proofs that the production of knowledge, from the points of view of the individual and of society, is a zero-sum game. This is probably where Smith most clearly breaks with the Renaissance tradition of Serra and others.[6] Today the opposite message is slowly sinking in: The forces driving the economic system are innovations created by new knowledge. Nations that stop innovating do not keep their standard of living; they lose it even though they may maintain the same level of efficiency. New knowledge does not, however, enter the economy in the manner assumed in new growth theory. Economic growth is activity-specific, a fact that has been recognized in all successful catching-up strategies from that of Henry VII's England starting in 1485 to those of Taiwan and Korea in our time.

Assumptions about the Mechanisms That Distribute Growth and Welfare

Another crucial dimension of economic growth is that it seems to be a product of a number of systemic effects, which are the starting points of positive feedback mechanisms in the economy. These effects can be seen only when the system itself is the object of analysis. The presence or absence of such factors determines how economic growth spreads in the economy, either as higher wages to the producer or as lower prices to the consumer. These two alternative mechanisms are the collusive and the classical modes, respectively, of distributing the benefits of technological change (Reinert 1994). In a closed system, it makes no practical difference which of the two modes operates to distribute the benefits from technical change. In international trade between two different labor markets with an asymmetrical trade pattern (trading increasing-return products for diminishing-return products), which of the two models operates makes all the difference.

The practical consequences for world income distribution created by the two different modes of distributing the benefits of technical change can best be seen in the traditional service sector. In this huge sector

---

[6] Analysis of Adam Smith and knowledge as a zero-sum game can be found in the original extended version of this essay, available as Working Paper 1997.5 of the Centre for Development and the Environment, University of Oslo, Norway.

there is normally very little difference in productivity between First World and Third World workers. A bus driver, a barber, or a chambermaid are about as productive in Bolivia or Haiti as they are in Norway or Italy. Why then do barbers or bus drivers in Bolivia or Haiti earn real wages that are only a fraction – 10–20 percent – of the real wages of barbers or bus drivers in Norway or Italy? Why does the invisible hand reward people with the same productivity at such different levels in different economies? Because of system effects: Much of the benefit resulting from technological change in increasing-return activities is spread in the collusive mode, that is, as higher wages in the local labor market rather than as lower prices internationally.

From the perspective of a poor sub-Saharan nation, what we in industrialized nations see as "economic development" basically appears to be a system based on "industry rent" from increasing-return activities that spreads throughout the national labor markets. The existence of increasing-return activities – and their accompanying barriers to entry – creates a national commonweal that gives the Norwegian bus driver real wages that are five times higher than those of his or her equally productive Bolivian counterpart. Such systemic effects originate in the fixed costs accompanying tools: The increasing sophistication of tools and of specialized human skills to use the tools leads to increasing minimum efficient sizes of operations with an ever-increasing number of professional specializations and an ever-increasing diversity of products and services.

The Philosophical Underpinnings of the Activist-Idealistic Tradition

Promoting new knowledge was a fundamental driving force for the economic policies of the Renaissance and later in the abundant mercantalist literature that did not deal with monetary issues but rather with the real economy. The same points were made by the central authors of German cameralism and French Colbertism. If one lists the economic interventions in Renaissance economics, it becomes clear that what united these seemingly diverse economic policies was the promotion and protection of new knowledge. These policies further rested on the assumption that some types of knowledge were more valuable than others. Consequently, it was in the state's interest to create and protect the valuable types of knowledge.

*Schumpeterian Mercantilism: Strategies for Promoting and
Protecting New Knowledge in Renaissance-Type Economic Policies*

1. Establishment of scientific academies
2. Encouragement of and assistance to inventors
3. Diffusion of new knowledge/education
4. Establishment of an apprentice system
5. Patent protection for new inventions
6. State-owned factories as places of learning
7. Subsidies to firms in industries new to the nation or region
8. Tax breaks and bounties to firms bringing in new technology
9. Travel restrictions for skilled labor
10. Prohibition against the export of machinery
11. Prohibition against the use of machinery in colonies
12. Export duties on raw materials
13. Import duties on manufactured goods coupled with strategies to ensure national competition
14. Strengthening of the navy

The economic policies resulting from Renaissance economic theories were carried out with varying degrees of understanding of the
underlying principles. They were not based on what we would call scientific analysis, but rather on a mode of inference called "abduction."[7]
This tradition was continued in philosophy by Giambattista Vico
(1668-1744) and by C. S. Peirce and his followers, and in economics by
Nicholas Kaldor in "stylized facts."[8] According to Peirce, "[induction] can
never originate any idea whatever. No more can deduction. All the ideas
of science come to it by the way of abduction. Abduction consists of
studying facts and devising a theory to explain them. Its only justification is that if we are ever to understand things at all, it must be in that
way" (Peirce 1867, 5:146; quoted in Lawson 1989, 68).

As an example of sound policy generated through adductive reasoning, consider that, starting in the twelfth century, sailors in the Mediter-
ranean ate lemons to prevent scurvy (Villner 1986, 110-13). This was
a very effective policy, but the scientific explanation of why it worked
appeared only in 1929 with the discovery of vitamin C (Mervin 1981,
14-15). Likewise, it is entirely possible to establish good economic policies without fully understanding the factors involved. For example, iden-

[7] For a more general discussion of these issues see Reinert and Daastøl 1997.
[8] For a discussion of Kaldor's use of stylized facts see Lawson 1989.

tifying "progress" or the ability to pay more taxes with the use of machinery in an increasing number of industries would result in a beneficial public policy even if the causal relationship between the use of machinery and wealth were not clearly established. Intuitive abduction often precedes what we would think of as a more scientific type of knowledge.

Business decisions are made, mostly under conditions of great uncertainty, based on "management by gut feeling," that is, intuitive abduction about what is good for the firm. Early statesmanship seems to have worked in a similar way. Just as lemons helped protect sailors against scurvy eight hundred years before we established the exact mechanism by which they work, economic growth was successfully promoted using "new knowledge" and "use of machinery" as proxies for the underlying factors causing systemic growth.

THE THREE ROLES OF THE STATE

We can divide the state's economic roles into three main categories: providing institutions, distributing income and risk, and promoting economic growth. The state provides basic institutions such as private property and the rule of law. As the standard of living increases, secondary demands are created and the state extends into providing institutions for education, science, charity, sanitation, and the like.[9] The state also acts as a distributor of income and risk. The idea of distributing the inevitable risks of life is very old: Participants in the camel caravans of the Mideast had a risk-sharing system by 2200 B.C. Modern insurance traces its root to the middle of the fourteenth century. The idea of risk-sharing was already present at the beginning of the welfare state in the Byzantine Empire, where risk-sharing gradually developed into a state role in income distribution.

The first two roles are necessary but not sufficient conditions for economic growth. The objective of this chapter is to examine the more active role of the state in economic development. Historically, the state as a promoter of economic growth has functioned in the following ways: (1) getting the nation into the "right" business; (2) creating a comparative advantage in the "right" business; (3) supplying infrastructure; (4) setting standards; (5) providing skilled labor and entrepreneurship

[9] Although he does not divide the state's roles into these three groups, I follow the historical development of the state set out in Cohn 1895.

when needed; (6) creating demand; (7) pushing technology by being a source of demand for cutting-edge products; (8) emphasizing the value of education and knowledge; (9) setting high wages per se as a goal; (10) understanding the importance of the legal system in strengthening economic structures; and (11) acting as a capitalist and entrepreneur of last resort.

Getting the Nation into the "Right" Business. The importance of this point, neglected in today's economic theory, cannot be overestimated. Different economic activities present different windows of opportunity for adding new knowledge and thus for creating positive feedback systems. As long as there is a demand for both low- and high-skill activities, the world market may produce lock-in effects, trapping nations in the comparative "advantage" of being poor and unskilled. Historically, all industrialized nations have passed through an initial stage in which they have had a state policy based on the understanding that not all economic activities are equally feasible as starting points for the self-enforcing positive feedback system we call development (see Reinert 1980, 1994, 1995). Economic growth is activity-specific, limited to some economic activities rather than others. A recognition of the activity-specific nature of economic growth undermines the assumptions on which today's world economic order rests. The activity-specific nature of economic welfare explains why a notoriously inefficient planned industrial economy produced a higher standard of living in the former Soviet Union than a largely deindustrialized market economy does in Russia today.

Creating a Comparative Advantage in the "Right" Business. A common element of all successful strategies for catching up with richer nations has been the conviction that free trade is not desirable until the nation has created a comparative advantage in the "right" economic activities (which, among other things, means skill-based, not resource-based, activities).

Supplying Infrastructure. Infrastructures are key factors in extending markets and are "highways" that the positive feedback mechanisms need in order to spread geographically.

Setting Standards. This has been a very important task of the state. Standardization from the neoclassical point of view lowers transaction costs, and from the evolutionary point of view it forms a basis for standardized mass production. A visitor to the Renaissance towns of Italy even today can observe the iron bars fastened to the church wall on the main square; these bars established the standard units of measurement valid in the city. Today the setting of standards is important to hi-tech industries such as mobile telephony. The state also has an important role in setting legal standards and standards of social virtue, which are crucial to prosperity.[10]

Providing Skilled Labor and Entrepreneurship When They Are Needed. Early policy measures were aimed at bringing in skilled labor and entrepreneurs from abroad by granting exclusive rights for a limited time, or through bounties, tax relief, and so forth.

Creating Demand. Better income distribution of a growing economic pie ultimately made industrial production and Fordism possible. Nineteenth-century U.S. economists saw particularly clearly the function of raising labor skills in order to increase their market value, a policy called the "high-wage strategy."

Pushing the Technological Frontier. The state has frequently been a source of high-quality demand for national production of goods at the edge of what was technically feasible, particularly for infrastructure projects and warfare.

Emphasizing the Value of Education and Knowledge. The state promoted general literacy, universities, and the establishment of scientific academies. A crucial part of this policy was to create demand for the new knowledge and the new skills. In order to achieve this, the economic policy, through encouragement and protection, would target for every nation the kinds of economic activities that employed new knowledge.

Setting High Wages Per Se as a Goal. At the core of Renaissance-type economic thinking was an emphasis on human needs. The importance of wage levels to the gross national product (GNP) is illustrated by the fact that today wages are typically 70 percent of GNP; thus, maximizing wealth essentially means maximizing national wages.

Understanding the Importance of a Legal System Built to Strengthen These Economic Structures. A system of property rights assists the dynamic symbiosis between those who collect knowledge and those who collect money. This is the core of a system that creates a never-ending frontier of development (see Reinert and Daastøl 1997).

Acting as an Entrepreneur and Capitalist of Last Resort. There is no reason to assume that the supply of entrepreneurship at any time and in any culture will be sufficient. For the most part, the state moved into the role of capitalist or entrepreneur because of bottlenecks in the system rather than ideological preferences.

The extent and activity of the state (what we could call the "optimal state") should reflect the paradox that, having managed the economy in

---

[10] I am indebted to Arne Disch for this point.

order to exploit the synergies and economies of scope that result from the variety and activity of humankind, the state is likely to produce the perverse effects of uniformity and inertness. This uniformity and inertness threaten variety and activity, the synergies of which the state was established to foment and exploit in the first place. In the case of both the firm and the state, one important answer to the diseconomies of scale produced by size and growing complexity lies in the concept of "organizational capabilities." In the world of business, the managerial revolution was the reply to these challenges (Chandler 1977, 1990).

The state's role in industrialized countries is often seen as that of protecting "civil liberties," the form of freedom that we can call "freedoms to." The state's role in the early stages of economic development, however, is that of jump-starting the systemic effects to secure "freedoms from" – freedom from hunger, freedom from injustice, freedom from ignorance. With time, the actions of the state to provide freedoms from can encroach upon the individual's freedoms to. The Smithian revolt against Renaissance economic policy can be seen as a response to this problem. In England at the time, the policies of the "development state" had become bogged down in static, individual rent-seeking rather than synergetic, collective rent-seeking. Clearly, a big dose of markets was needed. As German, U.S., and Japanese economists in the nineteenth century were so eager to point out, however, this did not mean that nations that had not reached England's economic level could use the same policies there and then. The role of the state is highly context-specific.

NEW KNOWLEDGE, SYSTEMIC EFFECTS, AND POSITIVE FEEDBACK LOOPS IN RENAISSANCE ECONOMICS

Renaissance economics was understood by philosopher-statesmen such as Francis Bacon (1561–1626), who consciously used his utopian tract *The New Atlantis* as an essay in forecasting the future, a process he called "feigned history" (Crother 1960). In Bacon's *New Atlantis* (published in 1627) and his *Essay on Innovations* (ca. 1605), new inventions and innovations propel the development of society. Not only in Bacon's feigned history but also in real history, these early inventions and innovations resulted from the organizational capabilities of the state (on capabilities see Chandler 1990; Lazonick 1991). The roles of the state and of private entrepreneurs were complementary. The state used both carrots and sticks to get private entrepreneurs to enter targeted industries and – if this failed – moved in as the entrepreneur of last resort.

A principal historical role of the state from the Renaissance on has been to promote and protect new knowledge and innovations. The common theme of knowledge-oriented economic policies is concern for the creation and protection of new ideas. If we look at history from a simple neoclassical perspective, the importance of these policies is lost. The factors causing unequal economic growth are lost, creating the world of artificial harmony and worldwide factor-price equalization. One of Adam Smith's most important historical roles was laying the groundwork for "perfect markets" and "natural harmony" by making the quest for knowledge into a zero-sum game – using the metaphor of a lottery – from the point of view of both the individual and the state. Smith effectively removed from consideration the quest for imperfect competition through new knowledge, which was so important to Renaissance thinking.

Pre-Smithian economic thinking takes a holistic starting point – the people, the state – along with the fundamental assumption that the situation of each individual can be improved by measures that take into consideration the collectivity. In other words, it looks to systemic effects. The existence of such systemic effects is the fundamental reason why the state has a role to play in economic growth.

The goal of the state's economic policy is to increase the prosperity of the community. While noting that widespread wealth seemed to accumulate in the cities, not in the countryside, Renaissance economists also recognized that there were huge differences between cities, between the opulence of Venice and the poverty of Naples. In the best theoretical works of the time, the superiority of the city over the countryside, and of dynamic cities over lagging ones, was explained by the size and density of population, by geographical position, by the high quality of the dynamic city's economic activities (Giovanni Botero [1590] describes differences in "windows of opportunity"), by the diversity of economic occupations, and by the capacity of some economic activities to initiate positive feedback mechanisms (Serra 1613).

The Size and Density of the Population

"The power of a state is not the result of its territorial extension, but of its number of people and its good government." This statement is found with little variation in the writings of virtually all economists and philosophers of the time: Thomas Mun, Joshua Child, William Petty, and Charles Davenant in England; Antoine de Montchrétien, François Forbonnais, and Jacques Necker in France; and Gottfried Wilhelm von Leibniz, Christian Wolff, Johann Joachim Becher, and Johann Heinrich Gottlieb von Justi in Germany. One reason for the great seventeenth-century European interest in China was its large population density, which Europeans saw as proportionate to the degree of knowledge and wisdom of a nation.

The population argument makes sense if, as Adam Smith claims, "the division of labor is limited by the extent of the market." If there are fixed costs and a minimum efficient scale involved in establishing new professions, then it makes sense that a larger population contributes to a larger division of labor.[11] Adam Smith's key contribution, the concept of the division of labor, is not compatible with the assumptions of neo-classical trade theory: If there are no economies of scale – that is, no fixed cost – and there is perfect information, there is little reason for any division of labor at all.

The Quality of Different Economic Activities

Renaissance economics presented several levels of arguments for policy intervention. Some economic activities produce greater economic welfare than others; some economic activities give rise to systemic synergies, which produce and spread welfare locally or nationwide; these systemic synergies can develop into positive feedback systems. The most sophisticated and complete description is that of Antonio Serra (1613), who describes Venice as a true autocatalytic system in which increasing returns and diversity are at the core of positive feedback systems that generate wealth. Naples is an example of the opposite effect in Serra's system because the production of raw materials is not subject to increasing returns.

Today we would view washing dishes in a restaurant as having limited potential for income creation compared with practicing law; Renaissance economists extended this argument to apply to the commonweal as well. In other words, they believed that the factors that create differences in welfare within an economy are the same as those that create differences in income between nations. According to pre-Ricardian

---

[11] See the discussion of the role of minimum efficient scale in Chandler 1990.

common sense, no factor-price equalization would be achieved by putting all the people washing dishes in one nation and all the lawyers in another and opening up free trade between the two nations. In these theories, economic growth is activity-specific: It is available only in some economic activities subject to dynamic imperfect competition, not in others.

Giovanni Botero asked in 1590: Which is more important for making a nation wealthy, the fertility of its soil or industry? No doubt industry, he answered, "because the things produced by the able hands of man are many more, and have a much higher price, than the things produced by nature" (Botero 1590, 362; my translation). We find the same line of reasoning among the German cameralist economists.

Understanding economic development as activity-specific leads to two different policy measures by the state. One is a set of positive measures taken in order to bring domestic economic activities into the "right" industries, those in which there could be a buildup of new knowledge, use of machinery, and so forth. Understanding the activity-specific nature of economic growth also leads to a set of negative measures taken in order to prevent other nations from getting into the "right" types of activities. Prohibiting the use of machinery in the colonies was one such measure. English debates made no secret of the nation's strategy of keeping other nations from industrializing. In 1816 Henry Brougham explained the English strategy in the House of Commons: "It is well worth while to incur a loss upon the first exportation, in order, by the glut, to stifle in the cradle those infant manufactures in the United States which the [Napoleonic] war has forced into existence" (quoted in Curtis 1904, 1:40). This is a fairly typical nineteenth-century comment. Exporting natural resources constituted "bad trade" in the orthodoxy of English economic policy until long after the time of Adam Smith and David Ricardo (see especially King 1721). We find this same line of argument in the United States, Germany, and Japan in the nineteenth century and in Australia and Canada in the twentieth.

What, then, are the characteristics of growth-inducing – "good" – economic activities? Figure 4.1 shows a quality index of economic activities, ranking them according to their ability to provide increasing economic welfare to a nation on a scale from perfect competition (white) to monopoly (black). The latter is only a temporary state because new technologies fall toward a lower score as they mature. Differences in wage levels, both nationally and between nations, seem to result from

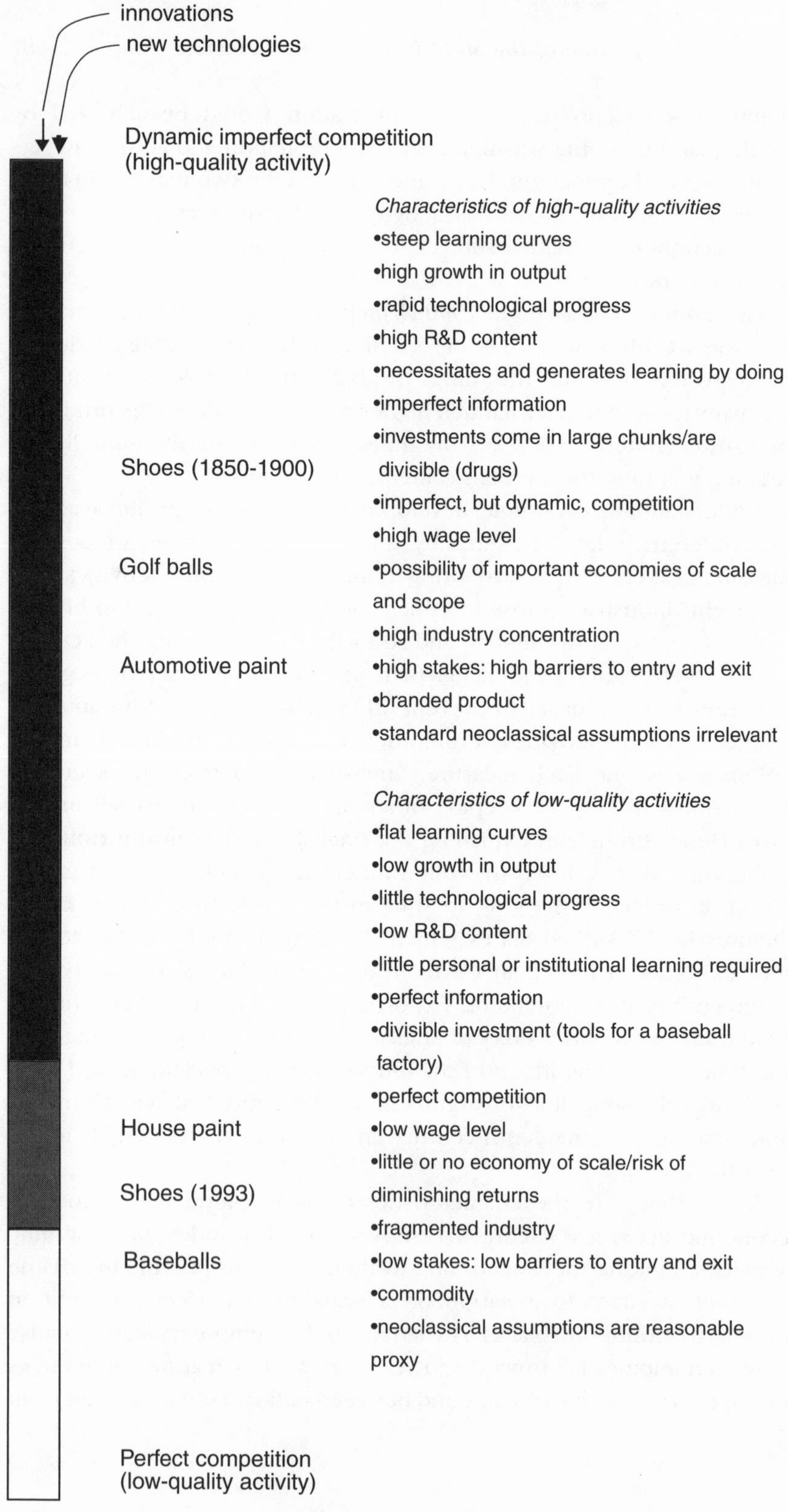

innovations
new technologies

Dynamic imperfect competition
(high-quality activity)

Characteristics of high-quality activities
•steep learning curves
•high growth in output
•rapid technological progress
•high R&D content
•necessitates and generates learning by doing
•imperfect information
•investments come in large chunks/are
 divisible (drugs)

Shoes (1850-1900)

•imperfect, but dynamic, competition
•high wage level

Golf balls

•possibility of important economies of scale
and scope
•high industry concentration

Automotive paint

•high stakes: high barriers to entry and exit
•branded product
•standard neoclassical assumptions irrelevant

Characteristics of low-quality activities
•flat learning curves
•low growth in output
•little technological progress
•low R&D content
•little personal or institutional learning required
•perfect information
•divisible investment (tools for a baseball
 factory)
•perfect competition

House paint

•low wage level
•little or no economy of scale/risk of

Shoes (1993)

diminishing returns
•fragmented industry

Baseballs

•low stakes: low barriers to entry and exit
•commodity
•neoclassical assumptions are reasonable
proxy

Perfect competition
(low-quality activity)

Figure 4.1. The quality index of economic activities.

varying degrees of imperfect competition caused by both static and dynamic factors. These factors, long identified by both businessmen and scholars in industrial economics, are correlated.

THE ROLE OF THE RENAISSANCE STATE IN THE LIGHT OF RECENT ECONOMIC THEORY

The state's involvement in economic growth starting in the Renaissance – although making no sense in the "fatally simple structure" of neoclassical economics, in Jacob Brunowski's phrase – is eminently compatible with new approaches in the evolutionary economics of complex systems (for example, the work of W. Brian Arthur and Paul David).[12] It is also compatible with the key elements of the new trade theory, with the theories of Paul Krugman in the 1980s and of Gene Grossman and Elhanan Helpman, and with the debate on strategic trade policy.[13] This is precisely because Renaissance economists did not see the economy as being deterministic, predictable, and mechanistic.

Synergetic and systemic economic effects, which modern economics views as typical of activities subject to increasing returns, were recognized by a multitude of pre-Smithian economists and were used to argue for specific state intervention. The mechanisms creating these cumulative causations were much more clearly described by Antonio Serra in 1613 than by Friedrich List in the 1840s or Gunnar Myrdal in the 1950s. The most surprising aspect of the new theories emphasizing increasing returns is that they are applied either to technological systems – where income distribution is not an issue – or to symmetrical trade, that is, trade between nations all involved in activities subject to cumulative causations. In such cases the logic of state intervention is infinitely less compelling than in cases of asymmetrical trade – in Third World countries that are historically locked into exporting products produced under conditions of diminishing returns and importing goods produced under conditions of increasing returns.[14] The existence of symmetrical trade between nations at the same level of development, all engaged in increasing-return activities, is an argument for free trade and no state intervention.

The new economic theories, based on increasing rather than dimin-

---

[12] A good overview of these theories is contained in Arthur 1990.
[13] See Grossman 1990; Helpman and Krugman 1985; and Krugman 1986.
[14] This argument is developed in Reinert 1980.

ishing returns, postulate a process-dependent, organic world where historical cumulative causations, positive feedbacks, and locked-in effects yield multiple solutions – some clearly less than ideal. The external economies of Alfred Marshall, the growth pools of François Perroux, the linkages identified by Albert Hirschman (1958), and the observation of Michael Porter (1990) that innovations thrive in clusters are all recognitions of important systemic effects of economic development. In all these theories, past history reinforces positive feedback systems and creates path dependence. Other recent works on technological change by authors such as Christopher Freeman and Giovanni Dosi analyze in detail the path-dependent nature of technological change.

An important insight from these modern theories is that small differences early in the history of an industry may have huge effects later on; they may influence whether the nation will become specialized in increasing- or diminishing-return industries. This opens up a huge area for state intervention of the kind that Schumpeterian mercantilism has long provided, from England in the 1480s to Korea in the 1980s. Because increasing returns are most typical in manufacturing, the new theories provide support for the century-old mercantilist preference for manufacturing over the production of raw materials. In Renaissance theories the use of machinery was often a proxy for good trade. This equation is being vindicated by recent theoretical developments pointing to the important role of machinery in economic growth (see De Long and Summers 1991).

The fundamental problem of neoclassical theory, and of the thinking behind the policies of institutions such as the World Bank, is that they are based on the implicit assumption that all economic activities are alike. These theories fail to account for the presence or absence of increasing returns and consequently of asymmetrical trade – trade between nations exporting products from increasing-return activities and nations exporting products from diminishing-return activities. New growth theory explicitly combines increasing returns with perfect competition, which is based on a fundamental misrepresentation of how new knowledge is produced and spread. Thus, although new growth theorists take into account the benefits of increasing returns, most perpetuate factor-price equalization. A few articles on new growth theory, however, take inherent differences between economic activities as the starting point for explaining the relative wealth of nations. The most notable among these are by the Nobel Prize winner in economics Robert Lucas, Jr. (1988, 1993).

These differences between economic activities make a strong state an "obligatory passage point" for economic development.[15] When we view a nation as a complex system, we can see the need for input coordination. In the development of technological systems – just as in the development of nations – obligatory passage points "represent instances of power, because they discipline the interactions of actors" (Bijker 1995, 266). As nations evolve, some "components" of the system fall behind others, limiting the system's efficiency. In the study of large technological systems these are called "reverse salients," a dynamic conception of what in a static system would be called a "bottleneck," and where, at certain stages, innovative energy should be focused.[16] In all industrialized countries an active state has historically been an obligatory passage point, performing the necessary functions of removing reverse salients and coordinating and coercing the various "reactants" that together produce economic wealth.

The state's role of coercing entrepreneurship in order to establish a textile industry in England beginning in 1485 is an expression of the same obligatory passage point to development as that expressed when the Korean government forced Samsung out of trading activities and into manufacturing semiconductors in the early 1980s. Other policy measures – some types of bounties, cheap credit, temporary protection of the local market, and so on – are also strikingly similar in Renaissance England and 1980s Korea. The same reasoning underlies these two state actions five hundred years apart: the fundamental Renaissance notions that new learning is the basis for economic development and that this new learning is able to create development through positive feedback systems in some economic activities rather than in others. In both cases, resource-based activities were understood to be unable to lift the nation out of poverty. This is the activity-specific element of economic growth: Only nations that have a large enough percentage of activities subject to dynamic increasing returns have been able to develop.

Based on the abundant evidence of similar production- and learning-based, activity-specific strategies for early economic development since the late 1400s, I argue for an alternative five-hundred-year canon of economic theory. In this canon, where growth is activity-specific, the state has played the necessary role of midwife for all developed nation-states in much the same way that entrepreneurs have played the initial role of

---

[15] For a discussion of the concept of obligatory passage points see Bijker 1995.

[16] For a discussion of reverse salients see Bijker, Hughes, and Pinch 1989, especially 4.

midwife for all large corporations by providing strong input coordination. Both companies and states grow up, however, and the role of the
autocratic leader is reduced. Once positive feedback systems have put
a nation on the path of dynamic increasing returns, the state's role is
reduced to the more indirect actions of maintaining the national innovation system and generating demand for new skills. In other words, the
closer a nation finds itself to the positive feedback systems of knowledge generation operating near the world's "knowledge frontier," the
more the nation has to depend on indirect measures to influence the
economy. The biggest "latecomer advantages" of being able to catch up
to a known technological frontier have been lost. For this reason, the
Ministry of Trade and Industry (MITI) plays a very different role in the
Japanese economy today than it did in the first decades after World
War II.

Once the vested interests of the ruling classes have been moved from
resource-based activities into manufacturing, the positive feedback
system also embraces the political system. Private rent-seeking has been
brought into the arena of collective rent-seeking. In some economic
activities, much more than in others, there is a community of interest
between the vested interests of the entrepreneur and the vested interests of the nation as a whole. This point was made by nineteenth-century
U.S. economists, particularly Henry Carey (1851), who also made it clear
that such effects could not be produced in the absence of manufacturing industry.

The most important historical role of the state has been to guide the
economic activities of the nation into such positive feedback activities.
Thus, Alfred Marshall (1890, 452) correctly recommended "a tax . . . on
the production of goods which obey the Law of Diminishing Returns,
and devoting the tax to a bounty on the production of those goods with
regard to which the Law of Increasing Returns acts sharply." We find the
same kind of reasoning applied to the fundamental mechanism causing
uneven economic development in Frank Graham's (1923) theory of
international trade. Unfortunately, with the mathematization of general
equilibrium theory, all such elements were gradually thrown out of economic theory as "not compatible with equilibrium" or "as inconsistent
with free competition, and therefore as outside the scope of the present
discussion."[17] The nations producing behind the barriers to entry created

---

[17] This is the way the famous trade theorist Jacob Viner (1937, 473) dismisses these
arguments.

by the largest effects of increasing returns and with the most exclusive new information were the very nations forcing on the world a model assuming no increasing returns and perfect information.

Since the end of World War II, Cold War economics has strengthened this development even further: The mathematization of general equilibrium economics and the political need for an economic theory providing an ideological defense against Communism reinforced each other. The historical coincidence is that both of these forces demanded that elements that created anything other than harmonious and even economic growth be eliminated. Economic theory developed along the "perceived line of least mathematical resistance" (Krugman 1990, 4).

THE ROLE OF PUBLIC ENTERPRISES IN RENAISSANCE ECONOMICS

One important role of the Renaissance state was the creation of public enterprises. Although in the 1990s the historical role played by these enterprises was repudiated, these enterprises in fact played a vital role in economic development. Here I shall largely follow the role of state enterprises as treated by Werner Sombart (1913, 2:847–57). Sombart points out that the reasons given for the establishment of state-owned industries in the historical record do not do justice to their role:

The importance of [state-owned enterprises] for the creation of modern industry cannot be overestimated. These served to set, not only a prototype example of industry, but also the pace and pattern for the new form of organisation. It was the state-owned enterprises which, due to the demands they created, often served as catalysts for the development of capitalist industries. These enterprises are so essential that they cannot be left out of an account of the development of capitalism, which – although their conceptual roots lay elsewhere – they furthered in thousands of ways. (2:847)

The main motivations for state-owned enterprises (SOEs) were:

1. *Administrative Reasons.* On occasion the state administration found that in certain industries the only practical way of instituting the necessary controls was by state ownership. This was most often done for reasons of financial policy, particularly in the case of mining of precious metals.
2. *To Meet the Needs of the Ruler and the Court.* Many state-owned manufactures were set up seemingly with the sole objective of pro-

viding luxury goods to the king. Rulers and ruled took pride in showing off the skill level and production capacity of their nation – whether in producing china, silk, or tapestries – in much the same way that nations are proud of their athletes today. The mass production of luxuries had the effects of making such goods more accessible further down the social ladder and, more important, of building up technical and managerial skills, which spread to other activities.

3. *Reasons of Statesmanship and to Enhance the Commonweal.* The reasons included creating employment, increasing exports, reducing dependence on foreign nations, and the like. Often state ownership became the entrepreneurship of last resort. The state used tax incentives and tariffs to promote industries deemed mandatory to the commonweal, making them attractive to investors.

4. *Reasons of National Defense.* The importance of national defense for technological development has been enormous. Defense-related state industries have included the manufacture of gunpowder and armaments, but also industries closer to the core of industrial and commercial development, such as steel production and shipbuilding. The technologies and logistics needed to supply large armies also contributed to developing managerial skills, scale, and scope in the state-owned production and distribution of goods such as bread and clothing. The shortage of natural raw materials needed for warfare led to research and inventions in the field of synthetic materials.

State-owned industries were thus part of the obligatory passage point of the developmental state. These companies were – as Sombart emphasizes – "places of learning," not only for technical skills but also for organizational and social capabilities. These skills are indispensable to economic development. Military demand seems to have had the same positive effect in the United States as in Europe. Eli Whitney financed the development of the cotton gin from his profits from selling rifles to the Revolutionary army, and the concept of production using interchangeable parts – paving the way for industrial mass production – originated in part in the production of rifles in the United States. The need for national security supplies forced nations into increasing-return activities even though their natural comparative advantage may originally have been elsewhere. National security considerations helped create a new comparative advantage in the production of skill-intensive, increasing-return goods.

The starting point of many technological trajectories was state demand, not only for warfare but also for infrastructure construction, power generation, a national telephone system, and so forth. Examples abound: That the Japanese automotive industry had its origins in the demand for trucks for the imperial army is typical (see Odigari and Gota 1993). Import substitution for reasons of national security seems to have played an extraordinarily important role through the centuries. Over time this led to a convergence of industrial structures, establishing a common platform of technological knowledge in all advanced countries. From this common platform, the processes of specialization and globalization today mutually benefit the advanced countries.

THE LOSS OF THE STATE AND THE RETURN OF THE CENTAUR

One of the most moving paintings of the Renaissance is Sandro Botticelli's *Pallas and the Centaur*, painted in the late 1480s. This work shows Pallas, the ancient goddess of wisdom, mildly caressing the head of a centaur, symbolizing humankind's past ignorance and violence. The expression of embarrassment on the centaur's face is precious – he is obviously ashamed of his wild and ignorant past. The symbolism – the victory of reason, wisdom, and peace – shines through the painting's harmonious atmosphere.

The economists of that time – and pre-Smithian economists in general – recognized the ongoing tension between the wisdom and peace of Pallas and the violent ignorance of the centaur. Channeling the passions and energies of the centaur into productive rather than destructive activities was one of the main challenges of the Renaissance (see Hirschman 1977). This was a matter that could not be left to a self-organizing invisible hand; as in Chandler's works on managerial capitalism, there is a conscious and visible hand (human wit and will) that holds this system together. Historically, mercantilism has been at the base of each and every successful nation. The invisible hand of the market starts operating only when conditions have been created that bring the vested interests seeking private rates of return into line with the interests of the public rate of return – when the interest of the individual is in line with the interest of the collectivity. This happens when a critical mass of labor in a nation is employed in activities subject to increasing returns and when the fruits of these increasing returns are allowed to filter out, to a large extent, as higher wages inside the producing nation rather than as lower prices for foreign customers.

Today, however, we see many nations that are trapped in an "under-development equilibrium" not unlike the "unemployment equilibrium" of the period between the two world wars. To get the world out of the unemployment equilibrium, John Maynard Keynes had to slay the dragon defending the gold standard. Belatedly economists came to recognize, with Keynes, that national welfare can be positively influenced by monetary stimuli. What is the formula used to get a large part of the world's population out of the "poverty equilibrium"? Economic development should be seen as the product of a set of reactants, all of which have to be present in order to set off the desired reaction, leading to a self-reinforcing growth system. The "dragons" that must be slain are the assumptions of perfect information, perfect competition, and constant returns to scale – a set of assumptions that must be rooted out en bloc, not cautiously investigated one by one and then put back into the theory, as is done in new growth theory.

The factors that determine the differences in living standards between nations are essentially the same factors that determine the differences in living standards within nations: levels of knowledge and skill, which create successions of temporary oligopoly power based on dynamic imperfect competition. Successful state interventions have created dynamic imperfect competition – a process of dynamic and collective national rent-seeking – which enormously increases the size of the pie. The state has given temporary help with strings attached. Unsuccessful state interventions may at first glance look similar to the successful ones because they protect national manufacturing industries. But less successful state interventions – such as those in India and many Latin American nations – have created static rent-seeking through relatively permanent protection with no strings attached, leading to "shallow" industrialization – inefficient monopolies with a limited potential to increase the pie. In spite of its inefficiencies, however, a relatively inefficient industrial sector produces a much higher GNP than no industrial sector at all; this is one of the lessons of the "transitology" of formerly Communist states. Deindustrializing inefficient nations is not a viable option if one has any concern for human welfare. This dilemma is very similar to that facing Germany in the 1830s, with more than thirty small states, each with an extremely protective tariff. The solution in Germany was a first stage that removed the tariffs between the states and created stiff competition among states with fairly similar skill levels. Within this symmetrical trade pattern the nation continued to build skills, and later graduated to open competition in the world markets. In this way the state completes its most important historical function: to establish the nation solidly in economic activities subject to increasing returns and to set up a dynamic national system in which innovations are an essential by-product of the way the national industry competes.

REFERENCES

Amsden, A. 1989. *Asia's next giant: South Korea and late industrialization*. New York.

Arthur, W. B. 1990. Positive feedbacks in the economy. *Scientific American* (February): 80–5.

Bacon, F. n.d. [1930s?]. New Atlantis. In *Famous utopias*, ed. C. M. Andrews. New York.

Bijker, W. 1995. *Of bicycles, bakelites, and bulbs: Towards a theory of sociotechnical change*. Cambridge, Mass.

Bijker, W., T. P. Hughes, and T. Pinch, eds. 1989. *The social construction of technological systems*. Cambridge, Mass.

Botero, G. 1590. *Delle cause della grandezza della città*. Rome. Translated as *The cause of greatness of cities* (London, 1606).

Bücher, K. 1918–19. *Die Entstehung der Volkswirtschaft*. 2 vols. Tübingen. The first volume originally appeared in 1893. An English translation of the first volume was published as *Industrial evolution* (Toronto, 1901).

Carey, H. 1851. *Harmony of interests*. Philadelphia.

Chandler, A. 1977. *The visible hand: The managerial revolution in American business*. Cambridge, Mass.

1990. *Scale and scope: The dynamics of industrial capitalism*. Cambridge, Mass.

Cohn, G. 1895. *The science of finance*, trans. T. Veblen. Economic Studies of the University of Chicago, no. 1. Chicago.

Crother, J. G. 1960. *Francis Bacon: The first statesman of science*. London.

Curtis, F. 1904. *The Republican Party: A history of its fifty years' existence and a record of its measures and leaders, 1854–1904*. 2 vols. New York.

De Long, B., and L. Summers. 1991. Equipment investment and economic growth. *Quarterly Journal of Economics* 106(May): 445–502.

Graham, F. 1923. Some aspects of protection further considered. *Quarterly Journal of Economics* 37: 199–227.

Grossman, G. M., ed. 1990. *Imperfect competition and international trade*. Cambridge, Mass.

Helpman, E., and P. Krugman. 1985. *Market structure and foreign trade*. Cambridge, Mass.

Hirschman, A. O. 1958. *The strategy of economic development*. New Haven, Conn.

——— 1977. *The passions and the interests*. Princeton, N.J.

——— 1991. *The rhetoric of reaction: Perversity, futility, jeopardy*. Cambridge, Mass.

King, C. 1721. *The British merchant or commerce preserv'd*. 3 vols. London.

Krugman, P., ed. 1986. *Strategic trade policy and the new international economics*. Cambridge, Mass.

Krugman, P. 1990. *Rethinking international trade*. Cambridge, Mass.

Lawson, T. 1989. Abstraction, tendencies and stylised facts: A realist approach to economic analysis. In *Kaldor's political economy*, ed. T. Lawson, J. G. Palma, and J. Sender, pp. 59–78. London.

Lazonick, W. 1991. *Business organization and the myth of the market economy*. Cambridge, England.

Lucas, R., Jr. 1988. On the mechanics of economic development. *Journal of Monetary Economics* 22: 3–42.

——— 1993. Making a miracle. *Econometrica* 61: 251–72.

Lundvall, B.-Å. 1994. The learning economy: Challenges to economic theory and policy. Paper presented at the European Association for Evolutionary Political Economy Conference, Copenhagen (October).

Marshall, A. 1890. *Principles of economics*. London.

Mervin, L. 1981. *Vitamin C*. Willingborough, Eng.

Nelson, R. R. 1995. Recent evolutionary theorizing about economic change. *Journal of Economic Literature* 33(1): 58–9.

Odigari, H., and A. Gota. 1993. The Japanese innovation system: Past, present and future. In *National innovation systems: A comparative analysis*, ed. R. R. Nelson, pp. 76–114. New York.

Peirce, C. S. 1867. *Collected papers of Charles Sanders Pierce*, ed. C. Hartshorne and P. Weiss. Cambridge, Mass.

Polanyi, K. 1957. *The great transformation: The political and economic origins of our time*. Boston. Originally published in 1944.

Porter, M. 1990. *The competitive advantage of nations*. London.

Reinert, E. S. 1980. *International trade and the economic mechanisms of underdevelopment*. Microfilm. Ann Arbor.

——— 1994. Catching up from way behind: A third world perspective on first world history. In *The dynamics of technology, trade, and growth*, ed. J. Fagerberg, B. Verspagen, and N. von Tunzelman, pp. 168–97. London.

——— 1995. Competitiveness and its predecessors: A 500-year cross-national perspective. *Structural Change and Economic Dynamics* 6: 23–42.

Reinert, E. S., and A. Daastøl. 1997. Exploring the genesis of economic innovations: The religious gestalt-switch and the duty to invent as preconditions for economic growth. *European Journal of Law and Economics* 4: 233–83.

Roscher, W. 1882. *Principles of political economy*. Chicago.

Schumpeter, J. 1954. *History of economic analysis*. New York.

Serra, A. 1613. *Breve trattato delle cause che possono far abbondare i regni d'oro e argento dove non sono miniere*. Naples.

Sombart, W. 1913. *Studien der Entwicklungsgeschichte des modernen Kapitalismus.* 2 vols. Munich.

Villner, K. 1986. *Blod, Kryddor och Sott.* Stockholm.

Viner, J. 1937. *Studies in the theory of international trade.* New York.

Wade, R. 1990. *Governing the market: Economic theory and the role of government in East Asian industrialization.* Princeton, N.J.

PART II

National Cases

5

∽

The Rise and Fall of State-Owned Enterprise
in Germany

ULRICH   WENGENROTH

The history of state-owned enterprise (SOE) in Germany has to be written on three different levels. Since unification in 1871, Germany has been a decentralized federal state; thus state ownership occurred on the national, state (*Länder*), and municipal levels. For historical reasons, the states were very strong and independent when it came to regulation of industry and infrastructure. This independence was vigorously defended by the southern states, notably Bavaria, in view of what was often felt to be suffocating Prussian dominance in national affairs. Prussia held about two-thirds of German territory during the German Empire and the Weimar Republic. The economic and political center of both Prussia and Germany was Berlin, which often made it difficult to draw a line between national and state interests. Given its sheer size, Prussia, unlike the other states, always had the option of pursuing its plans on either the state or the national level. Whatever Prussia did, its policy had a national dimension. Prussia's SOE, therefore, must be compared with national enterprise elsewhere. SOE in the other German states, by contrast, often served the function of protecting what was left of sovereignty. On the level of the individual states, this latent antagonism was reproduced between state governments and municipalities, frequently making municipal enterprise a guarantor of local sovereignty. Thus, there was not one agent of state ownership in

Germany but three, and it was not unusual for them to compete against each other.

SOE IN IMPERIAL GERMANY

Leaving aside land ownership,[1] education, institutionalized health care, and social security, Germany entered the twentieth century with the typical set of SOEs: arms factories and naval yards, postal, telegraph, and telephone service, the water utility, and a few mining operations that had escaped mid-nineteenth-century privatization. No state investment in a manufacturing industry, let alone nationalization of existing industries, had occurred for decades. Unlike many other industrial nations, however, Germany's major states owned railways. Around the turn of the century, municipalities, states, and private industry were creating mixed enterprises for the gas and electricity utilities and streetcar companies. Finally, there was a growing number of local savings banks backed by municipal guarantees. Whereas the mixed ownership of utilities had been a compromise necessitated by tight budgets, the savings banks were an effort to support capital formation among small businesses and to provide rudimentary banking services to the less well off. With very few exceptions, German SOE was concentrated in infrastructure and provided what many believed to be public goods from natural monopolies. This, however, had not always been evident. The two major SOEs, the post office and the Prussian railways, had taken over from private operators.

Postal Services

For more than three centuries the Fürstlich Thurn und Taxische Post (Princely Mail of Thurn and Taxis) had provided services for the German territories and their European neighbors. Operating from the independent city of Frankfurt, its legal framework was embedded in more than 300 individual treaties, many of them bills of fiefdom, with German and European sovereigns (Probst 1989, 123, 140). In 1866-7, toward the end of the Austro-Prussian War, the Thurn and Taxis Post

---

[1] In the transition period from mercantilism to liberalism, large parts of the royal and princely estates were taken over by the German states rather than being privatized. After the foundation of the empire, Prussia owned about 8 percent of Prussian territory; Bavaria and Saxony each owned 12 percent of their respective territories; and Baden held 14 percent of its territory (Ambrosius 1984, 26).

was high-handedly brought to an end when Prussian troops occupied Frankfurt and forced the pro-Austrian Thurn and Taxis to hand over their business to Prussia and its allies. Ever since then, the royal prerogatives of the mail and telegraph had been scrupulously observed and maintained. With the foundation of the German Empire in 1871, the Reichspost was created, inheriting all operations outside Bavaria and Wurttemberg, where the respective *Länderpost* (state post) continued to exist in close cooperation with the Reichspost. When Emil Rathenau tried to obtain a concession for Bell's telephone in Berlin in 1880, his plans were upset by the postmaster general, who claimed the royal prerogative for all public communications networks, whether mail, telegraph, or telephone (Pohl 1988, 26–7). Frustrated, Rathenau turned to the next major American invention, Edison's electric light, and set up what was to become the Allgemeine Electrizitäts-Gesellschaft (AEG).

The Reichspost became a rapidly growing business with a budget of more than 500 million marks ($100 million) in the 1890s (Vogt 1989, 219). It successfully developed the telephone business and introduced the postal check service on the eve of World War I. This was very much against the opposition of the banks. At the end of the war – prior to inflation – the transfer volume stood at more than 130 billion marks from nearly 10 billion transactions (Vogt 1989, 231). The value of post and telegraph operations had increased fiftyfold between 1850 and 1913, while the German economy had grown fivefold (Tilly 1976, 579). In spite of its enormous budget, the Reichspost was never a major contributor to the empire's revenues: in 1901 it contributed 2.1 percent and in 1913 4.1 percent of total revenues (Witt 1970, 378). Profits were deliberately kept low by reducing prices and subsidizing peripheral regions of the empire through a system of standard rates. Heinrich von Stephan, postmaster general from 1870 until his death in 1897, was an entrepreneur rather than just an administrator. He created one of the most dynamically growing enterprises in the German Empire, even if his yardstick was cheap and extended services rather than profits. Few would question that he succeeded. His conflicts with Parliament over the postal budget, and especially over the plowing back of profits for investment, were notorious. Von Stephan was a systems architect and an empire builder in the best tradition of late-nineteenth-century tycoons. Historians of the German postal services claim that none of his successors matched him in these genuinely entrepreneurial qualities (Vogt 1989, 221).

Railways

The end of private railway companies had been less dramatic. During the liberal 1860s, about half of the German railway system had been operated by private companies, most of them in Prussia. In the 1870s, widespread accusations of inefficiency, cartels, and corruption culminated in a strong campaign for a unified system. Bismarck's attempt to create a Reichsbahn for the whole empire, however, was blocked by the southern states. Instead, Bavaria and Saxony consolidated their state railway systems by acquiring the remaining private companies in their own territory. Thus left behind, Prussia nationalized most of its private railways between 1879 and 1885. This meant that the share of state-owned railways in Germany increased from 56 percent in 1870 to 82 percent in 1880 (Wessel 1982, 206-7). Largely through construction of new lines in eastern Prussia, this share was further increased to more than 90 percent by the turn of the century. On the eve of World War I, Prussian state railways were said to be the largest single enterprise in the world (Lotz 1917, 765-6).

Next to military requirements, the enormous coal consumption of the Reichsbahn was the main reason Prussia retained some of its coal mines after the deregulation of mining in 1865 and expanded its coal mining operations around the turn of the century.[2] This move can be understood as defensive backward vertical integration, since the major coal producers of Prussia had raised domestic prices with the formation of the Rhenish–Westfalian Coal Syndicate in 1893. Like other industrial enterprises in the steel and chemical industries, the Reichsbahn in its acquisition policy tried to bypass the cartel to contain rising transaction costs. Predictably, the cartel countered this policy and managed to abort the Prussian state's clandestine takeover of the extended Hibernia coal mine (Nussbaum 1963). Characteristically, the whole operation was conducted by the Prussian state like any hostile takeover in private industry. Rather than resorting to legislative action, the state employed Berlin banks to buy up the majority of Hibernia shares discreetly (Radzio 1990, 50-7).

---

[2] Burghardt 1995, 98-9. In 1913, 4 percent of Ruhr coal was produced by state-owned mines, whereas almost all the coal from the less important Saar region and a substantial amount of the coal from Upper Silesia came from state mines. Unlike coal mining in the dominant Ruhr region, that in the Saar and Silesia had never been privatized to the same extent.

Unlike the Reichspost but like the other state railways, the Prussian railways were of enormous fiscal importance. Immediately after nationalization in Prussia, they contributed 35 percent to the state budget. By the turn of the century, this share had increased to 50 percent (Ambrosius 1984, 33). Since expenses for labor and investment did not amount to more than 25–35 percent of the Prussian budget, the railways' net contribution was larger in many years than all state taxes combined.[3] Because railway revenues depended heavily on the business cycle, the Prussian minister of finance frequently ran into difficulties and had to introduce early forms of deficit spending in 1901 and 1908 when the railway surplus failed by a large margin to reach its targets (Ambrosius 1984, 34). Not surprisingly, the dependence of the Prussian budget on the railways led to continuous conflict between the Ministry of Finance and the administration of the railways, with the former usually gaining the upper hand. Earlier hopes that nationalization would bring significantly lower freight rates did not materialize. The policies of the two largest SOEs in imperial Germany, the Reichspost and the Prussian railways, were strikingly different in this respect. That there was more fiscal envy of the railways than of the post office is understandable, however. The postmaster general delivered less than 100 million marks compared with the more than 800 million marks provided by the German railways in 1913 (*Handbuch* 1930, 86). The Prussian and state railways ruthlessly exploited their monopoly for the sake of high revenues. They were more efficient than the private companies they had replaced, especially when it came to reliability and extension of service.

Gas and Electric Utilities

With the post office being run by the empire and the railways by the states, the third major field of SOE before World War I, the gas and electric utilities, was a predominantly local affair.[4] In both fields private enterprise dominated early development, and town and city councils moved in only after the technology proved itself and profitable operations were guaranteed. Since the gas works had started earlier in the

---

[3] Ambrosius 1984, 33; Fremdling 1993, 427. Annual gross profits (without interest payments, annuities, and reserves) were approximately 500 million marks (Schletzbaum 1990, 74). In the years before the war, most of these surpluses were invested in new lines and rolling stock.

[4] In 1913 more than 90 percent of the water cycle, which will not be dealt with here, was in the possession of local authorities (Ambrosius 1984, 41).

century, the first phase of municipalization took place between 1860 and 1874, with a second phase from 1885 to 1900. Cost-effective supply for the rapidly growing urban areas was as much a consideration as fiscal motives, especially during the second phase (Brunckhorst 1978, 228). The same was true for electrification. Here the local authorities benefited greatly from their experience with gas. The city councils were at first prudent in the face of an unproven technology; they began to license local networks in the 1880s. German manufacturers of electric power plants developed the *Unternehmergeschäft*, whereby the electrotechnical industry would finance the power plant and installation, and recover its costs through both operational profits and sale of the plant after a number of years. Contracts between municipalities and the electricity industry often also stipulated that the privately built electric power system would fall to the municipality free of charge after a longer period of, say, ten to fifteen years, thus reducing the strain on local budgets that had often been depleted by the need for other infrastructural investment in the rapidly growing urban areas. On the eve of World War I, 37 percent of all installed electric power generators were wholly state-owned – mostly by municipalities (Ott 1986, xxxiii). The share of mixed enterprise, which became ever more dominant after the war, is still unknown.

Regional electrical networks, linking several municipal distributors, first experienced this new form of ownership after the turn of the century. Even if twenty-four of the twenty-five regional companies had started as private enterprises, municipalities and counties soon acquired shares in these companies in order to gain better control over their prices and investment. The outcome was mixed enterprises, legally structured as private companies mostly controlled by local government, which held the majority or at least a substantial share of capital (Ott 1986, xxxvi). These mixed enterprises existed for both gas and electricity.

The common policy with these regional and municipal companies was to provide a nonsubsidized, cost-efficient service to local trade and industry as well as to private consumers. Operations had to be moderately profitable so as not to burden municipal budgets. Unlike the Prussian railways, they were intended not to be sources of income, but rather to provide public services. Cost reductions were usually passed on to the consumer in the form of reduced rates. Municipal ownership of the energy supply was not the end of competition; rather, city councils and state parliaments endeavored to generate positive externalities for their local business. Preference tariffs for gas and electricity for small-scale industry were much-used instruments of local trade promotion (Wengenroth 1989).

Savings Banks

The first local savings banks date from the late eighteenth century. Their number grew steadily throughout the nineteenth century and stood at 3,133 in 1913, with total deposits of close to 20 billion marks, compared with 21 billion marks for all the private German credit banks (Tilly 1976, 591). These savings banks were introduced to encourage saving by the petite bourgeoisie, artisans, and workers. They had no capital of their own but were guaranteed by the municipality; they did not pay a trade tax. The rationale behind their creation was to eventually reduce the demands being made on local poor relief funds. When the first legislation for national social security was introduced in the 1880s, this motive was put in the background and the savings banks increasingly transformed themselves into a German-type universal bank for small business. This process was legally settled in 1908, when the savings banks were authorized to issue checks and do transfer business (Born 1977, 204-8). Their major competition did not come from the established private banks but from the postal savings and check service, which appealed partly to the same clientele. It was the postmaster general's plan to start a post savings bank on the British model. This drove the local savings banks to form regional and eventually national associations in the 1880s. Savings banks, like gas and electricity utilities, were profitable for municipalities.

SOE IN THE WEIMAR REPUBLIC

World War I speeded up the concentration and association of German industry and greatly strengthened the state's influence on private enterprise. More than 200 *Kriegsgesellschaften* (war companies), in which the state had a major share, were created during the war (Hardach 1973, 68). Some new industries such as aluminum came out of the war as state monopolies. Ideas of *Gemeinwirtschaft*, a rational, planned form of capitalism in which market forces were minimized, had eroded the acceptance of economic liberalism and private capitalism among many politicians and the German public. With socialist governments prevailing in the revolution of 1918, nationalization of key industries was on the agenda. Whereas most private industries successfully weathered the early storm of state socialism, existing SOE was expanded and consolidated in the immediate postwar years. Moreover, some private sectors deemed essential for German industry's competitive advantage or as a backbone of future rearmament gained strong state support. One spectacular case was civil aviation. Germany was a leader in the late 1920s, with very low fares and twice as many passengers as in the United States. In 1928 there were 111,000 air passengers in Germany versus 53,000 in the United States. German airfares were equivalent to first-class rail tickets, whereas American airfares stood at about four times rail fares. All this was financed by state subsidies, which in 1928 amounted to three times the amount of revenue from ticket sales.[5]

In 1925 the central state took over 80 percent of the ailing Junkers company, which in 1926 became one of the two founder firms of Lufthansa (James 1997, 7). Air transport, as an industry of the future and a backbone of modern warfare, was a state business in private garb from the very beginning.

Shaped by the legacy of the war, a lasting fabric of German SOE was created in the 1920s. It survived the turmoil of the Nazi dictatorship, as well as defeat and national disintegration at the end of World War II.

Post Office and Railways

The Weimar Constitution of 1919 abolished all the prerogatives of the southern states in the postal services and railways and created a unified Reichspost and a unified Reichsbahn. A third nationalization project, for a unified electrical network, never materialized. Although Parliament had voted to nationalize the electric power system on New Year's Eve 1919, this law was never implemented, nor was it revoked during the Weimar Republic (Boll 1969, 57–8; Herzig 1992, 134). With the tacit consent of all parties, the project was eventually brought to a halt through a large number of committees and councils. In this case, the terms of the Treaty of Versailles might well have contributed to stemming the early tide of nationalization, since all Reich assets were subjected to reparations demands.

The Reichsbahn had a disastrous start. It lost 50,000 locomotives and 150,000 carriages to the Allies, and its future revenues had to be pledged

---

[5] James 1997, 4–5. By 1939, however, subsidies were down to one-third of company receipts (ibid., 11).

as security for reparations payments. Between 1924 and 1932 the Reichsbahn contributed about $1 billion to the reparations account (*Handbuch* 1930, 86). The possibility that the revenues of a nationalized electrical network might come under similar pressure could not be ruled out. Since it was the policy of successive governments to demonstrate Germany's inability to meet Allied reparations demands, a second Reichsbahn was viewed as more beneficial to France than to Germany. The Reichspost, on the other hand, having been less profitable during the empire and demonstrably loss-producing in the immediate postwar years, was under no threat.

After the war, both the Reichsbahn and the Reichspost were reorganized as independent institutions and their capital was formally separated from the Reich's property. The Reichspost and the Reichsbahn had to account for their operations like any private enterprise, and submit annual profit and loss accounts and balance sheets. Deficits or additional capital needs had to be met by issuing bonds rather than by resorting to the treasury (Sautter 1951, 471–7). In contrast to the prewar experience, the Reich tried to detach itself as much as possible from the vicissitudes of the business cycle, which were reflected in the revenues of its two largest enterprises. The combined turnover of these two continued to be huge, peaking at 7.6 billion marks ($1.8 billion) in 1929, with a favorable balance of 1.1 billion marks. This was about equal to the annual dividends of all German joint-stock companies for the same year (*Handbuch* 1930, 86–7). According to 1925 labor statistics, the two had a combined labor force of 1.1 million.[6]

Large-Scale Electricity Supply

Compared with these two giants, all other enterprise owned by the Reich was less significant, even though it was large by industrial standards. Despite the abortive nationalization scheme, the Reich owned one of Germany's largest electricity supply companies by the end of the 1920s, Elektrowerke AG. This company had its raw material base in the lignite fields of central Germany, which had been developed for electricity production during the war. In the second half of the 1920s, Elektrowerke sought participation in most of the local and regional electricity supply companies of central Germany and provided them

---

[6] Reichsbahn: 755,541, Reichspost: 355,086. *Statistik des Deutschen Reiches*, vol. 413, part V, p. 6.

with cheap electricity from its large-scale plant. Because of its central location in the German electricity supply, Elektrowerke successfully developed a regional grid, benefiting from economies of scale and thus greatly expanding production by lowering prices (Herzig 1992, 134-5). It is peculiar that the "national" Elektrowerke operated as a regional company very much like other regional companies, which were mixed enterprises or owned by one of the states. In Prussia alone there were three other electricity supply giants, and these were organized quite differently. They were the mixed enterprise of Rheinisch–Westfälisches Elektrizitätswerk (RWE), with its stronghold in the Ruhr district and the lignite fields west of Cologne; Vereinigte Elektrizitätswerke Westfalen (VEW), a combination of several municipal utilities in competition with RWE; and the state-owned Preußische Elektrizitäts AG. After the death of RWE's founder, Hugo Stinnes, in 1924, the Prussian state acquired a large share in this company. Nevertheless the relation between RWE and the Prussian state was never good, and it took lengthy negotiations before the two could agree on a territorial settlement in what was to become known as the *Elektrofriede* (electricity peace) of 1927 (Herzig 1992, 135). According to the director of RWE, the spectacular battle between Prussia and his company was one between "state socialism" and a mixed enterprise fundamentally governed by the principles of private enterprise (Herzig 1992, 136).

During the Weimar Republic the electric power industry witnessed every conceivable form of ownership, from 100 percent state-owned through a great variety of mixed enterprise to 100 percent private with many interlocking directorships, joint operations, and subsidiaries. The mixed RWE, for example, built a large power plant together with Baden-werk AG, a limited liability company controlled by the state of Baden, which had privatized its utilities in 1921 without surrendering control (Boll 1969, 24). Eventually most utilities cooperated in some way in the creation of a German power grid, which had been the focal point of the ill-fated nationalization law of 1919.[7] With the exception of the three southern states, Baden, Bavaria, and Württemberg, the "territories" of these companies were not always congruent with those of the states from which they operated, betraying a kind of capitalistic momentum in their development. In the southern states, independence from the

---

[7] After a national scheme had failed, three groups were eventually formed: West (RWE, Badenwerk, Württemberg), East (Elektrowerke, Berlin, Silesia), and Center (Bayernwerk, Preußenelektra). Bruche 1977, 85.

suffocating grip of the coal barons was as much a consideration as industrial modernization. Three out of five railway carriages crossing the Bavarian border before the war had carried coal (Blaich 1981, 2). Development of hydroelectricity (or "white coal," as it was called) was therefore seen as a precondition for local trade and industry to compete on equal terms in the domestic markets. The centralization of electricity generation in the hands of the state always smacked of socialism, however. It is no surprise, therefore, that the project of Bayernwerk, the Bavarian SOE established in 1921, served as a model for the aborted socialization project of 1919 (Blaich 1981, 175).

Municipal Gas and Electric Utilities

In 1930 municipal companies produced 84 percent of German gas and 45 percent of German electricity (*Handbuch* 1930, 14, 55). Both grew increasingly dependent on regional suppliers, however, with electricity leading the way. Economies of scale favored the centralized production of electricity and gas, which turned many of the municipal companies into mere distributors (Herzig 1992, 134-6; Körting 1963, 488-99; Löwer 1992, 185-7). Nevertheless they remained in control of the local infrastructure and urban development, giving city and county councils, which typically owned them, a source of independent income as well as an instrument of *Gewerbeförderung* (local trade promotion). The earlier autonomy of municipal governments with regard to energy policy was dwindling, however. In the interwar years, energy had become an issue for the major states and the central government. This was increasingly true after the *Energiewirtschaftsgesetz* (energy economics legislation) of 1935 stipulated that all investment in power plants and electricity networks had to be approved by the Ministry of Economics to make sure that the most efficient solution was chosen (Boll 1969, 77-8). This effectively prevented local suppliers from modernizing and forced them under the tutelage of large regional suppliers such as RWE, Bayernwerk, or Elektrowerke AG.

State Holding Companies

Toward the end of the 1920s, the Reich, Prussia, and Saxony created holding companies to take care of their many industrial possessions. The Reich had VIAG (Vereinigte Industrieunternehmungen AG – United Industrial Enterprises, Ltd.), which, with others, controlled Elektrowerke AG and the aluminum industry, both of which had been part of the state-run war economy. In 1929, the stock capital of VIAG stood at 160 million marks, with dividends of 16.1 million marks paid in the same year (*Handbuch* 1930, 287). The Prussian VEBA (Vereinigte Elektrizitäs- und Bergwerks-Aktiengesellschaft – United Electricity and Mining, Ltd.) was even larger. Its industrial stock was valued at 180 million marks, the lion's share of which was in agricultural and forestry estates worth about 4.8 billion marks. The Saxon holding, Sächsische Werke AG (Saxon Works, Ltd.) was valued at 1 billion marks. One of the companies it owned was the former financial holding company Siemens-Schuckert. Other holdings included the Meißen porcelain factory, the vast Saxon lignite deposits, and gas and electricity utilities (*Handbuch* 1930, 290–3; Radzio 1990, 27).

VEBA was particularly strong in coal mining. During the war, the Prussian state had finally managed to win control over Hibernia, which, together with Preußag and Bergwerks-AG Recklinghausen, amounted to one of the largest coal-mining conglomerates in the Ruhr district. Although Prussia had lost extensive hard coal deposits in the Saar region and in Upper Silesia as a result of the Treaty of Versailles, it still produced 10 percent of all German hard coal (*Handbuch* 1930, 125). Since Prussia no longer had its own railways or an independent army, the earlier motives behind the state's coal policy had become obsolete. At the end of the 1920s the Prussian state was a bona fide entrepreneur in the energy sector – and certainly one of the most powerful. In contrast to the prewar practice, however, all the German states and the Reich chose the legal form of limited-liability or joint-stock companies for their industrial possessions with the exception of postal services and railways. This was a far cry from the nineteenth-century past. German state enterprise in the 1920s was meant to operate in a market and was organized accordingly.

The Tacit "Nationalization" of Vereinigte Stahlwerke

The German state, whether the Reich or individual states, had acquired industrial enterprises and utilities either for fiscal reasons or to provide nondiscriminatory services to an increasingly industrial and urban economy. Given the steady growth of the German economy before World War I and after stabilization of the currency in 1924, there had been little need to come to the rescue of faltering branches of industry. Concentration and mergers would have taken care of failing enterprises.

The most spectacular move in this respect had been the creation of Vereinigte Stahlwerke (United Steelworks) in 1926. It was a merger of desperation, which brought half of Germany's steel production under one roof to share the burden of overcapacity and a great number of sub-optimal plants. The first measure taken by the new company was to close ten blast furnaces, seven steel works, eleven rolling mills, and four tube mills. The second step was to reduce coal-mining operations by closing sixteen pits. Production continued to expand, however, since only now was the remaining plant run at anything near capacity (Stremmel 1996, 13–14). Predictably, this did not ease the situation, and Vereinigte Stahlwerke became locked into a severe profit squeeze, which made the investment necessary for further reduction of production costs extremely difficult. To increase cash flow, Vereinigte Stahlwerke (which had a stock capital of 835 million marks) borrowed 942 million marks until September 1931. The Reich eventually had to bail out Vereinigte Stahlwerke's controlling group and took 23 percent of the shares at 364 percent of their market value in a very controversial operation (Stremmel 1996, 16). This put the Reich in a controlling position, but it never made use of it (Mollin 1988, 48–53). There had been no nationalization policy, and when the opportunity arose, it was allowed to slip. The motive behind this unprecedented rescue operation seems to have been fear that foreign investors would try to gain control of Germany's second largest enterprise (Seebold 1981, 31).

SOE IN THE NAZI YEARS

The Nazi government generally continued the policy of its predecessors toward SOE. Even if there were some centralizing efforts, as in legislation for the electric power industry, little changed materially in the early 1930s. The Nazi government tried to employ existing private and state-owned industry to meet its own aims. Only when there were major conflicts over autarchy and war preparation did the party intervene in industry and eventually create its own enterprise. Uncooperative industrialists such as the aircraft manufacturer Hugo Junkers were removed from their positions and replaced with Nazi governors. This was not an explicit nationalization policy, but simply an attempt to control production and investment policies in the interests of rearmament. As long as private industry was willing to cooperate, there was no interference by the state. The Nazi Party's newspaper, *Völkischer Beobachter*, boasted in 1936: "National Socialist economic policy corresponds to the technical age. It lets capitalism run as the motor, uses its dynamic energies, but shifts the gears" (translated in Hayes 1987, 79).

A somber but typical example of the success of this approach was the history of IG Farben's management, which moved from great skepticism vis-à-vis the Nazis in the early 1930s to compliance at Auschwitz. IG Farben, together with the state-owned VEBA, provided one of the pillars of autarky in war preparation – the hydrogen plants to convert coal into oil and eventually into gasoline for cars and aircraft. Less successful, or rather too late for the war, was the synthetic rubber program, with its fourth plant under construction in Auschwitz. Other branches of industry were less responsive to the Nazis, although this should not be misinterpreted as a form of political resistance.

The Nazi Industrial Empire

The steel industry of the Ruhr was openly hostile to the Nazi Party's plan to substitute low-grade domestic ore for the high-grade ore imported from Sweden. Such was the self-confidence of the steel barons in 1936 that the party eventually gave in and erected its own steel works on the ore basin in central Germany. The Hermann Göring Works, named after the second man in the party hierarchy, was to be the backbone of autarkic steel production in the coming war. The American engineering firm Brassert designed the plant and supervised construction, which began in 1938. Brassert and the Nazi Party intended the Hermann Göring Works to become the largest steel works in the world, but this ambition was never fully realized.

Another Nazi industrial project was Volkswagenwerk. Volkswagen suffered a fate similar to that of the domestic low-grade ore producers. None of the major German car manufacturers was willing to manufacture the Beetle. There had been other prototypes for a *Volkswagen* (people's car), the most advanced of which was probably that of Mercedes Benz. None of them, however, was approved by Hitler, who was an ardent admirer of Ferdinand Porsche. Against the advice of the whole German automobile industry, Hitler decided that Porsche's car would become the future Volkswagen and that the party-state itself would run the plant if necessary. This was the eventual outcome, and as in the case of the steel works, American engineers from the Ford Motor Company designed the Volkswagen plant close to the site of the Hermann Göring Works. Unlike Brassert, the Ford people finished their job, and Henry

Ford was awarded the highest award the Nazi Party would give to a foreigner.

The party organization running the Volkswagen plant was the Deutsche Arbeitsfront (DAF, German Labor Front), which had forcefully replaced the trade unions and taken over all of their possessions – banking, insurance, printing and publishing houses, and some home-building associations. The Volkswagen plant was to become the largest DAF industrial enterprise (Mommsen and Grieger 1996, 128). The real estate of the trade unions was sold to finance the project. During World War II, the Volkswagen plant produced the Kübelwagen – the German Jeep, based on the original Volkswagen, which had to go through extensive redesign for this purpose (Flink 1988, 262–7). During the war, tanks, aircraft engines, and missiles, manufactured by forced labor, were to be the main activity of Volkswagenwerk (Mommsen and Grieger 1996, chapters 6–8).

While Volkswagen remained a separate enterprise, the Hermann Göring Works became the nucleus of the greatest industrial conglomerate in the German state before unification in 1990. The Hermann Göring Works and its three branches (Reichswerke AG für Berg- und Hüttenbetriebe "Hermann Göring," Reichswerke AG für Waffen- und Maschinenbau "Hermann Göring," and Reichswerke AG für Binnenschiffahrt "Hermann Göring") consumed the heavy industries in occupied territory and ruthlessly expanded their control of arms manufacture. By 1941–2 the Hermann Göring Works comprised more than 300 companies in Germany and occupied Europe.[8] At the same time, it was a model of the future Nazi economy, which would overcome "plutocratic" capitalistic principles and replace them with a giant state industrial concern governed by the *Führerprinzip*.

A second state-owned conglomerate was Montan GmbH. Montan had been created in 1916 by private businessmen to serve as a holding company for mining and metallurgical undertakings. After the war it was a shell company. The Heereswaffenamt (Arms Office of the Army) turned it into a leasing and administrative holding company for the army's own clandestine industries in 1934. Montan served as an umbrella organization for state-owned arms factories and chemical explosives plants until 1945. Like the Hermann Göring Works, Montan expanded very rapidly during the war, until it comprised about 120 plant sites and more than 200,000 workers, many of them slave

[8] A complete list appears in Meyer 1986, 203–18.

laborers (Hopmann 1996, 19–22, 111, 117). It has been estimated that the Nazi state controlled 50 percent of all German stock capital toward the end of the war (Boelcke 1980, 472–3). In spite of their huge size and strategies, the Montan and Hermann Göring concerns were short-lived; they were a phenomenon made possible only by a belligerent dictatorship. At the end of the war they collapsed, together with a huge number of slave labor camps run by the SS. Whether the latter can meaningfully be described as SOEs seems debatable. Their brutality in squeezing labor out of doomed prisoners, with the extermination of workers as much an objective as production itself, was so remote from anything associated with "enterprise" that it is ignored here.[9]

SOE IN THE FEDERAL REPUBLIC OF GERMANY

The Nazi Inheritance

Whereas in Soviet-occupied East Germany all major enterprise was nationalized to form part of a socialist economy, the West German state was left with what it had inherited from the collapsing Reich. This included all the Weimar Republic SOEs on the national, state, and local levels, together with the domestic remains of the Hermann Göring Works, Montan, and Volkswagenwerk. The Montan armament empire was destroyed by the Allies. Although the Hermann Göring Works had been largely dismantled as well, the iron ore mines and part of the steel plant were still in existence in an area where unemployment was high in the postwar years. They were put back into operation under the name Salzgitter AG. Volkswagenwerk had been offered for sale by the British military government. It failed to find a purchaser, however, because nobody in the trade believed in a future for the odd Volkswagen.[10] The new state of Niedersachsen and the Federal Republic became owners of the plant by default. The plant was reactivated to create desperately needed jobs. Montan, stripped of its industrial possessions, continued to exist as a state-owned holding company for real estate under the name Industrieverwaltungsgesellschaft (IVG) until 1993, when it was fully privatized. From 1951 on, IVG sold off parts of its inheritance from Montan. For several years, IVG was instrumental in scouting for highly contro-

---

[9] On the "operational principles" of SS factories see Allen 1996.

[10] In March 1948, Ford president Ernest R. Breech reported to Henry Ford II on the plant that Ford engineers had designed a decade earlier: "Mr. Ford, I don't think what we are being offered here is worth a damn!" Flink 1988, 321–2.

versial nuclear waste disposal. The real estate still held by IVG in 1994 was valued at about 2.4 billion marks (Hopmann 1996, 217).

The Prussian Inheritance

Although most of Germany's SOE after World War II had its origins in the Weimar Republic, a major shift was brought about by the dissolution of the state of Prussia. Its major industrial possessions in the West fell to the federal government in Bonn, creating a concentration of SOE at the national level that – aside from the Nazi war period – had not existed before. Three-quarters of the Federal Republic's industrial possessions were concentrated in only six major companies, including Salzgitter AG (formerly the Hermann Göring Works), VIAG (as in the 1920s, but downsized), VEBA (formerly the Prussian holding company), Volkswagenwerk, and, after the return of the Saar from French control, Saarbergwerke (formerly the fiscal Prussian coal mines). Lufthansa, at that time still a small company with great potential, was officially relaunched in August 1954 as a state enterprise. It operated from German airports that themselves were owned by the *Länder* and the large municipalities.[11] New postwar creations included a number of banks to facilitate reconstruction and to compensate for heavy war damage and expulsion from the eastern provinces.[12]

Early Privatization and People's Shares

In spite of these important entrepreneurial activities, there was no policy to expand state control over industry. Some of the industries fell to the state only by default and were kept going in the early 1950s to overcome unemployment. As soon as this objective was achieved and the companies proved healthy and competitive, the first wave of privatization set in. State-owned industries, which were in desperate need of further capital to support their expansion, were taken to the stock exchange. *Volksaktien* (people's shares) were first issued for Preußag, a subsidiary of VEBA, in 1959, to be followed by Volkswagenwerk in 1960 and VEBA in 1965 (Ambrosius 1984, 130; Radzio 1990, 163–4, 169–77). The idea of *Volksaktien* was to spread ownership widely by

---

[11] On the creation of the new Lufthansa after World War II see Reul 1995.
[12] Kreditanstalt für Wiederaufbau, Lastenausgleichsbank. On the compensation scheme see Kleßmann 1986, 240–3.

limiting the number of shares owned per person. Since subsequent trading of the shares could not be controlled, voting rights were limited.

The operation was predictably controversial. In financial and private industry circles the limitation of voting rights smacked of state social-ism, since the state kept control through minority shares. Prominent members of the Social Democratic Party and the trade unions, mean-while, criticized the "dissipation of federal property" (Radzio 1990, 172). The privatized companies had been very profitable, and their shares were heavily oversubscribed. The breathtaking early development of Volkswagen shares, in particular, fueled fantasies of a new era of demo-cratic capitalism.

State-Owned Conglomerates

Chapter 65 of the *Bundeshaushaltsordnung* (federal budget regula-tions) stipulated that the state could have a stake in a private company only if there was a political objective that could not be pursued more efficiently and economically by other means.[13] This regulation, however, was administered extremely flexibly. Instead of further reduc-ing its involvement, the federal government reorganized and diversified its industrial possessions in the 1960s. VEBA, Saarbergwerke (Saar coal mines), and Salzgitter AG developed into highly diversified conglomer-ates. Problems in coal mining in the 1960s and in older industries in the 1970s, however, meant that these rather traditional and domestically focused state concerns lost much of their appeal. The Saarbergwerke and Salzgitter steel works never recovered, whereas VEBA managed to get rid of its coal operations and transform itself into an energy and petrochemical concern. After painful losses in the oil sector and sweep-ing reorganization with the help of British Petroleum, VEBA eventually became strong enough for the state to withdraw. It took the economic minister's overruling of the Federal Cartel Office (Bundes Kartellamt), however, to forge this alliance. Having already reduced its share from 43.75 percent to 30 percent in 1984, the federal government sold its remaining minority share of 25.5 percent in March 1987 (Radzio 1990, 327–8).

In the case of VEBA, as in the related cases of Volkswagen and VIAG, where the state had moved out earlier, the federal government's policy since the 1950s had been to leave these companies to themselves

---

[13] Bundeshaushaltsordnung of 16.8.1964, Bundesgesetzblatt I, pp. 1284ff.

and see that they were run as bona fide industrial enterprises. As in the Weimar Republic, there was no effort to politicize SOE. The rights of Parliament were restricted to little more than selling the companies (Wagener 1972, 86). The same was true at the state level.

Electricity

Electric power was a field in which SOE on the national and regional levels cooperated closely. Of the nine large electricity supply companies that had created a common organization for the German power grid in 1948, four were 100 percent state-owned. The state held more than 50 percent of the stock in four more; only in RWE was the state's ownership no more than 30 percent (Boll 1969, 114–17). The three big players were RWE, Preußenelektra/VEBA, and Bayernwerk/VIAG. Since the former had always been largely private and the latter two experienced progressive privatization from the 1960s on, German electricity production gradually returned to its private roots. The major conflicts today are over territorial monopolies and opening the market to other European suppliers, especially France, with its overcapacity in nuclear power. In spite of the efforts of a Deregulation Commission, progress toward deregulated and fully privatized markets has been slow (Löwer 1992, 202–4). A similar situation prevails in the gas industry, where the substitution of imported natural gas for coal gas has helped to create a nationwide system similar to the electric power grid, with municipal suppliers acting solely as distributors. State-owned and mixed enterprises continue to provide more than 90 percent of the gas used at the local level (Ambrosius 1984, 123).

Getting out of Coal

The Federal Republic's unwillingness to solve structural problems by outright nationalization was evident in the case of coal. When the coal mines in the Ruhr region ran into severe difficulties in the 1960s, the federal government was instrumental in pushing to create a single private company, Ruhrkohle AG. The share of state-owned coal companies in Ruhrkohle AG was about one-quarter, largely representing the Prussian legacy from the years of the empire and World War I (Abelshauser 1984, 144). Instead of assuming direct entrepreneurial responsibility, the federal government paid subsidies to the private company on the condition that the sums be reinvested in the problem-stricken Ruhr region, which thus continued to be the greatest single recipient of public funds. Already between 1949 and 1957, 6 billion of the 7 billion marks invested in coal mining had come from the government (Abelshauser 1984, 174). In Ruhrkohle, coal mining ultimately achieved a public character without state ownership.[14] If Ruhrkohle was officially a private company, it continued to be a burden on taxpayers by effectively socializing the enormous costs of a staggeringly slow retreat from hard-coal mining in Germany. The subsidies for Ruhrkohle have exceeded the total federal investment in science and technology over the last thirty years and have even outstripped that other public investment disaster, nuclear power.

Recent Privatization

The Federal Republic's determination to end its role as an entrepreneur is most conspicuously demonstrated in the privatization of postal delivery, telecommunications, and railways. Both the Bundesbahn (federal railways) and the Bundespost (federal post and telecommunications) have been transformed into joint-stock companies. In the process, the Bundespost has been divided into two systems: telecommunications and mail services. The former, always the source of income, was completely privatized and deregulated in two stages between 1996 and 1998, while the latter is still unprofitable. The newly created Bundesbahn AG made a modest profit in its first year but failed to generate sufficient funds for the normal rate of replacement, let alone substantial future investment. Privatization in these cases is more an effort to deliver the federal budget from what looked like an endless drain of subsidies. Unlike the situation in the late nineteenth century, when the postal service and the railways were nationalized, government and industry no longer believe in the greater efficiency of a unified system operated by the state.

Only after a gestation period of three decades of fundamental criticism of SOE did privatization in West Germany gather momentum. The spectacular *Teilprivatisierung* (partial privatization) of the 1960s still went hand in hand with expansion and consolidation elsewhere. Disadvantaged regions like the inner German border and the Saar were supported by the heavy investment of state-owned companies (Salzgitter AG, Saarbergwerke) in doomed industries. The prolonged depression

---

[14] The Christian Democratic Union politician Kurt Biedenkopf (today minister president of Saxony), according to Abelshauser 1984, 148.

since the 1970s, however, reduced public funds for these forms of barely camouflaged social policy and forced the state to reconsider its industrial activities. Persistent budget crises probably did more to accomplish privatization than all the newly minted academic arguments in favor of it.

The political boost to speed this process came with German unification, when the industrial heritage of state socialism had to be disposed of. Treuhandanstalt, which had been created by the socialist Modrow government of the German Democratic Republic in March 1990, comprised 40,000 facilities in 8,000 enterprises, three-quarters of which were to be privatized. About 1,900 infrastructure utilities among them were handed over to the municipalities, creating the local form of state ownership prevalent in the West (Sinn and Sinn 1993, 121–8). Although it was the largest privatization scheme in German history, Treuhandanstalt is a singular case and contributes little to understanding the vicissitudes of SOE in a market environment as it existed in most of Germany since the mid-nineteenth century.

FROM ENTREPRENEUR TO LIQUIDATOR: A CONCLUSION

In the long perspective, the German state has gone from entrepreneur to liquidator of its SOE. In the nineteenth century, creating favorable externalities for domestic business was but one consideration, and often not the first. Railways were monopolies that were shamelessly exploited for the benefit of the Treasury, while coal mines were held or acquired to protect the profitability of this monopoly against the cartels of private industry. There was no difference between state railways and any other monopoly in the way they were run. Whether the great profitability of the railways came at the expense of domestic growth is still open to debate. The Imperial Post Office looked much more like a public service at first glance. One could argue, however, that it was more growth-oriented, maximizing profits through its exceptional growth rather than through large margins.

Neither service was taken over from a bankrupt predecessor. They were the result of politically motivated, forced nationalization. They were based on the view held in the early stage of German capitalism that for purposes of infrastructure development the state was a better and more efficient entrepreneur in the public interest than were private companies. In spite of their huge profits this was especially true for the railways, which were nationalized in 1880 to the great applause of private business. If there were complaints about the cost of rail transport or mail services – and there were – these never led to demands for privatization. State ownership in the years of the German Empire was not an issue of socialism versus the free market, as in the Weimar Republic. Even the municipalities' control of the gas and electricity supply companies was seen in terms of providing protection from greedy and inefficient private monopolies. When power plants were transferred from private investors to city councils, lower rather than higher rates were expected, without this being an issue of subsidies.

A major change in this predominantly harmonious relationship between private companies and SOE occurred during and after World War I, when the state greatly expanded its industrial possessions and went into large-scale electricity production. Only then did private companies, mixed-ownership companies, and SOEs compete with each other over market share. At the same time, the rhetoric of state ownership changed, with socialist governments taking over from the conservative regime of the empire. Efficient SOE now could be seen as a first step toward socialism rather than as just another positive and therefore welcome externality. State enterprise had lost its political innocence. Cheap public services were as much a threat to private industry as they were a blessing. This situation changed only slowly when the state ceased to be an aggressive entrepreneur and became the custodian of troubled industries. The bailout of Vereinigte Stahlwerke by a conservative government had a signaling effect. Government had ceased being a political and economic competitor and had become the guarantor of the integrity of large enterprise. When the Nazi government continued this policy and began heavily subsidizing IG Farben and other industries in preparation for the planned war against Poland and France, the prewar harmony seemed to have been reestablished.

This honeymoon was short-lived, however. In creating the Hermann Göring Works, Volkswagenwerk, and the Montan holding company, the Nazi government openly questioned the ability of private industry to provide for the material needs of the new state. While these party concerns increasingly dominated industry up to and during the war, the old fear of socialism, this time National Socialism, was back. German business came out of the war thoroughly disillusioned with state interference in the economy. With American protection from any threat of socialism, the West German state was left mainly with what was either unprofitable or an embarrassing heritage from dismantled Prussia or the Nazi economy. The postal service and railways fell into the first category, and industrial possessions in the energy sector and the unwanted Volkswagenwerk into the second. When the unparalleled growth of the West German economy quite unexpectedly made many of these possessions profitable, the central state began to privatize them, retaining the great loss producers: the railways and the postal service.

The surrender of increasingly profitable possessions was not undertaken lightheartedly, however. The government was in no hurry until the economic crisis of the 1970s and 1980s turned jewels into millstones. Only then did the federal government genuinely begin to divest its industrial possessions. Even the post and the railways, which had served as buffers for the labor market, were now slimmed down to be left alone. Behind all the rhetoric of efficiency and competitiveness, privatization has become a panacea to escape political responsibility for employment at a time when state budgets no longer allow for massive subsidies. For this reason, privatization has become so widespread that many states and municipalities rid themselves of their possessions even when these are still moderately profitable. This secures them much-needed funds when tax returns are low because of high unemployment, and it offers the states an opportunity to relieve themselves of future responsibility for employment before open conflicts develop. In view of continuing deindustrialization and intensifying global competition, no politician wants to be caught with expectations he or she cannot meet. A great coalition of the Left and Right is liquidating SOE for the fundamental reason that the future of employment looks less than promising.

REFERENCES

Abelshauser, W. 1984. *Der Ruhrkohlenbergbau seit 1945: Wiederaufbau, Krise, Anpassung*. Munich.
Allen, M. 1996. The puzzle of Nazi modernism: Modern technology and ideological consensus in an SS factory at Auschwitz. *Technology and Culture* 37(3): 527–71.
Ambrosius, G. 1984. *Der Staat als Unternehmer*. Göttingen.
Blaich, F. 1981. *Die Energiepolitik Bayerns, 1900–1921*. Kallmünz.
Boelcke, W. A. 1980. Öffentliche Produktion: Geschichte. In *Handwörterbuch der Wirtschaftswissenschaften*, ed. W. Albers, vol. 5, pp. 457–73. Stuttgart.
Boll, G. 1969. *Entstehung und Entwicklung des Verbundbetriebs in der deutschen Elektriziätswirtschaft bis zum europäischen Verbund*. Frankfurt.
Born, K. E. 1977. *Geld und Banken im 19. und 20. Jahrhundert*. Stuttgart.
Bruche, G. 1977. *Elektrizitätsversorgung und Staatsfunktion: Das Reg-*

ulierungssystem der öffentlichen Elektrizitätsversorgung in der Bundesrepublik Deutschland. Frankfurt.

Brunckhorst, H.-D. 1978. *Kommunalisierung im 19. Jahrhundert, dargestellt am Beispiel der Gaswirtschaft im Deutschland.* Munich.

Burghardt, U. 1995. *Die Mechanisierung des Ruhrbergbaus, 1890-1930.* Munich.

Flink, J. J. 1988. *The automobile age.* Cambridge, Mass.

Fremdling, R. 1993. Eisenbahnen. In *Technik und Wirtschaft*, ed. U. Wengenroth, pp. 418-37. Düsseldorf.

Handbuch der öffentlichen Wirtschaft. 1930. Berlin.

Hardach, G. 1973. *Der Erste Weltkrieg.* Munich.

Hayes, P. 1987. *Industry and ideology: IG Farben in the Nazi era.* Cambridge.

Herzig, T. 1992. Wirtschaftsgeschichtliche Aspekte der deutschen Elektrizitätsversorgung 1880 bis 1990. In *Die Geschichte der Stromversorgung*, ed. W. Fischer, pp. 123-66. Frankfurt.

Hopmann, B. 1996. *Von der Montan zur Industrieverwaltungsgesellschaft (IVG), 1916-1951.* Stuttgart.

James, H. 1997. Die Frühgeschichte der Lufthansa: Ein Unternehmen zwischen Banken und Staat. *Zeitschrift für Unternehmensgeschichte* 43(1): 4-13.

Kleßmann, C. 1986. *Die doppelte Staatsgründung: Deutsche Geschichte, 1945-1955.* Bonn.

Körting, J. 1963. *Geschichte der deutschen Gasindustrie.* Essen.

Lotz, W. 1917. *Finanzwissenschaft.* Tübingen.

Löwer, W. 1992. Rechtshistorische Aspekte der deutschen Elektrizitätsversorgung von 1880 bis 1990. In *Die Geschichte der Stromversorgung*, ed. W. Fischer, pp. 169-215. Frankfurt.

Meyer, A. 1986. *Das Syndikat: Reichswerke "Hermann Göring."* Braunschweig.

Mollin, G. T. 1988. *Montankonzerne und "Drittes Reich": Der Gegensatz zwischen Monopolindustrie und Befehlswirtschaft in der deutschen Rüstung und Expansion, 1936-1944.* Göttingen.

Mommsen, H., and M. Grieger. 1996. *Das Volkswagenwerk und seine Arbeiter im Dritten Reich.* Düsseldorf.

Nussbaum, H. 1963. Ein neuer Hintergrund der Hibernia-Affäre. In *Jahrbuch für Wirtschaftsgeschichte*, ed. Deutsche Akademie der Wissenschaften zu Berlin, pp. 226-43. Berlin.

Ott, H., ed. 1986. *Statistik der öffentliche Elektrizitätsversorgung Deutschlands 1890-1913*, vol. 1, *Historiscche Energiestatistik von Deutschland.* St. Katharinen.

Pohl, M. 1988. *Emil Rathenau und die AEG.* Mainz.

Probst, E. 1989. Das Zeitalter der Lehensposten im 19. Jahrhundert: Thurn und Taxis. In *Deutsche Postgeschichte*, ed. W. Lotz, pp. 123-47. Berlin.

Radzio, H. 1990. *Unternehmen mit Energie: Aus der Geschichte der Veba.* Düsseldorf.

Reul, G. 1995. *Planung und Gründung der Deutschen Lufthansa AG 1949 bis 1955.* Cologne.

Sautter, K. 1951. *Geschichte der Deutschen Post, Teil 3: Geschichte der Deutschen Reichspost 1871 bis 1945.* Frankfurt.

Schletzbaum, L. 1990. *Eisenbahn*. Munich.

Seebold, G.-H. 1981. *Ein Stahlkonzern im Dritten Reich: Der Bochumer Verein 1927-1945*. Wuppertal.

Sinn, G., and H.-W. Sinn. 1993. *Kaltstart: Volkswirtschaftliche Aspekte der deutschen Vereinigung*, 3d ed. Munich.

Stremmel, R. 1996. Ein "gesundes Gebilde von gemäßigter Größe"? Notizen zur Geschichte der Vereinigten Stahlwerke AG. In *Findbuch zu den Beständen Vereinigte Stahlwerke AG und Bergbau- und Industriewerte GmbH*, ed. M. Rasch, vol. 1, pp. 3-46. Duisburg.

Tilly, R. 1976. Verkehrs- und Nachrichtenwesen, Handel, Geld-, Kredit- und Versicherungswesen 1850-1914. In *Handbuch der deutschen Wirtschafts- und Sozialgeschichte*, ed. H. Aubin and W. Zorn, vol. 2, pp. 563-96. Stuttgart.

Vogt, M. 1989. Die Post im Kaiserreich. Heinrich (von) Stephan und seine Nachfolger. In *Deutsche Postgeschichte*, ed. W. Lotz, pp. 203-39. Berlin.

Wagener, H.-O. 1972. *Neue staatswirtschaftliche Funktionen bundeseigener Industriebeteiligungen*. Meisenheim.

Wengenroth, U. 1989. Motoren für den Kleinbetrieb: Soziale Utopien, technische Entwicklung und Absatzstrategien bei der Motorisierung des Kleingewerbes im Kaiserreich. In *Prekäre Selbständigkeit: Zur Standortbestimmung von Handwerk, Hausindustrie und Kleingewerbe im Industrialisierungsprozeß*, ed. U. Wengenroth, pp. 177-205. Stuttgart.

Wessel, H. A. 1982. Der Einfluß des Staates auf die Industrie: Dargestellt am Beispiel der staatlichen Telegraphenbehörden und der elektrotechnischen Industrie. In *Die Rolle des Staates für die wirtschaftliche Entwicklung*, ed. F. Blaich, pp. 203-23. Berlin.

Witt, P.-C. 1970. *Die Finanzpolitik des Deutschen Reiches von 1903 bis 1913: Eine Studie zur Innenpolitik des Wilhelminischen Deutschlands*. Lübeck.

6

Beyond State and Market

Italy's Futile Search for a Third Way

FRANCO AMATORI

In Italy state-owned enterprise (SOE) has assumed a particular role and weight since the first half of the twentieth century. Indeed, one of the most important Italian historiographers, Rosario Romeo (1988, 135), stated that in the late 1930s the country was second only to the Soviet Union in the extent of its state property ownership. A complete apparatus of SOEs was active in Italy from the 1930s on. This apparatus was made up of state companies such as the national railways, founded in 1905, which were considered "autonomous organizations inside the public administration that manage directly, in the name of the competent ministry, specific production or service activities that belong to primary state tasks" (Bianchi 1994, 591). There are also state concerns such as INA (the National Insurance Institute, created in 1912 to operate the state life insurance monopoly), concerns that "should manage, according to a style typical of private business, activities considered public but which, unlike the state companies, remain outside the public administration" (Bianchi 1994, 591). Finally there are also state shareholding companies such as IRI (the Institute for Industrial Reconstruction), which will be examined in this essay. State shareholding companies are "subject to private corporate law while the majority of the outstanding shares are controlled by a state concern."[1] This essay will focus on the last category, partly for reasons of space, partly because of the availability of detailed historiographical information about state shareholding companies, and finally because this is probably where Italy made the most original contribution to the phenomenon of SOE.[2]

SOE in Italy went through four distinct phases: (1) the creation and the first consolidation of IRI in the 1930s; (2) the formation of a real shareholding system in the period from immediately after World War II to the early 1960s, which offered great successes in the oil and steel sectors, as shown by the creation of ENI (National Hydrocarbon Concern) in 1953 and the Ministry of State Shareholdings in 1956; (3) the extension of the system, relying on four super-holding companies – IRI, ENI, EFIM (Autonomous Concern for Financing the Machinery Industry), and EGAM (Concern for Mining Companies), through the early 1970s; and (4) the contraction of the system in the last quarter of the century, during which the sense of crisis became increasingly evident, a process of privatizations began, the Ministry of State Shareholdings was dissolved, and SOEs were transformed into corporations.

1.   At the beginning of the 1930s, the relationship between the banks and industry reached a crisis point in Italy. The two most important universal banks,[3] Banca Commerciale Italiana and Credito Italiano, were compelled by the government to concentrate their industrial securities in two financial holding companies. At the same time (1931), the government both guaranteed them and created IMI (the Italian Securities Institute) for medium-term financing of industry. But these measures were not sufficient to cut the ties between banks and industrial enterprise. To reach this goal, IRI was created in 1933 to take over all the industrial securities of the banks. IRI was articulated in two sectors: the first would grant long-term loans to companies affected by the Depression, and the second was set up to sell the securities taken over from

---

[1] Bianchi 1994, 592. An excellent typology of Italian SOEs from a historical perspective can be found in Bonelli 1987. For a review of the subject see Colitti 1975.

[2] No one has yet attempted to write a complete history of the state shareholdings system in Italy. For a detailed outline of the field and a good general bibliography see Anselmi 1990; Maraffi 1990; Sapelli and Carnevali 1992.

[3] A universal bank, on the German model, not only collects deposits and lends money on a short-term basis, but also functions with a long-term horizon, buying shares in companies and even designating some members of the companies' boards (so that it can strongly influence the companies' strategies). The risk of this kind of bank is that it invests in long-term operations the money it takes in as deposits.

the banks to private buyers. In 1936, legislation prohibiting banks from giving long-term loans to industrial companies and from acquiring their shares went into effect. This law remained in effect until 1993.

In 1937 IRI became a permanent institution, partly as a means of implementing autarkic and rearmament policies but also because of the absence of interested private buyers. IRI was now configured as a super–holding company, entirely owned by the state, which controlled more than 50 percent of the sectorial holdings STET (telephone companies, founded in 1934), Finmare (navigation companies, 1936), and Finsider (steel, 1937), financial holding companies that in turn controlled corporations operating as private companies. The creator of this complex framework, Alberto Beneduce, was a former socialist and, starting in the late 1920s, Mussolini's most influential economic adviser. When IRI was created, it controlled more than 40 percent of Italian industrial bonds. At the end of the 1930s, even after having given back to private owners some important companies (such as Edison, leader in the electrical sector), IRI was still the major Italian operator in heavy industry (steel, machinery, shipbuilding, and electricity). (See Table 6.1.)

2.   After World War II, notwithstanding the ascendancy of a free market ideology, IRI and its state entrepreneur formula were confirmed. Furthermore, two new sectorial holdings were created: Finmeccanica (1948, for machinery-manufacturing companies) and Finelettrica (1952, for electrical companies). Enrico Mattei, the head of the Catholic war partisans, was appointed as commissioner to divest AGIP, the Italian General Oil Company, a minor SOE created in 1926 for the national oil supply. Mattei not only opposed performing this task but went so far as to make AGIP (which had been a relatively minor player) the original core of ENI (1953) so as to create a monopoly for the extraction and distribution of natural gas in northern Italy, which carried out an aggressive and effective policy in the areas of oil and chemicals.

In the meantime, within IRI, important achievements occurred in steel, where, thanks to a plan long elaborated by Oscar Sinigaglia, president of Finsider, Italy advanced from being the world's ninth largest producer to the sixth largest. At the end of the 1950s, IRI found itself on the front line to build up the national toll road system and to complete the telephone system. In another industrial sector it gave new life to Alfa Romeo, the auto manufacturer, allowing the company to achieve the number two status in the country after Fiat. Nonetheless, as a whole,

Table 6.1. The Beginning of the Entrepreunerial State (late 1930s)

IRI: Activity Sectors	% of National Output	Employment (Thousands)	% of National Employment
A. *Manufacturing*			
Iron, and steel; production of:		57.3	
Iron ore	67		
Cast iron	77		
Steel	45		
Pipes	75		
Shipyards (tons):		23.9	
Merchant ships	78		
Military navy			
Surface	91		
Underwater	72		
Synthetic rubber			—
Production	50		
Mechanical (total production)	23	65	
Tractors	39		
Cars	11		
Airplanes	22		
Weapons and munitions	50		
Total employment in manufacturing		146.2	2.72
B. *Nonmanufacturing*			
Telecommunications		6.8	
Subscribers	52		
Sea transports		—	
Tons	90		
Electrical energy		9.8	
Production	27		
Radio and TV broadcasting	—	1.5	
Total employment in nonmanufacturing		18.1	0.82
C. *Other activities*			
Banking activities	—	15.2	
Various activities	—	18.9	
D. *Total employment at IRI*		198.4	2.58
AGIP—% of national production	26–30	31–35	36–40
Hydrocarbons	0	10.74	9.37
Methane	0	0	18.98

Sources: Saraceno P. IRI: origini, ordinamento, attività svolta; Industry and Trade Ministry, vol. III, 1955.
IRI and ENI, balance sheets, various years.
ISTAT, Annuario Statistico Italiano, 1939.

the machinery-manufacturing sector represented the state entrepreneur's deadwood. Most of Finmeccanica's companies were burdened by excessive staffing, a lasting heritage of the war. With the sole purpose of protecting employment, FIM (the Fund for Machinery Industry) was created in 1947. Fifteen years later, with its central pivot of Breda, the large heavy machinery company, FIM was transformed into EFIM and given the same status as IRI and ENI.

Starting in 1956, there was a precise design for the chain of command. It came about with the birth of the Ministry of State Shareholdings, which had been promoted by Enrico Mattei (who needed to garner strong political support for his entrepreneurial actions) and by Amintore Fanfani (secretary general of the country's biggest political party, the Christian Democrats), who wished to free his party from the tutelage of private industrialists. At the top of this new chain was the ministry, which oversaw two interministerial committees, CIPI (for industrial policy) and CIPE (for economic planning). Below them were the super-holding companies, the sectorial holdings, and the companies. (See Table 6.2.)

3.   In 1962 the National Agency for Electric Power (ENEL) was founded as a state-owned company to monopolize the production and distribution of electric power. Even though ENEL was situated outside the state shareholding system, the system reached its maximum expansion with a well-established presence in manufacturing, banking, and services. Its anticyclical role and its efforts to maintain a high level of employment were increasingly emphasized. The most obvious examples of these emphases include the continuous growth of the big integral-cycle steel plant located in the southern city of Taranto, the creation of an automobile factory near Naples, the expansion of ENI not only into chemicals but also into unrelated sectors such as textiles, the transformation of EFIM into a multisectorial group (machinery, aluminum, glass, food), and the rescues by EGAM, active since 1972 especially in assisting the sick giant of the chemical and mining sector, Montedison. (See Table 6.3.)

4.   The economic crisis of the mid-1970s that followed the first oil shock, together with serious social conflicts that rocked the country for the entire decade, significantly affected Italian big business and the SOEs in particular. Starting in 1977, Parliament and the government established numerous commissions and committees charged with studying the difficulties of the state shareholding system and making recom-

mendations. All of them emphasized that it was necessary to return to an entrepreneurial spirit like the one that had infused the state share-holding companies in the 1950s. But reality was stronger and faster than a set of recommendations prepared by scholars. In 1978 EGAM, which had become a recipient of nothing but business disasters, was disman-tled. Thus began a process of privatization in which ENI gave up its textile companies and IRI divested Alfa Romeo. In 1988, under the weight of the unwise expansion process in Taranto, Finsider was de facto bankrupt. In 1992 EFIM, which had also grown far beyond its initial goals, was closed, IRI and ENI were transformed into public corporations,[4] and the Ministry of State Shareholdings was dismantled. At present, it seems that political forces as well as public opinion see a general privatization process as necessary. (See Table 6.4.)

THE STATE ENTREPRENEUR: AN INSTITUTION DEEPLY ROOTED IN ITALIAN HISTORY

Was it really necessary to create IRI in the 1930s? Ernesto Cianci, a scholar and businessman, examines this question in his fascinating book on the birth of the state entrepreneur in Italy (Cianci 1977). His book was published when the difficulties of the system were already appar-ent. I will now briefly elaborate on some of Cianci's arguments. Italy was the only nation in southern Europe to have achieved a stable level of industrialization before World War II in spite of a serious obstacle: Since the start of its economic development, the financial needs of industrial investors far exceeded the supply of private savings, as seen in the issuance of securities. Nevertheless, the general improvement in the economic outlook after 1935 could have allowed an alternative to direct state intervention to materialize. The alternative was a govern-mental policy able to mobilize completely the resources of private busi-ness. The first goal would have been to create better channels for the financing of industry, promoting a more courageous initiative by IMI, strengthening the traditionally weak Italian stock exchange, and foster-ing the creation of institutional investors. Also very important would have been a massive investment in both visible and invisible infrastruc-tures: education, means of transportation, and communications. Equally decisive could have been a liberal policy that at least mitigated the

---

[4] According to Italian civil law (articles 2446–8), this transformation imposes severe constraints on the members of the board of this kind of firm.

Table 6.2. The State Shareholdings System (PPSS) in the Economic Miracle Years

1959—PPSS Sectors of Activity	Investments (Billions of Liras)	%	Employment (Thousands)	%	Gross Revenues (Billions of Liras)	%
A. Manufacturing						
Iron, steel, and related activities	45.70	13.60	63.70	20.67	342.10	23.17
Cement	3.60	1.07	1.30	0.42	11.60	0.79
Mechanical	12.30	3.66	55.30	17.94	180.10	12.20
Shipyards	7.40	2.20	27.20	8.83	111.90	7.58
Energy and related activities	43.60	12.97	14.90	4.83	361.10	24.46
Chemical	9.30	2.77	5.50	1.78	—	—
Textiles	1.50	0.45	5.00	1.62	9.20	0.62
	123.40	36.72	172.90	56.10	1,016.00	68.82
B. Nonmanufacturing						
Nuclear and electrical energy	65.00	19.34	18.70	6.07	131.10	8.88
Telecommunications	67.10	19.96	28.90	9.38	103.10	6.98
Radio-TV broadcasting	5.60	1.67	7.10	2.30	45.60	3.09
Sea transports	9.60	2.86	13.30	4.32	63.70	4.31
Air transports	4.40	1.31	4.70	1.52	35.90	2.43
Infrastructures	43.90	13.06	1.50	0.49	1.40	0.09
Thermal baths	—	—	4.20	1.36	—	—
Cinematography	0.10	0.03	0.90	0.29	1.80	0.12
	195.70	58.23	79.30	25.73	382.60	25.91
C. Other activities						
Various activities	5.50	1.64	26.50	8.60	77.80	5.27
Banking activities	—	—	29.50	9.57	—	—
Foreign activities	11.50	3.42	—	—	—	—

D. Total results					
	336.10	100.00	308.20	100.00	1,476.40	100.00
A. Manufacturing national sector		4.12		2.31		—
B. Nonmanufacturing national sector		10.47		0.13		—
D. National gross figures		8.54		1.55		8.45

1959—PPSS State Holdings	Investments (Billions of Liras)	%	Employment (Thousands)	%	Gross Revenues (Billions of Liras)	%
IRI	247.90	76.35	250.30	92.09	1,038.90	74.32
ENI	76.80	23.65	21.50	7.91	358.90	25.68
Total results	324.70	100.00	271.80	100.00	1,397.80	100.00

Notes:

The gross revenues of the energy sector include those of the chemical sector.

Nonmanufacturing activities: transports, building industry, communications, and various other activities.

National gross figures: national gross investments; national employment; total gross revenues of the system are compared with the net national income (current prices).

Sources:

State Shareholdings Ministry *Planning Report*, various years.

Budget and Economic Planning Ministry *General Report*, various years.

IRI and ENI, balance sheets, 1959.

ISTAT, *Statistiche Industriali*, various years.

Table 6.3. The State Shareholdings System (PPSS) at Its Peak

1975—PPSS Sectors of Activity	Investments (Billions of Liras)	%	Employment (Thousands)	%	Gross Revenues (Billions of Liras)	%
A. Manufacturing						
Iron, steel and related activities	573.10	17.11	141.10	20.23	3,756.20	22.71
Cement	12.30	0.37	2.10	0.30	65.40	0.40
Mechanical	137.30	4.10	122.60	17.58	2,517.20	15.22
Electronics	64.50	1.93	46.00	6.59	24.20	0.15
Shipyards	55.10	1.64	32.10	4.60	395.30	2.39
Energy and related activities	445.40	13.30	49.20	7.05	3,124.70	18.89
Chemical	236.30	7.05	22.80	3.27	547.60	3.31
Textiles	35.70	1.07	22.90	3.28	123.40	0.75
Food	28.30	0.84	34.90	5.00	801.70	4.85
Various manufacturing	42.90	1.28	24.70	3.54	465.60	2.81
	1,630.90	48.68	498.40	71.46	11,821.30	71.47
B. Nonmanufacturing						
Telecommunications	985.50	29.42	73.10	10.48	1,364.60	8.25
Radio and TV broadcasting	8.50	0.25	12.10	1.73	308.30	1.86
Sea transports	123.20	3.68	10.60	1.52	210.20	1.27
Air transports	54.80	1.64	19.20	2.75	468.20	2.83
Infrastructures	275.20	8.21	25.00	3.58	509.70	3.08
Thermal baths	3.50	0.10	3.30	0.47	35.60	0.22
Cinematography	2.40	0.07	0.50	0.07	5.60	0.03
Various nonmanufactur	30.40	0.91	8.00	1.15	283.40	1.71
	1,480.00	44.18	148.50	21.29	3,150.00	19.04
C. Other activities						
Banking activities	—	—	50.60	7.25	—	—
Foreign activities	239.10	7.14	—	—	1,569.70	9.49

D. Total results	Investments (Billions of Liras)	%	Employment (Thousands)	%	Gross Revenues (Billions of Liras)	%
D. Total results	3,350.00	100.00	697.50	100.00	16,541.00	100.00
A. Manufacturing national sector		21.40		7.52		56.12
B. Nonmanufacturing national sector		11.57		2.92		38.68
C. National gross figures		14.07		5.09		35.25

1975—PPSS State Holdings	Investments (Billions of Liras)	%	Employment (Thousands)	%	Gross Revenues (Billions of Liras)	%
IRI	2,188.00	67.39	525.00	78.13	9,719.60	56.12
ENI	940.00	28.95	99.80	14.85	6,700.00	38.68
EFIM	113.00	3.48	43.60	6.49	900.00	5.20
EGAM	93.00	2.86	34.00	5.06	591.20	3.41
EAGAT (thermal baths)	3.50	0.11	3.10	0.46	—	—
EAGC (cinematography)	2.40	0.07	0.50	0.07	—	—
Total results	3,246.90	100.00	672.00	100.00	17,319.60	100.00

Notes:

Nonmanufacturing activities: marketable nonmanufacturing activities.
National gross figures: national gross investments and national employment. Total gross revenues of the system are compared with the total gross revenues of the Mediobanca sample, which supplies balance sheet data on the most important Italian public and private enterprises.

Sources:

State Shareholdings Ministry Planning Report, various years.
Budget and Economic Planning Ministry General Report, various years.
IRI and ENI, balance sheets, 1975.
ISTAT, Statistiche Industriali, various years.
Mediobanca, Dati Cumulativi Principali Imprese Italiane, various years.

Table 6.4. The State Shareholdings System Crisis

	1981	1985	1989	1992
Gross Investments (%)				
IRI/national	5.28	6.44	5.50	7.71
ENI/national	5.49	4.28	2.98	4.91
EFIM/national	0.30	0.17	—	—
Employment[a] (%)				
IRI/national	3.03	2.79	2.20	2.04
ENI/national	0.72	0.74	0.71	0.66
EFIM/national	0.25	0.23	0.20	—
Net revenues (%)				
IRI/Mediobanca sample[b]	17.63	18.16	19.29	23.54
ENI/Mediobanca sample[b]	22.43	16.95	15.15	15.45
EFIM/Mediobanca sample[b]	1.97	1.86	1.69	—
Net assets (%)				
IRI/Mediobanca sample[b]	7.89	8.12	8.01	1.95
ENI/Mediobanca sample[b]	7.60	9.94	14.80	12.51
EFIM[c]/Mediobanca sample[b]	1.25	0.66	0.65	(0.18)
Financial charges[e]/net revenues (%)				
IRI	17.84	11.20	11.66	13.91
ENI	5.02	3.41	4.31	5.18
EFIM	8.68	10.64	15.52	—
Private firms in Mediobanca sample[b]	5.46	4.10	2.89	4.15
Financial indebetedness/net assets				
IRI	1.35	1.22	2.15	9.49
ENI	6.32	2.02	1.07	1.59
EFIM[d]	8.88	6.98	6.57	(13.10)
Private firms in Mediobanca sample[b]	1.28	0.80	0.62	0.71
Cumulative profits (losses) in billions of lira	1971–8	1980–4	1985–9	1990–2
IRI	(3,216.10)	(13,604.20)	2,518.10	(3,895.20)
FINSIDER	(1,382.40)	(8,836.60)	(4,187.30)	(2,652.70)
FINMECCANICA	(1,164.40)	(2,027.60)	(706.80)	(219.00)
STET	318.30	463.90	4,945.50	4,205.00
ENI	(948.70)	(3,281.00)	5,492.00	2,388.00
AGIP	479.90	1,925.50	2,708.00	4,151.00
AGIP PETROLI[f]	—	(169.80)	(321.00)	287.00

Table 6.4 *(continued)*

ANIC, (ENICHEM),				
(ENIMONT)	(767.80)	(2,063.20)	790.40	(2,595.00)
LANEROSSI	(389.00)	(675.20)	—	—
EFIM	(438.10)	(1,265.30)	(819.20)	(2,457.50)
Ernesto Breda Holding	(13.50)	27.00	126.70	(655.00)
MCS (Sardinia Coal)	(315.30)	—	—	—
EGAM[g]	(599.00)	—	—	—

[a] National employment net of nonmarketable services.
[b] Mediobanca sample: cumulative and sectorial balance sheets data of the major Italian firms.
[c] EFIM data as sum of Ernesto Breda Holding, Aviofer, Alumix, Siv and, for 1981-5 only, Sopal.
[d] EFIM aggregated data for 1981 and 1985. 1989 and 1992 as in note *c*.
The negative figures in (parentheses) for 1992 are due to heavy losses, which eroded the net assets.
[e] 1981 fin. charges unavailable. IRI and ENI: 1982 data. EFIM: 1980 data.
[f] Founded in 1982.
[g] Operative from 1971 to 1976.

Sources:
State Shareholdings Ministry Planning Report, various years.
IRI and ENI, balance sheets, various years.
Mediobanca, R&S, 1993.
Mediobanca, Dati Cumulativi Principali Imprese Italiane, 1993.
ISTAT, Annuario Statistiche Industriali, various years.

country's heavy protectionism and, above all, dismantled industrial cartels made compulsory by a law of 1933. Finally, in order to make up for the weaknesses of Italian entrepreneurship, it would have been necessary to create a favorable environment for foreign investments. Certainly this mixture of measures would have been effective, but it must be recognized – as Cianci does – that, combined with the difficulties of attracting foreign capital to Italy in a period of fragmented markets, all this would have been heresy to the fascist government. Mussolini much preferred to have at his disposal a centralized instrument for his aims of power (as was provided by IRI) rather than have to begin a pervasive, long-term program of general improvements to the Italian economic system. Moreover, in addition to the contingent economic and political environments, there was the pressure of a long-lasting tradition of direct state intervention that goes back to the birth of Italy as a politically unified nation in 1861.

The ruling class, which led the unification process, greatly desired the nation to become once again one of Europe's great powers. But in the mid-nineteenth century the Italian peninsula was a backward area, with fundamental differences among the various regions and a lack of spontaneous forces able to realize the economic transformation that the political goals of its leaders demanded. Thus the state had to become the major economic actor of the country. It issued public debt bonds and imposed taxes, which had never been done in the preunification states. It sold 20 percent of the land that had previously belonged to the Catholic Church or the states. It conducted a monetary policy beyond the limits of the gold standard system. By doing so, it was able to create a civil service organization, modern infrastructures (such as railways, main highways, and ports), and public and military construction projects, as well as both the army and the navy. Not by chance, the first Italian big business grew side by side with the state, as was the case, for example, with the railway company Società Italiana per le Strade Ferrate Meridionali and with Società Veneta, a firm involved in major public construction works financed by the state. The system seems to confirm fully the statement of Franco Bonelli, a scholar of modern Italian economic history, who defined the Italian model as "precocious state capitalism" (Bonelli 1978, 1204; see also Romeo 1965).

In the 1880s the state intervened in the market economy so as to channel the country toward industrialization. Up to that point, the Italian economy had been based on agriculture and its exports, both dramatically challenged during the 1880s by the flood of agricultural products from overseas made possible by the revolution in transportation. The substantial drop in the prices of agricultural products rendered obsolete the model of economic development that had been valid in Italy since the beginning of the eighteenth century. It became necessary to respond to the emerging challenge with consistent political choices intended to direct the country toward industrialization. In fact, the state used a vast array of means, including protective tariffs, financial support, orders, and privileges; it also did something more, rescuing companies on the verge of bankruptcy whose existence was considered vital for the country.

All the major phases of Italian economic development are marked by industrial rescues. In 1887, at the end of the first trial of industrialization, only state intervention helped avoid the closure of the first large Italian corporation, the Terni steel plant, founded three years earlier (thanks to the same generous state support) in order to produce battleship armor for the navy (Bonelli 1975, 26). Again in 1911, at the end of the so-called Italian industrial revolution, it was the turn of almost the entire steel sector, whose companies had expanded unwisely while accumulating impressive debts (Bigazzi 1981a, 96–8). In 1922, following the growth caused by World War I, which definitively positioned Italy among the industrialized nations, the state set about rescuing the industrial activities of two major banks, Banca Italiana di Sconto and Banco di Roma (Cianci 1977, 43–54). Among the companies rescued was Ansaldo (heavy machinery, shipbuilding, automobiles, and the like), which at the time was the largest Italian corporation.

In each of these three episodes, the Bank of Italy (the country's most important issuer of currency and, after 1926, the only institution able to issue currency) played a crucial role. Particularly revealing was what happened in 1922. Eight years earlier, the Bank of Italy had promoted the creation of a consortium of banks – CSVI – to reinforce the financing of national industry. In order to rescue Banca Italiana di Sconto and Banco di Roma, an Autonomous Section of the consortium was created, which was nothing more than the Bank of Italy. Every time one of the companies that had previously worked with Banca Italiana di Sconto or Banco di Roma needed money to pay its debts, it issued a promissory note on the order of the Autonomous Section of the consortium, which signed it over the same day to the Bank of Italy, which in turn issued new banknotes to pay the debts (Cianci 1977, 44).

Given the three main actors in Gerschenkron's (1962) typology – the entrepreneur, the universal bank, and the state – it would not be realistic to think that only the state was active in the process of Italian industrial development. The universal banks were formed in Italy in the last decade of the nineteenth century on the basis of German capital and technical know-how. They backed the most important industrial initiatives with financial resources and management expertise in the start-up phase at the beginning of the twentieth century (Confalonieri 1974–6). But their stability was always rather precarious since, given the scarcity of Italian private savings available, they were compelled to collect money in highly unstable international markets (De Cecco 1995, 259). There was a serious contradiction between this uncertain source of financing and the long-term commitment required by the companies, a contradiction that could be resolved only by state intervention in the form of rescues, a sort of ex-post financing by the state (Bonelli 1978, 1231).

Early-twentieth-century Italy had capable entrepreneurs who understood the critical needs of their companies in production, distribution, and management, including Giovanni Agnelli in the automobile industry and GiovanBattista Pirelli in rubber, entrepreneurs who vigorously competed in both national and international markets.[5] But at least half of Italy's business leaders had the state, rather than the marketplace, as their primary reference point. They pursued the growth of their companies, often in unrelated sectors, not for economic reasons (for example, to cut costs per unit) but for strategic ones, to better their bargaining position with the state. This motivation is clearly visible in the choices of Arturo Bocciardo, leader of the multisectorial Terni of the 1920s (steel, electricity, chemicals), and of Guido Donegani, president during the interwar years of Montecatini, the Italian chemical and mining giant.[6] It is possible to talk of an Italian political capitalism as opposed to a managerial American, a personal British, or a cooperative German model.[7]

When IRI eventually tried to sell its assets to private business it did not find a crowd of potential buyers, especially in sectors such as steel, heavy machinery, telecommunications, and shipping, in which deep pockets were necessary not only to purchase but also to keep the business going. This explains the transformation of IRI into a permanent institution in 1937. In the end, IRI was so embedded in the evolution of the Italian economy that following the war, when the political and ideological climate was free-market-oriented as never before, even a strong advocate of private business such as Angelo Costa (then the president of Confindustria, the Italian confederation of industrialists) was forced to admit before the Economic Committee of the Constitutional Assembly that IRI was an economic necessity (Maraffi 1990, 146–7).

ORIGINS AND DEVELOPMENT OF THE STATE ENTREPRENEUR IN ITALY: MINDLESS NATIONALIZATION OR COHERENT STRATEGY?

Although there was a noticeable continuity between what happened in the 1930s and previous Italian economic-political history, the birth of IRI represented a decisive turning point. From then on, the state became the direct owner of companies operating in the market. This had never happened before, not even in the years of fascism. Mussolini wanted to *shape* the Italian economy, but he did not intend to nationalize it. Thus,

[5] On Giovanni Agnelli see Castronovo 1971; on GiovanBattista Pirelli see Bigazzi 1981b.
[6] On Arturo Bocciardo see Bonelli 1975; on Guido Donegani see Amatori 1990.
[7] The typologies of advanced countries (the United States, the United Kingdom, Germany) can be found in Chandler with Hikino 1990.

in 1926 the Autonomous Section of the CSVI was turned into the Istituto di Liquidazioni (Institute for Liquidations), a clear sign that all the activities that the state had taken over from Banca Italiana di Sconto and Banco di Roma were to be sold to private business (Cianci 1977, 57).

An important challenge for historians is to understand whether this major change – that is, direct state ownership – grew out of a conscious design or simply happened under the pressure of the bank crash.

Andrew Shonfield, in his comparative work on different national industrial systems, inclines toward the second alternative. He believes that in general in Italy the "proliferation of nationalized and semi-public enterprise is more the result of historical accident than of deliberate political decision"; in particular, IRI's transformation into a permanent public agency in 1937 appears to be "perhaps the most absent-minded act of nationalization in history" (Shonfield 1965, 178, 179). Pasquale Saraceno is an economist who in the early 1930s served as assistant to Alberto Beneduce, made substantial contributions in 1936 when the Bank Bill was drawn up, and worked for IRI for all his professional career. His opinion on the origins of IRI is not so extreme, but he too emphasizes the pragmatism of the early years and the special attention given to not scaring private business with a nationalization policy. According to Saraceno (1975, 8–9), this is the reason IRI's companies maintained the legal status of private enterprises. The weight of private business in the origins of IRI is stressed by Marco Maraffi, who sees IRI basically as a rationalization of Italian big business and considers the entire operation – as shaped by the country's major capitalists – as influencing the government. He offers as proof of his argument the quick privatization of the two giants Edison, the electric company that was the biggest Italian corporation at the time, and Bastogi, Italy's major financial holding company (Maraffi 1990, chapter 3). After all, in the late 1930s, Ettore Conti, a leading figure in the electric industry, wrote in his diary that "in this period in which we say daily that we want to go toward the people, in reality a financial oligarchy has been formed that resembles in the industrial era a form of the old feudalism. Production is greatly controlled by a few groups that are in turn managed by a single man. Agnelli, Cini, Volpi, Pirelli, Donegani, Falck, and a few others literally dominate the various branches of industry" (quoted in Romeo 1988, 152).

With the catastrophe of the early 1930s, totally unexpected in its dimensions, IRI needed a good dose of pragmatism. Until the eve of IRI's foundation, for example, documents circulated about the creation of a state holding company for long-term industrial financing, IFI (Cianci

1977, 244–5). And fascism was unable to ignore the interests of the elite of the industrial bourgeoisie.

Nevertheless, Shonfield, Saraceno, and Maraffi seriously underestimate the intellectual consistency and managerial capacities of the group that conceived and carried out the reform of the 1930s, especially those of its leader, Alberto Beneduce.[8] A long-time civil servant, Beneduce had been a close collaborator of Francesco Saveno Nitti, who more than once served at the head of one of the economic ministries and was the politician in prefascist Italy who, above all others, saw in the process of rapid industrialization a way to overcome the country's backwardness, especially in regard to the gap between the North and the South.[9] Before abandoning the antifascist camp to become Mussolini's closest economic advisor, Beneduce dedicated most of his efforts to the problem of directing diffused private savings to the long-term financing needs of industry. Especially when he served as the head of two state financial concerns, first Crediop (the consortium of credit for public works) and then ICIPU (the Institute for Credit for the Public Utility Works), Beneduce organized the financing of large electric plants through a system of state-guaranteed bonds. Although he was a socialist, Beneduce never displayed any sympathy for a nationalized economy in which companies would be a bureaucratic appendage of the state. Given these premises, Beneduce, to whom Mussolini gave full powers in the IRI operation, certainly had in mind precise guidelines, if not a detailed action plan at the beginning. These guidelines are demonstrated above all by the general framework of the reform. Drastically separating bank from industry, the state fully assumed its responsibilities as industry owner, directing industrial development (not managing it), and leaving the companies to compete in the market. As regards private interests, it appears that Beneduce recognized the importance of sociopolitical balances and understood perfectly that IRI had to have boundaries; after all, he also knew the scarcity of managerial resources at his headquarters. Nonetheless, he fiercely opposed the idea of underselling "his" companies to private ones, as in the case of Alfa Romeo with Fiat, or the synthetic fibers manufacturer Chatillon with SNIA, or the electric company SIP with Edison (see Castronovo 1995, 294–301). Finally, Beneduce's IRI developed a distinctive element of rationalization based on the industrial sector in a period previously characterized by confused multisectorial groups. Furthermore, IRI favored fostering the develop-

---

[8] My interpretation of Beneduce's work at IRI is largely based on Bonelli 1984.
[9] On Francesco Saveno Nitti see De Rosa 1984.

ment of the best managers and technicians at both the sectorial holding and corporate levels.[10]

We can debate whether there was a strategy or improvisation in the 1930s, but the question does not make much sense when we look at the postfascist, pluralistic Italy of the 1950s. In this period, strategy – or, more precisely, a series of strategies – clearly emerged as soon as the confusion of the immediate postwar period died down. The climate in the 1950s was characterized by three schools of thought interested in using the state entrepreneur to attain certain goals. We can define the first as "nationalism," a stream that cannot be identified with a political party but in the 1950s still represented a strong ideological and political line in Italian life. In the most dramatic moments of modern Italian history, from Il Risorgimento (the movement that brought about the political unification of the nation) through World War I and the partisan movement of World War II, a spirit of nationalism motivated many entrepreneurs and managers. Oscar Sinigaglia and Enrico Mattei, the most successful state entrepreneurs, are two excellent examples of the Italian "samurai." Sinigaglia was a young, self-made businessman who donated his company to the state when the war broke out in 1915 and served in a public agency that supplied the army.[11] After the war, he took a very active role in the movement to ensure the passage of the Istrian city of Fiume to Italy's control. Thereafter he continued to act in various key positions connected to state interventions in the economy until the mid-1930s, when the hostility of fascist Italy toward Jews forced him to step aside. Since the beginning of the century, Sinigaglia had promoted the Italian steel industry's ability to compete at an international level. He strongly believed in the value of private initiative, but seeing its failure to resolve the Italian "steel question" (which he considered one of the nation's fundamental economic issues), he saw the only hope of salvation in state intervention. As a result of his efforts, the government gave him a free hand against the strong lobbies of private steel manufacturers in obtaining European Recovery Program (the so-called Marshall Plan) funds so as to realize the plan to which we will turn later in this essay.

Enrico Mattei was the leader of Catholic partisans during World War II and thus was surely influenced by the ideas of social Catholicism.[12] He was, however, above all a nationalist, obsessed with the idea of

[10] On the steel sector see Bonelli 1982; on telecommunications see Bottiglieri 1987.
[11] On Sinigaglia see Toniolo 1984; Osti 1993, chapter 1.
[12] On Mattei see Colitti 1979. On nationalism among Italian entrepreneurs and managers see Webster 1978.

Italian inferiority on the international scene. His quarrels with the "seven sisters" in the petroleum industry are reminiscent of Mussolini's battle with the Western plutocracies. Mattei counted on all the Italian political parties to achieve his objectives: the institution of ENI in 1953, the legislation on hydrocarbons in 1958 that confirmed ENI's privileged position in distribution and research, and the support for his "foreign policy" aimed at improving the oil supply coming from Arab nations and the Soviet Union during the Cold War.

The second strategy-inspired center is to be found in the Christian Democrats, which was Italy's biggest political party for almost a half century after World War II. Christian Democracy was a federation of different political groups, and among these were some left-leaning wings that pushed for state intervention to promote economic development and focus particularly on overcoming the historical gap between the North and the South. Since the end of the 1940s, these leftist groups (one of whose leaders, Ezio Vanoni, was minister of finance) started to look at the role of SOE. Certainly these groups were among Mattei's most convinced supporters. But the most important sign from the Christian Democrats toward SOE came from the party's secretary general after 1954, Amintore Fanfani. He had to cope with the aggressive competition of a highly organized Italian Communist Party. In 1948, in the first parliamentary elections after the war, the fear of Stalin pushed the Christian Democrats to achieve a triumphant absolute majority. In 1953, only five years later, they had lost 10 percent of their seats, and Fanfani saw in SOE both a tool for attaining political consensus (especially in southern Italy) and a solid source of financial autonomy to build up a "Leninist" organization (made up of professional, full-time politicians) able to face the Communist challenge. In this respect it was important for the party to abandon the patronage of private big business, which could have steered the party in an excessively conservative direction. The political action of the Christian Democrats, in addition to legislation in favor of ENI, resulted in the institution in 1956 of the State Shareholdings Ministry in order to attain stronger political control over SOEs and then in the legislation drafted the following year that required at least 60 percent of new investments (and 40 percent of overall investments) in state-owned initiatives to be made in the South.

In the 1930s and the early postwar years the socialists and the Communists, who looked with suspicion on SOEs, considered this agenda a tool of Italian monopolistic capital. Nevertheless, they could not refuse to support Enrico Mattei in his fight against the multinationals, or to work for the passage of legislation designed to foster economic growth in the South, or to institute a ministry intended to separate SOE from private big business. De facto, leftist parties supported (or at least did not impede) these measures. Their only opposition was directed against the formation of a single national concern for energy, which Fanfani proposed to entrust with Mattei's ENI in the late 1950s. Here they drew the line; this was really too much of a national economy controlled by the Christian Democrats. In the end, thanks to the efforts of nationalistic entrepreneurs, sincere developmental ideologists, and ambitious party leaders, Beneduce's creation solidified and expanded.[13] But it was burdened with too many political goals to function well as an enterprise.

PROBLEMS OF A GIANT CONGLOMERATE

At the peak of its expansion in the mid-1970s, the state shareholding system appeared to be a giant conglomerate, that is, a mix of companies belonging to different, unrelated sectors, whether considered as a whole or as the various super–holding companies such as IRI, ENI, EFIM, and EGAM. Giant groups of unrelated companies are a reality of our time, existing both in advanced nations and in those trying to catch up with them (Shimotani and Shiba 1997). They arise for various reasons: (1) to avoid being trapped in a saturated sector, (2) to avoid the risk of antitrust sanctions, (3) to respond to the necessity of diversifying, given the impossibility of exploiting scale economies in a weak domestic market, or (4) for reasons having to do with the nation's particular historical evolution (as in the cases of IRI in Italy and the *zaibatsu*, family-owned horizontal groups of companies in nonrelated sectors, in Japan).

Since the end of World War II, the most significant typologies seem to be the American conglomerate and the Japanese *keiretsu* (the form the *zaibatsu* assumed after the American occupation replaced family ownership with broader shareholder ownership). They are differentiated by the type of control exercised by top management. In the American case, headquarters wanted to direct corporate policy and to reallocate resources among the various subsidiary companies on the basis of financial statements (so-called management by numbers). In the

---

[13] For a bibliography on the relationship between political parties and SOEs in the 1950s see Maraffi 1990.

horizontal Japanese model, by contrast, each company's autonomy was almost total. Every company made decisions on its own markets, investments, and time horizons. In fact, headquarters "management" consisted of periodic information meetings among the various presidents of the major firms making up the group or, more concretely, the group's principal bank, which guaranteed the solidity of the group's ownership and thus permitted management stability. The conglomerate's choice to separate top from middle and lower management was one of the weaknesses of American big business, whereas the *keiretsus* became a cornerstone of Japanese success (see Chandler 1990; Fruin 1992).

The lesson we can draw is that a big, highly diversified group must be as "headless" as possible and grant as much autonomy as possible to the management of the individual companies. In order to avoid a serious fracture between companies and headquarters, the latter must be lean and act as guarantor of the companies. Beneduce took pride in having limited the size of IRI's headquarters to a simple office in downtown Rome no larger than a typical family apartment and in having operated with a small staff. "IRI's presence was little noticed," writes Gian Lupo Osti, Sinigaglia's assistant and until the 1960s one of the most important managers of the state-owned steel sector, in his magnificent autobiography.

IRI was formed by few persons, about fifty if I recall correctly, all very capable and prepared. It was said that Menichella [Beneduce's closest collaborator], who was for a long time IRI's general manager, absolutely did not want IRI's people to be involved in strategic planning at the individual company level. They were to simply critically assess the forecasts prepared by the sectorial holdings, the end of year reports, and certify their veracity. He absolutely did not want IRI's controllers to visit company factories. "You will not understand anything" – Menichella used to say to his collaborators – "and company technicians will pull your leg." (Osti 1993, 115)

In fact, the 1950s became the golden era of state shareholding companies, when IRI was weak while the sectorial holdings were strong and the corporations below them were even stronger; this was also the era when ENI appeared to be an entrepreneurial company. At the same time, there was no strong, external political reference point. The realization of Sinigaglia's plan seems to be similar to any other great entrepreneurial action in a Western market economy. He opened up a big new plant on the right scale in the right place, he specialized the production of existing plants, and he shut down those that were obsolete. Particularly surprising in a state entrepreneur, the last action involved the dismissal of thousands of workers. To such a charge, Sinigaglia (who was very attentive to social problems) used to answer that by producing better steel at lower prices he would powerfully foster the development of the machinery-manufacturing industry and consequently the expansion of employment – in both the machinery and steel sectors – which would more than compensate for the previous loss of jobs. This did indeed happen, but such a line of reasoning became unthinkable a few years later inside the state shareholding system.

Mattei's contributions, too, appear to be those of a great industrial leader. Even if he started from the privileged position provided by the legislation on ENI and hydrocarbons, his model was rational and vertically integrated from oil and natural gas research and extraction to distribution, refining, and the sale of gasoline products. It was able to reduce costs per unit and to increase market share in both the oil and chemical fields. Particularly relevant was the success attained with the construction of the Ravenna petrochemical plant, thanks to which ENI succeeded in destroying Montecatini's monopoly in nitrogen fertilizers, to the advantage of Italian farmers. In the end, *big state enterprises able to compete in the market better than private ones and acting in the best interests of the country* became the winning formula of the golden age of state shareholding companies in the early 1950s.

The turning point, or what we might also call the trap, came with the creation of the Ministry for State Shareholdings and a precise chain of command. At the top of this chain, not visible in the organizational charts, was a silent partner made up of the political parties forming the government coalition.[14] Political parties have always played an important role in Italy, given the necessity for mediation and adaptation in the relationship between the state (considered as a universalist, bureaucratic body) and society because of the latter's weakness and fragmentation (see Sapelli 1990). The lifeline of political parties is consensus, but state shareholding companies were started up in a period that was dictatorial and offered no political competition, a fact that kept them relatively free of political strife. Things naturally changed after the war when competition heated up and the parties realized that an extended system of state companies was a formidable weapon.

---

[14] The expression "occult shareholder" (the Italian equivalent of "silent partner") is explicitly mentioned by the committee set up in 1981 by the then minister of state shareholdings, Gianni De Michelis, a politician fully involved in the system. On the relationship between political parties and companies see Balconi et al. 1995.

But something made the Italian case more complicated. The major opposition party was that of the Communists. In Italy it is a competitive party but its international connections made it unthinkable as the governing party, an alternative to the Christian Democrats and their allies (among which, from the early 1960s, was the Socialist Party). So a one-way spoils system arose in which a set of parties had enormous economic power and would not be punished in the next elections even if they used this power badly. The competition was concentrated among the members of the government alliance in order to occupy, thanks to their coalition power, the largest possible number of positions that permitted them to distribute favors and resources so as to increase their consensus and hence their power. From this perspective, the state shareholding system must above all grow larger without consideration of profits and losses.

Some may object that this infernal mechanism did not begin with the birth of the Ministry for State Shareholdings. Often in the first years the minister was little more than a yes-man to the heads of the super-holding companies. This may be true, but it is also true that property rights and legal channels to exercise them are important in the Western world. Once such a precise formal arrangement was formed, it carried a specific weight that was fully understood from the mid-1970s, when SOEs found themselves in trouble and needed financial support from the government and the Parliament, which were, in turn, controlled by the parties (Castronovo 1995, 495–500). The mix of politics and economics that characterized SOE after 1960 has not always been judged severely by scholars and practitioners. On the contrary, for a while it was deemed the appropriate cure in order to increase the economic and social welfare of the nation. A good example of this point of view is the essay by Pasquale Saraceno, who emphasized that in the only appropriate choice for the SOE is *economicità*, which can be translated as "economic health or fitness." This meant that the aim was not to maximize profits but to focus on economic goals established within a framework of social and political constraints. On the other hand, the law stated that these kinds of constraints were considered "improper financial burdens," for which the Parliament had to compensate with an endowment fund (Saraceno 1975, chapter 2). According to Saraceno, the structure of state shareholdings must not be seen as a hierarchy, but rather as a continuous exchange and confrontation between political goals and managerial needs. This intellectual position is appealing, but it does not hold up to reality. The top management of Finsider in the second half of the 1950s, made up of disciples of Oscar Sinigaglia, accepted Saraceno's philosophy and went to the southeastern port city of Taranto to construct a big steel plant. Taranto had been reduced to a pitiful state when orders from the navy for its shipyards dried up. At the end of the 1950s Italy needed greater productive capacity in steel, but for Finsider it would have been more convenient to simply increase the size of existing plants. Nevertheless, the economic and social conditions of Taranto demanded a response, and management accepted the new industrial location. They wanted to build a factory with a precise market goal – large pipelines for natural gas and armor plates for ships. Finsider's management understood clearly that simple quantitative expansion was not as important as targeting highly specialized production, which would be less subject to attacks by the new emerging countries in steel production. But quantitative expansion meant more employment and hence more political consensus. On this ground, Finsider started an alliance between political powers and a part of management that had never accepted Sinigaglia's ideas. The Taranto plant, which finally opened in 1965, was expanded enormously in the 1970s to produce cheap steel but had no market strategy. For Finsider it would be the beginning of the end (Osti 1993, chapter 3).

A similar tale can be told of Alfa Romeo, which was compelled to open a new factory near Naples. The company's president, Giuseppe Luraghi, who had brought it to its peak in the postwar period, accepted the challenge, preparing for the new production unit the manufacture of a small car that would seriously compete with those of Fiat. When he was forced to hire workers on the basis of political and territorial criteria rather than their skills and attitudes (and was subjected to other nonsensical requests), Luraghi found himself with no choice but to resign (Luraghi 1979). Detailed research on single companies demonstrates that in some cases, thanks to a strong esprit de corps and a favorable market situation, management's resistance was stronger and the companies were not overwhelmed. This seems to be the case for AGIP Petroli, a sectorial holding of ENI (Sapelli et al. 1993). But it does not change the overall picture of management held hostage by politicians and subject to progressive degeneration. Even ENI is an excellent illustration of how the nature of an enterprise can change. After Mattei's death in 1962, ENI, besides its core business of oil, engaged in industrial rescues in mining, in chemicals, and in totally unrelated sectors such as textiles. It became more and more a state holding company for economic development. Even more striking is the fact that ENI had to take over first the mining and machinery-manufacturing activities of EGAM (1977) and then, in 1980, SIR's and Liquichimica's plants (the so-called Italian smoking chemical ruins) under a set of laws passed by Parliament (Carnevali 1992, 85-7) (Figure 6.1). The Soviet-style expropriation of top management's prerogatives is impressive.

CONCLUDING REMARKS

In the last quarter of the nineteenth century three countries – czarist Russia, Meiji Japan, and the newly unified Italy (different in size and political weight but equally significant in their histories) – each saw industrialization as the sole, inescapable path to becoming a world power. But the technological level of the core of the world economy was such that the necessary price of admission to the process of industrialization was strong discontinuity. This, in turn, could be provoked only by a substitution factor with respect to spontaneous economic forces (Gerschenkron 1962). This factor was synonymous with the state's action through protectionism, privileges, financial help, orders, and finally direct entrepreneurial activity. In each of these three nations the state as an economic actor was enormously important. In post–October 1917 Russia the state took the socialist form of Soviet power. It abolished the market and made companies into single units of production, giving them larger dimensions. In this way it obtained great successes in basic industries and in the military field. In the long run, though, the market (with the consequent autonomy of companies) appeared as an institution that could not easily be given up. The Soviet experiment turned out to be both ridiculous and tragic (Yudanov 1997). In Japan, the state's pervasiveness in the national economy was particularly evident in the decade following the Meiji revolution and in the 1930s, when war preparation efforts put the economy under state control at the risk of freezing it. The lesson was understood very well after 1945. The state singled out strategic sectors to support but used a nonpartisan bureaucracy via guidelines rather than a series of legislative commands (McCraw 1986). Moreover, the state pushed the supported companies to compete in a global context, squaring the circle via a balance between state support and the verdict of the marketplace.

Italy seems to have pursued yet another path: the state not only as supporter but also as owner of companies expected to remain competitive in the market. In the 1930s the state as owner was a necessity. Allowing companies to act as private ones was probably a choice due

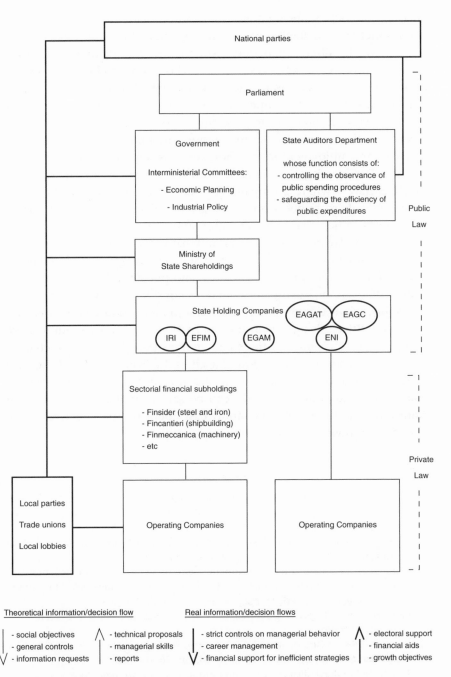

Figure 6.1. The theoretical and the real state shareholdings system

partially to sociopolitical equilibrium and partially to a strong tradition of competent and flexible public management that found its highest expression in Alberto Beneduce. After World War II, thanks to some strong entrepreneurial personalities who were highly devoted to national goals as well as to the development of a democratic system that included political competition, the state shareholding system grew progressively oriented toward fostering economic development. As time went by, this emphasis became more and more identified with an increase in employment in the short term, as required for political consensus. The marriage of the state with the market in an environment such as Italy's, where a bureaucratic state did not (and still does not) exist and where public institutions are dominated by political forces, merits only a negative judgment after sixty years of experience.

A present-day necessity is found in what Cianci described as an alternative policy in the 1930s: get rid of SOE, create appropriate financial institutions, foster antitrust measures, and put into effect an industrial policy that supports companies but does not shield them from the rigors of competition. Contemporary Italy is a modern industrial nation, but its competitive advantages in the international economy seem to have been achieved *in spite* of the state's actions (see Porter 1990, chapter 8). Perhaps Italy could have found itself in the front row, like Japan and Germany, had the state limited its role to steering development rather than managing companies. This can be said even if current European integration and the global economy cast doubt on the effectiveness of the policy choices of a state the size of Italy.

REFERENCES

Amatori, F. 1990. Montecatini: Un profilo storico. In *Montecatini: Capitoli di storia di una grande impresa*, ed. F. Amatori and B. Bezza, pp. 19–68. Bologna.

Anselmi, L. 1990. *Il sistema delle partecipazioni statali*. Turin. Revised version published in 1994 as *Le partecipazioni statali oggi*.

Balconi, M., L. Orsenigo, and P. A. Toninelli. 1995. Tra gerarchie politiche e mercati: Il caso delle imprese pubbliche in Italia (acciaio e petrolio). In *Potere, mercati, gerarchie*, ed. M. Magatti, pp. 299–338. Bologna.

Bianchi, P. 1994. Impresa pubblica. In *Enciclopedia delle scienze sociali*, 4, pp. 587–96. Rome.

Bigazzi, D. 1981a. Grandi imprese e concentrazioni finanziarie. In *Storia della società italiana: L'Italia di Giolitti*, 20, pp. 96–8. Milan.

1981b. La Pirelli e la Fiat nel mercato mondiale. In *Storia della società italiana: L'Italia di Giolitti*, pp. 126–34. Milan.

Bonelli, F. 1975. *Lo sviluppo di una grande impresa in Italia.* Turin.

1978. Il capitalismo italiano: Linee generali di interpretazione. In *Storia d'Italia. Annali I: Dal feudalismo al capitalismo*, pp. 1194-1255. Turin.

1984. Alberto Beneduce (1877-1944). In *Protagonisti dell' intervento pubblico in Italia*, ed. A. Mortara, pp. 329-56. Milan.

1987. The origin of public corporations in Italy. *Annali di storia dell'impresa* 3: 202-11.

ed. 1982. *Acciaio per l'industrializzazione.* Turin.

Bottiglieri, B. 1987. *STET.* Milan.

Carnevali, F. 1992. Il gruppo ENI dalle origini al 1985. In *Uno Sviluppo tra politica e strategia. ENI (1953-1985)* by G. Sapelli and F. Carnevali, pp. 85-7. Milan.

Castronovo, V. 1971. *Giovanni Agnelli.* Turin.

1995. *Storia economica d'Italia.* Turin.

Chandler, A. D., Jr. 1990. The enduring logic of industrial success. *Harvard Business Review* 68(2): 130-40.

Chandler, A. D., Jr., with T. Hikino. 1990. *Scale and scope: The dynamics of industrial capitalism.* Cambridge, Mass.

Cianci, E. 1977. *Nascita dello Stato imprenditore in italia.* Milan.

Colitti, M. 1975. Lo sviluppo del settore pubblico dal dopoguerra ad oggi. *Economia Pubblica* 5-6: 3-22.

1979. *Energia e sviluppo in Italia: La vicenda di Enrico Mattei.* Bari.

Confalonieri, A. 1974-6. *Banca e industria in Italia, 1894-1906.* 3 vols. Milan.

De Cecco, M. 1995. Lo stato investitore. In *Le istituzioni dell'economia*, by M. De Cecco and A. Pedone, reprinted in *Storia dello stato italiano dall'Unità ad oggi*, ed. R. Romanelli, pp. 253-69. Rome.

De Rosa, L. 1984. Francesco Saverio Nitti (1868-1953). In *Protagonisti dell'intervento pubblico in Italia*, ed. A. Mortara, pp. 205-40. Milan.

Fruin, W. M. 1992. *The Japanese enterprise system.* New York.

Gerschenkron, A. 1962. *Economic backwardness in historical perspective.* Cambridge, Mass.

Luraghi, G. 1979. La verità sull'Alfa Romeo. *Epoca* (August 11): 5-10.

Maraffi, M. 1990. *Politica ed economia in Italia.* Bologna.

McCraw, T. K. 1986. *America versus Japan.* Boston.

Osti, G. L. 1993. *L'industria di Stato dall'ascesa al degrado*, interview by R. Ranieri. Bologna.

Porter, M. E. 1990. *The competitive advantage of nations.* New York.

Romeo, R. 1965. Lo Stato e l'impresa privata nello sviluppo economico italiano. *Elsinore* 14-15: 114-32.

1988. *Breve storia della grande industria in Italia.* Milan.

Salerni, D. 1979. *Sindacati e forza lavoro all'Alfa Sud.* Turin.

Sapelli, C. 1990. Lo stato italiano come "imprenditore politico." *Storia Contemporanea* 2: 243-96.

Sapelli, G., and F. Carnevali. 1992. *Uno Sviluppo tra politica e strategia. ENI (1953-1985).* Milan.

Sapelli, G., L. Orsenigo, P. A. Toninelli, and C. Corduas. 1993. *Nascita e trasformazione d'impresa: Storia dell'Agip Petroli.* Bologna.

Saraceno, P. 1975. *Il sistema delle imprese a partecipazione statale nell'esperienza italiana*. Milan.

Shimotani, M., and T. Shiba, eds. 1997. *Beyond the firm*. New York.

Shonfield, A. 1965. *Modern capitalism*. London.

Toniolo, G. 1984. Oscar Sinigaglia (1877-1953). In *Protagonisti dell'intervento pubblico in Italia*, ed. A. Mortara, pp. 405-30. Milan.

Webster, R. 1978. La tecnocrazia italiana e sistemi industriali verticali: Il caso dell'Ansaldo (1914-1921). *Storia Contemporanea* 2: 205-39.

Yudanov, Y. 1997. Large enterprises in the USSR: The functional disorder. In *Big business and the wealth of nations*, ed. A. D. Chandler, Jr., F. Amatori, and T. Hikino, pp. 397-432. New York.

7

State Enterprise in Britain in the
Twentieth Century

ROBERT MILLWARD

Both the rise and the fall of state enterprise in Britain are shrouded in
myths. The scope and incidence of public ownership cannot readily be
explained as a manifestation of socialism, as many have assumed. It is a
common but also unsubstantiated view that the nationalized industries
were a particularly inefficient sector of the British economy in the
1950s, 1960s, and 1970s (Aldcroft 1986, 223; Alford 1988; Cairncross
1985, 465, 467; Pryke 1981; Shackleton 1982). The major drive to state
enterprise in Britain took place just after World War II. Yet it largely
excluded manufacturing, commerce, and land, a fact difficult to recon-
cile with a perception of the nationalizations as the centerpiece of the
socialist vision of the 1945–51 Labour government or as reflecting a
desire to commandeer the means of production. Even in the nineteenth
century, the rise of municipal ownership predated the so-called gas and
water socialism associated with the Webbs and the Fabians. From the
middle of the nineteenth century to the late twentieth century, public
ownership was concentrated in the infrastructure of the economy and
reflected in part the difficulties of regulating that sector under private
ownership. As for the second myth, detailed studies suggest that the performance of the nationalized sector in the period 1950–85 is not a clear-
cut issue. It is possible to show that the productivity growth record was
as good as if not better than that of the (private) manufacturing sector

Table 7.1. Vesting Date of State Enterprises in the
United Kingdom

1868	H.M. Telegraph
1914	British Petroleum
1926	British Broadcasting Corporation
1927	Central Electricity Board
1940	British Overseas Airways Corporation
1946	Bank of England
	British European Airways
1947	National Coal Board
1948	British Transport Commission
	British Electricity Authority and Area Boards
1949	British Gas Council and Area Boards
1951	Iron and Steel Corporation
1966	British Airports Authority
1971	Rolls Royce
1974	National Water Council
	British Leyland, Jaguar
1977	British Aerospace
	British Shipbuilders

and better than the performance of comparable American infrastructure
industries. The financial record, however, was poor and was instrumental in the decline of state enterprise.

These points will be developed and put into a long-term historical perspective on the role of state enterprise. The term "state enterprise" is open to several interpretations, but the focus here will be on
enterprises that aim to at least break even financially and that sell
goods and services to large numbers of buyers (thus, public firms producing armaments under government contracts will be ignored). The
emphasis will also be on enterprises operating at a national level, so that
regional units like the London Passenger Transport Board or municipal
undertakings like the Leeds Gas Corporation enter the story only as part
of the explanation of the role of public ownership in Britain. Table 7.1
lists the enterprises that meet those criteria. In sheer size, the nationalization of coal, railways, electricity, and gas in the 1940s dominated,
accounting for nearly 2 million employees and 20 percent of all U.K.
capital formation. In contrast, with the exception of steel, which flitted
between different organizational forms, public ownership in manufacturing was always on a small scale, notwithstanding the publicity asso-

ciated with the more recent temporary government forays into the car industry.

REGULATING THE INFRASTRUCTURE

It is useful to start by looking at the early experience with public ownership since this was closely linked to the regulation of infrastructure industries. In the 1920s and 1930s these industries were already regulated at the national level. The railways and parts of the gas, electricity, water supply, and tram industries were privately owned but subject to state supervision of rates, fares, and tariffs. Some parts were already publicly owned. The Post Office, with its penny post, had been a government department for centuries, and partly with the aim of achieving similar system integration, the telegraph was nationalized in 1868.

Of particular relevance for our story was that much of the *local* infrastructure in electricity, gas, trams, and water had been taken into public – that is, municipal – ownership in the nineteenth century. Why and how had this happened? It is an important issue, since the dominant philosophy was laissez faire, and neither Parliament nor the entrepreneurs in the infrastructure industries wanted the involvement of either central or local governments. A standard response to this puzzle (Falkus 1977, 145–6; Robson 1935, 309–10) has been that these activities contained strong elements of natural (albeit then local) monopoly and that this explains both the early-nineteenth-century arm's-length regulation of railways, gas, and water supply and the later drive to municipalization. However, that same economic phenomenon can be, and has been, associated with many different outcomes. The nationalization of railways in nineteenth-century Belgium and Prussia may be contrasted with central planning of the network in France and regulation of varying degrees of looseness in the United States and Britain (Dobbin 1994). Three matters, only indirectly connected to natural monopoly, seem to have prompted early government involvement in Britain. One was the limited-liability status that many railway, gas, and water companies needed in order to raise the huge amounts of needed capital, and in the early nineteenth century this required parliamentary approval. Second, the need for rights of way prompted companies to seek compulsory purchase orders from Parliament. This was a clash of property interests that Parliament could not avoid. Exclusive rights over routes were never granted, but since the first incumbent had a de facto monopoly, ceilings on tariffs, fares, and freight rates were imposed in line with previous practice on the canals. In the case of the water supply, there were, of course, externalities of great significance, as nineteenth-century urbanization polluted many water sources. But regulation of the water supply did not start until the middle of the century and was prompted as much by the cholera epidemics and health reports of the 1830s and 1840s as by any conscious decision to plan the development of water resources.

Indeed, the laissez-faire stance of mid-nineteenth-century Parliaments and the associated reluctance to intervene in local government matters led to a *weak* regulatory regime. Price ceilings were not followed by any serious inspection and monitoring mechanisms. In addition, legislation on health and water supplies was permissive, and improvements in this area were largely a function of the strength of local government bodies only just emerging from an inefficient and semicorrupt past (Millward 1991, 109–15). This had two broad effects. First, when tramways and electricity came on the scene in the 1870s and 1880s, parliamentary legislation was much tougher and contained explicit recognition of the interests of local governments. Second, the reformed and standardized local government structure that emerged from the 1872 and 1875 Public Health Acts and the later, more general 1888 and 1894 Local Government Acts was accompanied by pressures for closer regulation and indeed municipal ownership of the local infrastructure.

The rise of municipal ownership was affected by a wider range of factors than simply the regulation of prices, nor was this simply, or even mainly, a matter of ideology. Much talk of "gas and water socialism" is misleading in that it relates to the turn-of-the-century discussion of London government, the influence of the Webbs and the Fabians, and the growth of metropolitan utilities. It is true, as Table 7.2 shows, that there was a massive spurt in municipal activity at this time. The metropolitan boroughs were established under the 1894 Local Government Act, and many of them subsequently took to generating electricity. From 1895 to 1900 the number of statutory electricity undertakings in Britain shot up from 91 to 229, of which 71 percent were owned by local government. The tramways spurt followed in the next five years; there were already 213 undertakings in 1900, which increased to 311 by 1905, half of which were municipally owned. But municipalization was clearly not just a London matter and actually started a good half century earlier. The

Table 7.2. Number of Statutory Local Utility Undertakings in the
United Kingdom, 1845–1956[a]

	Electricity		Trams		Gas		Water		
	PR	LG	PR	LG	PR	LG	PR	MUNIC[b]	LG
1845	—	—	—	—	na	na	67[c]	10	na
1851	—	—	—	—	125	20	na	na	na
1855	—	—	—	—	136	31	na	39	na
1865	—	—	—	—	176	59	147[c]	61	na
1871	—	—	na	na	255	75	na	na	250[d]
1875	na	na	37[e]	7[e]	269[f]	103[f]	na	127	na
1879	na	na	51	9	na	na	na	na	na
1885	na	na	129	27	364	160	na	195	na
1890	na	na	127	29	416	178	na	na	na
1895	52	39	116	38	429	203	na	237	na
1900	65	164	114	99	453	240	na	na	na
1905	na	na	136	175	482	270	na	306	na
1914	na	na	108	171	519	312	200	326	820[d]
1926[g]	233	360	71	170	463	321	na	na	na
1934[g]	na	na	na	na	412	314	173	na	878
1938[g]	208	373	na	na	405	298	na	na	na
1946[g]	191	374	na	na	409	271	na	na	na
1956?	—	—	—	—	—	—	90	na	925

[a] PR is the private sector. LG are local authorities, including all joint boards. The data for trams refer to the ownership of track; for electricity, to undertakings supplying electricity for light or power. Southern Ireland is excluded after 1919. Company data generally refer to financial years ending in the years specified; for local authorities, the financial years often end in the following spring.
[b] Undertakings owned by the corporations of municipal boroughs.
[c] England and Wales only.
[d] Data probably exclude southern Ireland.
[e] Data refer to 1876.
[f] Data refer to 1874.
[g] Excludes southern Ireland.

Official Sources: Board of Trade, *Annual returns of all authorised gas undertakings* (1851 on) and *Annual returns of street tramways and light railways* (1877 on); *Return on electricity*, 1902; Balfour Committee on Industry and Trade, 1928–9; Ministry of Fuel and Power, *Engineering statistics*, 1948.
Secondary Sources: Dakyns 1931, 18–26; Falkus 1977, 134–61; Foreman-Peck and Millward 1994, chapters 2, 4, 5, 6, 8; Garcke 1896; Hassan 1995, 189–211; Robson 1935.

most dramatic growth in statutory water undertakings was from about 1845 to the early 1870s, by which time there were 250 systems run by local government. For gas, the most rapid growth was from the 1850s to the 1880s, during which period the share of the municipals grew from 13 to 39 percent, remaining at roughly that level until the 1940s – although the initial spurt was most noticeable in Scotland and the share of municipal undertakings in England and Wales continued to rise in a fairly smooth fashion until the 1930s. Hence, well before the term "municipal socialism" was bandied about, a huge part of the shift to public ownership had already taken place. In any case, the political makeup of town councils dominated by businessmen and rate payers can hardly be called socialist.

Nor is it possible to rely on the natural monopoly argument since many towns continued to rely on private companies, as Table 7.2 shows. Recent research suggests that a key factor in the drive to municipal ownership was the huge expansion of investment in the local sanitary and transport infrastructure, which had been prompted by the rapid rise in urban populations (Millward and Sheard 1995; Millward and Ward 1993). Many urban utilities that were brought into municipal hands saw their local natural monopoly status regulated not so much by the lowering of prices as by the channeling of trading profits to municipal coffers as an additional tax source providing relief for the rates. This is why services were left to the private sector when alternative income sources were available, as in many of the ports (such as Liverpool, whose dockland property provided a good income for the town council) and in those towns (such as Oxford, Eastbourne, and York) that had a good middle-class tax base. When it came to the water supply, by the turn of the century 80 percent of the companies were municipally owned and most undertakings were run at a loss. The Manchester Corporation, for example, openly used profits from the municipal gas works to subsidize its water undertaking.

Municipal enterprises generated a number of problems, and by the 1920s there were pressures to abandon them. This was not because they had performed poorly. There is no clear evidence that they hindered economic development – indeed, it seems that the local infrastructure performed better than the more loosely regulated railway companies (Foreman-Peck 1987). Nor did private utilities perform any better than municipal ones; all the evidence shows that they performed equally efficiently in the cost-effective sense (Foreman-Peck and Waterson 1985; Millward and Ward 1987). Rather, the issue is that municipal undertakings were part of an institutional mix in the infrastructure that was being undermined technologically by moves to a more regional and national focus, and this was prompting central government intervention.

THE ROAD TO NATIONALIZATION

By the interwar period, indeed, the fundamental problems of the infrastructure industries had changed in two fundamental ways. First, the scale of the natural monopoly and externality issues had been enlarged by technological developments, especially in the electricity supply, and by the advent of motor vehicles and the associated regulatory problems of transport. Second, the whole thrust of industrial policy was transformed by the depressed economic conditions of the 1920s and 1930s. The central questions are how much of the 1940s nationalization package can be explained by the perceived failure of the interwar policy and how far that perception was to be found in the civil service, the professions, and the Conservative Party as well as in the Labour Party.

Two interrelated factors disrupted the minimalist laissez-faire stance inherited by Parliament from the nineteenth century. One was the catastrophic decline in the staple exports of coal, cotton, shipbuilding, iron, and steel. The other was technological development that was to prompt fundamental changes in the infrastructure of the economy. The former is well known in terms of its impact on output and employment levels. It is relevant to stress only that, compared to the nineteenth century, the widened electoral franchise meant that members of Parliament in these regions could exert pressure on government. The benchmarks were seen as the United States and Germany, and in particular the large size of business organizations. Where specific international comparisons were made, as in the coal industry, a government response was unavoidable.

Contemporary changes in technology rendered larger business units more economical, while improvements in accounting, telephones, and road transport led to administrative changes allowing bigger business units for marketing and finance.

This was particularly significant for the infrastructure industries because the institutional mix inherited from the nineteenth century militated against a simple set of amalgamations to capture these gains. As Table 7.2 shows, in 1926 there were 233 separate companies involved in supplying electricity, 463 in gas, and 71 in tramways, and data for the nearest year indicate 173 water supply companies in 1934. Alongside these companies were local authority undertakings. They had come to dominate the water supply – 878 in total – but there were also 360 in electricity, 170 in tramways, and 321 in gas. Each was jealous of its own empire, and the local authorities in particular were reluctant to amalgamate with their neighbors, whether public or private (Hannah 1979, 337; Wilson 1995). Yet by the 1920s, technical progress in electricity was making large generating stations more economical, provided that transmission grids could be developed and electrical current standardized. The importance of integrating the water supply, drainage, and sewerage in the development of river basins was recognized but also could not be accommodated within the inherited structures. Domestic air routes had the luxury of being serviced by twenty separate companies, in part because of the government's desire to sustain a peacetime capability in this embryonic but strategically important industry. On the railways much had been anticipated by the 1921 Railways Act, which regrouped the motley collection of nineteenth-century companies into four regional undertakings. The act also converted the nineteenth-century rate structure, based not on the costs of transporting commodities but on their value, into a rigid formula and rendered the companies vulnerable to competition from their new rivals, road passenger and freight vehicles owned by a huge number of tiny firms, untouched in the 1920s by regulation and able to deal with customers individually.

Thus interwar governments inherited a minimalist stance on industrial matters and yet were faced with a catastrophic decline in exports that was eventually interpreted as a sign of industrial decline, as well as problems in the infrastructure industries that could not be resolved by private action alone. The industrial policies that followed have been described as timid and contradictory. For much of the 1920s and the early 1930s, British governments were reluctant to intervene in what was seen as the private preserve of businessmen or local authorities. The story of the bank relief to the cotton and steel industries, the proliferation of price-fixing schemes, the limited success of the amalgamation movement in manufacturing and coal, the tariff protection of the steel industry, and the general inconsistency between protection and rationalization are now standard textbook material (Hannah 1976).

With one or two exceptions, this arm's-length approach to manufacturing and coal carried over to the infrastructure industries. The exceptions were the establishment of the Central Electricity Board (CEB) and the London Passenger Transport Board (LPTB) following the tradition from the early years of the century when the Metropolitan Water Board and the London Port Authority were created. Most of the infrastructure industries, together with coal, were subject to constant investigations by government committees and royal commissions. In coal, the Sankey Report of 1919 was followed by the Samuel Commission in 1926, both advocating the establishment of large business units. The electricity supply industry saw similar proposals from the Williamson Committee in 1918 and the Weir Committee in 1926. The huge potential gains from regional and national transmission grids could not be resisted, and from 1926 through the late 1930s the CEB set up a national grid and closed the technical efficiency gap with the United States (Foreman-Peck 1994, 409). The distribution of electricity from the grid was unreformed and accounted, as in gas and water supply, for a large number of the undertakings recorded in Table 7.2. The issue had been highlighted by the Weir Committee, but nothing had materialized by 1936, when the Mcgowan Committee reported. This committee also preferred voluntary amalgamations around the larger undertakings, and although it did envisage regional public boards in the long run, the initial support for voluntarism meant that nothing had been achieved by the end of the 1930s. For the water supply, regional advisory committees were set up to coordinate the efforts to develop joint schemes and to investigate local needs and resources out of which a national policy might emerge, but they were weak bodies, insufficiently comprehensive in coverage and legal powers. Production economies were less obvious in gas and so, despite reforming comments from academic sources, the main government investigatory body, the Heyworth Committee, did not report until 1945, although by then it was sure that potential marketing and financial economies pointed to rationalization of area undertakings and it advocated outright public ownership. Finally, the widespread dissatisfaction with Imperial Airways and the proliferation of airlines on domestic routes led to the 1938 Cadman Report on Civil Aviation, which promoted the principle of two area monopolies. In the end, Imperial Airways and British Airways were merged in 1939 into the British Overseas Airways Corporation.

Thus the first part of the explanation for the 1940s nationalizations is the failure of the interwar regulation of the infrastructure industries. The second part is the widespread recognition that new industrial policies were needed (for details on this issue see Gourvish 1991; Hannah 1979, chapter 10; Supple 1986). The perceived failure of arm's-length regulation of these industries in the interwar period had two implications for the reorganization that was to come: rationalization of the various industrial units and legislation with teeth would be needed to forge the new undertaking. In theory these industrial units might have

been floated off as new, large, integrated private companies along the
Thatcherite lines of the 1990s, perhaps subject to regulation of prices
and profits where the market was monopolized. But this solution also
was not palatable given that very history of unsuccessful arm's-length
regulation of private companies. A shift in ownership was called for,
reinforced by the way the employers' own solutions had been discred-
ited. This was not simply the failure of the voluntary amalgamation
phase. By the late 1930s and early 1940s, many of the employers' associations were finding it necessary to formulate their own proposals for
reform, but these were invariably poorly received. In 1944 the Joint
Committee of Electrical Supply Associations put forward an agreed-on
response to the Mcgowan Committee's proposals, and the *Times* characterized it as "the product of a united front of those who want to be
left alone, both local authorities and companies" (Hannah 1979, 143).
The same newspaper saw the Foot plan for the coal industry as no "more
than the creation of a 'self-governing' trade association" (Kirby 1977,
194). The four railway companies had extensive financial interests in
airline companies and in 1944 published their proposals for a private
monopoly – "a gift . . . in return for which the 'chosen carrier' would
consent to exist in a cozy relationship with other transport systems"
(Lyth 1990, 3).

  This nonetheless leaves two puzzles in the account of which industries were nationalized. If the quest for large business units and the
aping of the United States and Germany were important, why was manufacturing left largely in private hands – not only declining industries
such as cotton and shipbuilding but also new strategic sectors such as
aircraft and armaments? The usual economic pressures on governments
and the need to decide priorities were heightened in the immediate
post–World War II years by Britain's severe balance of payments problems. Of prime importance was the need for manufacturing to maximize exports. Industries such as cotton and cars were given targets, and
as long as they met those targets, the firms were left alone – Britain was,
after all, the major car exporter in the late 1940s. Governments during
the war had not ventured far into public ownership, and in the most
widely publicized case, the aircraft manufacturer Short Brothers was
taken over only after it failed to meet flow production targets. The aircraft and armaments industries indeed were perceived to have had
a "good war" and for that reason were also unlikely to be touched in the
late 1940s. There was a second reason why the 1945–51 Labour
government did not extend public ownership far into manufacturing.

Recent research suggests that many in the party recognized that competition was vital for industries where the product changed rapidly – model changes in cars being the classic case – and that the risks were better taken by private enterprise (Bowden 1995). Moreover, party officials had no well-articulated philosophy of dealing – say, by equity shares – with atomistic industries such as cotton or oligopolistic ones such as cars and steel. And, despite many impressions to the contrary (and refuting the Olson [1982] thesis into the bargain), trade unions, outside coal mining, and railways did not necessarily see their best interests in public ownership. This was certainly the case in steel, and the great uncertainties and inexperience that troubled Labour leaders in this area allowed them to be outgunned by the employers' leaders (Ranieri 1995). The industry was nationalized, very reluctantly for many, at the end in 1951, and the transfer was sufficiently unpopular to be the only major reversal that the Conservatives effected over the next thirty years.

The second puzzle is coal. This is not an infrastructure industry and certainly not a natural monopoly, and even economies of scale at the coalfield level have been disputed. Yet it was the first major industry to be nationalized. Here there probably *is* some scope for invoking a neosocialist diagnosis. The coal industry played a special role in British industrial history. It had some unique operating characteristics, experienced the cold winds of market forces more strongly in the hundred years up to 1940 than perhaps any other industry, and caused bitter relations between miners and owners. The central elements of the coal story for our purposes relate first to working conditions. Coal mining is dirty and dangerous, and the mining communities, located away from the main areas of urban growth in nineteenth-century Britain, were insular and defensive. The economics of collieries implied steeply rising short-run marginal costs, and the strong cyclical and war-related variations in the demand for British coal in the second half of the nineteenth century made prices and wages more volatile than in any other sector (Benson 1982). The other factor is that the British coal industry was old. It expanded immensely in the late nineteenth century on the back of an ever-growing labor force working more and more difficult seams with declining marginal productivity. Greasley (1995) shows that by the 1940s the industry had reached severe production limits. Output shrank absolutely during World War II, while many leading collieries saw their share prices rise to 120–50 percent of their 1930s levels (Howlett 1994). The running of the industry was roundly condemned by a 1945 government investigatory body, the Reid Committee (composed mainly of engineers from the major mining companies!). The miners had clamored for nationalization for years, and now they got it.

THE NEW NATIONALIZED INDUSTRIES, 1945–85: GOALS AND INSTITUTIONAL ARRANGEMENTS

Although significant groups in British society outside the Labour Party favored public ownership, the final form it took in the 1940s was very much influenced by the incumbent Labour government. The institutional arrangements also prove important in understanding subsequent performance – at least the financial record. Thus, the Labour government was engaged in economic planning, but the planning was to be much more by administrative dictate than by the use of the price system. Hence all the constituent parts of transport were taken together into the British Transport Commission (BTC), which was expected to provide an integrated transport system. There was a distinctly *national* focus to all the new public firms, and this was linked to the postwar reconstruction program. All the new boards listed in Table 7.1 were to have a public responsibility to raise investment in both physical and human capital. Finally, the new nationalized industries were, in the same spirit, to provide a set of common services, that is, to meet items of consumer budgets with low income and price elasticities.

Hence we find that the Nationalisation Acts of 1945–9 had two central features. The first was that the new corporations were to serve the public interest and a public purpose was written into the acts, which embraced the provision of common services and the development of investment programs. Thus the BTC was required to provide "an efficient, adequate . . . system of . . . transport," the British Electricity Authority (BEA) "to develop . . . an efficient, coordinated and economical system of electricity supply," and the National Coal Board (NCB) to make "supplies of coal available . . . as may seem to . . . [the new board] best calculated to serve the public interest" (Coal Industry Nationalisation Act 1946; Electricity Act 1947; Transport Act 1947).

Consonant with these aims was the constitution of the boards, whose members were to be as disinterested as the corporations' objectives. Such had been the philosophy behind the CEB and the British Broadcasting Corporation (BBC), of particular note being the absence of union representatives, notwithstanding the long-standing pleas of unions such as the Union of Postal Workers. Similarly the new corporations were not to pursue profit. Finance was to come from fixed-interest stock – either the industry's own or government bonds – and any surpluses earned were required by the statutes to be devoted to the public purpose, that is, reinvested in the industry. The investment programs were not simply a commercial matter and had to be approved by the relevant minister of the sponsoring department, who also could "give to the Board directives of a general character . . . in relation to matters appearing to the Minister to affect the national interest" (Coal Act 1946).

Second, the new undertakings were expected to be commercially oriented, innovative, and enterprising. Thus, like the CEB and the LPTB, they were to have their own corporate legal status free from Treasury supervision, able to appoint their own employees and to be sued in the courts. "Cheap and efficiently supplied services" are words that recur in all the statutes and have to be seen in conjunction with another injunction, variously worded, along the lines of "revenues shall not be less than sufficient for meeting all outgoings properly chargeable, on an average of good and bad years." Vague though this wording might be for accountants, it was widely interpreted to mean breaking even, taking one year with another, and was much more easily monitored than the even vaguer public purposes.

With hindsight we can see that there were clear dangers in the loose specification of objectives and the absence of explicit mechanisms for reconciling the financial target with those objectives. Much of the last twenty years of British public services in, for example, health and education has been devoted to developing accountability and management mechanisms to cope with these issues. The "public purpose" objective was inherently vague. Many interpreted it to mean that the industries were expected to behave differently from ordinary commercial enterprises; in particular, they were rarely allowed to set prices to clear markets when capacity constraints yielded high marginal costs (e.g., the fuel crisis of the late 1940s and the oil price increases of the 1970s). In addition, the managers of the new public boards viewed the injunction to provide "adequate services" as meaning the setting of uniform prices (per passenger mile or per freight ton mile or per kilowatt hour or per cubic foot of gas) independent of how costs varied across areas and routes. This requirement generated price structures significantly out of line with costs. The other key word in the acts, "efficiency," is associated with two concepts for economists. One is the allocation of resources, where classic definitions of efficiency involved prices equal to marginal costs, which would, however, have flown in the face of the preceding interpretation of adequate services and uniform prices. The other concept was x-efficiency, and many have followed Alchian (1965) and De Alessi (1974) in seeing the citizen's inability to sell ownership rights unilaterally and the associated diminished pressure on management as likely to generate higher costs and poorer services than those of private firms. All could agree, however, that although the breakeven requirement could be spread over good and bad years and although the public boards could always be bailed out by government, there was no doubt that Parliament intended that financial losses should not be a persistent characteristic of the new public corporations.

PRODUCTIVITY: AS GOOD AS THAT OF THE PRIVATE SECTOR?

Commentators on the productivity performance of the nationalized sector in post–World War II Britain have perhaps been unduly influenced by some of the preceding a priori considerations. It is, in fact, perfectly possible to show that the sector performed just as well as the private sector and probably even better than the American infrastructure industries, where private ownership was more common. Several recent articles have summarized their findings on the lines of "the post-war model of nationalisation . . . has had its day" (Dunkerley and Hare 1991, 415–16) as a result of deficiencies in management control or management and organizational slack (Hannah 1994, 186). One article was actually entitled "Nationalised Industry Performance: Still Third Rate?" (Molyneux and Thompson 1987). Yet in all cases these authors could not document a clearly inferior productivity record – their precise judgment being that the performance was "mixed." In part these writers reflected the general public's sensitivity to the performance of industries whose price levels have important effects on low-income budgets, with few substitutes available. The clamor in the 1990s against the salary levels and share options enjoyed by the managers of the newly privatized utilities is consistent with this view. But the somewhat gloomy view of the performance of nationalized industries also stemmed from two features of the late 1960s and the 1970s. One was the unsuccessful attempts at public ownership in manufacturing, and the other was the control of prices in the 1970s and the resulting huge financial deficits, matters we shall turn to shortly.

Looking first at the productivity performance, much reliance has had to be placed on rigid measures like total factor productivity since cross-sectional cost function or production function estimates are not possible in Britain, where whole sectors were either public or private. There were some glaring examples of poor performance in manufacturing, but these were closely associated "with economic depression . . . [in the 1970s, when both political parties] nationalised more firms though Labour proved the more enthusiastic. A remarkably high proportion of these 'lame ducks' proved to be dead ducks, whose factories and workers faced closure and redundancy after brief subsidized half life in a terminal care hospice, not the intended convalescence and recovery" (Hannah 1994, 181).

In the main part of the nationalized sector, however, the record was much better. Since the infrastructure sector in Britain was dominated by nationalized firms and manufacturing by private ones in the period 1950–85, one test of the performance of state enterprise is whether the productivity growth records are any different and whether the different product types can be controlled by making comparisons with the United States. Table 7.3 displays the results of this exercise and constitutes a slightly revised version of earlier estimates (Millward 1990). It is clear that total factor productivity growth in Britain in the three broad groupings – (1) mining, (2) gas, electricity, and water, and (3) transport and communications – exceeded growth in the United States. Labor productivity data sometimes tell a different story – for example, the growth of coal output per employee was much bigger in the United States, but at the industry level, total factor usage is more relevant. Lumping all three sectors together, the public-enterprise sector in Britain shows a productivity growth rate similar to that of the British manufacturing sector, which was only slightly higher than that of U.S. manufacturing (after allowing for the different subperiods covered in the U.S. data; see the note in Table 7.3).

What about productivity levels? Several writers have implied that whatever the growth record, British productivity was below that in other countries. Hannah has recently recorded American labor productivity levels in the 1970s some two to three times higher than those in Britain in gas, electricity, water, buses, railways, postal service, and telecommunications, and the levels in Germany were twice as high. However, these are partial (that is, labor) productivity measures, and in any case, the key question is what these levels were like before nationalization. Table 7.4 confirms the very high level of output per capita in the U.S. infrastructure industries in the 1970s relative to those in Britain.

Table 7.3. The Productivity Growth Record, 1951–85 (Annual Average percent Growth Rate of Total Factor Productivity)

	1951–64	1964–73	1973–85
Mining			
U.K.	1.5	2.2	−1.0
U.S.	0.5	1.9	−4.3
Gas, electricity and water			
U.K.	3.3	4.3	1.8
U.S.	3.7	2.4	1.2
Transport and communications			
U.K.	2.4	3.7	1.4–2.4
U.S.	1.0–3.7	1.6–3.0	0.1–2.3
U.K. public enterprise			
Output	2.1	2.7	0.9
Labor productivity	2.8	5.3	2.4
Total factor product.	1.9	3.4	1.2
U.K. manufacturing			
Output	3.2	3.0	−0.8
Labour productivity	3.0	4.6	2.6
Total factor product.	2.0	3.1	1.3
U.S. manufacturing			
Total factor product.	2.0	1.8	1.4

Sources and Methods: The U.S data are taken from Griliches 1988 and relate to 1949-66, 1966-73, and 1973-85; "utilities" are assumed to cover gas, electricity, and water. Kendrick (1987) is an alternative source and his figures are higher, but the relative position of manufacturing and the other industries is the same. The U.K. data for 1951-73 are taken from Matthews et al. 1982. The mining data for 1973-85 are derived from Pryke 1981 and from Molyneux and Thompson 1986. The rest of the data are calculated from the figures for each sector on gross domestic product (GDP) at 1980 factor cost, the share of income from employment in GDP, gross capital stock at the 1980 replacement cost (all in Central Statistical Office 1979 and 1986), and estimates of man hours, derived (Millward 1988) from Department of Employment, *Employment Gazette* 1987 (Historical Supplement).

The comparison figures for 1938 and 1950 show two other things. First, the extractive, utility, transportation, and communications industries have *always* had lower labor productivity in Britain, including the period before nationalization. Second, the British performance in this respect *improved* for gas, airlines, and railways during the 1950s, 1960s, and 1970s, and Table 7.3 implies that the total factor productivity level improved relative to the United States in all the infrastructure industries.

Table 7.4. Sector Output per Head, 1938–77: U.S. Index (U.K. = 100)

	1938	1950	1968	1970	1972	1975	1977
Agriculture	103	222	242	240	207	222	209
Extractive and utilities							
Extractive	415	—	668	692	806	594	342
Coal mining	380	374	855	892	1,038	697	760
Utilities	180	—	426	397	345	321	307
Gas	163	—	736	705	492	332	279
Electricity	193	—	406	371	345	354	457
TOTAL	360	769	517	—	—	—	323
Manufacturing	215	292	289	285	293	282	291
Construction	115	150	206	163	165	165	170
Transport and Communications							
Transport	270–300	458	240	222	216	204	213
Railways	297	771	—	395	—	—	—
Airlines	—	388	—	—	152	—	—
Communications	270	264	284	291	302	323	334
TOTAL	280	412	262	251	250	252	264
GRAND TOTAL (all industry)	181	299	278	268	271	266	266

Note: The employment data underlying the calculations are generally total numbers of employees. The output data tend to refer to gross output for 1938 and net output for later years. Aggregates involve calculations using U.K. prices and weights. The 1938 figure for coal relates to tonnage per man shift and the 1950 figure to tonnage per worker. All the other 1950 data on extractive and utilities exclude (for both countries) output sold within that sector. The data for airlines relate to ton-miles per employee.

Sources: Data for 1968–77 are taken from Smith et al. 1982. The aggregate figure for all industry for all years is also taken from Table 3.7 of this source. The 1950 data are from Paige and Bombach 1959. The 1938 data are from Rostas 1948 and relate to various years in the period 1935–9.

FINANCES AND DECLINE

If the early expectation that nationalized industry would be efficient is interpreted in terms of productivity there is, myth to the contrary, a defensible record. Another early expectation, indeed a requirement, was that the industries would break even financially. Here the record was poor, and when it became disastrous in the 1970s, it proved to be meat and drink for the privatizers. What is clear from our analysis so far is that the source of the financial difficulties did not lie in any obvious way in x-efficiency, at least insofar as that is reflected in productivity measures.

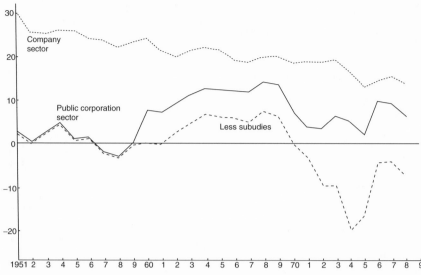

Figure 7.1. The share of profits on income in public and private industry in the United Kingdom, 1951–79. *Sources*: Data relate to gross trading surplus as a percentage of domestic value added, both measured net of capital consumption, and all taken from Central Statistical Office, *U.K. National Income and Expenditures*, various years.

The broad financial picture is that in the 1950s the revenues of the nationalized industries as a group generated a surplus above operating costs and depreciation but not enough to cover interest charges, which was important given the large amount of fixed-interest stock. The 1960s saw an improvement, with the surplus rising to 4 percent of net fixed assets, which was about enough to cover interest charges. The 1970s then saw huge deficits and government subsidies (Figure 7.1).

The explanation of these deficits is not a straightforward matter. Figure 7.1 shows the share of profits in net output for all public corporations in Britain (that is, all the nationalized industries plus some other publicly owned firms). This is not an ideal measure of profitability, but it does provide a continuous picture over the relevant part of the postwar period and, from other evidence on the capital output ratio, clearly mirrors the movements in the rate of return on capital. The secular improvement in the late 1960s is clear, and Figure 7.1 also shows that this contrasts with a secular decline in the private sector. Two government white papers in the 1960s stressed the importance to the nationalized sector of financial probity, and the subsidies granted in that decade were largely linked to those railway services that were unprofitable but deemed economical on other grounds. Dunkerley and Hare (1991, 407) have viewed the declining profitability and rising prices and costs of the nationalized industries in the 1970s as a manifestation of failing management and control systems. They ignore two matters, however. First, the oil price hike of the 1970s hit the infrastructure industries very hard. Other research shows that the faster rise of costs in the nationalized sector was due to the rise in the prices of fuel, raw materials, and other purchased items; unit labor costs were growing less than in manufacturing, reflecting, among other things, the productivity trends mentioned before (Foreman-Peck and Millward 1994, 316–17). Second, it is now generally accepted that the governments of the early 1970s imposed price controls more effectively on the public sector than on the private sector (Hannah 1994, 181). In the 1970s, the prices of the nationalized industries were not allowed to keep pace with cost levels inflated more than in other industries by oil price increases. The result is shown in Figure 7.1. Operating costs exceeded value added throughout the 1970s, and the profit share (even including the subsidies explicitly introduced to offset the price controls) declined precipitously from its late 1960s level. Whether this whole episode was the fault of central government was irrelevant in the late 1970s. The huge price increases that did take place in conjunction with the mounting deficits were readily translated into a verdict of failure, and the nails were in the coffin.

THE ROAD TO PRIVATIZATION

Critics of the nationalized industries could be found, from the early 1950s on, not only within the Conservative Party but in academia and the press as well. By the 1970s, the troubles and tribulations of British Railways and the NCB had become part of the British way of life, allowing even sports journalists to pepper their reports with clichés about the inefficiencies of the industries (Edmonds 1987, 30). There were also the more deeply rooted doubts of the intellectual Right, manifest in Britain in the activities of the Institute of Economic Affairs (IEA), which played a role not unlike that of the Fabians for the Left in the early decades of the twentieth century. The IEA published well-regarded pieces of applied economics with a clear bent toward the application of market tests to public-sector issues such as payment for roads, municipal housing, and fuel (Gray 1968; Roth 1966; Tugenhadt 1963). The

Institute's Advisory Council included well-respected public finance specialists such as Alan Peacock, Jack Wiseman, and Alan Prest, who from the early 1960s provided intellectual ammunition for a more market-oriented public sector, a torch taken up later by Littlechild (1978). At the same time, a stream of economics literature was emanating from the United States, rooted in questions of property rights and public choice. Alchian (1965), Demsetz (1968), and De Alessi (1974) illustrate the articles flooding the academic journals with new approaches to the public sector, and authors such as Milton Friedman and James Buchanan became contributors to IEA publications.

The critique has three elements. The first is an objection to using nationalized industries for redistributive purposes. If it is desirable to provide economic help to single parents, inhabitants of the Scottish highlands, and old-age pensioners, it is better to do it by the tax and transfer system than by offering gas, coal, and rail travel at prices that distort the real resource cost to the economy and destabilize the finances of the industries. A more fundamental approach (Alchian 1965) sees the essence of public ownership as involving the removal of the beneficial effects of private share dealings. The shareholder can unilaterally sell shares and exert pressure on management. In public firms, all that the dissatisfied taxpayer can do is emigrate or mount a political campaign. Officials who run state industries or supervise government departments or who exert influence as politicians are not – so the argument goes – disinterested individuals (Littlechild 1978). If they are politicians, they will try to use public institutions for political purposes (holding down electricity prices for voters, blocking the closure of a steel plant in a member of Parliament's district). Even civil servants are not disinterested, since they want large empires and will encourage industry managers to have large investment programs and low prices. These views were held sufficiently strongly to undermine even the case for public ownership of natural monopolies. In 1985, the then Conservative minister for industry said that his government would "encourage competition where appropriate, but where it does not make business or economic sense, we will not hesitate to extend the benefits of privatization to natural monopolies" (Moore 1986, 96).

In the 1970s, this line of attack was already falling on receptive ears. The traditional defense of the nationalized industries lacked wide support. Some had drawn intellectual support from the Marxist characterization of capitalism as a society of two antagonistic classes, workers and owners of the means of production. That characterization ill fitted the role of the nationalized industries in Britain, and the common ownership of the means of production, eradicated only recently from the Labour Party's constitution, had probably never been central to the 1940s nationalizations (Millward 1997). More pragmatic arguments for public ownership had rested on two issues. In the interwar period, untrammeled capitalism appeared to many to have failed. The reduction of unemployment and poverty became key objectives of post-1945 governments, and the state ownership of fuel and transport would provide essential services at low cost to working-class families. By the 1970s, the failure of capitalism was no longer so obvious. Indeed, the socialist economies of Eastern Europe were looking weak even though the apocalyptic events of the early 1990s in Russia were then unimaginable. Finally, the argument for public ownership also rested on some of the market failure problems common to the infrastructure industries – natural monopolies and environmental spillovers – as well as perceived advantages in coordinated investment programs in different sectors. Whether public ownership, and in particular nationalization, was the best way of tackling these issues was becoming more debatable in the 1970s, and the disastrous financial performance helped those who wanted change.

A program of specific privatizations had been discussed in think tanks for several years, but when the Conservatives came to power in 1979 they were initially quite timid. In their first four years, the only firms privatized were relatively small – British Aerospace, Britoil, Amersham International, Cable and Wireless (Steel and Heald 1985). What really gave the Conservatives confidence (apart from the Falklands War) was privatization in a different sector: the sale of municipal housing, which, at subsidized prices, proved very popular (Murie 1985). Eventually British Telecom was privatized in 1984, British Gas in 1990, the various electricity boards in 1990 and 1991, and British Coal and British Rail at the end of the Conservatives' period in office.

There were three basic aims: to raise efficiency, to spread share ownership, and to contribute to a reduction in the overall public-sector budget deficit (Heald and Steel 1982). A provisional assessment of the outcome is of considerable interest in the light it sheds on the shift to state enterprise earlier in the century. Large productivity gains were made in the 1980s, but in several major industries such as gas, electricity, and telecommunications, many of the gains were realized before the actual act of privatization. Further gains in both productivity and profitability in telecommunications and electricity generation occurred, but several commentators felt that this was due as much to a different market structure (more telecommunications competition from Mercury Telecommunications Ltd., for example) than to the change in ownership. A study by Parker (1993) of the period up to 1992 suggests that changes since privatization in output per capita and profitability were small and that the deterioration in some sectors has to be set against the gains in others. A review by Bishop et al. (1994, Introduction) sees the productivity gains that have occurred as due not so much to the threat of bankruptcy as to a more transparent separation of commercial and public interest activities. In electricity, for example, competition has been allowed to flourish in nonnuclear power generation, but the national grid's natural monopoly elements have been explicitly recognized.

It is the financial side that has seen the more dramatic and perhaps long-lasting changes. This is not so much a matter of the change in share ownership or the Conservatives' vision of a property-owning democracy. It is true that the number of persons owning shares rose from 7 percent of all adults in 1979 to 25 percent in 1992, but many people sold their shares quickly to realize capital gains, and by 1992 less than 50 percent of investors owned shares in more than one company (Parker 1993). The major power in shareholding still lies with the insurance companies, unit trusts, merchant banks, and other financial institutions. Rather more significant was the impact on the government's deficit and the internationalization of the ownership of the infrastructure industries. Privatization had the potential to eliminate from the public sector those enterprises whose claims on public spending, in the form of investment programs, were less than the contribution they made in terms of operating surpluses. However, the sales of public-sector assets were treated by Conservative governments almost like a receipt on the current account, lowering the government's borrowing requirement in the year of the sale but having no impact on future deficits. There was indeed an element here of what a former Conservative prime minister, Harold Macmillan, called "selling the family silver."

The silver was also often acquired by foreigners. The British stock market did not have problems coping with nationalization in the 1940s or with privatization in the 1980s. In the 1940s, owners of equity in private coal collieries, gas and electricity undertakings, and railway companies simply surrendered their shares and received government bonds, or a near equivalent, in exchange. The buyers and sellers were British. No resource effects of any significance were involved – simply an exchange of one piece of paper for another. The amount of compensation paid to groups like the former coal owners created resentment in some quarters, but that was the limit of the matter. In the 1980s and 1990s the sale of state assets involved foreign buyers, including French water companies and American electricity and telecommunication utilities. This had resource implications. A transfer of real resources into Britain was involved. By extension, any attempts to renationalize these companies would mean a loss of resources abroad. The government would have to use foreign currency to buy back these assets, so the transaction would be equivalent to an increase in imports of goods or services. This globalization of ownership will probably deter immediate renationalization, apart from the effects it is already having in introducing masters of the "regulation game" to the British scene.

CONCLUSIONS

Taking a very long-term perspective, we may draw the following conclusions:

1. State enterprise in Britain was strongly motivated by a desire to improve the efficiency (variously defined) of particular industrial sectors.
2. The focus was on infrastructure and reflected a continuation of attempts to regulate it from the early nineteenth century.
3. The available evidence suggests that the cost effectiveness of publicly owned utilities in Britain in the late nineteenth and early twentieth centuries was comparable to that of private utilities, and the productivity record of the publicly owned infrastructure industries in 1950–85 was as good as that of the British (private) manufacturing sector and better than that of the U.S. infrastructure industries.
4. Public ownership in British manufacturing had a distinctly worse record and provides some support for those in the Labour Party who argued as early as the 1940s for the importance of competition and private ownership in this sector.
5. The record on profitability in nineteenth-century municipal utilities is much better than that of twentieth-century nationalized industries. Over the last twenty years there has been something of a revolution in the accountability of British public services, and one question is whether that could have been extended to the

nationalized trading sectors. There are signs that what productivity
success the newly privatized industries have achieved is due in no
small part to the greater accountability of public services and thus
the greater transparency of the division between public and private
activities.

It is clear that the British experience of public ownership in the nineteenth and twentieth centuries has been closely linked to the coal and
infrastructure industries – railways, gas, electricity, and water. The forays
into manufacturing – motor vehicles in the 1970s, steel in the 1940s
and again in the 1960s and 1970s – have been tentative and largely
unsuccessful. In this respect, Britain looks very different not only from
Italy and Austria, but also from France, Germany, and the rest of continental Europe. The nineteenth-century rule of the sanctity of property
profoundly affected how intervention occurred, and elements of this
situation seeped through into the twentieth century. The fundamental
difficulty of the infrastructure industries – natural monopoly and environmental spillovers – remains and has shaped the way the new privatized utilities have been regulated. But that is another story.

REFERENCES

Alchian, A. A. 1965. Some economics of property rights. *Il Politico* 36: 816–29.
     Reprinted in *Economic forces at work*, by A. A. Alchian, pp. 127–49.
     Indianapolis, 1977.
Aldcroft, D. H. 1986. *The British economy*, vol. 1, *The years of turmoil 1918–39*.
     Brighton.
Alford, B. W. E. 1988. *British economic performance, 1945–75*. London.
Ashworth, W. 1991. *The state in business: 1945 to the mid 1980s*. London.
Balfour Committee on Industry and Trade. 1928–9. *Further factors in industrial
     and commercial efficiency. P.P.* 1928/9, xxx.
Benson, J. 1982. Coal mining. In *A history of British industrial relations
     1875–1914*, ed. C. Wrigley, pp. 187–208. Brighton.
Bishop, M., J. Kay, and C. Meyer, eds. 1994. *Privatisation and economic perfor-
     mance*. Oxford.
Board of Trade. Various years. *Annual returns of all authorised gas
     undertakings.*
     Various years. *Annual returns of street and road tramways and light
     railways.*
     1902. *Return relating to authorised electricity supply undertakings in the
     U.K. belonging to local authorities and companies for the year 1900. P.P.*
     1902, xciii.
Bowden, S. 1995. The motor vehicle industry. In *The political economy of nation-*

alisation in Britain 1920-50, ed. R. Millward and J. Singleton, pp. 88-115. Cambridge.

Cadman Report. 1938. *Report of the committee of inquiry into civil aviation.* Command 5685, March 1938, *P.P.* 193/18, viii.

Cairncross, A. 1985. *Years of recovery: British economic policy, 1945-51.* London.

Central Statistical Office. Various years. *United Kingdom national income and expenditure.*

Coal Industry Nationalisation Act. 1946. 9 and 10, Geo. 6, *Public General Acts and the Church Assembly Measures of 1946.* London, 1947.

Dakyns, A. L. 1931. The water supply of English towns in 1846. *Manchester School* 2(1): 18-26.

De Alessi, L. 1974. An economic analysis of government ownership and regulation: Theory and evidence from the electric power industry. *Public Choice* 19: 1-42.

Demsetz, H. 1968. Why regulate utilities. *Journal of Law and Economics* 2(April): 55-65.

Department of Employment. 1971. *British labour statistics: Historical abstract, 1886-1968.* London.

1987. *Employment gazette: Historical supplement.* London.

Dobbin, F. 1994. *Forging industrial policy:The United States, Britain, and France in the railway age.* Cambridge.

Dunkerley, J., and P. G. Hare. 1991. Nationalised industries. In *The British economy since 1945*, ed. N. F. R. Crafts and N. Woodward, pp. 381-416. Oxford.

Edmonds, F. 1987. *Another bloody tour.* London.

Electricity Act. 1947. 10 and 11, Geo. 6, *Public General Acts and the Church Assembly Measures of 1947*, vol. 2. London, 1947.

Falkus, M. E. 1977. The development of municipal trading in the nineteenth century. *Business History* 19(2): 134-61.

Foreman-Peck, J. 1987. Natural monopoly and railway policy in the nineteenth century. *Oxford Economic Papers* 39: 699-718.

1994. Industry and industrial organisation in the inter-war years. In *The economic history of Britain since 1700*, ed. R. Floud and D. McCloskey, 2, pp. 386-414. Cambridge.

Foreman-Peck, J., and R. Millward. 1994. *Public and private ownership of British industry, 1820-1990.* Oxford.

Foreman-Peck, J., and M. Waterson. 1985. The comparative efficiency of public and private enterprise in Britain: Electricity generation between the world wars. *Economic Journal* 95 supp: 83-95.

Garcke, E. 1896. *Manual of electrical undertakings and directory of officials*, vol. 1, *1896, London journals.* London.

Gourvish, T. 1986. *British railways, 1948-73: A business history.* Cambridge.

1991. The rise (and fall?) of state-owned enterprise. In *Britain since 1945*, ed. T. Gourvish and A. O'Day, pp. 111-34. Basingstoke.

Gray, H. 1968. *The cost of council housing.* London.

Greasley, D. 1990. Fifty years of coal mining productivity: The record of the British coal industry before 1939. *Journal of Economic History* 50(4): 877-902.

1995. The coal industry: Images and realities on the road to nationalisation. In *The political economy of nationalisation in Britain, 1920-50*, ed. R. Millward and J. Singleton, pp. 37-64. Cambridge.

Griliches, Z. 1988. Productivity puzzles and R and D: Another non-explanation. *Journal of Economic Perspectives* 2: 9-21.

Hannah, L. 1976. *The rise of the corporate economy*. London.

1979. *Electricity before nationalisation*. London.

1994. The economic consequences of the state ownership of industry, 1945-90. In *The economic history of Britain since 1700*, ed. R. Floud and D. McCloskey, 3, pp. 168-94. Cambridge.

Hassan, J. 1995. The water industry: A failure of public policy? In *The political economy of nationalisation in Britain, 1920-50*, ed. R. Millward and J. Singleton, pp. 189-211. Cambridge.

Heald, D., and D. Steel. 1982. Privatising public enterprises: An analysis of the government's case. *Political Quarterly* 33. Reprinted in *Privatisation and regulation: The U.K. experience*, ed. J. Kay, C. Mayer, and D. Tompson, pp. 58-77. Oxford, 1984.

Heyworth Report. 1945. *Report of the committee of inquiry into the gas industry, 1945*. Command 6699, May 1945, *P.P.* 1945/6, xii.

Howlett, P. 1994. British businessmen and the state during the Second World War. In *World War II and the transformation of business systems*, ed. J. Sakudo and T. Shiba, pp. 133-53. Tokyo.

Kendrick, J. W. 1987. Service-sector productivity. *Business Economics* 22(2): 18-24.

Kirby, M. W. 1977. *The British coal mining industry, 1870-1946*. London.

Littlechild, S. C. 1978. *The fallacy of the mixed economy: An Austrian critique of economic theory and policy*. London.

Lyth, P. 1990. A multiplicity of instruments: The 1946 decision to create a separate British European Airline and its effects on airline productivity. *Journal of Transportation History* 11(2): 1-17.

1995. The changing role of government in British civil air transport, 1919-49. In *The political economy of nationalisation in Britain, 1920-50*, ed. R. Millward and J. Singleton, pp. 65-87. Cambridge.

Matthews, R. C. O., C. H. Feinstein, and J. C. Odling-Smee. 1982. *British economic growth, 1856-1973*. Oxford.

Mcgowan Report. 1936. *Report of the committee on electricity distribution*. Ministry of Transport, May 1936.

Millward, R. 1988. The United Kingdom services sector: Productivity change and the recession in long-term perspective. *Service Industries Journal* 8(3): 263-76.

1990. Productivity in the U.K. services sector: Historical trends 1856-1985 and comparisons with U.S.A. 1950-85. *Oxford Bulletin of Economics and Statistics* 52(4): 423-35.

1991. The emergence of gas and water monopolies in nineteenth-century Britain: Contested markets and public control. In *New perspectives on the late Victorian economy*, ed. J. Foreman-Peck, pp. 96-124. Cambridge.

1997. The 1940s nationalisations: Means of production or means to an end? *Economic History Review* 50(2): 209-34.

Millward, R., and S. Sheard. 1995. The urban fiscal problem, 1870-1914: Government expenditure and finances in England and Wales. *Economic History Review* 48(3): 501-35.

Millward, R., and J. Singleton, eds. 1995. *The political economy of nationalisation in Britain, 1920-50*. Cambridge.

Millward, R., and R. Ward. 1987. The costs of public and private gas enterprises in late nineteenth-century Britain. *Oxford Economic Papers* 39: 719-37.

1993. From private to public ownership of gas undertaking in England and Wales, 1851-1947: Chronology, incidence and causes. *Business History* 35(3): 1-21.

Ministry of Fuel and Power. 1948. *Engineering and financial statistics of all authorised undertakings 1946/7*. Electricity Supply Act (41-213-0-47).

Molyneux, R., and D. J. Thompson. 1986. The efficiency of the nationalised industries since 1978. Institute of Fiscal Studies Working Paper no. 100.

1987. "Nationalised industry performance: Still third rate?" *Fiscal Studies* 8(1): 48-82.

Moore, J. 1986. The success of privatisation. In *Privatisation and regulation: The U.K. experience*, ed. J. Kay, C. Mayer, and D. Thompson, pp. 94-7. Oxford.

Murie, A. 1985. What can the councils afford?: Housing under the Conservatives. In *Implementing government policy initiatives: The Thatcher administration, 1979-83*, ed. P. Jackson, pp. 169-87. London.

Olson, M. 1982. *The rise and decline of nations*. New Haven, Conn.

Paige, D., and G. Bombach. 1959. *A comparison of national output and productivity of the United Kingdom and United States of America*. Paris.

Parker, D. 1993. Privatisation ten years on: A critical analysis of its rationale and results. In *Britain's economic miracle: Myth or reality?*, ed. N. M. Healey, pp. 174-94. London.

Pryke, R. 1981. *The nationalised industries: Policies and performance since 1968*. Oxford.

Ranieri, R. 1995. Partners and enemies: The government's decision to nationalise steel, 1944-8. In *The political economy of nationalisation in Britain, 1920-50*, ed. R. Millward and J. Singleton, pp. 275-305. Cambridge.

Reid Report. 1945. *Report of the technical advisory committee on coal mining*. Command 6610, 1945, *P.P.* 1944/5, iv.

Robson, W. A. 1935. The public utility services. In *A century of municipal progress: The last one hundred years*, ed. H. J. Laski, W. I. Jennings, and W. A. Robson, pp. 299-331. London.

Rostas, L. 1948. *Comparative productivity in British and American industry*. Cambridge.

Roth, G. J. 1966. *A self-financing road system*. London.

Samuel Commission. 1926. *Report of the royal commission on the coal industry*. Command 2600, 1926, *P.P.* 1926, xiv.

Sankey Commission. 1919. *Coal industry commission act: Interim report*. Command 84, 1919, *P.P.*, xi.

Shackleton, J. R. 1982. Privatisation: The case examined. *National Westminster Bank Review* (May): 59–73.

Smith, A. D., D. M. W. N. Hitchens, and S. W. Davies. 1982. *International industrial productivity: A comparison of Britain, America and Germany.* Cambridge.

Steel, D., and D. Heald. 1985. The privatisation of public enterprises, 1979–83. In *Implementing government policy initiatives: The Thatcher administration, 1979–83*, ed. P. Jackson, pp. 69–91. London.

Supple, B. 1986. Ideology or pragmatism?: The nationalisation of coal, 1916–46. In *Business life and public policy: Essays in honour of D. C. Coleman*, ed. N. Mckendrick and R. B. Outhwaite, pp. 228–50. Cambridge.

Transport Act. 1947. 10 and 11, Geo. 6, *Public General Acts and the Church Assembly Measures of 1947*, vol. 2. London, 1947.

Tugenhadt, G. 1963. *Freedom for fuel.* London.

Weir Committee. 1926. *Report of the committee appointed by the Board of Trade to review the national problem of the supply of electricity energy.*

Williamson Committee. 1918. *Report of a committee appointed to consider the question of electric power supply.* Command 9062, *P.P.* 1918, vii.

Wilson, J. 1995. The motives for gas nationalisation: Practicality or ideology? In *The political economy of nationalisation in Britain, 1920–50*, ed. R. Millward and J. Singleton, pp. 144–63. Cambridge.

8

∞

The Rise and Decline of State-Owned
Industry in Twentieth-Century France

EMMANUEL CHADEAU

The question of public enterprise, especially state-owned[1] and state-controlled enterprise,[2] is crucial in contemporary French history. France witnessed three peaks in nationalization under left-wing governments (1936–7, 1945–6, 1982) and had an earlier tradition of state-created, state-owned, and state-controlled firms. By the early 1980s the state was involved in all major industries, including energy, machine tools, glass, car manufacturing, chemicals, pharmaceuticals, shipping, banking, insurance, and aircraft manufacturing.[3] More than 90 percent of energy production (electricity, gas, oil, coal), 75 percent of insurance and

---

[1] Due to the brevity of this essay, the question of local publicly owned firms has been excluded. Many of these were, and are, involved in electricity or gas supply, public transportation, port authorities (including airports) and, from the 1960s, real estate and housing development. State- or locally controlled and managed cooperatives have also been excluded, as have associations dedicated to various economic activities and affiliated with public firms or even public administration.

[2] France has had many firms in which the state owns few or no shares, but appoints the CEO and other managers and controls or scrutinizes their management.

[3] This is to say nothing of television. In 1986 there were four television channels, three of which were state-owned and the fourth privately owned but state-controlled through a 25 percent share owned by the public news agency Havas. From the late 1940s, most television films and entertainment broadcast on public channels were produced by a state-owned production company with its own studios in Paris. The employees were public servants and had jobs for life.

banking, and 35 percent of industrial production (including 45 percent of car manufacturing, 90 percent of aircraft and jet engine manufacturing, and 60 percent of telecommunications) belonged to public firms. Only a few industries were completely independent of public firms: retailing, food,[4] clothing,[5] and newspapers.[6]

This achievement in the public economy contrasted with the huge and rapid turn toward privatization that took place beginning in 1986-7. Over a ten-year period, the state sold many of the firms that had been nationalized in 1944-6 or 1982-3. Even some of the firms that had been established or nationalized by the state before the socialist-inspired nationalization program of 1936 were returned to private ownership – for example, tobacco production. There has been a considerable public debate about the advantages and disadvantages of both nationalization and privatization. The performance of state-owned enterprises (SOEs), by both micro- and macroeconomic criteria, has been discussed widely. Experts have contributed many reports and books to the argument about how best to manage SOEs. Although France had previously been a homeland for the public sector, attitudes changed very quickly in the second half of the 1980s. SOEs fell from favor, and there was a strong move toward privatization and deregulation. It is worth asking why so many people regarded nationalization and state control or management as an efficient remedy for economic slumps and the proverbial "shortsighted market" – and why these later came to be seen as obstacles to prosperity and efficiency.

BACKGROUND

The first peak in nationalization came in 1936-7. It was introduced by the left-wing Parliament elected in June 1936 and by a government led mainly by socialists and the "advanced" wing of the Radical Party.[7]

---

[4] Although several public banks or insurance companies owned and operated large vineyards, especially in the Bordeaux area.

[5] Textiles had been partly nationalized in 1982, through the fiber branch of Rhône-Poulenc Co.

[6] Although French daily newspapers had long been unprofitable, and they were heavily subsidized through postal rates.

[7] The main socialist leaders were the prime minister (Président du Conseil), Léon Blum, the minister of finance, Vincent Auriol, and the state undersecretary for mining, Paul Ramadier. The "new radical" leaders were the war minister, Georges Daladier, the air minister, Pierre Cot, and the vice prime minister, Albert Sarraut. The government was accepted by a Chambre des Députés in which the Communist and Socialist parties held 40 percent of

Nationalization involved many aircraft and armament factories. Aircraft production was reorganized into six new mixed-capital state-dominated firms. Firearm and tank production was reorganized into state workshops.[8] An act passed on 24 July 1936 put the Bank of France under tighter governmental control. As previously, the governor of the bank remained a cabinet appointee, but the executive council of the bank, the Conseil des Régents, was reformed. Until July 1936 the executive council had been chosen by the governor from among the 200 main shareholders – mainly bankers or prominent industrialists. The executive council now became a Conseil General (advisory board), with two members appointed by the whole assembly of shareholders and nine by the cabinet (Andrieu 1990, 31–41; Dauphin-Meunier 1937; Dromer 1978). In July 1937 the industrial assets of the five main railroad companies were purchased and amalgamated with the old Cie des Chemins de Fer de l'Etat within a new Société Nationale des Chemins de Fer Français (SNCF) responsible for a 35,000-km national trunk and secondary line network.[9] Railroad nationalization followed the 1933

---

the seats, the radicals (left-wing or moderate) 25 percent, and the traditional right-wing parties the remaining third. Despite being more conservative, the senate tolerated the government's economic decisions until the spring of 1937.

[8] Nationalization was enacted on 11 August 1936. In the aircraft industry the final cost was FF. 451 million in payments to expropriated companies or entrepreneurs. A further FF. 250 million was paid to the large arms companies that had been expropriated – the Oscar Brandt factories, Schneider (guns), and Renault and Saint-Chamond (tanks) specialized workshops. The two main aircraft engine manufacturers, Gnome & Rhône and the Hispano-Suiza Cies, which were both listed on the Paris stock exchange, were not nationalized. Hispano-Suiza's main shareholders were Swiss citizens (the Birkigt family) and depended for licenses on a family trust located in Switzerland. For this reason, it was agreed that French manufacture and current French production would be shifted to a local subsidiary, the Société Française d'Exploitation des Moteurs Hispano-Suiza, and this subsidiary paid for the main French plants, work force, licenses, and models. The French state bought 10 percent of the shares and could appoint two members of the board. The Air Ministry made an unsuccessful attempt to buy 10 percent of Gnome & Rhône Co. shares on the stock exchange. Twelve aircraft manufactures remained private or family properties. For further details see Chadeau 1987, 308–98 and annexes. For a case of a resistant private owner see Chadeau 1990, 290–308. For a comparative essay on the establishment of the public sector in European aircraft manufacturing in the 1930s see Chadeau 1996, 216–61. The transfer of gun and tank plants to public workshops was dealt with by Frankenstein 1981, 270ff. This last underestimates the transfer cost because during his research the author was denied access, for legal reasons, to the confidential archives of the Treasury and the Chamber of Counts (Cour des Comptes).

[9] Railway nationalization occurred on the expiration of the charter granting the network to private companies. Assets were exchanged through a combination of time-limited but guaranteed shares and bonds issued by the new company. Some of the huge previous debt was refunded by the state, and some was paid off through expropriated shares. The old

regulation of the transport industry, when the main private airlines were amalgamated into Air France, a mixed-capital firm, and when one of the largest shipping companies, the Compagnie Générale Transatlantique, was partly purchased by the state. Many people interpreted these events as proof that nationalization was a socialist good that came out of economic decline.

A new, larger round of nationalization occurred in 1945–6. This program was characteristic of the dominant desire of the early postwar period to give back to the nation the main means of production and exchange. France was a devastated country, and the nationalization program, aided by strong pressure from the Communist Party and its affiliated trade union, the Confédération Générale du Travail (CGT), received overwhelming parliamentary approval. The Free French government of General de Gaulle embarked on a heavy program of nationalization in March 1944, the details of which had been planned by the Conseil National de la Résistance (CNR, National Resistance Council). This program was implemented by the Free French on their return to Paris between August 1944 and June 1946. The capital of the Bank of France was taken over by the state, and the four biggest commercial banks (Société Générale, Crédit Lyonnais, Comptoir National d'Escompte, and Banque Nationale du Commerce et de l'Industrie) were nationalized on 2 December 1945. Another act in 1946 nationalized thirty-six insurance companies, about half of the industry. Two important manufacturing companies, Gnome & Rhône (aircraft engines) and Renault (cars), together valued at 2 billion francs,[10] were confiscated under Communist pressure as a result of two pieces of legislation that came into force on 15 January and 31 July 1945.[11] A further act on 14

companies (Cie du Nord, de l'Est, du PLM, du Midi, Paris-Orléans) kept many nonindustrial assets (for instance, housing and real estate near network locations, especially in Paris) and could later use their compensation as collateral to raise money as holding or portfolio companies.

[10] The final valuation of the Société Anonyme des Usines Renault (SAUR) net assets was made in early 1949, when Louis Renault's inheritance taxes were shared between his family and the 1945 Régie Nationale des Usines Renault (RNUR). It was then valued at about FF 1,220 million (source: Renault family archives, Paris). The value of Gnome & Rhône can be estimated from the fact that its main shareholder, "Commodore" Paul-Louis Weiller, received FF 550 million for his 76 percent share in the company's capital after his share of the 1939–40 dividend (FF 23 million). Source: private archives, Paris.

[11] It soon appeared that these nationalizations were not the result of the CNR program, but rather of pressure from the Communist Party and its affiliate trade union, the CGT. They were suspected of active cooperation with German armament efforts. In fact, Renault factories had built about 32,000 trucks for the Germans between 1941 and 1944. Their main

July 1945 made the state almost the sole shareholder in Air France.[12] A few months later, on 26 April 1946, the coal mines, which had already been confiscated earlier in the summer of 1944, were incorporated into the public Charbonnages de France company. The latter was a financial and management holding company for its regional subsidiaries, the "Houillères de Bassin," which had been appointed to operate the coal mines and associated industrial assets (coke and gas plants, chemicals, and so on), together with their 200,000 employees (Trempé 1987). On 6 April 1946 another holding company, Electricité et Gaz de France (EGF), became responsible for two new public companies, Electricité de France (EDF) and Gaz de France (GDF), which had been set up to operate the expropriated electricity and gas suppliers. By the summer of 1946 it seemed that the claim of the CNR program had been met and that the main means of production had come back to the nation. Significantly, however, the most radical suggestion was not implemented. This concerned the nationalization of iron- and steelmaking, which had a capacity of 8 million tons and an effective production of 4.5 tons. These escaped legislation that would otherwise have brought not only basic industry under state control, but also a large part of intermediate industry (due to the large mechanical subsidiaries of iron- and steel-makers' groups).

The third peak in nationalization was the unsurprising result of the

domestic competitors, Peugeot and Citroën, had built similar or even larger numbers of trucks for the Wermacht, but they were not nationalized. The contracts for these 100,000 trucks formed part of the official cooperation between the Vichy government and the Germans and were not evidence of a special relation between the Renault company or its founder and leader, Louis Renault, and the Germans. Gnome & Rhône's largest shareholder and chief executive from 1922 to 1944, engineer Paul-Louis Weiller, had been fired and eventually jailed by the Vichy government late in 1940 because of the Jewish origins of his family and because of his well-known acquaintance with the prewar political establishment, especially the moderate left wing. From 1940 to 1944, the Gnome & Rhône company built several thousand engines for the Luftwaffe or as a subcontractor for BMW. All the contracts were ordered by the Vichy air administration in a French–German state joint program signed in June 1941. In both cases, nationalization was urged as a revenge for the prewar period, when both firms and their leaders were very active in the struggle against the growing influence of the Communist Party in French strategic industries. See Archives Nationales, Paris, Haute Cour de Justice, 3W 217–21, François Lehideux, 1945–9; Chadeau 1987, 349ff.

[12] The first Air France, created in 1933, had its fleet, crews, and ground staff incorporated into the Air Transport Administration, a branch of the Vichy Air Ministry, in 1941. Many officers and employees of the former Air France joined the Free French and the Free French Forces (Forces Françaises Libres). The Air France of 1945 can therefore be considered a new firm.

Table 8.1. Industrial Companies Nationalized in France in 1982

Name	Main Activity	Turnover (FF, billions)	No. of Employees (1,000s)
CII-Honeywell-Bull	Computers	7.3	21.2
Cie Gale d'Electricité (CGE)	Elect. equip.	56.7	180.4
Saint-Gobain	Glass, tubes	43.4	135.6
Matra	Elect./missiles	6.7	34.0
Rhône-Poulenc	Chemistry	30.2	89.3
Pechiney-Ugine Kuhlman (PUK)	Aluminium	41.0	86.1
Usinor	Steel	24.7	51.5
Sacilor	Steel	17.5	38.5
Dassault	Aircraft	12.5	5.8
Thomson-Brandt	Elect./household	43.7	29.0
ITT–France	Telecommunications	3.8	14.4
TOTAL		287.5	795.8

Data are for the year 1981.
Source: French Ministry for Economy and Finance.

1981 socialist–communist government appointed by President François
Mitterrand after the two ballots of May and June 1981. It was spectacular (see Table 8.1) because it left out the two main water supply companies operating within France, the Générale des Eaux and Lyonnaise
des Eaux, but touched groups involved in European and worldwide
competition. It particularly affected advanced aerospace companies
(Dassault, Bull, Matra, Thomson-Brandt), some multinational firms (Saint-
Gobain, Bull, Pechiney-Ugine Kuhlman [PUK], Rhône-Poulenc), and
multinational subsidiaries (ITT–France). Aside from these equipment or
manufacturing companies, more than thirty banks (including small local
ones) and financial groups were also nationalized. Both nationalization
acts were intended to complete the program initiated in 1945–6 and to
bring about the nation's control over the wealth it created.

BETWEEN PEAKS: A CONTINUOUS FLOW

The fact that nationalization reached peaks when radical, socialist-led,
left-wing governments were in power, and that they were supported
by the Communist Party, suggests that the destiny of French industry
depended strongly on political issues and on collectivist ideas. Such a

Table 8.2. Main Industrial State-Owned Firms Created in France, 1918–70

Year of Birth	Activity	Name of Company	Merged Later in
1919	Chemistry	Potasses d'Alsace	EMC[a]
1922	Chemistry	ONIA[b]	EMC
1924	Oil refining	CFR[c]	CFP (Total)
1928	Oil fields	CFP[d]	Total Group
1941	Oil fields	SNPA[e]	Elf-Aquitaine
1943	Oil fields	BRP[f]	Elf-Aquitaine
1945	Oil fields	ERAP[g]	Elf-Aquitaine
1959	Missiles	SEREB[h]	Aerospatiale
1967	Computers	CII[i]	Bull
1969	Nuclear fuel	COGEMA[j]	
1973	Nuclear eng.	Framatome	

[a] Entreprise Minière et Chimique.
[b] Office National Industriel de l'Azote.
[c] Compagnie Française de Raffinage.
[d] Cie Française des Pétroles.
[e] Sté Nationale des Pétroles d'Aquitaine.
[f] Bureau de Recherches Pétrolières.
[g] Etablissement des Régies Autonomes des Pétroles.
[h] Sté d'Etudes et de Réalisation d'Engins Balistiques.
[i] Compagnie Internationale d'Informatique.
[j] Compagnie Générale des Matières Nucléaires.

theory cannot, however, explain the continuous establishment of state-owned or state-controlled firms from the end of World War I to the end of the 1960s (see Table 8.2).

STATE AND INDUSTRY: A LASTING DEBATE

Nationalization and public enterprise were part of a continuous process of economic development that had begun in the early nineteenth century. For a long time, historians interpreted nationalization as a consequence of the older mercantilist tradition – but mercantilism more properly belongs to the age of the French monarchy, especially during the reign of Louis XIV (1643–1715). The real roots of nationalization lie in the new order established during the French Revolution and, more specifically, the Napoleonic Age (1798–1815). It was during these periods that private property and the private economy was subjected

to the law. If, on the one hand, the revolutionary age liberated employment and entrepreneurship from the old guilds or trade associations,
the Civil Code and further legislation extended public property to the
subsoil and ground transport infrastructures (roads, canals, harbors,
and so on). In parallel, properties and real estate previously in the possession of the Catholic Church, the crown, noble families, or chartered
companies (especially the Ferme Générale, which brought together
influential tax collectors and financiers) were transferred to the state or
to local authorities. This meant that during the early industrial period,
coal, iron, and other mines, railroads, shipping, armament production,
and postal services were publicly operated or awarded by the state to
private interests. The Bank of France, which was a company of private
bankers and merchants, had held the monopoly for issuing currencies
and credit discounts since 1801. Its monopoly was limited in time and
submitted to tight political control.[13] Similar grants were provided by
Parliament, under government control, each time a mining company,
and later a railroad, wanted to establish operations. In parallel, the
public works administration had a monopoly on road, bridge, and canal
building, which were all paid for out of public funds (national or local)
and were publicly operated.

   As a result, debates about the comparative advantages of public or
private operation, or ownership of the right to operate, governed the
way many companies and industries were established in nineteenth-
century France. All the chartered or state monopolies, from mining to
the postal service, were subject to a specific regulatory code enacted
or periodically revised as a result of parliamentary debate and administered by public servants. Strong regulation gave public servants, especially engineers and state controllers such as the Inspecteurs des
Finances, a prominent role in economic debates. These high-ranking
civil servants and military engineers were not just advisers and experts
with access to the government and Parliament. They were the people
who set the boundaries between private and national interests. They
were able to do so not merely by virtue of their skills and specialist train-
ing (first in the famous Ecole Polytechnique and then in the Ecoles des
Mines, des Ponts et Chaussées, des Eaux et Forêts, du Génie militaire
ou du Génie Maritime, and so on, or in the law faculties), but also
because they prepared the rules and ensured that public or private oper-

---

[13] The Banque de France charter was renewed in 1848 and 1897, the last time for forty
years, the grant being revocable by Parliament.

ators complied with them. The 1811 Mining Code, for example, established the rules and duties applicable to private companies operating mines (ranging from technical rules to security and statistical duties). It also set out in detail how the mining department and the mining advisory board (Conseil Général des Mines) should be organized, with its local branches and its central offices in Paris. A similar organization also existed for public works (including railways) and other industries, and this led, in the first half of the nineteenth century, to a common interest in the development of both public utilities and private enterprise. The "Saint-Simonians" were very influential within both public and private administration from the 1830s to the end of the Second Empire (1870). They were credited with having made the theory into an ideology; for having applied the ideology to railways and bank establishment and management; and for having been a strong influence on governmental changes toward modernity and big business.

The first change occurred in the 1880s and 1890s, when France achieved a parliamentary regime and local democracy. Many Republicans – especially the left-wing ones, who were influential in the Paris area and in the rather backward small southern towns – imagined that the age of cooperation between the state and big business was over. They believed that the public interest had to be supplemented by local democracy[14] to protect the "little man" from the influence of large firms or big business and to promote equality in popular welfare. Some of the debates of the 1880s illustrate how one ideal was replaced by another.

---

[14] The political reform achieved by the new 1875 Constitution and the ballot reforms of the early 1880s made the local community and local borough (the canton) the center of political life. Representatives were elected from boroughs of between 40,000 and 90,000 inhabitants (excluding women, who could not vote in pre-1944 France). Senators had the final power in making law, and were elected for eighty-seven districts (ninety after the recovery of eastern districts in 1919) by a constituency grouping local mayors (more than 36,000), some deputy mayors, and borough delegates, themselves polled by universal suffrage from the borough inhabitants. (A countryside borough consisted of two or more villages or small towns. France had more than 6,000 boroughs.) The assembly of borough delegates in each of the eighty-seven main districts (the Conseil Général) voted on the local budget (roads, secondary schools, etc.). Such a system had been built to counterbalance the previous influence of the state administration – both ministries and central power delegates in districts (the *préfets*) – and to establish the bicameral Parliament as a pivotal power more powerful than the cabinet and the president of the republic. National policy resulted mainly from expressions of local will or compromises between opposing local interests, and parliamentary parties became networks of local representatives who rose from local tenure to become representatives or senators. Entering the cabinet (even for a few months) was considered the supreme achievement in a political career. It could be achieved through consistently successful performance in the various assemblies.

In 1881–3 it seemed that the first large program of public works (mainly local railroads and new canals) launched by the new regime would have to be halted because of its cost. This was the Freycinet Plan, which took its name from its main promoter, the Republican representative and engineer Charles de Saulces de Freycinet. Debate over which part of the newly established networks should be granted to the existing large private networks divided Republicans as well as conservatives. The debate coincided with the rechartering of the large companies, which were forced to accept the new networks and their low return rates as the price for rechartering (Caron 1997). In the end, the added costs of the transfer were balanced by an enlarged Treasury guarantee of company loans, although this was accompanied by greater state control over company rates.

The second debate occurred in 1888–9, when half of the Western Railroad Company network that operated from Paris seemed threatened with failure. The question of its nationalization was raised, and Parliament was divided over who should pay for the company's future losses. The company was controlled by the public works administration, and it was argued that "public utility" considerations meant that the nation should bear the whole burden of both the previous and future losses. Very few politicians noticed that the company's failure had followed the publicly funded opening of new lines between 1878 and 1883. Ten years earlier, in 1879, there had been a debate involving the postal service. It had been a branch of the Home Office (Ministère de l'Intérieur) since its establishment in 1849 because mail and telegraph operations were closely connected with local government and politics.[15] The Republicans decided to free the postal and telegraph services from central and local police influence. It was then decided to make the service a state administration (in order to keep control over the news) and to put post offices under local administration rather than commercial control. Letter carriers remained public servants under a centralized hierarchical authority, and the possible losses of the service were charged to the annual budget. The advent of the telephone caused a debate about the relative roles of public utilities and commercial services. Telephone systems were first established in 1882 on a local scale, and were operated by competing start-up companies backed by equipment manufacturers. A law of 1889 provided that the new network should be

---

[15] Before July 1881 the reporting and circulation of news were under strict government and police control – the police being one of the main branches of the Home Office.

established on a local scale (the communal or district scale) and funded from local budgets – but that it should be operated by the postal service from post offices. The Republicans considered that such a complicated system joining very small networks together would protect the state's sovereignty over news circulation. They also believed that it would protect the ideal of the state's administrative monopoly over an advanced technology, and the role of the post office and of letter carriers as important features of local life.[16] (In spite of concern over maintaining the state's sovereignty over news circulation, the *préfets* and their offices in district *préfectures* were not the first to connect to the system.)[17] Debates about the telephone system were followed by debates about electric power. The problem of the 1880s was to decide how networks should be funded. Up to 1907, the first stage of regulation gave very extended power to local communities to establish power plants and distribution networks in their territories. Each town or district could fund private or community-owned companies. Both kinds of enterprise were subject to dual control: state administration for technical issues and town administration for financial matters. It was only between 1907 and 1911 that anxiety over the small size of these companies allowed for a reform permitting larger networks operating from bigger power plants, more capital-intensive operators, and larger, publicly funded companies (Beltran 1996).

The debate was fueled by the events of World War I. The war revealed the weakness of many French industries. The German occupation of industrial districts in the north and the east meant that France had to rely on Allied support for supplies of coal, iron, raw materials, machine tools, and explosives. On the one hand, transportation improvements revealed that France's national security was dependent on supplies from foreign oil fields and refineries. On the other hand, industrial

---

[16] As a result, cooperation between local networks in larger ones, the normalization of technology, lasted until early 1900. Firms that had pioneered in introducing telephone technology to France disappeared. Access to the network depended on when the post office was open. Some authors have argued that the regulatory rules that made user access to the network very expensive were responsible for the low density of telephone coverage in early-twentieth-century France. This view is disputed by the official historians of the French postal service. Eventually, the postal service became part of the public administration in 1923, but with its own separately voted budget.

[17] Fermaut-Minier (1990) shows that in the industrial district of northern France, demand for telephones came first from industrial companies and traders and second from the state administration. Industrial companies were connected before the powerful prefect of Lille, the capital of northern districts.

mobilization revived the traditional cooperation between the state administration and firms. It also revealed the employers' union's inability to meet the demand of the armament administration and the war ministry. The main partners of the state administration became industrial tycoons, such as Louis Renault, Eugène Schneider, André Citroën, and Louis Loucheur,[18] who were able to respond to the demand and to head up larger groups of affiliates and subcontracting firms (Carls 1993; Godfrey 1987). A new debate about mass production and the role of large firms sprang up in the war years. Should mass production be entrusted to large firms? Could France accept the establishment of huge private or listed manufacturing companies in industries such as automobiles, electric machines, machine tools, chemistry, and so on? This question was justified because during and after the war manufacturing firms favored both forward and backward integration with public enterprise: electric machinery and parts suppliers with power plants and power distribution. They also favored integration with industries partly dependent on public enterprise: car manufacturers with steelmaking. The previous "equilibrium" of large public firms in basic activities such as transportation and mining, and small or middle-sized firms in manufacturing, had nearly come to an end. Significantly, the socialists tried to reshape the relations between industries in July 1918, before the end of the war. They wanted legislation to put coal mines under state control.[19] Wartime oil and ammunitions shortages pushed the state in the 1920s, for security reasons, to create its own oil companies (for research abroad and refining in France) and its own nitrogen plant, and then to protect both from foreign competition.

CIRCUMSTANCES

The circumstances of each period encouraged enlarged public ownership and control. In the 1880s, as in the 1930s, several scandals showed the influence of big money on political life. Some of the scandals fostered a climate of rejection of large private firms and the role of banks in financing large technical projects. In 1881 and 1888, for example, there were two important failures: that of the Banque de l'Union Générale and that of the Compagnie du Canal de Panama. Both of these failures seemed to prove the dangerous influence of bankers or financiers on the government, and the corruption of newspapers and

[18] This is the reason Loucheur was appointed minister for armaments in September 1917.
[19] All of the project papers are in the Léon Blum Papers in Paris.

politicians. Both events stimulated the public perception that big money was open both to foreign influence, particularly British and German, and to the influence of cultural minorities such as the Jews. It was a common belief shared by left- and right-wing radicals in the 1920s and 1930s that any large failure or bankruptcy hid a political scandal and that only a stronger state – that is, a stronger state bureaucracy – would protect France. State control and public ownership were also encouraged by left-wing parties, and this attempted bolstering of organized mass socialism was combined with socialist influence over the non-industrial lower middle class such as low-ranking civil servants, small shopkeepers, and farmers. The ideal of socialist achievement was not focused on a "social economy" and cooperative association; rather, the objective was a more powerful state able to protect the "little man" (citizen and consumer) from the "big guys." In the 1930s and 1970s, employers' associations were unable to establish sufficiently large or complete mergers in the face of sectorial or general slumps.[20] This, coupled with their "provincialism"[21] and their inability in the 1930s to negotiate with trade unions and to promote collective agreements, weakened the employers' cause and encouraged the proponents of large-scale nationalization. In the 1970s, the Left accused large industrial corporations of redundancies,[22] unprofitability, management failure, and dependency on public subsidy (steelmaking, chemicals) or government orders (computers, electronics, aircraft or missiles manufacturers). They were thought to have shortsighted strategies for confronting international competition, to have insufficient investment – especially on French soil – and to be too ready to turn for capital to conglomerates, investment banks such as Suez or Paribas.[23]

METHODS OF PUBLIC SECTOR ENLARGEMENT

Three main methods were used to enlarge the public sector. The most common method, degranting, was used by the state in the case of the Banque de France, railways and other transportation, electricity, gas, and coal mining. Degranting reopened public debate about financial policy.

---

[20] Electricity companies in the 1930s, steel and chemical companies in the 1930s and 1970s.
[21] Especially in the case of mining companies in the 1930s.
[22] Steelmakers laid off 35 percent of their work force between 1973 and 1979. The work force dropped from 160,000 to 105,000.
[23] Examples of this literature include Boublil 1977; Club Socialiste du Livre 1980; Lorenzi and Le Boucher 1979 (on the CII-Bull Company); Morin 1975; and *Programme Commun de la Gauche*, Paris, May 1972.

Would a degranted company provide greater efficiency and lower costs than a public enterprise firm? Degranting gave the state a virtual monopoly over an industry. The nationalization of electric power in 1946, for example, came about through legislation that degranted the whole distribution network. The legislation gave the state three-quarters of the electricity plants and prevented other suppliers (for instance, railways or aluminum makers) from selling the power generated by their own plants. The second method was purchase through legislation. This was used to nationalize banks and insurance companies in 1945-6 and again in 1981-2. It was suitable for nongranted industries and allowed for firm-by-firm selection of those that were to enter the public sector. Finally, one of the most original methods for enlarging the public sector was through the start-up of new public firms. This was used in so-called strategic industries such as oil, chemicals, and nuclear power. It was responsible in 1922 for the establishment of the Office National Industriel de l'Azote, which later became part of Entreprise Minière et Chimique. It was also responsible in 1924-8 for the establishment of the Compagnie Française de Raffinage and the Compagnie Française des Pétroles, which later became the Total Group. The same method was used in 1941-5 to establish the first components of the future Elf company. Start-ups were used again in 1968-73 with the industrial subsidiaries of the CEA (Commissariat à l'Energie Atomique), such as COGEMA (Compagnie Générale des Matières Nucléaires) and Framatome.

GOALS

Some of the goals set for the industrial public sector were widely publicized, for instance those dealing with the concept of equity. The nationalization of the subsoil, and then its granting or degranting, were done to protect the nation, considered as the new sovereign, against the private owners' interests. During World War I, coal and subsoil supplies in general were much-needed strategic resources that had to be protected against waste and the shortsighted policies of owners. In the case of roads (including railroads, canals, and later air routes), the prevailing idea was that of equity of access from one place to another within French territory and equity of access to any good. From the 1930s on, it was claimed that public enterprise resulted in cheaper equipment and operation because it did not have to make profits for private owners or shareholders. This meant that when public enterprise was profitable, its profits could be returned to the whole nation. The theory of equity considered French soil as a commonwealth in need of protection from division. This theory was extended to include all other goods, including imports, that could protect the nation when times were bad; in this way, oil and nitrogen became part of national security and strategic needs. The same theory of equity lay behind the nationalization of the oil and chemical industries after World War I and the nationalization of electricity and gas in 1946.

Less publicized but still important goals were the growth of the gross national product and the protection of France from foreign technical or commercial competition – war being considered a specific period of competition. This explains why the state administration established oil firms from the 1940s to the 1970s, not just to provide domestic refineries on overseas fields, but also as credible challengers to the U.S. and U.K. "majors" (Catta 1990; Péan and Séréni 1982; Soutou and Beltran 1995). The firms nationalized after World War II were already presented as the principal agents for reconstruction and modernization, and they benefited from public investment and protected rates from the beginning of the Marshall Plan up to the 1950s (Monnet 1976; Roussel 1996; Rousso 1986). The first task of Electricité de France was the unification and standardization of the power distribution network. Its second, to be achieved through the huge 1946–54 new dam program, was to meet the rapid growth of the electricity market and consumption.[24] Coal mines were governed by a "battle for coal" spirit and a thrust toward modernization that was coordinated at ministerial levels and highly subsidized. The main goals were to reduce French dependence on external supplies and to supply cheaper coal to domestic industry (Thullier 1987; Trempé 1987). Publicly owned firms, especially energy and transport companies, became the main investors in France and also the main long-term borrowers on the Paris financial market after the end of the Marshall Plan in 1952 (Cazes 1991). They were, at the same time, some of the largest companies in Europe, promoting their own technologies[25] and large-scale management for the heavy orders they gave to many industrial suppliers.

---

[24] Beltran et al. 1985. In this postwar context, a view from the inside is provided by Marcel Boiteux (1993), who spent his whole career at EDF, beginning in 1949.

[25] Especially EDF, SNCF, and the publicly owned aircraft manufacturers, with the twin-engine short-range carrier Caravelle (1955) or the first non-U.S. or non-U.K. helicopters in Europe (1955–7).

This experience conditioned the 1981 nationalization of many large industrial firms. All of them were considered by the Left as having failed to match international competition. They were seen as failing in the case of foreign competition because they remained smaller than their principal competitors in the United States, Britain, Japan, and Germany. They were also seen as having failed in the case of domestic competition because they were suspected of neglecting employment and capital expenditure within France. Nationalization was perceived as a way of protecting France from the globalization of the economy and from competition among European Economic Community (EEC) firms. According to the 1981 reformers, the new public firms would achieve two goals. First, they would win back the domestic market, which had supposedly been invaded by foreign goods.[26] Second, they would enhance employment. In 1983–5 reformers publicly stated a third goal. The new nationalized companies had to streamline all the firms within their own field of activity, which was now called their "profession": glass and materials at Saint-Gobain, chemicals and pharmaceuticals at Rhône-Poulenc, computer hardware at Bull, and so on. This so-called stream politics was intended to help all industries to meet domestic demands. It was designed to reshape industry as a result of the orders given by large publicly owned firms to their subcontractors and subsidiaries and through technological spinoffs (Boublil 1977; Zinsou 1985).

A fourth goal has been identified by historians and political scientists (Birnbaum 1977; Brun 1985). This consisted of founding a mystical relation between the masses and the state. The state here included the politicians and high-ranking civil servants who were appointed as public-sector managers. The intention was that the masses would be enlightened by the state. At the end of the nineteenth century, the birth of the state-owned railroads Chemins de Fer de l'Etat anticipated the 1906 and 1920 Railways Craftsmen Charter, which defined employee status and carriers. The charter applied to all company employees before complete nationalization in 1937 (Baudouï 1991). In 1936 and 1937

---

[26] One episode of this "reconquest" occurred in 1983, when the government – one year after Thomson-Brandt, the main television manufacturer, had been nationalized – indirectly prohibited imports of Asian magnetoscope sets by forcing the imported ones to undergo a long "customs clearing" wait at Poitiers, a small town in west-central France. Poitiers was where the Frank warrior Charles Martel defeated Muslim invaders in 732.

nationalized aircraft companies were given workers' delegates on their boards of directors (Chadeau 1987, chapter 8; Chapman 1991). From 1945 on, Régie Renault was legally instituted[27] as a social model in which trade unionists and managers shared control over the labor force.[28] Renault was an industrial relations "laboratory" for a long time. Longer holidays, higher wages, and social institutions were tested there before their full legal adoption. In 1981–2 Régie Renault was the model. Every new state-owned firm had workers on its board and was encouraged to become a new Renault. In general, the public sector after World War II became the main base for French trade unionism (the state bureaucracy being its second home). In some companies, such as Electricité de France or Gaz de France, up to 1 percent of annual turnover was remitted to the social institutions headed by employees' representatives (Association pour l'Histoire de l'Electricité en France 1997, especially 303–15). All of these enterprises practiced employment for life, and some of them recognized the shop-steward principle of craftsman recruitment.

ORIGINS OF DECLINE

Denationalization broke out suddenly in 1986–7, after the victory of the Right (an alliance of Liberal, Social Christian, and Gaullist parties) in the general ballot for representatives of March 1986. In two years, some of the industrial firms nationalized in 1981–2 (Saint-Gobain, Pechiney, Rhône-Poulenc, Matra, CGE-Alcatel) were sold back to investors, as were some of the "new" public banks (Suez, Paribas, etc.). Some firms that had been nationalized in 1945, such as the second biggest commercial bank, the Société Générale, were also sold for symbolic reasons. Although President François Mitterrand's reelection in June 1988 halted the move back to private firms, the conservative Cabinet led by Edouard Balladur in 1993–5 deepened it, as did the Juppé Cabinet in the first two years of President Jacques Chirac's term in office (June 1995 to May 1997). By December 1996, only a few groups of the industrial public sector that had been created over six decades remained: Aerospatiale and Snecma, Air France and Air Inter, the SNCF, Thomson-CSF,

---

[27] By the 16 January 1945 nationalization legislation. Original text and file in French National Archives, Paris, AN F12 10103, file "Renault."

[28] Dreyfus 1981. Dreyfus was Renault's CEO from 1955 to 1975.

Charbonnages de France,[29] EDF, Gaz de France, the CEA subsidiaries,[30] and France Telecom.[31]

The decade of privatization had been long prepared for through the development of doctrines preaching denationalization among the French political and civil service elite. The huge nationalization program of 1981 was merely the last attempt to promote ideas that were already outdated in many circles. Reaganomics and Thatcherism were not the major influences on the debate between the supporters and opponents of privatization. The strongest influences were the past experience of state-enterprise management and the problems raised by government control of a significant part of industry. These issues were very closely related.

The golden age of publicly owned firms ended in the 1960s, when the ambitious government-led Gaullist or neo-Colbertist industrial policy, established ten years earlier, had reached its limits. The main limit was the challenge of free industrial exchange inside the EEC. This pushed President Georges Pompidou and his government from 1969 to 1974 to concentrate on the establishment of large, private companies that could compete against their German, British, or Dutch counterparts. Less significance was given to doctrinal debates about the essential role supposedly played by the public sector in stimulating growth and modernization. It was clear that serious reforms would have to be implemented in strategic industries under state control if they were to become compatible with the new market. From 1958 to 1968, the public aircraft industry had contracted from five to two firms – Aerospatiale and the enlarged Snecma, both inaugurated in 1969 – in order to carry out large projects. Such large projects included joint ventures with European and American partners such as Airbus, designed in 1967 and launched in 1969, the Ariane launcher in 1972–3, and the Snecma/ General Electric/MTU collaboration on the CF6 engine in 1969 (Chadeau 1995a, 1995b). After the French withdrawal from Algeria in

[29] CDF had lost all its chemical subsidiaries between 1982 and 1986. In 1997 it operated only three small coal fields with 12,000 coal miners, compared with 450,000 in 1959 and 230,000 in 1968.

[30] In the financial sector, the following remained state-owned: two main commercial banks, Crédit Lyonnais and Crédit Industriel et Commercial Group (CIC), one main insurance company, GAN (Groupe des Assurances Nationales, the main shareholder of the CIC banking group), and a few small (and unprofitable) banks.

[31] France Telecom was born in 1987 as a commercial public institution. Earlier it had been the telephone branch of the Post and Telephone Administration. In October 1997, 11 percent of its capital was sold to investors and to the German Deutsche Telekom.

1962, the public oil industry had to be reshaped. ERAP and BRP, together with their research and oilfield subsidiaries, had to match tougher competition abroad from the majors and tougher domestic competition from the state-controlled CFP. Finally, several mergers brought about the 1967 establishment of Elf-ERAP, which was committed to enlarging its role in foreign markets and to applying for membership in the majors club (Soutou and Beltran 1995).

State ownership and control showed its weaknesses, in terms of delay, when the so-called old sectors of industry encountered unfavorable long-term conditions. At the end of the 1950s, the protected coal mines were seriously challenged on prices, investment costs, and labor force productivity, as well as by imported coal and by the oil industry. A large downsizing program was announced by the minister for industry, Jean-Marcel Jeanneney, in December 1959. It called for closing many mines over the following ten to fifteen years. The plan could not be seriously considered, however, until 1964 because the coal miners, as well as the managers of coal districts, refused it. The plan was fully implemented only after 1968, following tough negotiations. In the interval, CDF chemical branches were grouped into a new subsidiary, SCC (Société Chimique des Charbonnages, known under its trademark, CDF-Chimie). SCC itself had to face the challenge of competition from another state-owned chemical company, EMC (Entreprise Minière et Chimique). Both enterprises tried, with the help of public subsidies, to compete not only with the oil refining groups, but even with traditional private chemical groups (Péchiney–Saint-Gobain, Kühlmann). Finally, in the 1970s, they both had to join the oil companies to build a new large unit. Confusion resulted from this situation in which public companies competed against each other in some markets, cooperated in others, and planned giant plants. As the chemicals market slumped in 1974, all the companies attempted to save themselves, and to protect their plants and the planned new one. At the end of the 1970s, French chemical companies were in the red, weighed down by overcapacity. Through the 1981 nationalization of Rhône-Poulenc, the PUK Group, and Saint-Gobain, the government attempted to clear the whole sector, but between 1983 and 1986 the whole sector was sold, mainly to the oil group Elf and its subsidiaries or to foreign companies.

The coal mining and chemical industries' difficulties publicized a major problem that had been noted in 1967 by some experts in a white paper on public industry: the inadequacy of state control in the development of long-term strategy in an open economy (Nora 1967). During Georges Pompidou's term in office, it was decided to modernize the relations between public firms and the state in order to save the public enterprises and to protect the Treasury from further public-enterprise deficits or investment needs. An agreement signed by both partners in 1971 promoted a new kind of management. Larger public firms had to include their investment and employment programs within a market forecast. They were further obliged to turn to the financial market – international as well as domestic – for long-term loans and to initiate financial planning. Many of them discovered that they did not even have a financial department, and they had to invent one. They were expected to scrutinize prices and costs. When necessary, they were asked to transform some or many of their branches into subsidiaries. In exchange for these changes, they were permitted to set some of their own rates and prices within a range previously negotiated with the state.

The new system meant that after 1976 most of the largest public companies were obliged to create a balance among debt, employment, wage rates, investment, and capital expenditure. Over the next ten years, public industrial companies lost between a quarter and a third of their work force, and although the socialists tried to oblige old and new state-owned firms to recruit more workers in 1981–2, the trend could not be halted because of the huge gap between worker productivity generally and worker productivity in public firms.

At the beginning of the 1980s, none of the attempts to save public companies from themselves could hide the dangers threatening them. One of these problems was their huge need for capital programs, which exceeded the capacity of the state to provide new equity capital. The 1981–2 nationalization cost FF. 37 billion in share redemptions. A further FF. 27 billion was spent over three years in reshaping. At the same time, the added need for share capital in both the old and new public sectors exceeded FF. 35 billion. Public-sector long-term debt was estimated at approximately FF. 400 billion – an annual charge of FF. 50 billion supported by customers or clients. The state could not afford either to increase capital or to subsidize added losses, and new techniques for raising equity capital were used. These new techniques were the cause of a reform of the Paris financial market. The international capital market supplied public firms through bonds convertible into shares and other means, which suggested that the financing of many state-owned firms would soon be transferred from government to banks and private funds.

A new doctrine began to be heard in government circles in praise of greater autonomy for state-owned or state-controlled firms. This ran counter to the long tradition of governmental guidance. The new doctrine appeared at the time of France's negotiations with its European partners over the 1986 European Unit Act; this was approved by Parliament early in 1987. The new doctrine was popular with the leaders of many publicly owned companies, since it gave them more freedom in return for the attention they now had to give to strategic planning, employment policy, and financial results. The last macroeconomic link between public firms and government policies was then cut, and only their monopolistic position in France remained. The Maastricht Treaty condemned this last protecting wall.

In the 1970s and early 1980s, the circumstances that had sustained the vogue for nationalization in the past now helped the return to capitalism. In the early 1970s, Régie Renault seemed to be protected, by its very nature, from market injuries. Its main domestic competitors, Citroën and Peugeot, were forced first to merge and then to request huge bank loans. In the early 1980s, however, Renault itself was in the red, its cars were below market-quality standards, and it was forced to dismiss workers, to sell off subsidiaries, and finally to close its historic plant at Billancourt, which had been the symbol of Parisian working-class struggles since the 1930s. Nationalized steelmaking, previously a symbol of gaining back the domestic market, survived in the 1980s only through massive dismissals, investment abroad, and furnace or plant closures. Just before the first European sky-opening agreement on regional lines in 1993, Air France and Air Inter air carriers had recruited an extra 10 percent of personnel in nonoperative branches; suddenly they had to reduce employment and/or wages while losing both money and their monopoly on dozens of routes. The final touch was given by the huge Group Crédit Lyonnais, a historic institution in European banking, where top management mistakes, fraud, and insane governmental guidance destroyed both the bank and the faith of those who believed in the superiority of state-managed business over the "shortsighted" market. In the last years of the twentieth century, even socialist politicians turned their backs on state-owned industries except those operating undeniable public utilities: telecommunications, railways, and electric power. These were all sectors where only the power of trade unions could balance the temptation for better resource allocation and European-scale operations.

CONCLUSION

The French taste for nationalization is related to the attempts made by the whole country to protect itself from international competition and market rules. Nationalization implied a formal pact between the state bureaucracy elite and the radical trade unions, both of which were candidates for managing the domestic economy through the control of publicly owned firms. Public firms were viable in an environment of increasing public expenses tempered by inflation and budget deficits. Public enterprises permitted France to match technological competition from abroad within a protected domestic market and to execute market operations limited to domestic needs. Nationalization and industrial policy can be understood as part of a more general desire to preserve the French supremacy dating back to the period when the country had been the richest in Europe, led by "enlightened" monarchs following mercantilism. As François Furet (1997) suggests, nationalization and its resulting corporatism, its denial of free exchange and fair competition, played a part in hiding "the dawn of the special part [France] gave herself in the historical scene, since the Ancien Régime and the Revolution." Did the French taste for nationalization delay or hasten the country's international decline or did it simply accompany it? The answer to this last question remains open.

REFERENCES

Andrieu, C. 1990. *La banque sous l'Occupation: Paradoxes de l'histoire d'une profession*. Paris.
Association pour l'Histoire de l'Electricité en France. 1997. *La nationalisation de l'electricité en France, 1946-1996*. Paris.
Baudouï, R. 1991. *Raoul Dautry*. Paris.
Beltran, A. 1996. L'electricité à Paris et en région Parisienne, 1880-1945. Diss., Université Paris–IV–Sorbonne.
Beltran, A., M. Bungener, and J.-F. Picard. 1985. *Histoire(s) d'EDF*. Paris.
Birnbaum, P. 1977. *Les sommets de l'etat*. Paris.
Boiteux, M. 1993. *Haute-tension*. Paris.
Boublil, A. 1977. *Le socialisme industriel*. Paris.
Brun, G. 1985. *Technocrates et technocratie en France (1914-1945)*. Paris.
Carls, S. D. 1993. *Louis Loucheur and the reshaping of modern France, 1916-1931*. Baton Rouge.
Caron, F. 1997. *Histoire des chemins de fer en France*, vol. 1, *1740-1883*. Paris.
Catta, E. 1990. *Victor de Metz, de la CFP au groupe total*. Paris.
Cazes, B. 1991. Un demi-siècle de planification indicative. In *Entre l'etat et le*

marché: L'économie française des années 1880 à nos jours, ed. M. Lévy-Leboyer and J.-C. Casanova, pp. 473–506. Paris.

Chadeau, E. 1987. *L'industrie aeronautique en France: De Blériot à Dassault (1900–1950)*. Paris.

1990. *Latécoère*. Paris.

1996. *Le rêve et la puissance: L'avion et son siècle*. Paris.

ed. 1995a. *Airbus: Un succès industriel européen*. Paris.

ed. 1995b. *L'ambition technologique: Naissance d'Ariane*. Paris.

Chapman, H. 1991. *State capitalism and working-class radicalism in the French aircraft industry*. Berkeley.

Club Socialiste du Livre. 1980. *Socialisme et industrie*. Paris.

Dauphin-Meunier, A. 1937. *La Banque de France*. Paris.

Dreyfus, P. 1981. *Renault: Une nationalisation réussie*. Paris.

Dromer, L. 1978. *La réforme de la Banque de France du 24 juillet 1936*. Paris.

Fermaut-Minier, C. 1990. L'implantation du téléphone dans le Nord, 1882–1914. Diss., Université Charles de Gaulle–Lille 2.

Frankenstein, R. 1981. *Le prix du réarmement français (1936–1939)*. Paris.

Furet, F. 1997. L'enigme française. *Le Débat* 96.

Godfrey, J. F. 1987. *Capitalism at war: Industrial policy and bureaucracy in France, 1914–1918*. Leamington Spa., Eng.

Lorenzi, J.-H., and E. Le Boucher. 1979. *Mémoires volées*. Paris.

Monnet, J. 1976. *Mémoires*. Paris.

Morin, F. 1975. *Les groupes industriels français*. Paris.

Nora, S. 1967. *Rapport au Premier Ministre sur la gestion et les perspectives des entreprises publiques*. Paris.

Péan, P., and J.-P. Séréni. 1982. *Les emirs du pétrole*. Paris.

Programme Commun de la Gauche. May 1972. Paris.

Roussel, E. 1996. *Jean Monnet, 1888–1979*. Paris.

Rousso, H., ed. 1986. *De Monnet à Massé: Enjeux politiques et objectifs économiques dans le cadre des quatre premiers plans (1946–1965)*. Paris.

Soutou, G.-H., and A. Beltran, eds. 1995. *Pierre Guillaumat: La passion des grands projets industriels*. Paris.

Thuillier, J.-P. 1987. Les charbonnages et le plan, 1946–1958. In *De Monnet à Massé: Enjeux politiques et objectifs économiques dans le cadre des quatre premiers plans (1946–1965)*, ed. H. Rousso, pp. 89–102. Paris.

Trempé, R. 1987. *Les trois batailles du Charbon (1936–1947)*. Paris.

Zinsou, L. 1985. *Le fer de lance: Essai sur les nationalisations industrielles*. With an introduction by Laurent Fabius. Paris.

9

⌯⌯

The Rise and Decline of Spanish
State-Owned Firms

ALBERT CARRERAS, XAVIER TAFUNELL, AND
EUGENIO TORRES

Before the outbreak of the Spanish Civil War in 1936, there were very few public firms in Spain.[1] Those that existed were closely linked to military activities. Government intervention was focused on the regulation of some markets. The need to raise revenues induced the Primo de Rivera dictatorship to nationalize oil distribution in 1927, but the state monopoly was sold out to a consortium of private interests, mainly banks. Other "fiscal monopolies" existed in tobacco and matches production and distribution. There were a few firms with mixed ownership: CAMPSA and a couple of banks (Banco de Crédito Industrial and Banco Exterior de España). In all these cases the management was private, and the minority partnership of the state meant only that the firm had some duties to this special shareholder. Also during the Primo de Rivera dictatorship, in 1924 a law was passed (Estatuto Municipal) that authorized town councils to create municipally owned firms.

All in all, even taking into account these developments, free enter-

---

[1] Throughout this essay we will use the terms "state-owned" and "public" interchangeably. This essay has been prepared with the support of the Spanish DGICYT PB93-0405. We thank Francisco Galicia and Javier Pueyo for their efficient research assistance. A complete account of public firms in Spain is Comín and Martín Aceña 1991. An updated summary is found in Martín Aceña and Comín 1994. On the complete development of public firms and the public sector see Comín 1996.

Table 9.1. Economic Weight of State-Owned Firms

	1963	1979	1985	1990
France	19	18	24	18
Germany	11	13	12	10
Italy	12	20	20	19
Spain	12	10	12	10
United Kingdom	10	19	13	4

Note: Arithmetic mean of the weight in employment, in gross capital formation, and in gross domestic product (in percentages).
Source: Toninelli 1997a, quoting Macchiati 1996.

prise and free domestic markets were the rule. The Civil War was, in this respect as in many others, a watershed event.

In this essay we will concentrate on two issues: the historical development of Spanish state-owned firms and their growth pattern compared with that of the private sector. In the first part, the opening section will outline the great wave of creation of public firms, lasting from 1940 to the end of the 1950s, and their political and economic origins. The second section will describe the changing role of public firms and how a phase of semiparalysis was followed by strong state activism once the industrial crisis of the 1970s began to be felt by private firms. The third section will focus on the privatization schemes that have been deployed during the last decade or so.

The second part of the essay will deal with a series of case studies, organized by sector, comparing public and private growth patterns. We will compare industrial sectors where technological decline has brought public firms to complete obsolescence to sectors where financial failure was not correlated with technological limitations and to nonindustrial public firms that have managed to grow fairly well and that have become the "jewels of the crown" for the Spanish state.

We begin with a summary assessment of the overall importance of the Spanish public firms. For years when comparable figures do exist (that is, since 1963), the proxy indicator for the economic weight of state-owned firms does not rank very high in the Spanish experience (Table 9.1). It was quite stable around 10–12 percent from the early 1960s to 1990. Always smaller than their French counterparts, these firms are most similar to their German sisters. The stability of their size seems to be their main feature. Indeed, the most dramatic developments happened before 1963, when public firms were created from scratch, and since 1990, when they have been sold to private owners.

EBB AND FLOW OF THE SYSTEM OF PUBLIC FIRMS

The Great Wave of Creation of Public Firms

After World War II, Franco's style of state intervention was framed within a fascist (Mussolinian) pattern. Generally speaking, an autarkic approach, identical to that of Nazi Germany and fascist Italy, dominated public life. Franco replicated Mussolini's innovations in specific ways of dealing with firms. The creation of the INI (Industrial National Agency) followed very closely the Italian IRI.[2]

Franco also opened the way for the nationalization of many privately owned firms, mainly if they were in foreign hands. The nationalistic mood implied an effort to regain national (i.e., Spanish) control over most economically significant activities and, possibly, state control over all sectors related to national security. Railways were nationalized between 1941 and 1944 and telecommunications in 1944. Most motor and parts building companies were nationalized or gently pushed out of the country. The same was true for shipbuilding. Oil refining was initially developed only by new publicly created firms.

In one decade (1940–51) public firms increased dramatically in number, entering many sectors and immediately becoming the largest firm (or the monopolist) in quite a few of them. The period of maximum activity was from 1945 to 1951, when the president of the INI (J. A. Suanzes), while keeping this responsibility, was named minister of industry. For six years he was able to implement most of his initiatives. He represented autarkic ideas in a very concrete way. He was a seaman and naval engineer, a close friend of Franco, who worked as an engineer with Vickers, the British shipbuilding firm, at the SECN, the Spanish Society for Shipbuilding, and was convinced of the need to rid Spain of foreign interests. Like many other politicians of the 1940s and 1950s in developing countries, he was determined to implement state-led industrializing policies (Ballestero 1993).

Spanish public firms were created through two different means: nationalization of previously existing assets and creation of new firms.

---

[2] There are two major books on the history of the INI: Schwartz and González 1978 and Martín Aceña and Comín 1991.

Table 9.2. Main Firms under Public Ownership as of 31 December 1948, Ranked by Their Total Assets

Company[a]	Sector	Assets[b]	Year[c]	Rank[d]
RENFE (N)	Railways	6,440	1941	1
CTNE (Telefónica) (N)	Telecom.	2,477	1944	2
CAMPSA (M)	Oil distrib.	1,222	1927	6
EN Bazán (INI)	Shipbuilding	650	1947	16
ENCASO (INI)	Oil distil.	598	1942	18
Tabacalera (N)	Tobacco	583	1945	19
EN Elcano (INI)	Maritime transp.	485	1943	24
ENASA (INI/N)	Engineering	474	1946	25
Banco Exterior de España (M)	Banking	266	1929	54
ENDESA (INI)	Electricity	187	1944	74
FEFASA (INI/M/R)	Chemicals	181	1944	76
CASA (INI/M)	Engineering	149	1943	93
ENHER (INI)	Electricity	144	1946	95
BYNSA (INI/M)	Engineering	134	1943	102
Marconi Esp. (INI/M)	Engineering	125	1942	109
TorresQuevedoSA (INI)	Telecom.	116	1944	119
ENDASA (INI)	Aluminum	109	1943	128
HispanoAviac. (INI/M)	Engineering	89	1943	152

[a] INI = INI firm; M = mixed ownership (private/public); N = nationalized; R = rescued firm.
[b] In millions of pesetas.
[c] Year of incorporation (or, if relevant, year of nationalization or of rescue or of beginning of public ownership).
[d] Position in the overall ranking of the 200 largest Spanish firms.

Sources: Carreras and Tafunell 1993; Martín Aceña and Comín 1991.

A third means – bailing out failing private firms – was rare during the first wave. Two different legal strategies were used. Most of the brand new firms appeared within the INI. Big firms in nonindustrial sectors usually remained legally independent (RENFE, CTNE, CAMPSA, Tabacalera, Banco Exterior de España).

As can be seen in Table 9.2, all but two (CAMPSA and Banco Exterior de España, both of mixed ownership) of the biggest state-owned companies in existence by 1948 had been created in the previous few years. The nationalized firms were huge. RENFE and CTNE were the two top firms by asset size, and Tabacalera was the nineteenth. Four recently created INI firms ranked sixteenth to twenty-fifth in position, growing strongly in their first years of life. Even smaller firms (ENDESA and those following it) displayed a noticeable diversity of interests and initiatives.

Indeed, heavy industry was the preferred target of INI leaders: oil, electricity, steel and metals, engineering, shipbuilding, and chemical manufacture. These were the industrial priorities. Transportation of all kinds and telecommunications were the other preferred public investment targets.

The extent of public involvement was extraordinary in Spanish economic history, although it occurred simultaneously with the European postwar wave of nationalizations. This coincidence arose because of Spain's delay in implementing its industrial plans. The increasing isolation of the Franco regime after 1945 induced the Spanish government to insist on the autarkic approach and on a closely state-monitored economy. All the defense-related sectors became extremely important for the Franco regime. The concept of strategic sectors was dramatically enlarged, and embraced most of the energy-producing sectors and heavy industry.

After 1951, when Suanzes was removed from the Ministry of Industry – although he continued as chairman of the INI for twelve more years – the INI projects were completed, but Suanzes lost his influence to launch new ones. During this second period (1951–63), industrial state-owned firms reached their maximum size. By 1960, the picture of Spanish state-owned firms was quite impressive (see Table 9.3). No fewer than eight firms out of the top eleven – quite an astonishing performance! The growth of ENSIDESA, ENCASO, ENDESA, and ENHER was impressive, as was the multiplication of initiatives. Thirty-one state-owned firms out of the two hundred largest Spanish firms is not irrelevant, but the important element was the large number of big firms: the four top firms, seven of the top ten, twelve of the top twenty-five, fifteen of the top fifty. The sectorial distribution did not change compared to that of 1948. It is the extent of state involvement that matters and, even more, the insistence on the size of the enterprises. The INI liked to show private firms how important its technical skill was, and it looked fiercely for scale economies. Never before and never after 1960 would there be a Spanish industrial firm larger – relative to industrial output, to gross domestic product (GDP), or to national wealth – than ENSIDESA in 1960. Taken together with the other big INI firms, the outcome was an extraordinary upsurge of industrial firms at the top levels of the Spanish ranking.

Interestingly enough, by 1962, when they were at the zenith of their domestic size, Spanish public firms were very small in international terms. According to the Dunning and Pearce (1981) sales ranking of the world's largest industrial enterprises, in 1962 there was not a single Spanish industrial state-owned firm among the top 497.

Table 9.3. Main Firms under Public Ownership as of 31 December 1960,
Ranked by Their Total Assets

Company Name	Sector	Assets	Year	Rank
RENFE (N)	Railways	61,040	1941	1
ENSIDESA (INI)	Steel	22,204	1950	2
CTNE (Telefónica) (N)	Telecom.	15,806	1944	3
ENCASO (INI)	Oil distil.	15,408	1942	4
CAMPSA (M)	Oil distrib.	8,391	1927	7
EN Bazán (INI)	Shipbuilding	8,363	1947	8
ENDESA (INI)	Electricity	6,133	1944	10
ENHER (INI)	Electricity	5,469	1946	11
REPESA (INI/M)	Oil refining	3,822	1949	21
Tabacalera (N)	Tobacco	3,424	1945	24
SEAT (INI/M)	Motor cars	3,411	1950	25
ENASA (INI/N)	Trucks	3,209	1946	27
Hidroel. Monc. (INI/M)	Electricity	2,657	1951	31
MTM (INI/M/R)	Engineering	2,285	1956	36
ASCASA (INI/R)	Shipbuilding	1,309	1952	60
GeneralEl. (INI/M/R)	Engineering	1,250	1954	62
FEFASA (INI/M/R)	Chemical	1,201	1944	63
GESA (INI/N)	Gas and elect.	1,172	1952	66
ENDASA (INI)	Aluminum	1,134	1943	71
ENIRA (INI)	Chemicals	856	1952	87
TorresQuevedoSA (INI)	Telecom.	593	1944	117
Banco Cto. Ind. (M)	Banking	577	1920	121
HidroGalicia (INI/M)	Electricity	528	1954	126
FRIGSA (INI/M)	Food	459	1951	140
ENMASA (INI/N)	Engineering	423	1951	145
IFESA (INI/M)	Food	346	1956	165
BYNSA (INI/M)	Engineering	343	1943	167
Aviaco (INI/M)	Aviation	334	1954	170
ENCelulosasPon. (INI)	Chemicals	315	1956	181
Banco Ext. España (M)	Banking	269	1929	197
ENCelulosasHue. (INI)	Chemicals	266	1955	199

Notes and Sources: As for Table 9.2.

Maturity and Decline

By 1958, the need for a liberal turn in Spanish economic policy was
urgent. The 1959 reforms freed many markets, but the INI empire
managed to survive the harsh criticism of all the foreign reports (linked
to foreign aid) on Spanish development potential. Indeed, Suanzes
resisted until 1963, when the liberal turn was politically exhausted and

Table 9.4. Main Firms under Public Ownership as of 31 December 1974, Ranked by Their Total Assets

Company Name	Sector	Assets	Year	Rank
CTNE (Telefónica) (N)	Telecom.	289,622	1944	1
RENFE (N)	Railways	169,981	1941	2
ENSIDESA (INI)	Steel	126,307	1950	6
EMPETROL (INI)	Oil	74,499	1974	13
Iberia (INI)	Aviation	56,330	1943	17
ENDESA (INI)	Electricity	54,245	1944	18
AESA (INI/M)	Shipbuilding	50,115	1969	20
ENHER (INI)	Electricity	47,670	1946	21
SEAT (INI/M)	Motor cars	46,538	1950	23
CAMPSA (M)	Oil distrib.	45,878	1927	24
EN Bazán (INI)	Shipbuilding	28,401	1947	31
Tabacalera (N)	Tobacco	27,343	1945	33
HUNOSA (INI/R)	Coal mining	22,261	1967	38
Banco Ext. España (N)	Banking	15,598	1962	51
HISPANOIL (INI/M)	Oil mining	14,421	1965	56
ENDASA (INI)	Aluminum	12,892	1943	63
ENCE (INI)	Chemicals	11,302	1968	75
ENASA (INI/N)	Trucks	10,410	1946	78
GESA (INI/N)	Gas and elect.	10,149	1952	81
ENUSA (INI)	Energy	9,642	1972	86
ASTANO (INI/M/R)	Shipbuilding	9,642	1972	87
Banco Hipotecario (N)	Banking	7,655	1962	114
ENTURSA (INI)	Services	5,785	1964	144
MEVOSA (INI/M)	Motor cars	4,686	1972	163
SKF Española (INI/M)	Engineering	3,857	1970	181

Notes and Sources: As for Table 9.2.

a new wave of politicians, more technically than economically oriented, achieved full control of economic and industrial policy.

The period 1963 to 1975 (from the end of Suanzes to the end of Franco) was one of slow downsizing of INI activities. The INI increasingly became the holder of loss-making, previously private assets. Other state-owned nonindustrial firms took much greater advantage of Spain's hypergrowth: telecommunications, civil aviation, oil, electricity and gas distribution, and even banks.

As is evident from Table 9.4, from 1960 to 1974 the state-owned firms strongly resisted downsizing and privatization during the years of the Spanish economic miracle. There was a smooth decline but not a dramatic fall. New state-owned firms were created. Some were brand new, according to the old INI tradition (ENUSA, ENTURSA). Others were the outcome of mergers and acquisitions under INI's absolute control (EMPETROL, HUNOSA, ENCE) or with INI's active, although not exclusive, involvement (AESA, Hispanoil, MEVOSA, SKF) or even simple acquisitions (ASTANO). Some old names covered important acquisitions (ENSIDESA, ENDESA).

During the transition to democracy (1975 to 1982) and also during the first years of the socialist government (1982–5), the oil shocks and the industrial crisis made life at the INI even more complicated. The "crisis" character of the INI was fully developed. The number of firms entering the INI grew quickly, hoping for unlimited financial support.

The oil crisis hit the INI firms very hard. The government avoided the first adjustment to the rise in oil prices, and Spain became a wonderful place to find cheap energy subsidized by the government. Some huge investments were planned with this factor in mind. Cheap energy lasted from 1974 to 1979. The political weakness of the transition (from dictatorship to democracy) governments was no longer a problem in 1979. The democratic Unión de Centro Democrático (UCD) government passed along all increases in oil prices to the final consumer, and Spain was no longer an attractive place to invest in aluminum, steel, nuclear energy, or petroleum refining. The INI heavy industries paid a very high price for this policy, as did all private firms in Spain. The crisis was all the more difficult for having been delayed. From 1979 to 1983 the INI became an active rescuer of failed industrial firms. Its largest size, in number of firms and in amount of losses, was probably reached by 1983 or 1984.

The Privatization Years

The INI was committed from 1984 to a policy of reprivatization. Much public money was invested in the "cleaning" of financially "dirty" (that is, loss-making) companies. From 1986 on, and following the booming effect of Spain's entrance into the European Economic Community (EEC), the INI inaugurated a policy of selling most of the firms that could return to profitability. The downsizing of the INI was its major trend until its legal dissolution in 1995. In the meantime, its name was changed to TENEO (1992), and a major reorganization of industrial state-owned assets occurred. Jointly with the slow dissolution of INI, the socialist government undertook the partial privatization of most of its profitable non-INI assets: oil production, refining, and distribution (REPSOL), electricity production and distribution (ENDESA), banking (Argentaria), and telecommunications (Telefónica). The privatization experience began with CTNE around 1970, still under the Franco regime, but it remained exceptional until the late 1980s, when REPSOL and ENDESA exploited it successfully.

In 1990, just before the end of INI's history, the main characters were almost the same as they were sixteen years before (Table 9.5). By 1990 there were almost as many state-owned firms among the top two hundred as in 1960: thirty instead of thirty-one. The size reduction of the public sector was more a question of ranking than of absolute numbers; there is a clear-cut increase in number compared with 1974. But whereas there were ten public firms among the top twenty-five in 1974, there were only seven in 1990. A few firms related to transportation and communication services with monopolies remained in the leading positions (CTNE, RENFE, IBERIA). Another subset managed to survive as profit-making entities. They grew thanks to governmental assistance in the regulation of home markets (ENDESA, REPSOL). Only ENSIDESA continued the decline of the old INI guard. Generally speaking, the main feature of this period is the continuity of the Spanish public-firm landscape.

The socialist long governments of 1982–95 succeeded in reforming many state-owned firms with the goal of finding a proper future for them (public or private) in a more competitive environment (De la Dehensa 1992, 1993). Table 9.5 must be read keeping in mind that some big public firms were being privatized. Table 9.6 shows the proportion of the capital switched to nonpublic ownership between 1985 and 1997.

By 1997 Spanish public firms were undergoing a renewed privatization process. This privatization was not ideologically oriented but pragmatic. Financial and budgetary reasons, compliance with the EEC's competition law, political fashion – a number of reasons have converged into a strong political will (Cuervo 1997a). Some firms were completely sold: SEAT, ENASA, ENTURSA, and ARESBANK. A second group underwent almost complete privatization: SKF (98.8 percent), ENAGAS (91 percent), and REPSOL (89 percent). The third group was partially privatized: ARGENTARIA (50 percent), Telefónica (31.7 percent), and ENDESA (29.2 percent). The last group was a mixture of ongoing privatizations that were to continue after 1990 (ARGENTARIA and

Table 9.5. Main Firms under Public Ownership as of 31 December 1990, Ranked by Their Total Assets

Company Name	Sector	Assets	Rank
CTNE (M)	Telecom.	3,292,835	1
RENFE (N)	Railways	1,200,005	4
ENDESA (INI)	Electricity	1,026,405	6
REPSOL (INH)	Oil mining	439,286	12
CAMPSA (M)	Oil distrib.	389,692	13
Iberia (INI)	Aviation	379,495	15
ENSIDESA (INI)	Steel	358,823	16
BANCO. EXT. ESP. (N)	Banking	209,637	28
ENHER (INI)	Electricity	206,563	30
CASA (INI)	Engineering	186,371	35
Tabacalera (N)	Tobacco	181,351	37
ENAGAS (INH)	Gas	179,957	38
REDESA (INI)	Elect. distr.	164,905	43
HIDRUÑA (INI)	Electricity	150,651	46
UNELCO (INI)	Electricity	119,520	55
INESPAL (INI)	Aluminum	112,091	60
B. ARABE ESP. (INI)	Banking	109,428	63
ENRESA (INI)	Electricity	108,858	64
AESA (INI)	Shipbuilding	98,126	67
ENUSA (INI/M)	Electricity	97,582	68
EN Bazán (INI)	Shipbuilding	80,213	78
GESA (INI)	Gas and elect.	69,973	89
TELEVISION ESP. (S-O)	Television	67,232	94
F. N. MONEDA (S-O)	Mint	59,901	101
SINTEL (M)	Telecom.	51,605	119
BWE (INI)	Engineering	51,590	120
ENCE (INI/M)	Chemicals	50,358	123
SIDME (INI)	Steel	38,831	156
Aviaco (INI)	Aviation	32,408	177
AUXINI (INI)	Engineering	30,703	186

Notes: As for Table 9.2. S-O = state-owned but not included in any other category.
Sources: As for Table 9.2, plus *Anuario El País* 1992; Fomento de la Producción 1991.

ENDESA) and of firms that completed a privatization that had begun much earlier (Telefónica). The privatization process was not insignificant. Ranked by their assets, the firms that went totally or partially private were, in 1990, the first (Telefónica), the sixth (ENDESA), the twelfth (REPSOL), the twenty-third (SEAT), the twenty-eighth

Table 9.6. Privatization of Public Firms by 1997

Company Name	Rank in 1990	% Sold (1985–97)	% S-O
CTNE	1	31.7	0
ENDESA	6	29.2	66.9[a]
REPSOL	12	89.0	0
CAMPSA	13	—	—[b]
Iberia	15	0	99.9
ENSIDESA	16	—	—[c]
BANCO EXT. ESPAÑA	28	50.0	25.1[d]
ENHER	30	—	—[e]
CASA	35	0	99.3
Tabacalera	37	0	52.4
ENAGAS	38	91.0	9.0
REDESA	43	0	100
HIDRUÑA	46	?	?
UNELCO	55	—	—[e]
BANCO ARABE ESP.	63	100	0
ENUSA	68	?	60.0
GESA	89	—	—[e]
SINTEL	119	?	?
ENCE	123	49.0	51.0
SIDME	156	—	—[f]
AVIACO	177	?	67.0
AUXINI	186	0	60.0
Rank in 1974			
SEAT	23	100	0
ENASA	78	100	0
ENTURSA	144	100	0
MEVOSA	163	?	?
SKF	181	98.8	0

Notes: The table includes only public firms listed in Tables 9.4 and 9.5 (the largest by their assets in 1990 and 1974).

% sold (1985-97): Proportion of capital sold between 1985 and March 1997.

% S-O: Proportion of capital under state ownership by March 1997.

[a] A further 25 percent was sold during the fall of 1997, and the sale of another portion was announced for the spring of 1998.

[b] CAMPSA was dissolved after Spain joined the EEC. It was sold to private and public oil refining companies.

[c] ENSIDESA and Altos Hornos de Vizcaya merged in 1991 to form CSI, out of which ACERALIA was formed in 1997 and privatized completely during the summer of 1997.

[d] Banco Exterior de España, jointly with the other state-owned banks, is part of ARGENTARIA. The proportions shown in the table correspond to ARGENTARIA.

[e] Absorbed by ENDESA in 1983. ENDESA's privatization ratios apply to each of them.

[f] Absorbed by CSI. Its remnants are part of ACERALIA.

Sources: Our own preparation based on Barea and Corona 1996; Cuervo 1997b; Martín Aceña and Comín 1991; *Anuario El País* 1992.

(ARGENTARIA), the thirty-eighth (ENAGAS), and so on. It should be emphasized that the list of nonprivatized firms was almost as impressive: RENFE (fourth), Iberia (fifteenth), CASA (thirty-fifth), TABACALERA (thirty-seventh), and so on.[3]

In chronological terms, it is necessary to distinguish three periods (Barea and Corona 1996; Cuervo 1997b). The first period begins in 1985, when the INI actively began to promote the privatization of many firms that were nationalized in the previous few years to subsidize employment. These firms were never considered to be of national interest, and their reprivatization was considered necessary by everybody but the trade unions. The government accelerated the privatizations by financing losses and looking for partners who could take over ownership and management. This was the same scheme that was used to privatize the former RUMASA companies.

By the late 1980s, privatization began to reach profit-making state-owned firms – the jewels of the Spanish state. Telefónica, ENDESA, and REPSOL underwent a first round of privatization in 1988 and 1989. As the public deficit soared in 1993, 1994, and 1995, the financial need for privatization became overwhelming and the government launched a new round of privatization, including the same companies and ARGENTARIA.

The third period began in 1996 and is related to the change in government. The new policy has been one of explicit support for privatization to increase efficiency and private ownership. The need to comply with the strict deficit rules of the European Monetary Union has strengthened the privatization will of the government, which is very interested in reducing the public deficit. The creation of SEPI (Spanish Society of Industrial Shareholdings) and of AIE (State Industrial Agency) following the dissolution of the old INI suggested how the government planned to deal with the privatization process. All the firms that could be profitable went to SEPI and are being privatized. All the loss-making firms and the historical INI debt went to AIE and are being digested according to political rules.

Although fears about the loss of public control or, even more, about the loss of national control have been voiced by some politicians, businessmen, and trade unionists, the government is fully committed to the completion of the privatization of all profitable firms in public hands.

---

[3] But TABACALERA underwent a partial privatization during 1998 and CASA is looking for a buyer.

By the end of the twentieth century, Spain closed a long cycle of birth, growth, decline, and near disappearance of public firms.

PUBLIC VERSUS PRIVATE GROWTH
PATTERNS: CASE STUDIES

Up to this point, the story we have been telling has been very general. We will go into greater detail to better illustrate the main strategic moves of the firms operating in fields where private and public firms coexisted.

The Iron and Steel Industry

During the first half of the twentieth century the iron and steel sector was dominated by Altos Hornos de Vizcaya (AHV). Born from a merger in 1901, this company immediately overcame its Asturian competitors and managed to destroy its main challenger, the Compañía Siderúrgica del Mediterráneo, which began operations in 1923 but was absorbed in 1940.

The supply structure and the behavior of the main firms in the sector underwent no important changes until ENSIDESA appeared in 1950. At that moment, AHV had one-third of all the installed capacity in steel production. Another third belonged to seven other firms, located in Asturias and in the Basque country, all with more than thirty years of activity. The remaining third was shared by many small, nonintegrated firms (Fraile 1992). In an environment dominated by strong oligopolization and autarky, with weak industrial and economic growth, the iron and steel industries showed no interest in increasing their output. Indeed, installed capacity and output remained below their 1930 level (the highest of the pre–Civil War years) until the mid-1950s. Furthermore, the private firms of the steel sector declined, one by one, all the administration's proposals to create a large steel complex with mixed capital (private and public). Nonetheless, political leaders and those of the INI felt that an increase in the steel supply was essential in order to increase industrialization. With this idea in mind, they decided to create a large, integrated iron and steel industry on the Asturian coast, ENSIDESA.[4] By 1957, the first year of its operation, ENSIDESA reached a hegemonic position, in capacity terms, that it maintained up to the early 1990s. It

---

[4] It was incorporated in 1950, but the steel works began production only in 1957.

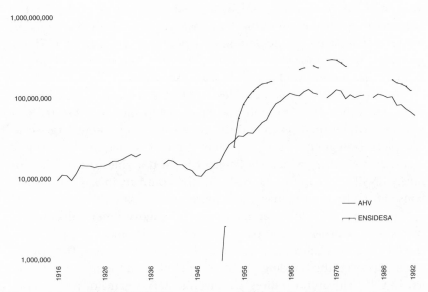

Figure 9.1. AHV and ENSIDESA real assets, 1916–92 (in 1980 pesetas). *Sources:* "Anuario Financiero y de Sociedades Anónimas," supplemented as needed with the companies' annual reports. The assets of the firms have been converted into 1980 constant pesetas by the GDP deflator (Leandro Prados, "Spain's Gross Domestic Product, 1850–1993; Quantitative Conjectures," working paper, Madrid, Universided Carlos III, pp. 175ff., series BPGDFC8).

exceeded the yearly output of AHV by 1961, and for the following ten years produced more than a quarter of the Spanish output. During the 1970s its market share jumped to more than 40 percent because of the absorption of UNINSA. Figure 9.1 shows the sudden appearance of ENSIDESA in the steel sector and how it quickly surpassed AHV.

Undoubtedly, ENSIDESA lacked the dynamism that the Basque iron and steel firms possessed between 1880 and 1913. ENSIDESA was always very poorly managed, weighed down by bureaucratic obstacles and governmental controls. Investment suffered drastic cutbacks due to pressures exerted by private iron and steel companies (Fraile 1992). Nevertheless, state initiative had the virtue of spurring on the main iron and steel industries to modernize, especially when the liberalization of iron and steel imports followed.

AHV undertook a plan of technological transformation that, regardless of the enormous accumulation of obsolete technical materials and knowledge, allowed it to sell shares to U.S. Steel. The building of another integrated iron and steel plant in the old installations of the CSM in Sagunto at the beginning of the 1970s was an excessively risky strategy for AHV. It signaled the beginning of a period of crisis from 1975 on, when the demand for steel plunged drastically. The strategy of diversification that began simultaneously was insufficient.

Duro-Felguera, one of the oldest coal blast-furnace plants, merged with two other Asturian iron and steel companies in 1961 to form UNINSA, which then promoted the construction of a new, large-scale, complete (integrated) iron and steel plant. This required enormous financial resources, which its backers were not able to provide, and finally ENSIDESA was forced to absorb the company in 1973. The problems caused by poor management increased dramatically.

To complicate the steel landscape, the government decided to promote new projects to expand steel capacity during 1974, just when the oil crisis was signaling a new era of declining demand. The government approved the building of a new steel plant in Sagunto, on the old site of CSM. The authorization was given to AHV, the major private competitor of ENSIDESA. A few years later, the government (a very different one) was obliged to pursue the opposite goal: the downsizing of the steel sector, including the closing of some plants. A new episode began then, by 1981, which was extremely painful in social and financial terms.

Almost twenty years later, after two complex rescaling plans, there are still major doubts about the sustainability of the Spanish steel sector. In the meantime the two giant firms (AHV and ENSIDESA), after having been radically streamlined, have disappeared through merger. A new public firm was born in 1991: Corporación Siderúrgica Integral (CSI). Its financial situation is healthy, but its assets are insufficient and its technical expertise is not state of the art. In 1997 a new company was formed out of the profit-making parts of CSI: ACERALIA. Immediately afterward it underwent a full privatization process.

Shipbuilding

The main firm in the shipbuilding sector during the first third of the twentieth century was the Sociedad Española de Construcción Naval (SECN, Spanish Society for Shipbuilding). It was founded in 1908, with warships as its first business goal, in answer to the recently passed Escuadra Act. Northern banks and iron and steel company interests contributed to the formation of the firm, constituting a case of vertical integration (like most of its Spanish competitors) under the leadership of Vickers, the British shipbuilding firm involved in a multinationalization strategy.[5] SECN, which had purchased the assets of the Astilleros del Nervión shipyard, acquired and maintained a position of hegemony in the sector from the beginning. It finally abandoned its dominant position in 1969, when it merged with Euskalduna.

After the Civil War, the new regime was reluctant to put the navy into the hands of a company (SECN) that was under foreign control. This brought about the INI's creation of E. N. Bazán in 1947 and the marginalization of SECN, which received a declining number of orders. E. N. Bazán was oriented exclusively to warships. This firm had to deal with the same problems as all the shipyards that depended on public demand: excess productive capacity, high costs, and the like. However, the distinctive mark of public intervention in this sector was the increasing direct participation of the state, which culminated in 1969 in virtual nationalization.[6] In part, the INI was forced to take over private shipyards that had declared bankruptcy due to poor management (Cadíz and ASTANO). On the other hand, the administration – through concerted action, approved in 1967 – propelled a strong concentration of the existing units in the hope of achieving scale economies that would allow Spanish shipyards to become internationally competitive and make the most of a moment of strong expansion worldwide. The 1969 formation of AESA (Astilleros Españoles) from a merger of SECN, Euskalduna, and Astilleros de Cádiz was a fruit of this policy. The new company was among the largest European shipbuilding firms. The shipbuilding industry of the country grew accordingly in an expanding international context: by the mid-1970s, Spain was the world's fourth largest producer. Nevertheless, it did not succeed in maintaining its position because its large shipyards specialized in oil tankers, the demand for which decreased after 1973, and, no less significant, because the INI did not undertake any form of economic rationalization within the companies comprising the group (a process that eventually led to the closing down of several plants). The last decade and a half has been devoted to finding ways to put a politically feasible end to the state-owned shipbuilding companies and to the whole sector.

---

[5] The British firm owned the largest number of shares. On its external investments see Segreto 1997.

[6] In the 1970s INI gained control of 90 percent of naval production. Comín and Martín Aceña 1991; Myro 1980.

The accumulated losses have been so huge as to prevent any privatization strategy.

The Automobile Industry

Since the 1970s, the automobile industry has been the most important of Spain's industrial sectors. Its development was very rapid; indeed, Spain has become one of the largest producers and exporters worldwide. Until the 1950s, vehicle manufacturing was at very low levels.[7] This has caused many authors to affirm that the Spanish automobile industry did not evolve until this decade (Castaños 1985; Tamames 1990). This conclusion is inexact since it ignores the fact that between the two world wars the industry had begun to take its first promising steps forward. Many small firms manufactured very short runs of automobiles using artisan methods, and some, more ambitious than others, were dedicated to the assembly of imported parts. The Hispano Suiza company was known for the exceptional mechanical and aesthetic quality of the vehicles it produced. For this reason, Hispano Suiza did not succumb to foreign competition, despite its low production rate (fewer than six hundred vehicles annually); naturally, this allowed it to specialize in luxury items. The great expertise of its technical staff made diversified production possible, and various types of industrial vehicles were also produced.[8] The accumulated know-how (as well as one of its plants) would serve as the basis on which ENASA (the most important Spanish state-owned manufacturer of industrial vehicles) would later be formed.

The second type of manufacturer – the automobile assembly plant – had two prominent representatives: the two largest worldwide producers, Ford and General Motors. The first company established a plant in Spain in 1920, and by 1930 more than 10,000 vehicles annually left its assembly lines (Estapé 1998). These were large production volumes compared to those of the automobile companies in other European countries of the period and those of the assembly plants functioning during the 1960s in many developing countries. Part of the production

---

[7] From the end of the Civil War (1939) to 1954, not even 1,000 private cars were produced annually. Industrial vehicles did extremely well the following year. See Carreras 1988.

[8] During World War I, extremely successful airplane motors were produced. Even earlier, in 1910, the company opened an affiliated company near Paris. Nadal and Tafunell 1992.

was destined for various North African and Southern European markets. Ford Motor Ibérica had, moreover, revolutionized the production and marketing methods of the newborn Spanish automobile industry. The increased profits obtained from its overwhelming competitive superiority and the growth potential that it offered to the Spanish market caused its main rival, General Motors, to follow its example, unfortunately with little success. Operations began in 1932, but the Civil War soon brought them to an abrupt halt.

The conflict and its outcome were incredibly traumatic for the vigorous automobile industry. Faced with the enormous difficulties of importing raw materials and intermediary goods, the hostility of the administration toward firms financed with foreign capital, and the overall economic disaster in general, the two North American firms abandoned the concern. Two firms fostered by the public sector, ENASA (trucks) and SEAT (private cars), replaced them, with the declared objective of substituting their own products for imported cars. The first company was created in 1946, with material assets and, above all, the personnel of the earlier Hispano Suiza. The second concern was established in 1950, with the majority of shares belonging to the INI and with the minor participation of Spanish private interests and the Italian Fiat, which contributed its technology for the manufacturing processes and products (San Román 1995). At that stage Ford left Spain, as it became clear that no agreement with the government was possible. Nevertheless, the establishment of SEAT was immediately followed by FASA (1951), a branch of the French Régie-Renault. However, a market so protected and so short of goods attracted foreign manufacturers. In a little more than a decade, three other companies that produced private cars and by-products entered the Spanish market – Citroën Hispania (1957), Chrysler-Barreiros (afterward Peugeot Talbot España, 1963), and AUTHI (1967) – all of them subsidiaries of foreign firms – Citroën, Chrysler (sold to Peugeot), and the British Motor Corporation. Finally, the Spanish automobile industry was completed with the incorporation, for the second time, of Ford (1972) and General Motors (1979). In the area of industrial vehicles, ENASA had to face competition from various manufacturers, of which the best known were Motor Ibérica (Ford's successor, which stopped manufacturing in Spain in 1954), SAVA, and IMOSA (later transformed into MEVOSA).

SEAT was the main engine in the motorization of the country: it put Spain on wheels. SEAT's hegemony was absolute between 1953 (when manufacturing began) and 1976: it produced 59 percent of all vehicles manufactured in Spain.[9] It was therefore able to achieve an efficient scale of production, even if quite inferior to what an optimal level could have been. SEAT, like ENASA in the industrial vehicle sector, was able to profit fully from the advantages derived from government policy, but it also suffered its long-term negative effects. Complete protection against foreign competition,[10] barriers to entry,[11] government price intervention (until 1979), scarce or nonexistent export possibilities due to the subordination of the licensed branch firms, and total technological dependence on outside sources all conditioned the direction and orientation of the automobile companies. SEAT (and ENASA) could rely on financial backing and government management interference, which explains why it developed into an overly bureaucratized and poorly run organization. Overall costs represented a very high percentage of SEAT's cost structure. The organization was bloated, and business management neglected rationalization. The second automobile company (FASA-Renault) did not have these problems, and its successful policies regarding its manufactured models allowed FASA-Renault to oust SEAT from its first-place position in the domestic market in 1979.

Ford's return upset the sector once again. All the established firms were producing at high unit costs because the runs were not long enough for the excessive variety of models and variants and the low productivity of the plants. The new Ford factory (and that of General Motors a few years later) was conceived completely differently, responding to maximum internationalization of the product. The plant was designed to produce a single type of vehicle to be sold throughout Europe. The scale economies that had been realized, and the programming and automation of factory production, allowed drastic cuts in costs. New strategies of contract negotiation and quality control, together with the

---

[9] Yearly production details of the various factories – not fully coinciding – are given in Argandoña 1972 and Castaño 1985. Nineteen seventy-five was the first year in which SEAT's share of vehicle production was below 50 percent. Before 1963, this figure was above 60 percent, despite the fact that, on average, no more than 25,000 vehicles were manufactured annually.

[10] Imports were practically vetoed until 1979 and were not effectively – and quickly – liberalized until Spain became part of the EEC in 1986. From 1976 to 1979 the importation of private automobiles represented just 3.1 percent (in units), a percentage slightly less than that of ten years before. See the data in Castaño and Cortés 1980.

[11] Plant installation required administrative authorization, which implied an increased percentage of national materials for parts and products used and a minimum capacity of determined production. The government used this last requisite to limit possible undesirable competition, as happened with Volkswagen in 1965.

impact of new advertising techniques (one campaign launched for one single model simultaneously throughout Western Europe), rapidly gained public approval.

SEAT's financial situation deteriorated rapidly. Fiat decided to withdrew from SEAT. In the late 1970s and early 1980s, the losses became unmanageable and there were no prospects at all for a relaunching of the firm. The INI decided to make an extra effort to sell the firm. Once a reasonable buyer was found – Volkswagen – the Spanish state cleared all SEAT debts and sold it for one peseta. The other major state-owned automobile manufacturer (ENASA, a truck maker) underwent a similar process. The difference was that in this case Fiat was the buyer.

The Oil Industry

Oil refineries grew large in Spain, as in many other countries – not surprisingly, since the oil industry is one of the most capital intensive. The uniqueness of the Spanish case lies in the obstacles presented by public intervention in the field.

From its beginnings, the historical development of the oil industry has been marked by the oil monopoly. When it was established in 1927, the Spanish market for oil and its by-products was small, although very promising.[12] Numerous companies marketed by-products of imported oil. Two of these were the big names in the field: Standard Oil (through two branch subsidiaries) and Royal Dutch Shell (also through a subsidiary). These, plus a middle-sized Hispanic–French company (Porto Pi), had begun a fierce competitive fight for a greater share of the market.[13] This situation was dramatically altered by governmental intervention in 1927. From that moment on, a monopoly existed regarding imports, refining, and the distribution of oil and its by-products. CAMPSA was formed to manage the monopoly, with a majority of private capital but strong government participation as well. The companies active in the field were expropriated. However, CAMPSA alone fully carried out one of its tasks: distribution (transportation and storage). This was the main task entrusted to it, which was, naturally, closely linked to the fiscal goals of the administration. It did nothing to augment the crude oil refinery business, which was extremely limited

---

[12] Consumption remained insignificant until 1920 because there were only about a thousand cars in the country at the time. Carreras 1988.
[13] Tortella 1990. There is a more detailed description in Tortella 1991.

at the time.[14] There was no subsoil exploration or surveying for hydrocarbons, which should have been one of its tasks. The company left
completely unattended the final step of the distribution process: the sale
of fuels to the consumer. CAMPSA was inefficient with regard to management and operative costs (Fernández-Cuesta 1986). This situation can
be attributed to the fact that the fixed assets it managed belonged to
the state, which also controlled investments. With a captive market and
fuel sold by individual dealers, CAMPSA limited itself to the sale of oil-
based products and refrained from investing (in marketing as well). This
attitude changed only with the entry of Spain into the EEC. Forty years
earlier, in 1947, when the company lost its monopoly on research,
importing, and refining, it retained a monopoly on distribution and
marketing.[15] This fact conditioned the possibilities of expansion and the
strategy of the oil industries. Forced to sell their products to CAMPSA
at fixed prices and in fixed quantities and forced to buy part of their
crude oil from a public firm (HISPANOIL), they were not able to carry
out vertical integration.[16]

The only firm (CEPSA) that developed a growth strategy analogous
to the one implemented by the oil industries of other countries was able
to do so thanks to a small window of opportunity provided by the legislation passed in 1927: the Canary Islands remained under free-market
rules. CEPSA, founded in 1929, acquired all rights to the production of
crude oil in an area of Venezuela and took the refinery – with North
American technology – outside the territory covered by the oil monopoly in order to furnish the nonpeninsular Spanish zone and to supply
fuel to the monopoly. Ten years later, CEPSA threw itself into exploration
and research. Not only was this firm a pioneer in the field, but it was
the only private national company that had an important role, one

[14] The figures on imports of crude oil and principal by-products are given in Tortella 1990,
    95. This author believes that the company operated rationally, since the reduced size of
    the Spanish market did not justify the heavy investment for a first plant that was needed
    to install a refinery using the cracking process.
[15] In line with community law, at the end of 1992 Spain abolished its previous monopoly
    on gasoline sales. In 1985 the CAMPSA service stations, together with the remaining
    assets, were divided up among the company's shareholders, and from this time on, all
    national or foreign companies were free to create their own chains of gasoline stations.
[16] In reality, the refineries did not sell all their production to CAMPSA. Several special prod-
    ucts used by the petrochemical industry were sold outside the monopoly, as were
    exported fuels. Furthermore, the refineries had already been authorized, for some time,
    to sell lubricants and other primary commercial products to the consumer by paying a
    state tax. See Santamaría 1988, 69. In any case, fuels purchased by CAMPSA represent an
    important fraction of refinery sales. See Myro 1980, 187.

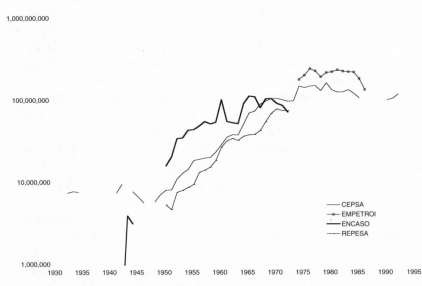

Figure 9.2. CEPSA, ENCASO, REPESA, and EMPETROL real assets, 1931–92 (in 1980 pesetas). *Sources:* See Figure 9.1.

involving high investment costs and great risks. Nevertheless, CEPSA was unable to grow during most of the 1940s (see Figure 9.2). A little later, it participated actively in the creation (1949) of the first oil import-ing refinery built on the Spanish peninsula (REPESA), putting aside the autarkic dream of obtaining hydrocarbons from the distillation of the country's mineral resources (Comín and Martín Aceña 1991, 203–12).

This was the initial project backed by the INI to increase the national production of fuel and lubricants, which gave birth to ENCASO in 1942. The same process used in Nazi Germany was to be used to obtain hydrocarbons by synthesis. Financial restrictions and lack of tech-nology and technical assistance destroyed a project that was out-landish at its start from an economic point of view. However, a large part of the funds invested in the 1940s were concentrated here by the INI. The alternative project of constructing a mixed refining industry was repeatedly proposed by CEPSA to INI (the industrial public holding company). Once official consent was received in 1947, in order to reform the Monopolio de Petróleos on a new basis, CEPSA took on the responsibility of finding a foreign partner (Caltex Oil) to provide technological and financial assistance in exchange for a crude oil supply.

When in 1964 it was authorized to construct its own refinery plant, CEPSA quickly developed and expanded a conglomerate of petrochemical industries, reinforcing its commercial structure (Santamaría 1988). The high level of vertical integration and product diversification achieved, in addition to the well-known economic efficiency of the head of the group – the refinery – allowed CEPSA to become a multinational company, which was exceptional in the Spanish business context. As in other similar cases, the successful Spanish firms have become very attractive to larger multinational companies and have been unable or unwilling to resist their extremely attractive offers. During the last decade, CEPSA's ownership has been switched to the French Elf-Aquitaine.

Between 1964 and 1968 the government authorized the installation of three refineries (including CEPSA's) maintained with private national and foreign capital – the latter with a growing number, although still a minority, of shares. With this scope in mind, two oil companies, Petróleos de Mediterráneo (PETROMED) and Petróleos del Norte (PETRONOR) (the third part was taken over by the chemical plant RIO TINTO), were created. Moreover, between 1961 and 1969, the construction of three more refineries was approved, with the majority of capital coming from the public sector: in La Coruña (Compañía Ibérica Refinadora de Petróleos, PETROLIBER, a mixed company following the REPESA model); in Puertollano (ENCASO); and in Tarragona (E.N. de Petróleos de Tarragona, ENTASA, to which another refinery in the same area with its corresponding firm would be added – Asfaltos Españoles, ASESA – whose capital was distributed in equal parts by CAMPSA and CEPSA). A total of ten refineries and seven companies came into being.

The Spanish oil industry finally gave birth to another modern enterprise in the public sector through the creation and merging of firms. The first step was taken in 1974, when EMPETROL was formed as a result of the merger of three refineries in which the INI held the majority of the company's capital (ENCASO, REPESA, ENTASA) – incorporating in 1985 the last independent public (state-owned) refinery, PETROLIBER. This horizontal integration in the public sector was intended to improve management and reduce operational costs. The creation of the Instituto Nacional de Hidrocarburos (INH) – a holding company that grouped together all oil-related companies in which the state possessed shares – allowed an intensification of the organizational rationalization already undertaken. This culminated in 1987 with the creation of REPSOL. This company is the head of a group of companies formed by REPSOL EXPLORACION, REPSOL PETROLEO, REPSOL QUIMICA, and REPSOL BUTANO that concentrates all the public oil business in each of its separate phases of production. REPSOL is an extremely well integrated firm horizontally as well as vertically. This has made possible the adoption of organizational schemes and commercial and financial strategies similar to those of the large European oil companies (of which REPSOL is one). At that stage, REPSOL began a privatization strategy that started in 1989 and was completed in 1997 after six selling rounds (1989, 1992, 1993, 1995, 1996, and 1997).

The Electrical Industry

Public intervention in the electricity market took two forms: price regulation and firm creation.[17] Price regulation consisted of freezing electricity rates at the 1936 level. As the real price of electricity declined dramatically (with inflation from 1936 on), demand for electricity boomed even during years of economic stagnation or decline. Private firms did not invest because the frozen prices were not profitable. At this stage, the INI decided to enter the electricity market. It created two main firms in the 1940s: ENDESA in the field of thermoelectricity generation and ENHER in the field of hydroelectricity.

In 1951 increases in electricity prices were approved by the government. A new way of defining an automatic acceptable revision of prices was also developed, and the private electrical firms began to invest again. In the early 1950s the INI acquired or created more firms: Hidroeléctrica Moncabril, GESA, HidroGalicia, and so on. A few years later, some of these late arrivals were absorbed by ENDESA or sold to private owners.

In the early 1980s, during the socialist government, the basic high-voltage network was nationalized and a new state-owned firm was created: Red Eléctrica Española, S.A. (REDESA). Given the poor financial condition of some of the electrical companies (resulting from their overly optimistic investments in nuclear plants during the 1970s), a complete reorganization of the private and public assets was undertaken. ENDESA was the main winner of this game. Since 1984 it has become a much larger firm. ENHER also got a larger portion of the Catalan market, thanks to the financial problems of its traditional main

---

[17] On business developments of the electrical industry as well as the oil industry, see the description of the energy industrywide approach in Sudrià 1993.

competitor, FECSA, the successor to the old Barcelona Traction, Light, and Power company. Other regional companies were also absorbed by the INI electrical sector. ERZ is the main one.

Starting in 1988, ENDESA began to go private. A second wave of privatization, up to 29 percent of share capital, occurred in 1994. During the fall of 1997 another 25 percent of shares went on the market, reducing state ownership to 41 percent.

Transportation and Communications

State-owned enterprises in the transportation and communications sectors[18] flourished under the Franco regime. Before the Civil War the railway companies were privately owned. They were running into financial trouble, and there was much talk of nationalization in the 1930s. The concessions of the main companies expired around 1945, and it was clear that they were not interested in investing in their railways less than twenty years before the end of their contracts. After the Civil War the government decided to go ahead with the nationalization. It was approved in 1941 and executed from then to 1944. Although the railways were no longer profitable, an indemnification was approved: the shareholders were paid the historical cost of their investments. That is, they got back all the money invested in the railway companies. This extremely generous arrangement meant that more than 2 billion pesetas were paid to the shareholders. At that mature stage in the life of the railway companies, the banks were important shareholders. During the 1920s and 1930s, most of their loans were transformed into shares as the companies failed to repay them. The banks were lucky enough to have the state repaying their bad loans! The take-off of the private Spanish banks began there.

RENFE was the new state-owned railway company. Another, smaller state-owned company was created – FEVE – from all the narrow-gauge railways. RENFE and FEVE received no attention at all from the regime that had paid so much for them. Net investment in them was negative for a decade, and they were still in very bad shape in 1960. Even so, the railway assets were so huge that despite RENFE's decline, it remained near the top in the asset ranking of Spanish firms (first in 1960, second in 1974, fourth in 1990).

In the maritime sector, where private management was standard

---

[18] Carreras 1988.

throughout the world, the INI decided to create a large firm devoted to invigorating Spanish cargo liners. The new firm, Empresa Nacional Elcano, began with generous financing (Valdaliso 1998). Nevertheless, it became one of the major failures of INI's management.

The airlines were another project of INI. Iberia was acquired and relaunched in 1944 and Aviaco a bit later. For more than half a century they have remained under public management. Their current prospects are extremely doubtful, but they enjoyed some years of prosperity.

Not only transportation but also communications were a government priority. The INI's contribution to telecommunications policy was twofold. Marconi Española, devoted to the radio industry, exploited the Marconi patent under public management. Much more important was the Empresa Torres Quevedo, responsible for all the telecommunications services in Spanish-ruled Morocco. It did not outlast Spanish rule in Morocco, ending in 1956. Much more important for the Franco regime was CTNE (Telefónica), an ITT-owned company. CTNE was nationalized (for 50 million gold pesetas in 1944, paid in cash when the Franco regime was very short of it) and managed outside the INI structure. It has remained a separate entity, and it was the first company that underwent partial privatization in the late 1960s and early 1970s. By 1985 it was the public firm with the lowest share of state ownership: 32 percent. This portion was completely sold out in three rounds: in 1988, 1995, and early 1997.

Other Sectors

Competition between public and private firms happened in other sectors. The most relevant one was banking (Martín Aceña 1991). A mixed (public and private) banking sector appeared during the 1920s: Banco Exterior de España, Banco de Crédito Local, and Banco de Crédito Industrial. These specialized banks were fully nationalized in 1962. In the mid-1980s they underwent a double process of privatization and reorganization, out of which a new banking entity was created: Corporación ARGENTARIA. The new bank immediately became one of the largest Spanish banks and set about domestic reorganization and multinational expansion. Its privatization began in 1993 and was speeded up in 1996 and 1997.

Tabacalera, the holder of traditional monopoly rights for tobacco manufacturing and marketing in Spain, underwent major strategic changes following the entrance of Spain into the EEC (Torres 1997). It diversified investments, jumped into the food and beverage businesses, and prepared for privatization. Although it was once a mixed-ownership firm, state interest was always dominant, but state ownership was dramatically downsized in 1998.

CONCLUSIONS

In the long run, the great wave of creation of state-owned firms produced great disappointment. In most of the manufacturing sectors, the outcome has been entrepreneurial failure. Lack of technological resources and know-how has weakened or destroyed almost all the firms. The change in economic environment following the 1973 oil crisis meant the end of the golden years for all these public firms.

Not everything was a failure. Some state-owned firms managed to survive, mainly in those sectors where a monopoly was granted (oil, telecommunications, electricity, and so on). When competition appeared – as in the case of air transport – and monopoly rents vanished, most of the state-owned firms experienced tremendous problems. A few of them managed to resist and to adapt to the liberalization trend after Spain joined the EEC. REPSOL and Argentaria are cases in point, and CTNE is trying to follow suit.

Among those that survived (because of their monopoly situation or government protection) and entered competitive markets, we find firms that are attempting to survive multinationalization of their activities. The giant state-owned firms that remained profitable made a tremendous effort to expand their activities worldwide. In practical terms, this has meant an expansion to South America. Private successful firms (such as the largest banks) and formerly state-owned firms (Telefónica, ENDESA, REPSOL) coincide in their venturing into South America.

Meanwhile, the loss-making remnants of the former INI have been granted new life through all kinds of national and European-wide subsidies. Even the current pro-privatization government feels unable to cope with regionwide public firms such as HUNOSA, the Asturian coal firm. The government become aware that eliminating subsidies is out of the question; only the handling of subsidies matters.

REFERENCES

Anuario El País. 1992.

Argandoña, A. 1972. Economías de escala y eficiencia: Estudio de dos sectores de la economía española. *Revista Española de Economía* 2: 125–62.

Ballestero, A. 1993. *Juan Antonio Suanzes, 1891–1977.* Madrid.

Barea, J., and J.-F. Corona. 1996. La reforma de la empresa pública. *Papeles de Economía Española* 69: 278–309.

Carreras, A. 1988. La segunda revolución tecnológica. In *España: 200 años de tecnolog lá*, ed. J. Nadal, A. Carreras, P. Martín Aceña, and F. Comín, pp. 101–96. Madrid.

Carreras, A., and X. Tafunell. 1993. La gran empresa en España, 1917–1974: Una primera aproximación. *Revista de Historia Industrial* 3: 127–75.

Castaño, C. 1985. La industria del automóvil en España: Efectos de los procesos de cambio tecnológico sobre las condiciones del mercado de trabajo. Ph.D. diss., Universidad Complutense, Madrid.

Castaño, C., and G. Cortes. 1980. Evolución del sector del automóvil en España. *Ínformación Comercial Española* 563: 145–57.

Comín, F. 1996. *Historia de la Hacienda pública*, vol. 2, *España (1808–1995)*. Barcelona.

Comin, F., and P. Martín Aceña, eds. 1991. *Historia de la empresa pública en España*. Madrid.

Cuervo, À. 1997a. La empresa pública: Razones que explican su ineficiencia y privatización. *Economistas* 75: 88–100.

———. 1997b. Las privatizaciones en España. *Cuadernos de Información Económica* 119: 10–23.

De la Dehesa, G. 1992. Privatización europea: El caso de España. *Información Comercial Española* 707: 55–71.

———. 1993. Las privatizaciones en España. *Moneda y Crédito* 196: 131–41.

Dunning, J., and R. Pearce. 1981. *The World's Largest Industrial Enterprises*. New York.

Estapé, S. 1998. Economic nationalism, state intervention, and foreign multinationals: The case of the Spanish Ford subsidiary, 1936–1954. *Essays in Economic and Business History* 16: 75–94.

Fernandez-Cuesta, N. 1986. La liberalización del sector petrolero español. *Economía Industrial* 248: 41–56.

Fomento de la Producción. 1991. *Las 2.500 mayores empresas españolas*. Barcelona.

Fraile, P. 1992. *Interés público y captura del Estado: La empresa pública siderúrgica en España, 1941–1981*. Madrid.

García Delgado, J. L., ed. 1993. *España, economía*. Madrid.

Macchiati, A. 1996. *Privatizzazioni: Tra economia e politica*. Rome.

Martín Aceña, P. 1991. Los orígenes de la banca pública. In *Historia de la empresa pública en España*, ed. F. Comín and P. Martín Aceña, pp. 331–73. Madrid.

Martín Aceña, P., and F. Comín. 1991. *El INI: Cincuenta años de industrialización en España*. Madrid.

———. 1994. La empresa pública en España antes de la guerra civil. In *Introducción a la Historia de la Empresa en España*, ed. G. Núñez and L. Segreto, pp. 115–40. Madrid.

Myro, R. 1980. El INI en la industria española: Especialización sectorial, eficiencia económica y rentabilidad. Ph.D. diss., Universidad Complutense, Madrid.

Nadal, J., and X. Tafunell. 1992. *Sant Martí de Provençals: Pulmó industrial de Barcelona, 1847–1992*. Barcelona.

Núñez, G., and L. Segreto, eds. 1994. *Introducción a la Historia de la Empresa en España*. Madrid.

San Román, E. 1995. El nacimiento de la SEAT: Autarquñia e intervención del INI. *Revista de Historia Industrial* 7: 141-65.

Santamaría, J. 1988. *El petróleo en España: Del monopolio a la libertad*. Madrid.

Schwartz, P., and M.-J. Gonzalez. 1978. *Una historia del Instituto Nacional de Industria (1941-1976)*. Madrid.

Segreto, L. 1997. *Marte e Mercurio: Industria bellica e sviluppo economico in Italia, 1861-1940*. Milan.

Sudrià, C. 1993. El sector energético: Condicionamientos y posibilidades. In *España, economía*, ed. J. L. García Delgado, pp. 267-95. Madrid.

Tamames, R. 1990. *Estructura económica de España*. 16th ed. Madrid.

Toninelli, P. A. 1997a. Il ruolo dello stato nella economia. In *Lo sviluppo economico moderno: Dalla rivoluzione industriale alla crisi energetica (1750-1973)*, ed. P. A. Toninelli, pp. 561-96. Venice.

    ed. 1997b. *Lo sviluppo economico moderno: Dalla rivoluzione industriale alla crisi energetica (1750-1973)*. Venice.

Torres, E. 1997. Intervención del Estado: Propiedad y control en las empresas gestoras del monopolio de tabacos, 1887-1985. Paper presented to the VI Congreso de la AHE, Girona, September.

Tortella, G. 1990. CAMPSA y el monopolio de petróleos, 1927-1947. In *El INI: Cincuenta años de industrialización en España*, ed. P. Martín Aceña and F. Comin, pp. 81-116. Madrid.

    1991. El monopolio de petróleos y CAMPSA, 1927-1947. *Hacienda Pública Española*, Monografías 1: 171-90.

Valdaliso, J. 1998. *La empresa nacional "Elcano" de la Marina Mercante y la actuación del INI en el sector naval durante la presidencia de J.A. Suanzes*. Madrid.

10

⌾

Fifty Years of State-Owned Industry in Austria, 1946–1996

DIETER STIEFEL

THE REASONS FOR NATIONALIZATION IN 1946

Austria has a long history of state ownership dating back to the mercantilist era. The state controlled monopolies on salt and tobacco for a long time, and at the end of the nineteenth century the water supply, electricity, railways, and city transportation also came under public ownership in various ways. This absorption by the state might have been due to the "relative backwardness" (Alexander Gerschenkron) of the country or, alternatively, might have been a tribute to Austria's close relationship with the German tradition of confidence in the institution of the state as such. The liberal tradition had always been weak. The left-wing Socialist Party (SP) and the conservative Christian Socialists always favored public ownership in certain areas, and private business and public ownership coexisted without friction. The revolutionary period after World War I witnessed the socialist experiment of socialization, which soon failed, partly because of conservative opposition (März and Weber 1978). During World War II the fascist German government established important publicly owned war industries in Austria, and these transformed the economic structure of the country. If public ownership of part of the credit, trade, and agricultural systems (municipal savings banks, cooperative banks, agricultural cooperatives) is also included, it is evident that Austria had for a long time experienced no real problems with public ownership in a mixed market system.

Public ownership, however, reached unforeseen proportions after World War II. In 1946 the Austrian Parliament decided to nationalize seventy-one large business enterprises, 20 percent of the country's industry. These included iron, steel, and oil production, part of the chemical industry, and machinery and mining. This was followed in 1947 by the transfer of the three leading banks and 85 percent of the electrical companies to public ownership as well. Austria thus suddenly became a country with one of the highest levels of nationalization in the Western world. The reason for this dramatic step was the political issue of German property. After the war, the Allied powers were not sure if a reestablished Austria could be held responsible for World War II. Austria had not existed between 1938 and 1945, but its population had taken an active part both in the war itself and in Nazi crimes. The Allies decided not to impose war reparations on the Second Republic but to take possession of the German property in Austria instead (Sandgruber 1995). This demand, which seemed fair enough, would have brought a major part of the Austrian economy under foreign control.

How was it possible for German capital to penetrate Austria to such an extent? The explanation dates back to World War I. Very few countries had suffered as much as Austria from the loss of capital and wealth. The impoverishment brought by World War I, the disintegration of the Habsburg Empire and the consequent diminishing importance of Vienna, postwar inflation and the breakdown of the currency in 1922, and the Depression all had a devastating effect on private capital. This was the situation when Austria joined the German Reich in 1938 (*Anschluß*). As an immediate result, Jewish capital lost its influence (*Arisierung*). The Germans not only invested heavily in important war industries (such as Hermann Göringwerke, Linz, which later became VOEST), but also bought Austrian businesses. German shareholding in Austrian industry (*Aktiengesellschaften*), which had stood at no more than 8–12 percent before the *Anschluß*, totaled 57 percent in 1945 (Klambauer 1978a).

After the war, the Allied powers wanted to destroy German influence in Austria totally. As a result of the developments just described, however, there was no Austrian private capital that could have been used to take over these industries. Thus, the only alternatives were foreign ownership or nationalization. The Austrian Parliament responded to this situation by unanimously voting in favor of public ownership

Table 10.1. Share of Austrian SOE in Production, 1951
(Percent)

Brown coal	94
Copper	100
Iron ore	99
Pig iron	99
Sheet metal	90
Lead-zinc	100
Aluminum	71
Chemical fertilizer	90

Source: Langer 1966.

Table 10.2. Share of SOE in Economic Measures, 1951
(Percent)

Industrial employment	19
Industrial net product	22
Industrial exports	26

Source: Langer 1966.

(Koren 1964). This political step was taken regardless of the general attitude of members of Parliament toward public ownership. It was an exceptional law in an exceptional time. Nineteen forty-five brought to an end the thirty-year-long process of impoverishment, and only the state could raise the capital necessary for reconstruction. The state is not only the lender but also the capital supplier of last resort (see Tables 10.1 and 10.2).

The Allied powers were not pleased with the Austrian initiative to nationalize German property, but they endorsed it on the condition that the ownership rights of their own citizens would be settled by negotiation. The Soviet Union ignored the Austrian laws and took over a considerable industrial complex within its occupied zone (USIA), including all Austrian oil production. About 40 percent of state-owned enterprises (SOEs), including 28,000 employees, were beyond the sphere of Austrian influence. It was not until the signing of the State Treaty in 1955, when the occupying powers left the country, that the Soviet Union handed back these industries on the condition that a further payment be made by Austria (Klambauer 1978b).

THE POLITICAL ATTITUDE TOWARD PUBLIC OWNERSHIP

In spite of Austria's long tradition of state ownership, mainly in infrastructure, the situation in 1946 was absolutely new. The Austrian state
had never been responsible for such a large industrial organization
before – and this large industrial organization was no mere monopoly,
but faced competition from the private market. The economic knowledge of politicians and civil servants was undoubtedly inadequate.
The politicians naturally concentrated on general political questions
rather than on management needs. The two leading political parties, the
Socialist Party and the conservative People's Party (ÖOVP), had different attitudes toward the public ownership of industries beyond the
infrastructure. The left-wing party considered such ownership an important step toward the establishment of a socialist society, and they
wanted to enlarge the number of enterprises and the resources dedicated to them (Zimmermann 1964). Thus, they wanted to nationalize
not only the 71 business enterprises finally included in the law of 1946,
but also a further 125 industrial companies, comprising nearly all the
leading firms in every branch of the economy. The conservatives,
however, perceived this extent of public ownership as simply a result
of the war. They wanted a speedy return to what they perceived as nor-
mality, that is, to private ownership. Although the ÖOVP did not refrain
from using the possibilities of political influence that SOEs offered, it
was this different point of view that characterized the development of
SOEs in their fifty years of existence. The ÖOVP always maintained its
distance from nationalization. Even in 1946 the party gave its consent
to the nationalization law only in conjunction with a *Werksgenossen-
schaftsgesetz* (a production cooperative law). This would have offered
the possibility of transferring the shares of SOEs to employees. The attitude of the Christian Socialists was that the worker should also be the
owner of the means of production. Thus, the social problems of capitalism (*Soziale Frage*) should be solved by giving the work force a share
in industrial ownership. The implementation of the *Werksgenossen-
schaftsgesetz* would have entailed the quiet, steady denationalization
of SOEs. Socialist opposition, however, meant that it was never
implemented.

Political disagreement broke out once more in 1955. At the end of
the Allied occupation, the Soviet Union had to hand over its share of
SOEs. As the Soviet Union had a very broad understanding of German
property, only 18 of the 319 companies under Soviet control (USIA)

were named in the nationalization law of 1946. The question "What to do with the other companies – nationalize or reprivatize?" was the subject of a very intense election campaign. This time the ÖOVP achieved one of the greatest election successes in its history. As a result of its success, a reprivatization campaign was undertaken that lasted until 1962. The government was able to raise 1.5 billion schillings by selling off publicly owned enterprises. The nationalized banks were partly privatized in 1956. Forty percent of the share capital of the two leading banks, the Creditanstalt-Bankverein and the Länderbank, was sold as "people's shares" (*Volksaktien*). "*Volk*" meant that only a limited number of shares could be bought by individuals, thus ensuring a wide distribution of the share capital and preventing individuals or groups from acquiring a controlling influence in the banks. Finally, in 1972, most of the Austrian Siemens company had to be sold back to the German parent company for reasons of technological transfer. Only 40 percent remained under Austrian state control.

There has always been a difference in the general position of state ownership concerning banks, electricity, and industries. The management of the banks was able to restrict political influence more effectively than that of other nationalized enterprises, at least in the running of day-to-day business. The reason may be that the government not only owned the banks but also needed their help in financing the state budget. Thus, the nationalized banks were separated from the administration of nationalized industry. The banks were controlled by the Finance Ministry and were never subjected to the frequent reorganizations typical of other SOEs. The situation concerning electricity was even more complicated because these enterprises were not only nationalized but also regionalized, with each of the nine Austrian *Bundesländer* (federal states), no matter how small, establishing its own organization that had to cooperate with the state agency. This is why privatization in this field seems especially complicated. In this essay, I will concentrate on state-owned industry.

ECONOMIC PERFORMANCE

Austrian SOE (Table 10.3) was a success in its first twenty-five years. The reasons for this were two. First was its economic potential. The SOEs – iron, steel, machinery, and so on – provided the basis of mass production needed for economic reconstruction and the economic upswing (*Wirtschaftswunder*) that followed it. The productivity and export rates

Table 10.3. SOEs in Austria (ÖIAG-Konzern)

Year	Employees	Billion Schillings		
		Turnover	Investment	Export
1946	56,060	1.7	—	0.2
1950	83,095	6.5	1.0	1.5
1955	123,327	12.5	1.0	4.1
1960	130,877	23.0	2.7	8.2
1965	123,132	26.0	92.2	9.9
1970	110,760	44.0	3.8	14.8
1975	116,717	81.1	6.9	29.8
1980	116,602	114.3	9.3	47.0
1985	102,160	198.6	7.3	71.6
Percent of Austrian Industry in 1980				
	17	23	26	22

were higher than those of many private sectors. In addition, the nationalized sector of the Austrian economy included a large part of the
country's big business. These large enterprises could carry out projects
such as the construction of bridges, power plants, and factories, both
within Austria and abroad. The size of the work force doubled within
the first ten years, reaching a peak at the beginning of the 1960s with
more than 130,000 employees. At that time, SOEs were shown off with
pride to foreign diplomats or visitors. The VOEST was named the flag-
ship of the Austrian economy, and the opening of a new factory or a
new blast furnace was a formal state occasion. The technological success
of SOEs such as LD-Verfahren was recorded in school textbooks and
became part of Austria's sense of identity in the same way as its cultural
tradition in music. Further, SOEs were especially important to the socialist movement. Unlike the generally small and middle-sized businesses in
Austria, SOEs employed "real" industrial workers, who played a fundamental role in socialism's self-perception.

The other reason for the success of SOEs is to be found in the political environment. After 1945 the political culture of Austria was quite
different from that of the prewar period. Political conflicts had been
very intense before 1945. There had been the danger of a working-class
revolution in 1918, a short but intense civil war in 1934 in which the
socialist movement had been destroyed, and the victory of National
Socialism by means of the *Anschluß* with the German Reich in 1938.

After 1945, conflict was transformed into cooperation, although for decades the supporters of the various political parties still distrusted one another. The culture of cooperation, which evolved as a political instrument during the Allied occupation, became the general basis for political action. In the last fifty years, Austria has usually been governed by a coalition of the two big parties. The coalition has had an overwhelming majority in all the elected political institutions of the country. The economic side of this political culture was social partnership (*Sozialpartnerschaft*): employers' and workers' organizations settled their conflicts by negotiation (Prisching 1996). SOEs were one of the basic instruments of social partnership. They played a leading role in wage development, social improvement, and job security.

POLITICAL INFLUENCE

Proportional Representation

SOEs offered supporters of the two parties in power remarkable economic advantages (Hood 1994). There is little absolute proof, but it is common knowledge that in SOEs formal party membership was a necessary prerequisite for even minor jobs (Summer 1987). Austrians did not mind these political conditions because usually there were no additional obligations. The distribution of economic advantages (apartments, credits, jobs) through political connections was usual in Austria. This is how, in a country of 7 million inhabitants, each of the two leading parties could boast of having 500,000 party members, and the Austrian trade union movement had the highest level of membership of any Western country.

Political influence on recruitment of senior managers certainly existed, although in this connection it was important that the conservatives were the first to take responsibility for SOEs in 1946. As a consequence SOEs did not enjoy special legal status, but were organized within the framework of existing commercial law. This meant that they had the same legal framework as private industry and competed with the private sector both at home and abroad. The government only held the position of majority shareholder. The supervisory board (*Aufsichtsrat*) was appointed by the government as the representative of the owner, but management itself was, at least formally, installed by and responsible to the supervisory board rather than to the government. Legally, politics had no direct influence on the management of SOEs.

Informally, however, political influence was permanent and strong. It is important to understand that even the social partnership was informal and not enforced by law. Informality was an important element in Austrian political culture after the war. As one of its fundamental institutions, the social partnership depended on the goodwill of employers' and workers' organizations and the influence these organizations had on their members. Therefore it seems quite natural that senior management positions in SOEs were subject to bargaining by the political parties. Frequently, important management posts had to be filled twice, so a "red" director faced his "black" counterpart and vice versa. This political bargaining involving proportional representation (*Proporz*) was so common that it was even established by law. The Kompetenzgesetz of 1956, which was the legal basis of the work of the coalition government, laid particular emphasis on the requirement that personnel decisions in SOEs had to be based on the wishes and strength of the political parties in Parliament (7).

The recruitment of top management positions by *Proporz* is peculiar for a business enterprise. Normally, proportional representation is an instrument for solving ethnic or national conflicts. In the South Tyrol, for instance, the German-speaking minority has the legal right to a certain proportion of positions in the public administration. In the United Nations as well, positions in the various organizations have to be filled by members of different nations. But these organizations are neither profit- nor market-oriented and are intended to solve political conflicts. *Proporz* is therefore a political model that was transferred to the market sphere. As a result of its employment, SOEs were reorganized after nearly every national election.

After 1966 SOEs were removed from the direct control of one of the state departments. A shareholding company (*Aktiengesellschaft*) was set up in 1970, and this took over all the property rights of the state. The objectives were to weaken direct political influence and to allow SOEs to work more like private, profit-oriented businesses.

Despite political influence, the management of SOEs was not really different from that of private industry. In Austria, as in other countries, fluctuation between private and state enterprise was not uncommon (Parris 1985).

The argument for the superiority of private management in industry is more political than economic. Regarding the large number of business insolvencies in Europe in recent years, it should be clear that private enterprises as well as SOEs have had to face increasing difficulties over the last two decades (Kramer 1985). It is too easy to blame the management of SOEs for poor economic performance and to speak of incompetence. The management of SOEs was not only confronted with difficult economic developments, it was also constrained by political considerations that sometimes exerted a powerful influence on business policy. According to Rudolf Sallinger, longtime president of the employers' organization (*Bundeswirtschaftskammer*):

It has to be said that it is not easy for the management of SOEs. If management wants to take the hard but necessary measures to ensure redevelopment, politics interferes again and again. The economic necessities for structural changes are hindered or delayed by political interference. We can't go on like this. We want and we need SOEs. But we also need to give management a free hand, even if the necessary measures do not please either the government or political parties. (Sallinger 1985, p. 7)

Investment

Due to differences of political opinion, SOEs were never able to develop their economic potential in full. Their organization was changed after nearly every election, and sufficient risk capital could never be raised. Until 1952 they received an important share of the Marshall Plan funds (European Recovery Program, ERP), but after that date they ran into structural financing problems. The state as owner provided no additional funds for financing the necessary investment. The Socialist Party wanted financing to come from the state budget. The conservatives, however, believed that giving additional public funds to nationalized industries would mean a creeping enlargement of the public sector in the economy, so they blocked it. The ÖOVP argued that industry in a market economy had to be financed through the capital market, which would have entailed slow, silent privatization. This solution was also blocked by political opponents. Thus, after 1952, SOEs had to self-finance up to 80 percent of their own expansion, and this undoubtedly reduced their potential. Financial distress eased only after the establishment of the Österreichische Industrieholding Aktiengesellschaft (ÖIAG). Although the ÖIAG was 100 percent state-owned, it had the right to issue loans on the capital market. In the 1970s the ÖIAG supplied the SOEs with 4.6 billion schillings of risk capital. Of this, 3.6 billion schillings were in the form of national industry dividends that the state returned for investment purposes (see Table 10.4).

Table 10.4. SOE Investment Financing (Percent)

	1946–53	1946–70
European Recovery Program	45	9
State	4	3
Self-financing	51	88

Product Policy

Product policy, too, was subject to political restriction for a long time. The Austrian Chamber of Commerce, which looked after the interests of private industry, insisted that the role of SOEs should be to supply the Austrian economy with cheap primary products. Therefore the price of its products, regulated again through social partnership, had to be cheaper at home than abroad. In the 1950s the price of coal and steel was 10–20 percent less than that in the Federal Republic of Germany. It is estimated that this politically enforced price policy cost SOEs 2.2 billion schillings in iron and steel and 6.2 billion schillings in coal and chemicals, as well as hindering expansion into new final production. Private industry argued that if SOEs were really necessary, their role should be to offer an economic advantage to private business rather than to act as competitors. It seemed impossible that private industry should stimulate public-owned competitors through tax payments. Only at the beginning of the 1970s was this restrictive product policy changed. Until the mid-1980s, thirty-five SOE production lines were closed and twenty-seven new ones opened. In 1985, 20 percent of VOEST-Alpine activity came from products that had not been produced five years earlier.

Personnel Reductions

Finally, SOEs were not free to reduce their work forces or to close down money-losing factories. In this case the political influence of the state, local authorities, and trade unions remained invincible for a long time. Every decision to shut down – in cities such as Judenburg, Fohnsdorf, and Donawitz – brought strong opposition from all the local political parties and trade unions. All parties agreed in principle about the need to reorganize SOEs – so long as their own areas remained unaffected. As early as the 1960s, business consultants had recommended the reduction of production centers. Political opposition ensured that such early restructuring of SOEs did not take place. The reduction of Austrian steel production was delayed until activities elsewhere in the group had developed and steel workers were offered a chance to retrain for new jobs. The limitation of this policy is that growth industries are rarely as labor-intensive as declining industries. The scarcity of resources for investment in the public business sector means that hard choices have to be made between maintaining employment in traditional sectors and creating jobs in new areas (Parris 1985).

Kreisky's famous statement that he preferred a few billions of budget deficit to a few thousand unemployed was typical of the 1970s. The partial success of Keynesian policies in Austria cannot be denied (Nowotny 1982). The structural economic change of the 1970s had fewer political and social consequences in Austria than in many other countries. There was no breakdown of industry and no region of mass unemployment; rather, there was a slow and reluctant retreat. This policy was expensive, however, and some of the cost had to be borne by SOEs. The structural crisis of state-owned industry worsened. There is little doubt of the long-term overstaffing in SOEs. In 1952, during the first postwar recession, employment in industry generally declined by 12 percent, but it remained more or less unchanged in the public sector. In 1966 the ÖOVP government (the first noncoalition government after 1945) asked foreign business consultants to investigate Austria's SOEs. Their suggestion was to reduce the work force by 10,000, but this could not be done for political reasons. The greatest difference in employment policy became evident during the recession of the 1970s. In 1975 production in private industry was reduced by 7 percent; production in SOEs declined by 9 percent during the same period. As a consequence of declining production, overall industrial employment decreased by 7 percent – but the SOE rate of employment did not change at all. SOEs thus played an important role in the employment policy of the government. Without them, full employment would have ended much earlier. SOEs, unlike private industry, had to pay a kind of labor market tax at a time when they were facing a severe structural crisis. Their obligation to provide employment not only reduced their ability to produce income but also delayed necessary structural adjustment. "It can be argued that public enterprises should not attempt to solve their problems by sacking people, and sometimes the state puts pressure on them to behave in a socially responsible manner. But it is easy to be socially responsible with other people's money, and all too often that is what it

Table 10.5. Change in Industrial Employment
(Percent)

Year	Industry	SOE
1952	12	−0.3
1975	2	+1
1984	0.3	−5

Table 10.6. Number of Employees in SOEs, 1985–95

1985	102,160
1990	83,136
1991	82,381
1992	77,731
1993	64,859
1994	34,164
1995	18,888

comes to. Employment maintenance by a public enterprise may only be practicable so long as the taxpayer foots the bill" (Parris 1985, p. 48).

The picture changed at the beginning of the 1980s, when the government had to accept that it was not faced with a short-term economic downswing but rather a long-term structural change in the economy. Between 1980 and 1985, SOEs had to dismiss or make redundant more than 17,000 people. During this period private industry reduced its work force by 10 percent, but SOEs took the lead by making a reduction of 13 percent (see Tables 10.5 and 10.6).

REORGANIZATION

The golden years of the SOE came to an end in the 1970s. Management mistakes had aggravated their problems but were not the only reason for their decline. The main reason was the international economic depression and the changing structure of the world market. Costly political decisions were made. The government tried to solve the problems of the growing number of unprofitable SOEs by merging them with their profitable counterparts. A big industrial complex was established as part of this process. The "great steel solution" of 1973 saw the merger of VOEST and Alpine (VA); Böhler and Schöller-Bleckmann were affiliated to form the biggest Austrian business enterprise, with 67,000 workers.

This was followed in 1974 by the nonferrous metal merger and in 1975 by the foundation of the Vereinigte Edelstahlwerke (VEW). Thus, the ÖIAG controlled eight industrial groups comprising about 200 firms and more than 500 very different production lines. Instead of the sixty-seven industrial enterprises mentioned in the nationalization law of 1946 there were now eight industrial groups under the control of the ÖIAG. They were under complete public ownership. Three mining companies had already been closed down; the shipping company Donau-Dampfschiffahrts-Gesellschaft (DDSG) was under the control of the Ministry of Transport; Siemens (Austria) had come under majority control of the German parent company; four firms had to be given back to Western oil companies in 1955; and three private companies, not listed in the 1946 law, were taken over by the government because of economic problems in the period 1983 to 1985 – Elektro-Bau AG, Eumig Fohnsdorf, and Futurit Werke AG.

CRISIS AND PRIVATIZATION

The year 1985 was a turning point in the history of Austrian SOEs. The international discussions about privatization strengthened the ÖOVP's position at home. In nearly every country, state ownership was in decline (Hood 1994). It thus seemed natural to follow the international development. After forty years the reasons for nationalization, which had been genuine in 1946, no longer seemed relevant (Kehrer 1986). The Socialist Party still defended the existence and the extent of the nationalized sector, but mounting SOE losses meant that there was no alternative to partial privatization at the very least. Until the end of the 1970s, the world of the SOE seemed more or less in order. It is true that VOEST had stopped dividend payments in 1974, but on the whole, the results of the ÖIAG were balanced until 1978. From then on, the results of SOEs were generally negative. In view of the global recession and the need for reconstruction, the losses were still acceptable. It was not until the catastrophic business results of 1985 (Intertrading, Bayou, Pöls) that the losses reached a dangerous level. The losses for 1985 were higher than those of the previous years combined – and they were even higher than all the SOE dividend payments since 1946. Only twenty-one out of forty-one ÖIAG companies recorded no losses in their balance sheets. The oil company Österreichische Mineralöl Verwaltung (ÖMV) alone was responsible for 70 percent of the remaining dividend payments for the year.

Table 10.7. ÖIAG Losses (Billion Schillings)

1978	1979	1980	1981	1982	1983	1984	1985
0.7	0.1	1.0	1.1	0.8	2.6	2.5	12.5

In the first half of the 1980s, the losses amounted to more than 20 billion schillings (see Table 10.7). Altogether the state had to cover losses of more than 100 billion schillings (Nemeth 1992). When he was appointed finance minister, Ferdinand Lacina (SP) commented, "If it can be proved that nationalized enterprises cannot be managed profitably, that our model of public property rights does not function, then I not only fear for the existence of one factory or another, but for the whole political concept for which I stand." In Lacina's view, the demand for privatization was ideologically, not economically, motivated (in *Zukunft*, April 1986). It is one of the ironies of history that Lacina, one of the most committed defenders of state-owned industry, was forced to begin the process of privatization and liquidation as a socialist finance minister. Facing the huge and unforeseen SOE losses from 1985 on, the socialists had to accept the capitalist principle that the first aim of a business enterprise is to make a profit. Ten years earlier, this attitude would have been rejected as conservative or reactionary.

After 1985 Austrian economic policy veered toward privatization. The thirtieth and fortieth anniversaries of nationalization were celebrated in 1976 and 1986, but in 1996 the fiftieth anniversary was not publicly mentioned. Today privatization predominates and almost seems to be a value in itself. The first privatization strategy was the foundation of the Austrian Industries AG (AI) by the ÖIAG. It aimed to privatize SOEs by selling AI shares on the stock market. In 1993 this concept had to be changed as it became clear that SOEs would remain unsold until they were reorganized and became profitable once more.

The new ÖIAG law of 1993 and the privatization concept of 1994 made privatization the final aim of the ÖIAG. The ÖIAG had to undertake the process of reorganization itself, and this is why the process of privatization has lasted such a long time. Some companies, such as Bleiberger Bergwerksunion (lead mining), had to be closed down completely. Today privatization is in full swing; SOE shares are sold on the stock market or to private industries in Austria and abroad or to management buyouts. In many sectors, such as oil production, the state has reduced its influence by keeping only a blocking minority. In 1995 most of VOEST–Alpine Stahl AG was successfully sold on the stock market, and the state reduced its ownership to 43.3 percent (ÖIAG 1995). The sole purpose of the ÖIAG became the liquidation, consolidation, and sale of the remaining SOEs. In view of this aim, the results are very positive. The ÖIAG has reduced public ownership in Austrian industry, and it has reduced the losses and debts of the remaining SOEs. Losses on the ÖIAG balance sheet were reduced from 7.44 billion schillings in 1993 to 2.5 billion in 1994 and 1.7 billion in 1995. Whether companies are profitable or not, the final objective is still privatization. The degree of privatization in itself, rather than the return to profitability of nationalized companies, is seen as a success by the public. An important additional political motivation is the financial result of privatization. The Austrian government needs to reduce its budget deficit in order to meet the conditions of the Maastricht agreement. It seeks to do so through the successful sale of its property rights in banking and industry. The financial results of "selling the family silver" are potentially among the highest in the Western world. It could yield 30 to 50 billion schillings, which is 2 percent of the country's gross national product or a third of its annual budget deficit (*Der Standard*, Vienna, 4 December 1994; *Kurier*, Vienna, 2 December 1994). SOE employees have been cut to about 15 percent of their former number, and the process of privatization is still going on. The SOE was an important instrument for the economic reconstruction of Austria after the war, but today it seems no more than an episode in the economic development of the country.

REFERENCES

Hood, C. 1994. *Explaining economic policy reversals*. Buckingham, Eng.
Kehrer, K. 1986. *Wirtschaftspolitische Blätter*. Vienna.
Klambauer, O. 1978a. Die Frage des deutschen Eigentums in Österreich. In *Jahrbuch für Zeitgeschichte*, pp. 148–51. Vienna.
——— 1978b. "Die USIA-Betriebe." Diss., University of Vienna.
Koren, S. 1964. Sozialisierungsideologie und Verstaatlichungsrealität. In *Die Verstaatlichung in Österreich*, ed. W. Weber, p. 248. Vienna.
Kramer, H. 1985. *Österreichs Industrie im internationalen Wettbewerb, Entwicklungstendenzen und längerfristige Aussichten, Institut für angewandte Sozial- und Wirtschaftsforschung*. Vienna.
Langer, E. 1966. *Die Verstaatlichungen in Österreich*. Vienna.
März, E., and F. Weber. 1978. Verstaatlichung und Sozialisierung nach dem Ersten und Zweiten Weltkrieg. In *Wirtschaft und Gesellschaft*, p. 36. Vienna.
Nemeth, F. 1992. *Privatisierung als Antwort auf die Krise der verstaatlichten Unternehmungen in Österreich*. Vienna.

Nowotny, E. 1982. SOE as an instrument of stabilisation policy: The case of Austria. *Annals of Public and Co-operative Economy* 53.

ÖIAG (Österreichische Industrieholding Aktiengesellschaft). 1990–5. *Geschäftsberichte*. Vienna.

Parris, H. 1985. *Public enterprise in Western Europe*. London.

Prisching, M. 1996. *Die Sozialpartnerschaft. Modell der Vergangenheit oder Modell für Europa*. Vienna.

Sallinger, R. 1985. *Der Unternehmer*. Vienna.

Sandgruber, R. 1995. *Ökonomie und Politik: Österreichische Wirtschaftsgeschichte vom Mittelalter bis zur Gegenwart*. Vienna.

Summer, F. 1987. *Das VOEST Debakel*. Vienna.

Zimmermann, R. 1964. *Verstaatlichungen in Österreich, ihre Aufgaben und Ziele*. Vienna.

11

A Reluctant State and Its Enterprises

State-Owned Enterprises in the Netherlands in the "Long" Twentieth Century

M. DAVIDS AND JAN L. VAN ZANDEN

The rise and fall of state-owned enterprises (SOEs) should be seen in the context of broader changes in the socioeconomic structure of the Netherlands after about 1870. In an ongoing study of the Dutch economy in the twentieth century, Jan van Zanden has developed the concept of the "long" twentieth century to describe these changes. In the decades after 1870 three interrelated processes of structural change began; these processes dominated economic life during the twentieth century. These three changes are the rise of trade unions, the growth of the managerial enterprise, and the development of the welfare state. After about 1900 these changes accelerated, reaching full maturity after 1945. Since the early 1970s all three seemed to be in decline: union membership fell, the crisis in the welfare state led to large-scale cuts in welfare provision, and the large multinationals radically decreased their share of total employment due to downsizing, increased subcontracting, and intense competition from abroad. Economic development since the early 1980s has been characterized by (1) increased flexibility in the labor market (in spite of trade union resistance), (2) a government that officially aims at reducing its role in the economy, and (3) the decline of (large-scale) industry and the great increase in (small-scale) service employment (Van Zanden 1997).

The rise and decline of SOEs in the long twentieth century is another feature of these interrelated processes. The forces that contributed to the rise of the welfare state and trade unionism, for example, also favored increased direct state intervention in production through the establishment of SOEs and the nationalization of private enterprises. In a similar way, the shift to monetarism and supply-side economics during the 1980s, which in a way marked the end of the long twentieth century, also hastened the decline of SOEs. In our view, these developments can be interpreted on two levels. On the ideological level, what changes in the thinking on economics, and on the relationship between the economy and the state, led to a century of increased interventionism after 1870? What developments in the ideological sphere caused the 180 degree turn after about 1975? On the material level, what changes in the economy and in society at large stimulated the acceptance of those ideas and helped to force the rise of the welfare state, trade unionism, and big enterprise after about 1870? What caused the 180 degree turn after 1975? The brevity of this essay does not allow us to deal with these questions in detail, but we will sketch the main developments related to the rise and decline of SOEs.

COLLAPSE OF THE LAISSEZ-FAIRE CONSENSUS: 1870–1940

In the second half of the nineteenth century, the "liberal" consensus (in the European sense of the word) was particularly strong and well established in the Netherlands. Already in the seventeenth century, when Dutch merchants dominated international trade and industry, it was realized that the bourgeoisie (which had been in control of the state since 1572) benefited most from free access for all to the seas (the *libre marum* of Grotius). The thinking about economic matters in this very open economy had generally favored free exchange and limited intervention by the state. Experiments with interventionism during the first half of the nineteenth century (by King William I) were perceived as having failed and led to the near bankruptcy of the state in 1840. Since then, classical liberalism dominated economic thinking and a good part of economic policy making.

There are, however, some notable exceptions. When private enterprise failed to build an interconnected system of railways, for example, the government was forced to step in and finance their construction in the 1860s. The operation of the network was, however, delegated to a number of private companies, which were supposed to compete with each other to keep prices down. In 1890, after a reorganization of the railway companies, this became the accepted philosophy of railway policy: two companies were created that were obliged to compete with each other on all major routes. It was hoped that this would result in greater efficiency and lower prices (Van den Broeke 1989).

After about 1870 the liberal consensus increasingly came under attack as a result of the rise of a group of "radical" liberals who favored increased government intervention in the labor market (e.g., some basic social insurance, limitations on female and child labor) and in production. The most hotly debated issue was the ownership of public utilities, especially the gas companies (De Vries 1994). In a few big cities the British Imperial Continental Gas Company had acquired a monopoly in the manufacturing and distribution of gas, which (according to its left-wing critics) resulted in high prices for consumers and enormous profits for its owners. The first municipal gas company had started in Leiden in 1848, becoming an important source of income to the city. The question of whether or not to nationalize the British and other private gas producers became a major bone of contention between the orthodox liberals and the left-wing radicals, resulting in the victory of the latter. In the 1880s and 1890s almost all private gas companies were acquired by the municipalities (Brugmans 1969, 349). The same process occurred with the growth of the electricity industry. The pioneers of the 1880s and 1890s were rapidly overtaken by municipal firms after 1900 and by provincial firms after 1913. The latter came to monopolize the industry.

In these debates the interests of consumers loomed very large. The fact that Dutch industries had to pay high prices for these inputs as a result of the monopolization of gas production by private interests also played a role in the decision to nationalize them (Zadoks 1899).

Market failure also lay behind the establishment of a state-owned savings bank allied with the postal service (Rijkspostspaarbank) in 1881. Post offices were used as branches for its (limited) banking activities. Again it was noted that private enterprise was unable to cater to this need (De Ru 1981, 26).

Similar arguments played a role in the decision to set up the State Mines in 1901, again proposed by a left-wing liberal (radical), Cornelius Lely. Coal mining had developed quite slowly in the Netherlands during the nineteenth century. As a result, the country was largely dependent on imported coal. Moreover, the existing mines were mainly owned by foreigners (from Belgium, France, and Germany), as Dutch investors had not been very interested in the industry (which was located in Limburg in the southern tip of the country). Officially the reason for setting up a state-owned company, Staatsmijnen, was to accelerate its development and keep it in Dutch hands. The Limburg politicians who favored the new law, however, were afraid that coal mining would develop too quickly (after a breakthrough in mining technology had made the Limburg deposits quite profitable for exploitation), which would result in the large-scale immigration of foreign (Polish and Italian) workers (as happened in the neighboring Ruhr area). They favored exploitation by the state so as to be able to control the development of an indigenous labor force (Kreukels 1986, 23).

Unlike the case of the railways, no attempt was made to privatize the company in this case. In 1913, however, it was decided that Staatsmijnen was to be managed as a private enterprise, which gave its management relative freedom to pursue independent policies. This decision was the result of the Bedrijvenwet (Company Law) of 1912, according to which every semipublic firm had to be run along commercial lines and its financial administration made independent of government finances. This law became the legal basis for the relatively independent development of many semipublic companies in the Netherlands during the twentieth century (De Ru 1981, 30–1).

The limited ambitions of the Dutch state in the field of coal mining are also evident from the following. In 1921 the owners of the private Oranje-Nassau mines offered the company for state purchase, as they were disappointed by its output and the quality of its coal. The government, however, refused to buy the mine, stating that it favored a degree of competition among the different mining companies (Kreukels 1986, 26).

During World War I state intervention in all aspects of economic life increased enormously, even in a neutral country such as the Netherlands. Rather reluctantly, the state was forced to reorganize international trade, the food supply, agricultural production, the coal supply, and many other parts of the economy. As a result, state intervention became much more normal and accepted, although on many occasions the state was criticized for being late and inefficient and for allowing too much war profiteering.

Strategic considerations also played a role in the extension of the state's role in the economy after 1914. For example, the minister of economic affairs, the radical Willem Frederik Treub, decided to finance part of the establishment of the first Dutch blast furnace, NV Hoogovens, in 1917. Moreover, a detailed agreement with Staatsmijnen secured the delivery of relatively cheap coal to the new industry (Dankers and Verheul 1993, 27–30). Government support for the plan to set up this basic industry was aimed at reducing the nation's dependence on imported iron and steel. In the same year, the government participated in the formation of another basic industry, Nederlandsche Zoutindustrie (the Dutch salt industry), which began exploitation of the rich subterranean salt deposits in the eastern part of the country (De Ru 1981, 32).

A few other firms profited from the increased willingness of government to subsidize new strategic industries. Antony Fokker, who switched his production of airplanes from Germany to Amsterdam in 1919, and Albert Plesman, the founder of KLM (Royal Dutch Airlines), both profited from government support during the interwar years to compensate for their large deficits on current operations. The strategic importance of these companies, especially KLM, was related to the close relationship with the Dutch colonies. The government wanted to control the means of communication with the Dutch East Indies and was prepared to subsidize KLM to that end. In 1927 the state was more or less forced to buy a majority holding in KLM because no other sources of share capital could be found (Brugmans 1969, 486–7). However, like the Staatsmijnen and other semipublic companies, KLM was still managed like a private enterprise.

The experiment of having two railway companies competing against each other officially ended in 1917 (close cooperation between the two dated back to 1911), when both were merged into a single still-private company. In 1920 the government acquired a majority interest in that company, NV De Nederlandsche Spoorwegen, a "nationalization" that was forced through by the private owners of the company, who feared that the value of their stock would decline even more as a result of the continued losses of the firm (De Ru 1981, 34).

During the 1930s the number of state-owned firms increased rapidly, but most of them were quite small. A number of declining industries (canals and streetcar lines) were taken over by the state, and some new firms were set up with government financing as part of employment policy. This kind of state intervention was generally accepted.

How can the disintegration of the laissez-faire consensus in the first decades of the twentieth century be accounted for? The first attacks against it were led by left-wing liberals, who criticized the market for three related reasons: (1) its failure to develop strategic new industries (such as coal mines, blast furnaces, aviation, and, in an earlier phase, railways); (2) the excessive monopoly profits made by public utilities (and the railways); and (3) the market's failure to provide social security at low cost. Ideologically, these criticisms were based on the mainstream economics of the day, although some radicals were also influenced by socialist thinkers, Marx in particular. The socialists, who had little effect on public debate before the 1910s, favored planning and socialization of the means of production as a substitute for the anarchy of the free market. Their case was greatly enhanced by the experiments with planning during World War I, by the massive market failure of the Great Depression of the 1930s, and by the "successful" plans implemented by the Soviet Union after 1928 and Nazi Germany after 1933. However, as the Socialist Party became more reformist, support for these ideas declined in the 1930s. The ideas of John Maynard Keynes offered a neat solution to this dilemma and gained wide acceptance among social-democratic policy makers during the 1940s.

Behind these ideological developments were fundamental changes in politics and in the economy. The gradual extension of the franchise between 1890 and 1917 (when universal male suffrage was introduced) led to the rise of mass political parties. The liberals thereby lost domination of the government and had to give way to parties that did not have a well-developed economic philosophy; some Catholics favored corporate restructuring of society, but most Protestants still clung to the old liberal order of the nineteenth century. Nationalist arguments became more important in politics too, as the debates about the establishment of a national coal industry and subsidies for national champions (KLM, Hoogovens) show. At the same time, the state's scale and scope increased relative to the economy. During the decade after 1914, for example, the share of government expenditure in gross domestic product (GDP) almost doubled. This helped to make the government a natural agent to solve almost any economic problem.

A striking feature of the development of state-owned firms in the Netherlands is that most of them were managed as private enterprises. Thanks to the Company Law of 1912 and other legislation, their bookkeeping was comparable to that of private firms. In general, the state did not interfere with the appointment of personnel below the level of managing director, and party politics played only a modest role in the selection of directors by the government. State-owned firms were not regarded as prizes to be won by certain political parties in order to create and maintain a clientele. After World War II, the stress on the efficiency and market orientation of SOEs would become even greater.

1945–1982: CHANGING FORTUNES OF SOES

In the years after 1945, an intense debate took place about the future restructuring of the economy, especially between the Social Democratic Party, which advocated partial nationalization and macroeconomic planning, and the Catholic Party, which held corporatist views. The results of the debate were minimal. A new investment bank (Herstelbank) was set up as a joint venture between private banks and the government to supply venture capital to industry, especially to small and medium-sized firms, which did not have access to the capital market. The state was a 51 percent majority shareholder and guaranteed the payment of a 3.5 percent dividend on the rest of the shares of the Herstelbank, which channeled its funds into the industries specially favored by the industrialization policy (De Hen 1980, 258–9). The Central Bank was nationalized in 1948 but remained de facto almost completely independent (although the minister of finance had the right to provide guidelines to the president of the Central Bank). An industrialization policy was adopted in 1949, which aimed at creating a favorable environment for the growth of private enterprise. As part of this policy the government participated in the extension of two firms, Hoogovens and the Nederlandse Soda Industry (salt).

Throughout the 1950s and most of the 1960s this trend was reversed, and the government tried to privatize its enterprises. Shares in Hoogovens, the salt industry, and the Herstelbank were sold. A new law of 1955 mandated that, in order to prevent unfair competition, SOEs had in principle to pay the same taxes as private firms.

An interesting case is the transformation of Staatsmijnen into the chemical company DSM, which occurred in this period. During the 1950s, Staatsmijnen had already started large-scale activities in chemicals and related activities; in fact, its production of fertilizers dated back to 1930. Coal was still the most important basis for its chemical division, but it wanted to switch to cheaper oil and gas and to increase these very profitable activities (Messing 1988, 65–6). As a result, it had begun to see its mines as a liability and was in fact putting pressure on the government to start closing down the first mines (Messing 1988, 281). Finally, the discovery of enormous reserves of natural gas in the northern part of the Netherlands in about 1960 made it clear that coal would not be able to compete much longer with this new and very cheap source of energy. In 1963, after a number of requests by Staatsmijnen for subsidies for its mining activities, on which it had been taking losses since the coal crisis of 1958, the government decided to give the company a share in the exploitation of the gas reserves (De Voogd 1993, 162). The firm set up to exploit these reserves, the Nederlandse Aardolie Maatschappij, was reorganized to include Staatsmijnen as well as Shell and Esso, with shares of 40 percent, 30 percent, and 30 percent, respectively (Messing 1988, 276). In 1965 the decision was made to close down the coal mines over the next ten years. The enormous income from natural gas made heavy investment in new chemical activities possible, as well as the gradual closure of the mines after 1965. Part of the money was also used – under strong pressure from the government – to invest in other industrial ventures, for example, a new DAF automobile factory at Born (Wever and de Smidt 1987, 160). As a result of the expansion of DSM, the new name for Staatsmijnen after it became a joint-stock company in 1967, total employment fell by only a third between 1958 (44,411) and 1974 (29,500), when the last mine was closed.

Problems with declining industries forced the government to change course and to increase its involvement in industry after the mid-1960s. The main goal of policy became the restructuring of these activities in order to create larger, more competitive firms and to close down surplus capacity. In 1972 the Nehem (Netherlands Reconstruction Company) was created as an independent body to carry out this policy (Vrolijk 1982). During the 1970s subsidies for declining industries grew rapidly. After 1973 attempts were made to stem the downturn of the economy by large (Keynesian) plans to stimulate employment. Part of this money was also used to subsidize these industries. According to Organization for Economic Cooperation and Development (OECD) statistics, industrial subsidies as a percentage of sectorial GDP increased from 1.2 percent in 1970–4 to 2.1 percent in 1975–9 to 2.6 percent in 1980–4. A more or less comparable increase occurred in most other OECD countries (Ford and Suyker 1990). Part of these subsidies consisted of risk-sharing capital; as a result, the number of firms in which the government (or semipublic agencies) participated rose rapidly. By international standards, however, the share of SOEs in the Dutch economy remained relatively small (Table 11.1).

The industry that profited most from the industrial policy was shipbuilding. Between 1975 and 1979, more than 64 percent of the expenditure on "measures to restructure industry" went to this sector. After giving large subsidies to a number of shipbuilding firms in the years 1967–71 because of their urgent financial problems, the minister of eco-

Table 11.1. Share of SOEs in the National Economy of Four Countries, c. 1968 and c. 1974

	c. 1968				c. 1974			
	It.	Fr.	GB	Nl	It.	Fr.	GB	Nl
Share in employment	11.2	—	8.4	6.6	14.1	—	7.7	7.3
Share in GDP	13.9	12.2	10.8	7.6	14.7	11.3	10.8	10.0

Source: De Ru 1981, 342.

nomic affairs forced them to form one large company, Rijn-Schelde-Verolme (RSV). After a few rather prosperous years, the depression of 1974–5 led to new rounds of subsidies, during which RSV received ample funds to develop new activities outside shipbuilding, ranging from the manufacture of nuclear power stations to oil platforms. However, in spite of the massive subsidies (totaling 2,700 million guilders), the company was almost bankrupt in 1983. This led to a public scandal, which resulted in an official inquiry by the Dutch Parliament into the allocation of this money and the management of RSV (the first official parliamentary inquiry after 1946). The inquiry was broadcast on television in 1984–5 and became a media event. Members of Parliament exposed the follies of certain captains of industry, high-ranking public servants, and former ministers of economic affairs. The inquiry revealed the government's and RSV management's failure to plan and control the spending of government funds (Van Zanden and Griffiths 1989, 79–85). Others have noted, however, that the results of the inquiry were overly negative toward the management of RSV. Its problems were, in view of the worldwide decline in shipbuilding during this period, incapable of solution, and the strategy of developing new activities was the only alternative (De Voogd 1993, 230).

PRIVATIZATION IN THE 1980S AND 1990S

The depression of the early 1980s hit the Dutch economy very hard. Large firms went bankrupt, GDP declined for two years (1981–2), and unemployment increased enormously. This sharp crisis caused a number of important changes in policy making and in the relationship between the state and the economy. In 1982 the famous Wassenaar Agreement, a three-party agreement between the government, the trade unions, and the employers' organizations, heralded an era of wage moderation and of measures designed to increase the flexibility of the labor market. As a result of the public debate about the failure of industrial policy, this was gradually transformed into a more aggressive technology policy. From about 1982, economic policy and the cooperation between trade unions, employers' organizations, and the government were based on supply-side considerations. The main goals were improving the competitive position of Dutch industry and increasing active participation in the labor market (Van Zanden 1997).

Experiments with the privatization of a number of public companies were a logical part of this new set of policies. Already during the 1950s and 1960s, semipublic companies such as KLM, Staatsmijnen, and others had become increasingly independent of direct government control and were gradually transformed into private enterprises with declining state participation. Hoogovens is another case in point. In 1961 the minister of economic affairs had already decided to sell a large part of its share in the company (De Ru 1981, 79). During the 1950s and 1960s, state-owned shares in these companies were sold because there was no reason to continue state participation. The management of these firms also pressed for privatization because this would enhance the status of their companies and make it easier to attract new capital (Dankers and Verheul 1993). Ideological considerations hardly played a role in the lesser debates about these partial privatizations.

The new coalition government that took office in 1982, which was to implement the supply-side policies mentioned earlier, outlined as one of its major operations the privatization of SOEs in order to strengthen the market economy. Another, perhaps even more important reason for promoting privatization was that the government was desperately looking for money to finance its large deficit. According to Andeweg, the roots of Dutch privatization are corporatist/bureaucratic, not party-political, as a result of which it did not become "an ideological quest: the trumpets of 'popular capitalism' have never sounded in the Netherlands, and privatization was merely regarded as a pragmatic solution to specific administrative and economic problems" (Andeweg 1994, 199).

Some of the most important cases of privatization were those of the postal bank, the post, telegraph, and telephone company (see the next section), the government printing office, and the royal mint, all of which became private enterprises with some state ownership. The government also sold some of its shares in KLM, in the chemical company DSM, in Hoogovens, and in Fokker – but it remained closely involved in the management of the last company until its final dissolution in 1996. Total revenues of these operations were relatively small – about $2.75 billion between 1982 and 1992 (Andeweg 1994, 201). The basic reason for the relatively small scale of the process since 1982 is that the government-owned sector was already rather small at the beginning of the period, and for a number of administrative and bureaucratic reasons, progress has been much slower than was expected in 1982.

PRIVATIZATION OF THE PTT: TECHNOLOGICAL, ECONOMIC, AND POLITICAL BACKGROUNDS

A more detailed examination of the privatization of the post, telegraph, and telephone company (PTT) makes it possible to analyze the interaction between a state-owned company and government policy in greater detail. This change in the ownership of the PTT should be analyzed against the background of a number of developments in the economy and in society that changed the character of the industry. Most important in this respect were technological developments, the increased importance of the service sector, changes in economic policy in other countries (e.g., widespread deregulation in the United States and the United Kingdom), and European Union (EU) policy. These factors should not be considered separately; they are closely interrelated.

Technological Changes and the Service Economy

Since the 1970s, advances in technology have triggered many new developments in the fields of telecommunications and information technology. The transmission of signals, for instance, has expanded considerably. The introduction of fiber-optic lines offered the possibility of enlarging transmission capacity and, next to the physical infrastructure, satellite links and microwave or cellular systems emerged. Digitalization technologies made it possible to transmit sound, text, and images through digital pulses. This would suggest that specialized networks would no longer be needed for the transmission of the signals. Not only would this lead to multipurpose networks – such as integrated broadband networks and integrated services digital networks (ISDN) – but existing networks (e.g., cable television networks) could also be used to transport telecommunication signals.

Developments in the field of microelectronics, as well as digitalization, also had major consequences for the existing exchanges and terminal equipment. Not only did these provide the opportunity to offer more software-based applications, also called "value-added" or "tele-information" services (e.g., call-back and call-forwarding services, video-text, video- and teleconferencing, and electronic mail), but they also brought about a convergence of existing telecommunications and computer equipment. Moreover, as a result of the integration of telecommunications and information technology (telematics), historically separated modes of communication such as telephony, data communications, data processing, and broadcasting converged. The technological developments were significant because of the growing importance of the service sector since the end of the 1960s. Information and communication play crucial parts in the development of a service-oriented economy, which explains the expected profitability of the telematics sector. The phenomenal growth in user demand for telecommunications has to be understood in this perspective (Hulsink 1996, 99; Noam 1992, 51–3).

Political Changes: Deregulation and Liberalization

As pointed out earlier, general changes in the ideology and aims of economic policy took place during the 1980s. This did not happen only in the Netherlands. The United States and the United Kingdom were the first countries where the new economic doctrines (monetarism, supply-side economics) were put into practice. Private enterprise and competition were considered of prime importance in achieving an efficient and healthy economy (Hulsink 1996, 2). In these countries, measures aimed at privatization and liberalization were quite drastic. Deregulation of the telecommunication sector in the United States started in the 1960s. The divestiture by AT&T of its regional operating companies in 1984 was important: after the divestiture, AT&T was free to enter new markets, and other companies were allowed to enter the telecommunications market. At about the same time, the British government decided to privatize the public telephone company and, to a large extent, liberalized its home market. Not surprisingly, the American and British companies sought market expansion abroad, which led to demands for the liberalization of these markets in other countries.

In other Western European countries, national policies with regard to telecommunications, and hence the PTT, were influenced by these developments. The Dutch government increasingly acknowledged the importance of the telecommunications and information sector as an engine of economic growth. Moreover, the government itself had become an important information services customer and would benefit from more competition in these markets. Finally, the Dutch government was heavily influenced by the demands from large users and the information industry to liberalize the telecommunications market.

European Policy

Another important international development was the changing policy of the EU.[1] From the end of the 1960s and the beginning of the 1970s, the EU became increasingly interested in the telecommunications and postal services. The emerging interest, especially in telecommunications, can be attributed to new technological developments. Telecommunications was viewed not only as an important high-tech industry, but also as an important means to facilitate the economic unification of Europe. From the 1970s on, national governments had to pay more attention to decisions made in Brussels.

In this respect the basic idea of the EU – the creation of a European common market – was important. The existence of a European common market in the area of telecommunications would be necessary to strengthen Europe's competitive position in this field. According to the EU, the national compartmentalization of telecommunications in technical and economic respects meant that European companies were not able to achieve full economies of scale in production.[2] As a result, technological diversities and minimal compatibility between national telecommunications systems would put the European market at a disadvantage in competing with the other Triad powers (the United States and Japan), where deregulation had led to internationally oriented multinational companies. The monopolistic position of PTT organizations was seen as an obstacle that prevented the closing of the gap between the EU and its major competitors.

The EU began by encouraging cooperation in telecommunications

---

[1] Although different terms and abbreviations have been used over the years – "European Coal and Steel Community (ECSC)", "European Economic Community (EEC)", "European Community (EC)" after 1992, and now "European Union (EU)" – we use the abbreviation "EU" in this chapter.

[2] National boundaries imposed restraints on research and development (R&D) because a minimum scale was necessary, especially when R&D became increasingly capital intensive. If R&D in the field of telecommunications became more important and the knowledge-intensive policy of the non-European powers boomed, this could have a negative influence on international competitiveness.

research projects. In the 1980s an active antimonopoly policy was launched. Besides opening up competition in the markets for terminal equipment, the goal was the unrestricted provision of services within and among member states. The EU first focused on the telecommunications equipment market: the market for telephones, fax machines, private automatic branch exchanges (PABX), mobile telephones, and terminals for telex and data transmission.

Some modifications in the structure of European PTT organizations were also considered necessary for the liberalization of the telecommunications market.[3] The monopolistic nature of the administrations was to be abolished. Apart from dominance in voice telephony, only the monopoly on the PTT network infrastructure was accepted. To achieve competition in the telecommunications market, the regulatory function (including standardization and type approval) had to be separated from PTT organizations (Davids 1997).

Interest Groups

In the Netherlands, these technical, economic, political, and international developments had far-reaching consequences for the constellation of economic actors and their interests. Because of the emergence of telematics, new suppliers, such as computer producers, as well as service providers, became increasingly interested in developments in the telecommunications field. They strove for liberalization of the market for terminal equipment and tele-information services, which until then had been a de facto PTT monopoly. Moreover, they accused the PTT of using its power to prevent equal access to the market (Slaa 1987, 229).

Competition was seen as an important solution to the problem of lowering prices. Large professional users tried to reduce transmission costs by setting up private networks of so-called leased lines. They requested a more liberal policy on these leased lines, for which they could turn only to the PTT. Because of the increasing dependence of large corporate users on telecommunications and information technol-

---

[3] Article 90 of the Treaty of Rome formed the basis for the liberalization of terminals and services. Not only did it offer the opportunity to prohibit PTTs from having exclusive rights, which would confine competition, it also gave the European Commission the power to issue binding directives without seeking approval from the European Parliament or the Council of Ministers (Long 1995, 224; Sandholtz 1993). By using this article, the EU increasingly bypassed national governments.

ogy, they also organized themselves into interest organizations. The representatives of large corporate users often cooperated with traditional consumer organizations to further their interests vis-à-vis the PTT. They formed an important force in telematics policy making, demanding liberalization, the removal of legal or tariff barriers, and the introduction of cost-based services (Hulsink 1996, 106–7). In 1979 the large users and the information and computer industries formed an umbrella organization, the Center for Information Policy (Centrum voor Informatiebeleid, CIB). This organization was very active in communicating its wishes not only directly to politicians, but also to the general public through the media.

Private users in the Netherlands also raised various complaints. The most important consumer organization (Consumentenbond) joined professional users in urging privatization and liberalization. They hoped that the PTT would become more consumer-oriented when it was transformed into a private company and confronted with competition. Not every interest group supported these ideas. A small consumer organization (Konsumenten Kontakt) did not favor a liberalized market and a privatized PTT. Its view was that this would lead to the creation of unwanted consumer needs, which would be profitable only for the industry. A reduction of tariffs could better be obtained by reducing the yearly payment to the state rather than through liberalization.

Partly as a consequence of international pressure for deregulation, the telecommunications industry had to expand its activities. New markets also had to be found because of the high research and development costs associated with technological innovations. As a result, equipment manufacturers had to become more internationally oriented. The Dutch telecommunications industry, of course, welcomed the new markets that would result from deregulation. Although the links between the PTT and the national telecommunications industry were not very close, the latter did not favor the complete privatization of the PTT because then it could no longer be forced to favor the Dutch (Davids 1997, 368; Scherer 1993, 99). This explains why the Dutch telecommunications industry favored *gradual* liberalization.

The growing service sector and technological developments also had consequences for the labor force: specialists in the new technology were in short supply (Noam 1992, 44–5). This was one of the factors that complicated the role of the trade unions in making policy regarding the denationalization of the PTT. The trade unions in this sector were confronted with decreasing membership, declining internal coherence, and a subsequent loss of bargaining power.[4] The internal coherence of the various trade unions representing PTT personnel declined, especially when highly skilled employees became scarce in the technology-intensive telecommunications sector, whereas in the more labor-intensive postal sector, most jobs were of a semiskilled nature (Van den Besselaar and Visser 1993). Privatization and liberalization were welcomed but also feared because of anxiety over job losses.

With regard to postal services, interest groups were not that important.[5] This was partly a consequence of the market for postal services, which was only partially monopolized by the PTT. Only the transportation of letters weighing less than 500 g was the exclusive right of the PTT. The market for express mail, for example, had already been liberalized in the 1970s.

Challenges and New Opportunities for the PTT

It was necessary for the PTT to expand its market and seize the opportunities offered by the new telecommunications and information technology. Further, technical innovations gave the PTT the opportunity to diversify its services. To contribute to the growing demand for advanced telecommunications services, the PTT also had to increase the transmission speed of the existing network. More financial capital was needed to install digital exchanges and fiber-optic lines than the government was willing (or able) to offer. More autonomy was desirable, especially with regard to the company's financial policy. Partly as a result of the saturation of the private telephone market, it became increasingly important to pay more attention to the development of the professional market, which was growing rapidly. Its status as a state enterprise hindered its development of a business policy (Davids 1999; Slaa 1987, 228).

Another challenge relates to the company's personnel policy. Employing highly skilled personnel was expected to become increasingly important in the future. As a state company, the PTT had to abide by the regulations for civil servants, which lagged behind practices in the

---

[4] The declining bargaining power of the public-sector trade unions is illustrated by their inability to win more than a 0.5 percent reduction of the 3.5 percent salary cut that the Cabinet (Lubbers I Cabinet) had imposed on civil servants, despite a massive strike of civil servants, including the PTT staff, against the salary cut.

[5] This was also partly a consequence of the emphasis on telecommunications during this process.

private sector. It became increasingly difficult for the PTT not only to find but to keep its highly specialized employees.

PRIVATIZATION OF THE PTT: THE POLITICAL PROCESS

To respond to growing complaints about the lack of equal access to the market and the lack of consumer orientation, and convinced of the importance of a high-quality information and telecommunications sector, the Cabinet appointed an advisory commission in 1981. The Swarttouw Commission proposed to give the PTT a more independent status and to liberalize the market for terminal equipment and value-added services (such as electronic mail).

The recommendations did not result in real changes. The most important result was the appointment of another committee to advise on the new status and structure of the PTT, which took place in the summer of 1984. This committee, the Steenbergen Commission, proposed to transform the state company into a limited-liability holding company, all the stock of which would be government-owned. The demands of suppliers and users had to be met by transferring the regulatory and licensing functions (e.g., for local cable networks) from the PTT to an independent body for regulations and permits.[6] To avoid the possibility of cross-subsidization, three subsidiaries had to be made responsible for the postal services, the public utility telecommunications services, and the competitive telecommunications services, respectively. This was proposed not only to foster fair competition in these markets, but also to protect private users from high tariffs and the inevitable commercial risks of a fully competitive market. The committee also proposed granting an exclusive concession to the PTT for public utilities in the fields of telecommunications and postal services. The concession had to relate to the construction, exploitation, and maintenance of a telecommunications infrastructure and the connections with foreign telecommunications infrastructures. Postal services were also covered by the concession, but that did not change the existing situation greatly.

The monopoly on terminal equipment (e.g., telephone sets, car telephones, teleprinters) was to be abolished. The PTT had to give up its exclusive right to deliver terminal equipment. The resistance against this monopoly had increased. Moreover, terminal equipment was already readily available on the black market. To a great degree, the abolition of

---

[6] This office would be set up within the Ministry of Public Works (RVPT).

the PTT's monopoly was the legal implementation of an already exist-ing situation. The NV PTT would be obliged to provide leased lines on request. Third-party traffic with value-added services, all to be liberal-ized, would be allowed.[7] With regard to the leased lines and the value-added services, the wishes of the large users and new service providers were met.

Most of the Steenbergen Commission's recommendations were accepted by the Cabinet and Parliament. The most important exception was the legal separation of the telecommunications subsidiary. Due to the successful objections of the PTT, a decision to split up the company was postponed, and in 1992 this idea was dropped.[8] Denationalization has increased independence vis-à-vis the state. Being an NV enabled the PTT to borrow on the capital market, which had been a long-held ambi-tion. In addition, the PTT was finally separated from the national budget.

The denationalization of the PTT and partial liberalization took effect on January 1, 1989. The state was still the sole shareholder, but it was decided that it would be possible to sell shares publicly in the future. In June 1994 the first installment of shares (about 30 percent) was sold. Two years later, state ownership was reduced to 45 percent.

CONCLUSION

Two characteristics of Dutch society are the dominant laissez-faire orientation of its elite and the political tradition of compromise. In this case, compromises were made between the conviction of most politi-cians that government intervention should be kept to a minimum and the strong pressures (from party politics, trade unions, and sometimes employers themselves) pushing for a larger state role in the economy. One of these compromises was the Company Law of 1912, which was basic to the relatively independent development of these enterprises. Broadly speaking, the state was quite reluctant to take up this new role, and this reluctance has probably promoted the success of many state-owned firms.

A number of SOEs have contributed greatly to the economic devel-opment of the twentieth century. For example, the Netherlands was and

---

[7] The RVPT would give permission for the resale.

[8] The new holding company consisted of two bv's (*besloten vennootschap*, a type of limited liability company under Dutch law): the bv telecom and the bv post. Both bv's held exclu-sive concessions in certain fields.

is a distribution and transport center, of which the two main ports (Rotterdam harbor and Schiphol airport) are the hubs. Both were and are managed by state-owned companies, which have been very dynamic and highly competitive. In general, during the first six decades of the twentieth century the state was relatively successful in "picking winners" (Hoogovens, DSM, the salt industry, KLM, Fokker). In the late 1960s and 1970s, policies were dominated by the problems of declining industries and the success ratio declined accordingly.

The PTT is an example of a relatively strong state-owned firm. Its strength made it an important actor in the decision process toward privatization and liberalization. The company led the opposition against the disadvantages of its position as a state enterprise but had fewer problems with the more profitable effects of its legal monopoly position. The need to obtain compromises among the various interest groups involved in the privatization of the PTT had a large impact on the process itself and on its outcomes. The demands of the large users and the information industry to liberalize the telecommunications market were taken seriously; at the same time, the interests of the PTT and of the unions were not neglected. The role of the state was reduced, but this was achieved gradually. Other privatizations during the 1980s and 1990s, although they changed the character and role of the companies involved radically, were also characterized by complicated negotiations and small steps. These changes were, of course, aided by the relatively independent position of state-owned firms in the Netherlands.

REFERENCES

Andeweg, R. B. 1994. Privatisation in the Netherlands: The result of a decade. In *Privatisation in Western Europe*, ed. V. Wright, pp. 198–214. London.

Besselaar, P. van den, and J. Visser. 1993. The Dutch case. *Bulletin of Comparative Labour Relations* 25 (special issue: *Industrial relations developments in the telecommunications industry*): 97–184.

Broeke, W. van den. 1989. Preludium op een vijfsporenbeleid (1839–1939). In *Het spoor: 150 jaar spoorwegen in Nederland*, ed. J. A. Farber, pp. 52–87. Utrecht.

Brugmans, I. J. 1969. *Paardenkracht en Mensenmacht*. The Hague.

Commissie-Steenbergen. 1985. *Signalen voor straks: Een nieuwe richting voor PTT. Rapport van de Commissie Steenbergen*. The Hague.

Dankers, J. J., and J. Verheul. 1993. *Hoogovens, 1945–1993*. The Hague.

Davids, M. 1997. European co-operation in telecommunications and the Dutch PTT (1950s–1980s). In *Business and European integration since 1800:*

Regional, national and international perspectives, ed. U. Olsson, pp. 357-79. Göteborg.

1999. *De weg naar zelfstandigheid: De voorgeschiedenis van de verzelfstandiging van de PTT in 1989*. Hilversum, The Netherlands.

Ford, R., and W. Suyker. 1990. Industrial subsidies in the OECD economies. *OECD Economic Studies* 15: 37-84.

Hen, P. E. de. 1980. *Actieve en re-actieve industriepolitiek in Nederland*. Amsterdam.

Hulsink, H. 1996. *Do nations matter in a globalising industry? The restructuring of telecommunications governance regimes in France, the Netherlands and the United Kingdom (1980-1994)*. Delft.

Kreukels, L. H. M. 1986. *Mijnarbeid:Volgzaamheid en strijdbaarheid*. Assen,The Netherlands.

Long, C. D. 1995. *Telecommunications: Law and practice*. 2d ed. London.

Messing, F. A. M. 1988. *Geschiedenis van de mijnsluiting in Limburg*. Leiden.

Noam, E. 1992. *Telecommunications in Europe*. New York.

Ru, H. J. de. 1981. *Staatsbedrijven en staatsdeelnemingen*. Nijmegen.

Ru, H. J. de, and A. T. L. M. v.d. Ven. 1993. *Country study: Privatisation in the Netherlands*. Rotterdam.

Sandholtz, W. 1993. Institutions and collective action: The new telecommunications in Western Europe. *World Politics* 45(2): 242-70.

Scherer, J. 1993. Telecommunications laws in Europe. In *Telecommunications laws in Europe*, ed. J. Scherer, pp. 1-22. Deventer.

Slaa, P. 1987. *Telecommunicatie en beleid:De invloed van technologische veranderingen in de telecommunicatie op het beleid van de Nederlandse overheid inzake de PTT*. Amsterdam.

Voogd, C. de. 1993. *De neergang van de scheepsbouw en andere industriële bedrijfstakken*. Vlissingen.

Vries, H. de. 1994. *Nederlandse economen over een ondernemende overheid, 1850-1940*. Leiden.

Vrolijk, H. 1982. Opkomst en neergang van de Nederlandse herstructureringsmaatschappij. In *Interventie en vrije markt*, ed. H. Vrolijk and R. Hengeveld, pp. 49-92. Amsterdam.

Wever, E., and M. de Smidt. 1987. *De Nederlandse industrie*. Assen, The Netherlands.

Zadoks. 1899. *Geschiedenis van de Amsterdamse concessies*. Amsterdam.

Zanden, J. L. van. 1997. *Een klein land in de 20e eeuw*. Utrecht.

Zanden, J. L. van, and R. T. Griffiths. 1989. *Economische geschiedenis van Nederland in de 20e eeuw*. Utrecht.

12

⚬⚬

State-Owned Enterprises in a Hostile Environment

The U.S. Experience

LOUIS GALAMBOS

For more than a century, American historians have devoted considerable energy to explaining how and why their nation's experience is unique.[1] Self-absorbed and often self-congratulatory, they have sprinkled these historical exercises with moral judgments based on everything from the peculiarities of organized religion in the United States to the wonders of America's modern plumbing.[2] Although this essay on U.S. encounters with state-owned enterprises (SOEs) does not dwell on morality, it perforce deals with the question of uniqueness. My position on that question can be summarized as follows: First, the history of SOEs in the United States has many unique characteristics. Second, when we add municipal and state-level SOEs to those created by the federal government, developments in the United States do not appear to be as unique as many of its citizens have assumed they were. Third, the historical processes that fostered state-owned ventures and also the processes that turned the nation away from them were similar to the processes that

---

[1] I would like to thank those who have given me suggestions for improving this essay. They include the participants in the Milan meeting and a seminar at the Johns Hopkins University, the anonymous readers for Cambridge University Press, Jane Eliot Sewell, Steve Hanke, Julie Kimmel, and Madeleine Adams. The usual disclaimer applies.

[2] On American exceptionalism see Ross 1991, 1993. See also Bushnell 1995, especially xiii–xxiii.

shaped the rise and fall of SOEs in the other nations surveyed in this volume. The objectives were similar, and the factors shaping SOE performance were much the same.

We can evaluate these propositions after examining the two distinct cycles or phases of experimentation with SOEs that took place in the United States. The first, relatively short cycle – the developmental phase – took place during the first half of the nineteenth century, when stimulating economic growth provided the primary rationale for state enterprise. During this developmental cycle the difference between the level of SOE investment in the United States and in the leading economic powers of Europe appears not to have been particularly significant. Levels of investment were significantly different, however, during the second, much longer cycle – the planning phase – that began in the late nineteenth century and has extended to the present day. The goals of those individuals and groups promoting state enterprises in this phase were extremely complex and varied, but all of these undertakings involved the central assumption that political planning should replace markets as the primary force shaping investment in selected economic institutions. During this planning phase, the United States lagged behind the other industrial nations of the West in reliance on SOEs (see Figure 12.1). The United States was at one of the polar extremes, standing outside the normal Western experience with the provision of goods and services for sale through the agency of government. With one significant exception, SOE at the federal level neither rose very high nor fell very far in the twentieth-century United States during peacetime.[3] But the historical processes shaping these developments were similar to those in other Western nations, and after we add together the SOEs at the municipal, state, and federal levels, the results were somewhat less unique than either academic or popular perceptions indicate.

During both the nineteenth and twentieth centuries, the United States experienced many of the economic problems and political pressures that fostered SOEs elsewhere. The desire to accelerate economic growth, and real (and sometimes imagined) threats to national security, generated demands for SOEs in the United States, just as they did in Europe. Concern for public safety and market failure also fostered

---

[3] Rose (1989) compares aggregate aspects of the political economy of the United States and the other Organization for Economic Cooperation and Development (OECD) nations in the post–World War II era and places the United States in a group of six countries that are rich and do not have big governments.

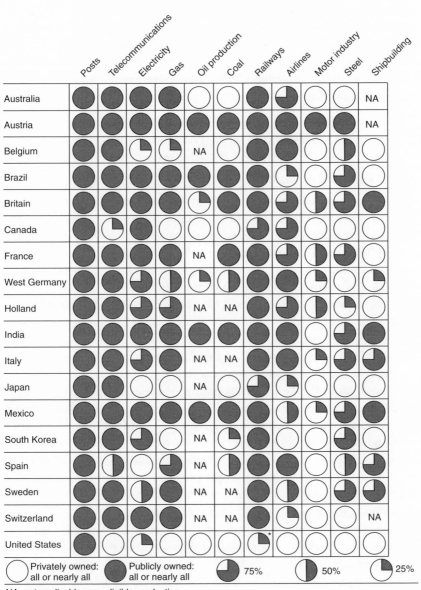

Figure 12.1. Extent of state ownership of business, 1978. *Source: Harvard Business Review*, March–April 1979, p. 161.

governmental enterprises. But the most formidable American experiment with SOEs resulted from the nation's unusual endowment of land and related natural resources. So unusual has been the business of the public lands that it was not even included in Figure 12.1. We will, nevertheless, explore that subject as we sweep over two centuries of American excursions into SOE.[4]

LAISSEZ FAIRE AND THE DEVELOPMENT
PHASE OF U.S. SOEs

As the United States emerged from its long colonial era, most of its citizens had a well-developed antipathy toward central government and a deeply rooted affection for individual effort, voluntary association, and material progress. As colonists, many of them had misbehaved frequently when called on to sacrifice self-interest to the interests of the mother country. As newly minted citizens of the United States, many of them simply converted suspicion of the British crown into mistrust of the U.S. national government. That suspicion spilled over to state-supported enterprises, which were associated with monopoly, corruption, and distant, undemocratic control.

Fortunately, the nation had a federal government, with most powers reserved to the individual states. This was fortunate because it was not very long before the American desire for economic expansion began to erode the mistrust of government and distaste for SOEs. With a federated system, Americans could hate government and deploy it at the same time, while feeling little regret for the loss of principle. President Thomas Jefferson – who fervently believed in a strict construction of the Constitution – showed the people how to navigate such moral dilemmas by making the Louisiana Purchase in 1803 – an act that embodied a loose construction of the Constitution.

Once acquired, the vast lands of the Louisiana Purchase made the U.S. government one of the great real estate organizations in the history of the world. For some years before 1803, the federal government had been attempting to work out a satisfactory way to handle its already

---

[4] Throughout, I deal almost exclusively with state enterprises that sold goods or services; thus I do not explore regulation in any detail, nor do I deal with the provision of tax-based government goods or services such as national defense or education or the growth of government in general. My focus is almost entirely on this narrowly defined concept of the SOE.

large holdings to the east of the Mississippi River. What the central government needed – as did most Americans for the next century – was
capital, and it attempted through sales large and small to convert the
nation's abundant land into revenue. Three official aspects of the
process were relatively stable over the long run: the land was surveyed
into six-mile-square townships and subdivided into 640-acre lots, later
called "sections"; the land was sold at auctions at an established
minimum price; and one section in each township was reserved to
support public schools. But even before the Louisiana Purchase, it
proved easier to establish policies for the sales than to convert the
country's land into money. Like their government, Americans were
capital-poor. Land sales sputtered along at a relatively low level until the
end of the War of 1812 (Feller 1984, 3–13).

After the war, expansion into the western lands accelerated, and with
the flood of people came a great increase in land sales. The rush into
the virgin lands beyond the Appalachian Mountains brought substantial
revenue into the federal treasury for the first time. Nevertheless, the
government was no more immune to the cycles of boom and bust than
were other commercial entities. The first panic and depression came in
1819, and others followed on a fairly regular basis. Yet following each
panic and downturn, a great rush of settlers moved into the Midwest
and Southwest in search of cheap land and natural resources. Having
little capital, the settlers wanted to buy the land on credit or they were
inclined simply to squat on the public domain and then demand title to
the land.

To take advantage of their newly acquired resources, Americans
needed better transportation. It is thus not surprising that they turned
to their state governments for help, making a series of decisions as pragmatic as Jefferson's purchase of Louisiana. Political principles notwithstanding, most were ready to support a formidable array of state-owned
transportation enterprises designed to link them to eastern sources of
manufactured articles and to distant markets. A distinctive brand of
urban-centered mercantilism spurred the construction of canals as the
commercial interests in each of the East Coast cities attempted to beat
their rivals to the lucrative western trade. It was customary to look on
that trade as a zero-sum game: What Boston won, Baltimore lost; what
New York acquired was surely taken from Philadelphia. Although the
development process proved not to be zero-sum, the city and state
of New York clearly surpassed their rivals in the nineteenth century.
By pairing its excellent seaboard port facilities with the Erie Canal,

New York City became the nation's leading commercial and financial center.[5]

Even New York, however, found that SOEs were difficult to run efficiently over the long term. The organizational capabilities of state governments were simply not up to the tasks of running a large canal system without corruption and waste, and the legislature in New York compounded the problems by extending the system in an effort to spread the political benefits around as much of the state as possible. Other states had similar difficulties without having the advantage of a backbone canal as effective as the Erie. The problems became insurmountable in the late 1830s after a downturn in the economy left several states unable to pay the interest on their canal bonds.[6]

The depression of the late 1830s also tightened the noose on what was left of one of the other SOEs in antebellum America, the Second Bank of the United States (BUS). Paradoxically, the powerful desire to promote economic expansion worked against this SOE while favoring the canal undertakings. As a creature of the central government and a monopolistic handler of federal funds, the Second Bank was politically suspect in many quarters. The BUS functioned in part as a central bank and in part as a private bank that competed with the state-incorporated banks. It restrained the state bankers in the South and West, and they joined hands with entrepreneurial, development-oriented interests to oppose an institution they considered a threat to the country's economic expansion. An economic success but a political failure, the Second Bank lost its federal charter in 1836 and went under during the depression following the Panic of 1837.[7]

Up to the end of the 1830s, the U.S. deployment of SOEs was similar to that of many other Western countries. The only significant difference was the dependence in America on state governments rather than federal authority to achieve the goal of accelerating economic growth, a goal that was shared throughout the West. In the twentieth century this goal was also shared by the developing countries of Africa, Latin

[5] There is an extensive literature on this subject. See, for example, Goodrich 1960; Goodrich et al. 1961; Hartz 1948; Miller 1962; Scheiber 1969.
[6] See, for instance, Jensen 1978, 43–60, which provides an excellent treatment of the crisis and its political implications in what was then a western state.
[7] Although the central government held only four-fifths of the bank's stock and the president of the United States appointed only five of the twenty-five directors of the bank, the institution was dependent on federal support and was closely identified with the government in Washington, D.C. Hammond 1957; Smith 1953; Sylla 1971–2; Temin 1969.

America, and Asia, all of which turned to SOEs for the same reason the state governments of the United States did in the early nineteenth century.

As the U.S. development cycle peaked and reliance on SOEs waned, however, the American situation became more exceptional. The experiences with canals and the Second Bank were significant because they were accompanied and followed by a long and unusually successful period of private-sector economic growth. In the nineteenth century U.S. private enterprise was by no means trouble-free, but for many decades the problems it generated seemed to most Americans to be far less important than the economic progress the U.S. brand of capitalism promoted. In the course of that long period of expansion, the states and the federal government eschewed the opportunity to become directly involved with railroads, with the telegraph and telephone, and with the nation's rapidly growing manufacturing sector. State governments actually surrendered the power to control the corporations they created by making incorporation a perfunctory administrative act. At best, the government became a source of subsidies used to accelerate development by private interests.

At the national level of government, the Post Office and the public lands were the only prominent SOEs that survived the turn toward private enterprise. The Post Office Department (a department as of 1829), which was equally devoted to generating political patronage and providing mail service, experienced considerable growth in the nineteenth century. By the late 1830s there was a post office for every 1,500 Americans, and in 1863 the government began to pay mail carriers to deliver to private residences. Home delivery was available only in cities and towns, however, and at the turn of the century most Americans were still picking up their letters at the post office. Secure by 1845 in its monopoly of letter-mail service, the Post Office failed to grow fast enough to fend off several innovators in the market for communications. Private express services and the telegraph took over substantial portions of the enterprise, as did the telephone after long-distance service was established. The Post Office Department suffered repeated political scandals, deficits, and charges of inefficiency, but Americans never lost their faith that more subsidized services could be squeezed out of this formidable SOE.[8]

---

[8] White 1958, 257–77. White concluded (276) that the record was "a baffling mixture of excellence and imperfection." Brock 1981, especially 55–147; John 1990, 1995.

Concern for development dominated the federal government's other prominent SOE, the land business. Under pressure from a land-hungry population and the business interests that would benefit from faster settlement, the government accelerated distribution of its holdings. Politicians gradually lowered the minimum price of government lands, and under the Homestead Act of 1862, any settler who could fulfill a five-year residency requirement could acquire 160 acres free.[9] Land was used as a subsidy for private undertakings such as the transcontinental railroads and state ventures such as the land-grant colleges.[10] Although private institutions were generally thought to be far more efficient than public organizations, Americans continued to use subsidies to promote private undertakings that could be linked – no matter how tenuously – to economic growth and thus to the general welfare of the nation.

The leading historian of nineteenth-century federal administration called the Department of the Interior, which handled the land business, the "Department of the Great Miscellany." Leonard D. White wrote, "The dispersion of function was so great that perhaps no man could have dominated the whole of this sprawling organism." Interior was under so much pressure from special interest groups that in 1881 Carl Schurz, the talented head of the department, called it "the most dangerous branch of the public service. It is more exposed to corrupt influences and more subject to untoward accidents than any other."[11] The contrast between these two public functions – performed by an inefficient, tainted Department of the Interior and a sluggish, periodically corrupted Post Office – and the spectacular growth of private enterprise lent further strength to America's bias against state ventures.

THE SECOND CYCLE: THE LONG PLANNING PHASE OF SOE DEVELOPMENT

Insofar as there was an American national culture in the late nineteenth century, it was extremely hostile to SOE. Throughout the country public officials were held in low esteem. Many Americans assumed that gov-

---

[9] Bogue 1980; Feller 1984, 188–98; Swierenga 1968.

[10] Bogue 1980, 589. Almost 29 percent of the land the federal government disposed of went to the states; 8.2 percent went to railroad corporations, which received 94.3 million acres (Fogel 1960).

[11] Quoted in White 1958, 175–208. Of the General Land Office, White wrote (196), "It would be difficult to discover a more dismal example of administrative confusion, laxness, and frustration."

ernment activities had to be isolated in some way from party politics to be efficient and free from corruption. Civic values were stunted in a culture that was oriented to material progress achieved almost exclusively through advances in the private sector. That distinctive culture exerted a powerful influence over the second cycle of SOE development, a planning phase that lasted for the next century.

That cycle began in the late nineteenth century when various groups of Americans began to define a number of "problems" for which the market seemed to have no solutions. Planning through public organizations provided an alternative that was widely discussed. The "problems" often involved market failure, but the discussions of that day were not framed in that way; instead, Americans complained about the "trusts" or the "labor problem" or just "the social problem." Since it was possible to substitute planning for markets in a variety of ways, much of the political debate was over the means – including SOEs – as well as the ends of public action. Many Americans were, for instance, concerned that corporate interests had become too powerful and were closing off opportunities for individuals and small enterprises. For the most part, they were satisfied when antitrust laws were employed to discipline some of the largest and most oppressive "trusts," but in some instances they sought direct controls on business.[12] Agrarian interests and shippers were thus pleased to see the federal government impose rate-of-return regulation on the railroads. Piece by piece, reformers with diverse agendas laid the foundation in America for a more vigorous, intrusive administrative state that they thought would be capable of implementing their plans to improve society.

One of the things that was different in this second cycle was the complex mix of motives for increased government activity at the state, municipal, and federal levels. The goals as well as the political processes were far more complex than they had been during the early nineteenth century. In this second cycle, economic development was still one of the important goals, but there were many others. Agrarian reformers wanted to protect farmers and their families from the great combines in transportation and manufacturing. There were also widespread concerns about the nation's unequal distribution of income and wealth, about the lack of equity and security in a market-dominated system, and about the exploitation of women and children in an urban-industrial society. In efforts to solve those problems, populist and Progressive Era

[12] Brock 1984; Galambos 1975; Keller 1977; Thorelli 1955.

reformers looked to new forms of planning, most often including regulation but sometimes SOEs as well. Left ideologists and political leaders, sometimes radical but most often moderate in their demands for change, helped to shape an environment in early-twentieth-century America that was critical of markets and corporate interests and favorable toward public planning.[13]

The planning impulse was felt at the local, state, and federal levels of government. As cities expanded, civic leaders and citizens discovered that their traditional sources of water and means of sewage disposal no longer sufficed. Wells were polluted, and concerns about public health lent urgency to calls for reform. Private firms frequently found it difficult to muster the heavy capital investments that were needed to improve the water and sewage systems or to obtain an urban right-of-way through condemnation. By 1900, forty-one of the fifty largest cities in the United States had public waterworks, and by 1910, 70 percent of cities with populations of more than 30,000 had shifted from private to municipal water services.[14] Expenditures for that type of service were large, and through the early decades of the twentieth century the total of municipal (nonschool) budgets for the entire country exceeded the budget of the federal government. In 1910 municipal capital outlays were almost 9 percent of U.S. net capital formation.[15] Municipal SOEs were employed in transportation, production of antitoxins and vaccines, the generation and distribution of electricity, gas distribution, and healthcare.[16]

---

[13] Alchon 1985; Faulkner 1951; Skocpol 1992; Skrownek 1982; Wiebe 1967.

[14] Black 1956; Chapin 1901, especially 1–51, 108–219, 262–305; Griffith 1974a, especially 178–95; Griffith 1974b, especially 85–99; Schultz and McShane 1978; Tarr 1984; Teaford 1984. Baker 1991, 91–118, provides a perceptive account of the political process involving "improvements" outside of the major East Coast cities.

[15] Anderson 1977, 9–13; see 66–86 for an excellent analysis of the water supply and sewage disposal crises in the last major American city to establish a municipal sewage system. For an equally perceptive analysis of Washington, D.C., see Lessoff 1994, especially 4, 21–27, 88–94, 106–7, 181–2, 184–98, 240–2. Philadelphia was the first U.S. city to develop an adequate municipal water supply but was slow to employ a modern filter system (Warner 1968, 99–111). On New York see Goldman 1997. See also Melosi 1973. For a good statement of the reform approach to a more active government see McDonald 1984, especially 60–3. For a perceptive analysis of the restraints on urban investment see Monkkonen 1984.

[16] Cheape 1980, 208–19; Duffy 1974, 71; Foster 1981, 65–90, 116–31; McKelvey 1973, 80–2, 110–12; Warner 1968, 191–4. Municipal ownership was not always possible; in Ohio it was not permitted under state law (Toman and Hays 1996, 71). It was 1941 before Cleveland took over its transit system (ibid., 284–5). In telephony, many cities and towns allied themselves with local independent phone companies or used the threat of creating

State governments opted to experiment with many of the same types of SOEs. They had their own hospitals and electrical utilities, sold transportation services and operated shipping facilities, sold insurance and ran grain elevators and banks. They edged into the recreation business, as did the State of New York, which for a number of years ran the Saratoga Springs spa.[17] The State of California ran packinghouses for the fishing industry and shops for repairing fishing vessels (Nash 1964, 336-7). The states also were deeply involved in the real estate business, distributing land they had acquired from the federal government. Although state governments edged into SOEs less often than municipalities, they were no more averse to public intervention in business in the years 1880 through 1930 than they had been during the developmental cycle of the early nineteenth century.[18]

The federal government's largest business continued to involve handling public lands, and, like other large enterprises in turn-of-the-century America, this one provoked substantial controversy. The problems that developed prefigured some of the major difficulties that SOEs would encounter later in the twentieth century in the United States and elsewhere. For many years the government succeeded in distributing federal lands and even making some money from the sales. But as settlement spread into the Far West, the effort to promote small-farm holdings, the Jeffersonian ideal, gradually gave way to a program of leasing land to ranchers, miners, lumber companies, and other business interests, none of which paid fair market prices for their use of these national

municipal SOEs to force concessions from the Bell System; see Hirsch 1989, 22, 25; Lipartitio 1989, especially 175-207. Hellman 1972, 233-351, provides city case studies of electrical systems. According to my working definition, hospitals became urban SOEs when they were transformed by modern scientific medicine and began to treat large numbers of paying patients as well as the poor of the cities; they stopped being SOEs when third-party payment became commonplace in the post-World War II period. Numbers 1984; Rosenberg 1987, 237-61; Starr 1982, 145-79, 347-78. For a contemporary engineering perspective on planning through public works see Whinery 1903. See also Blackford 1977, 86-90.

[17] Hellman 1972, 47-114; Nash 1980; State of New York, Conservation Department 1945; Stevens 1989, 149-56. California was the first state to embark on government ownership and operation of an entire port, an enterprise that was launched in San Francisco in 1863 (Nash 1964, 106-18). For later developments see Blackford 1977, 10, 11.

[18] There was, however, a major difference between the two cycles. In the later period, the entire economy was much larger and the government activity was thus a much smaller percentage of the total economic activity underway in the United States. A typical textbook survey of state government as late as 1960, however, gave no mention of SOEs at the state level. See, for example, Anderson et al. 1960.

resources. The amount of land involved was impressive: 30 percent of Montana, 45 percent of California, 66 percent of Utah, and 96 percent of Alaska were still owned and operated by the federal government as late as the 1970s.[19] In 1979 the federal government owned 744.1 million acres of land in the United States, about one-third of the nation's land area.[20] The business of managing U.S. federal public lands was the single largest SOE in any of the capitalist countries of the West, and the handling of those formidable assets was the subject of repeated, intense political debates. That was especially true after the New Deal of the 1930s gave a boost to irrigation, flood control, and power projects that pumped vast subsidies into the western states.

During the Great Depression of the 1930s, high levels of unemployment and bankruptcy, the problems of the banking system, and the breakdown of local and state relief institutions created a sense of crisis in a generation accustomed to sustained economic growth. As the private sector's status sagged, more and more Americans looked to the public sector for protection from the worst effects of the Depression. Security and equity became salient aspects of America's political culture. By 1940 federal government expenditures in the United States constituted about 9.6 percent of the nation's gross domestic product, a substantial change since the end of the 1920s.[21]

In 1933 the New Deal spawned one of the nation's most formidable SOEs by establishing the Tennessee Valley Authority (TVA), which was authorized to control floods, to generate power, and to promote the economic development of the entire region served by the Tennessee River and its tributaries. Modeled in part on the Power Authority of New York (established in 1931 with the aggressive sponsorship of Governor Franklin D. Roosevelt), the TVA gave full expression to the planning ideology.[22] Regional planning rather than private entrepreneurial activities

---

[19] White 1991, 136-54, 270-3, 395-429, 522-31, 565-8. As White explains (399): "Beginning in the 1890s, the central government ceased to be a nursemaid to the future states and a prodigal distributor of resources to the country's citizens and corporations. Washington instead became a manager of western land, resources, and, inevitably, people."

[20] President's Private Sector Survey on Cost Control 1983, Issues and Recommendations, 11.

[21] In 1890, the comparable figure was about 2.4 percent.

[22] Hellman 1972, 73-114, briefly surveys the Power Authority's history. Robert Moses, chairman of the Power Authority as of 1954, explained his particular variant on that ideology: "These are more than power projects," he said. "They are multiple purpose park, power, navigation, railroad relocation, arterial, reclamation, restoration and conservation programs extending for miles along the frontiers, and representing international and municipal cooperation on an unprecedented scale." Quoted in ibid., 99.

would thus pace the growth of this large, multistate area. Public power would provide the nation with a yardstick to measure what private firms were charging and accomplishing in other regions. Launched with great enthusiasm and fanfare, the TVA promised to become the model for a series of federal and state development agencies that would bring a regional perspective to planning and explore state-financed alternatives to those capitalist enterprises that had failed the nation in the early 1930s. President Roosevelt explained, "It is time to extend planning to a wider field, in this instance comprehending in one great project many States directly concerned with the basis of one of our greatest rivers." More would follow, he said: "If we are successful here we can march on, step by step, in a like development of other great natural territorial units within our borders."[23]

For a time it appeared that the TVA's performance was providing solid justification for FDR's optimistic prediction. After fighting off legal challenges to its authority and mission, the TVA successfully promoted public power, rural electrification, and regional economic growth in a substantial, five-state area (McCraw 1971). As historian Thomas K. McCraw noted: "Since 1933, in large measure due to the TVA programs, the Tennessee Valley has progressed at a faster rate than the nation and the South generally. It is today [ca. 1970] studied as the finest example of what can be done with interested and intelligent participation at all levels of the community from the federal government down to the small stream basins."[24]

The next major opportunity to replace markets with centralized planning and SOE came, however, not from domestic economic concerns but from national security problems stemming from World War II.[25] Prior to 1940, national security issues had done little to shape the public discourse over the proper role of the state in economic enterprise. During World War I the United States had largely used the regulatory model rather than the SOE model to guide its mobilization. The railroads and the telephone company provided exceptions to this rule, but U.S. involvement in the war was so brief that the government had neither

---

[23] Quoted in Hargrove 1994, 20. See also Hellman 1972, 115–87.

[24] McCraw 1971, 127. On the myth of grassroots participation in the TVA see Selznick 1966. See also Hargrove 1994, 54–9.

[25] On the transition from the issues of the New Deal to those of the 1940s see Katznelson and Pietrykowski 1991. As should be clear in the subsequent pages of this essay, I disagree completely with the authors' assertion (314) that the termination of the National Resources Planning Board (1943) "effectively removed planning from the repertoire of available options in the American political economy."

the time nor the need to create a structure of state-owned manufacturing facilities.[26] In the early 1940s, by contrast, the U.S. government had both the need and the time to occupy a new role in the industrial economy.

When the private sector was at first unable to achieve the level of investment needed to supply the nation's military needs, the U.S. Defense Plant Corporation quickly began to take up the slack. The government provided capital for new plants in the steel, rubber, aluminum, aircraft, magnesium, and shipbuilding industries and constructed new interregional gas pipelines in order to supply the East Coast with fuel during the war. By 1945, three-quarters of the country's $25 billion investment in new facilities and equipment came from the public sector, leaving the government in an ownership position in a substantial part of the nation's industrial sector. The government's power over private firms was as complete as an elaborate network of controls over prices, wages, raw materials, and transportation could make it.[27] So formidable was federal government involvement that a well-connected, media-savvy entrepreneur could manipulate the system to gain entry to the steel, shipbuilding, and aluminum industries – all of which had high barriers to entry (Adams 1997).

At the end of World War II the nation debated the future course of its economy far more seriously than it had in 1919–20, and this debate took place amid concern that America might well sag back into a paralyzing depression. Price control was one of the central issues, as was the disposition of the federal government's industrial holdings. There was strong support from some quarters for retaining in public hands both the investments and the controls, hence abandoning two vital aspects of U.S. peacetime capitalism. But as the debate unfolded, it became apparent that the outcome had been prefigured during the war when the Roosevelt administration had been forced to replace John Kenneth Galbraith, a brilliant New Deal economist/reformer, as head of the Office of Price Administration. To take his place, the administration turned to Chester Bowles, a business-oriented liberal who had made a fortune in advertising. By the end of 1946, most price controls were just

---

[26] Following the Armistice in 1918, there was a lively debate in the United States over whether the railroads should be nationalized. But the outcome was a return to "normalcy," which meant in this case private ownership under extensive regulation. On the mobilization see Cuff 1969, 1973.

[27] Vatter 1985, especially 26–31, 67–83. See also Bruchey 1990, 473–80. The government owned approximately $16 billion worth of industrial facilities in 1945.

a memory in a country edging into what would be one of its longest sustained periods of economic expansion.[28] The government quickly sold off its industrial holdings, much to the benefit of a host of entrepreneurs who fully understood that Mr. Kaiser had not been entirely selfless when he went to Washington to join forces with the New Deal.[29]

The so-called American Century, which lasted only from 1945 until the late 1960s, was an era of great prosperity. The gloomy predictions of the "stagnationist" school of Keynesian economists turned out to be wrong; the U.S. economy quickly recovered from the conversion to peacetime conditions, and Americans enjoyed two decades of economic expansion. The country's mood was relatively conservative, as President Harry S. Truman discovered when he proposed that the national government create more SOEs on the TVA model. Congress rejected Truman's proposal. Planning along moderate Keynesian lines, however, was as acceptable to the Republican Eisenhower administrations (1953-61) as it was to the Democratic administrations of Truman (1945-53), John F. Kennedy (1961-3) and Lyndon B. Johnson (1963-9).[30]

The federal government's two major SOEs continued to expand during the American Century, but both provoked substantial controversy. When the Hoover Commission on the Organization of the Executive Branch of the Government reported in 1949, it provided Congress and the nation with a succinct evaluation of the Post Office: "a. The administrative structure is obsolete and over centralized. b. A maze of outmoded laws, regulations and traditions freezes progress and stifles proper administration. c. Although the Post Office is a business-type establishment, it lacks the freedom and flexibility essential to good business operation. d. Rates have not kept pace with wages and other costs, and rate-making machinery is inadequate. e. The service is used to hide subsidies. f. Political appointment of first-, second-, and third-class Postmasters and certain other officials produces inefficiency and militates against the incentives of promotion."

---

[28] Rockoff 1984, 85-176. As Rockoff explains, the business community led the charge against Galbraith and Leon Henderson, both of whom were identified as "the professors."

[29] Adams 1997; Vatter 1985, 64, 83-8. In addition to plant and equipment, the government had between $50 and $70 billion in "surplus" property. The best treatment of the still somewhat mysterious purchase of the government's interregional pipelines is found in Castaneda and Pratt 1993, 33-53.

[30] Collins 1981; Graham 1976, 94-187; Stein 1969.

These and other problems left the Post Office operating in 1947 with a total deficit of $263 million, 20 percent of its revenues. The deficit grew in 1948 and was expected to reach 30 percent of revenues by 1949. "The Post Office," the commission concluded, "should be taken out of politics" (Hoover Commission 1949, 220–5). In 1970 Congress finally attempted to follow this mandate and depoliticize the organization by making the U.S. Postal Service an independent government enterprise. After this reorganization failed in the 1970s to eliminate either the deficits or the postal politics, the result was yet another round of critiques and proposals for reorganization.[31]

The federal government's land/water business had a somewhat less troubled history during the expansive American Century. In 1949 the Hoover Commission found problems in land management stemming from "a long and wasteful conflict and overlap" between the Departments of Agriculture and the Interior; "these problems of conflicting, confusing, and duplicating activities of the bureaus concerned call," the commission said, "for basic organizational changes." So, too, did the development of subsoil and water resources, activities involving projects totaling $15 billion and about 100,000 employees, as well as the personnel of independent contractors. "There is," the commission noted, "no adequate check in the Government upon the validity or timing of development projects and their relation to the economy of the country."[32]

But the pressure from the cities, agricultural interests, businesses, and federal agencies was too great to resist. As one leading historian of the U.S. West explains: "The period from the late 1940s through the 1960s was the golden age of the Bureau of Reclamation. The bureau raced the Army Corps of Engineers and local public utility districts to dam the free-flowing rivers of the West. . . . Funding for western water development rose from $33 million in 1939 to $230 million in 1949 and stayed at that plateau. By 1975, the bureau had spent $6 billion on western irrigation projects" (White 1991, 522–8). Struggles among the various public bureaucracies and between the agencies and private interests using the vast land resources managed by the government finally forced Congress to take action in 1960. Still, the controversies over subsidies continued, as did the expansion of federal services. Little wonder that

---

[31] See, for instance, Sherman 1980. For a positive evaluation see Tierney 1988.

[32] Hoover Commission 1949, 251–3, 263–6. See also Macneil and Metz 1956, 109–19, on the second Hoover Commission.

this happened because "the West had found in the federal government the engine for development it had long sought; the growth it so cherished seemed to stretch endlessly before it."[33]

States and municipalities also tapped federal resources during the postwar era. Urban development programs carried cities into the real estate and rental businesses in new ways as efforts mounted to salvage decaying central business districts. The intent of these policies was not to create SOEs; for the most part, the municipal enterprises were incidental to renewal plans. But incrementally the plans broadened the scope of municipal government and made it increasingly dependent on a continued flow of dollars from Washington, D.C.[34] Similar changes took place within and between state governments. One of the most dynamic institutions in the 1940s and 1950s was the New York Port Authority under the leadership of Austin Tobin.[35] Because the Port Authority had its own cash cow (bridge tolls), Tobin was not constrained by the availability of federal funds, but he did have to contend with two state governments (of New York and New Jersey) and the political leaders of several municipalities. Showing the political, legal, and entrepreneurial skills that we usually associate with leaders of great national endeavors and multinational firms, Tobin built an empire of Port Authority SOEs. They included marine terminals, airports, a commuter rail line, bus and truck terminals, and finally, the World Trade Center in New York City.[36] Looking down on the Empire State Building from the top floor of the World Trade Center, one senses that the building is an appropriate symbol of the political culture of a short-lived American Century.

THE END OF THE PLANNING PHASE IN THE UNITED STATES

Prosperity notwithstanding, many Americans remained hostile to the administrative state, and during the half century following World War II, voters gradually turned against further extensions of governmental authority. The shift in general public and elite attitudes was a widespread

[33] White 1991, 529–31. See the evaluation in President's Private Sector Survey on Cost Control 1983, Executive Summary, iii–ix.
[34] Fox 1986, 80–106; Mollenkopf 1983, 32–4, 80, 159–221. As Mollenkopf observes, "by 1978 direct federal aid constituted 50.7 percent of locally raised revenues in forty-eight large central cities (33)."
[35] On the Authority before Tobin see Bard 1939.
[36] Doig 1987, 124–73. It is helpful to compare Tobin's career with that of Robert Moses, who followed a similar path to power. See Caro 1974.

phenomenon with motives and goals as complex as those that drove the beginning of that long cycle in the 1890s and early 1900s.[37] In the postwar era, many Americans became disenchanted with the regulatory state, the welfare state, and SOE. By the 1980s and 1990s, the long planning phase of SOE development appeared to have ended. Retrenchment had become the essence of reform.

The end of this cycle, like its beginning, came in a series of waves, starting in the 1950s with the Eisenhower administrations. Eisenhower and many of his congressional supporters were moderate reformers who, for the most part, wanted to prevent further extensions of national authority, but in a few areas they sought retrenchment. One of their targets for retrenchment was the public electrical power system in general and the TVA in particular. Eisenhower could not understand why the federal government should subsidize energy supplies to one part of the country. In his vision of America, it was better to leave decisions about electric power to private, market-oriented interests in the Tennessee Valley and elsewhere.

The TVA, however, still had strong support, and this effort to shift the U.S. focus from public to private enterprise was unsuccessful. Eisenhower's attack on publicly owned electric power – like his efforts to curtail agricultural subsidies and to restrain the expansion of the Federal Power Commission's authority – failed. Although the nation would eventually return to all of these subjects in settings that would place the defenders of the administrative state on the defensive, the opponents of SOEs would all find, as Eisenhower did, how difficult it was to terminate a deeply entrenched system of subsidies. This was especially true in a democratic society in which all of the subsidized factions were defended by active interest groups.

Interest-group politics ensured that the Iron Law of Subsidies would not be repealed. The Iron Law predicts that (1) all interests will struggle to preserve their particular subsidies, even though they may oppose subsidies in principle; (2) their resistance will vary in direct proportion to the pressure exerted by those seeking to reduce subsidies; and (3) all subsidized interests will frame their opposition to change in terms of the public interest. In America's twentieth-century polity, organized interests receiving direct or indirect subsidies were able to marshal their

---

[37] As Bennett and Bennett (1990) point out, however, even those who thought "the federal government controls too much of our daily lives" (more than half of those polled in the late 1980s) still had their own wish list of specific federal activities they wanted increased.

resistance to change through three-sided alliances between legislators whose constituents received the subsidies, interest groups that lobbied against change, and agencies that delivered the subsidies. These triocracies (or iron triangles) stabilized American government at the federal, state, and local levels, ensuring that the end of the long planning cycle would be much slower than the final stages of the developmental cycle of the early nineteenth century had been.[38] Eisenhower spent eight years fighting the Iron Law and in most cases had to settle for a tie, having taken some of the political momentum out of the drive toward expansion of the state at the federal level.[39]

The second major wave in this conservative, market-oriented movement came in the 1970s and 1980s under dramatically different conditions. One of the new conditions calls for very little explication. Between 1965 and 1975, the United States steadily lost its preeminent position in the global economy as more efficient, innovative firms in other countries attacked U.S. markets at home and abroad.[40] The competitive struggles that followed that crucial decade forced some of America's leading firms out of business entirely and left others struggling to cut costs, improve efficiency, and innovate more quickly and effectively. The end of the prosperous American Century left Americans looking for new ideas but uncertain about which direction the country should take.

Whatever direction that was, it was not likely that it would involve a substantial increase in the role of SOEs.[41] The government's conduct in the Vietnam War left many Americans skeptical of public authority. Watergate and the associated scandals of the early 1970s strengthened

---

[38] I have explored these subjects in Galambos 1982. See also Noll and Owen 1983, 26–65.

[39] Eisenhower's efforts can be traced through the following: Alexander 1975; Ambrose 1984; Galambos et al. 1996; Greenstein 1982.

[40] Galambos 1996. My conclusions about the impact of international competition run counter to those of Cameron (1978), but he was analyzing the postwar years 1960–75, when, as many of the authors in this book note, nations were employing government aggressively in an effort to spur economic growth. Their experiences did not encourage a similar response in the 1980s and 1990s.

[41] The exception to this rule is the federal government's move into the railroad industry after regulation failed; see Saunders 1978. As Saunders notes (299), the Penn Central petitioned to end all passenger service west of Buffalo, New York, and Harrisburg, Pennsylvania: "The ploy worked. Congress panicked, and the result was the Amtrak law that established the National Railroad Passenger Corporation, which took over the operation of nearly all noncommuter passenger services in the United States on May 1, 1971." The U.S. Surface Transportation Board apparently brought that unsuccessful SOE experiment to a close in 1998.

the perception that public authority was untrustworthy. Uneasy about
their future, Americans seemed prepared in these difficult years to
reconsider the basic structure of the corporate commonwealth that had
emerged from a century of demands for government programs to ensure
equity and economic security for particular groups and particular institutions. Americans began to ask new questions about the administrative
state.

Answers were available in the professional literature of scholars
whose work was seldom read by anyone except other professionals in
their fields. Economists had for some years been examining, in theory
and practice, the manner in which regulatory systems, public bureaucracies, and SOEs performed.[42] Political scientists and economic sociol-
ogists had been studying bureaucracies in both the public and private
sectors, providing insights into interest groups and the subsidy systems
they helped to sustain.[43] Because most of this literature was turgid,
detailed, jargon-filled, and sometimes written in mathematics instead of
English, it was inaccessible to all except the hardiest nonprofessionals.
During the years prior to World War II, it would probably have had little
impact on public thought or public policy. Since the 1940s, however, the
United States had developed a new amalgam of professionals and public
institutions, an amalgam that historian Brian Balogh (1991b) has called
the "prominstrative state." That blend of institutions provided new
conduits that carried professional ideas into the public sphere, where
they could be translated into terms accessible to a general audience.

These conduits were important because they had a decisive influence
on the second wave of reaction against the state and SOEs. Profession-
ally trained staff members in both the legislative and executive branches
provided an important means of intellectual transfer. Another conduit
was agency staff. Principals made final decisions, but staff members
increasingly shaped the alternatives that the principals considered. Over
time, elaborate networks of experts developed around salient issues,
and those issue networks were sensitive to ideas that were gaining
acceptance in professional circles (Heclo 1978, 90–3). Nobel Prizes in
economics mattered in these networks.

The result was an unusual political movement, which began without
widespread public support, without elected political leadership, and

---

[42] See, for instance, Buchanan 1977; McAvoy 1970; McCraw 1984, 222–309; Posner 1974;
Stigler 1971.
[43] See, for example, Rourke 1972.

without a general agenda. Insofar as the movement had a unifying theme, it was various forms of "antistatism." Although opposition to an active government had a long history in America, the antistatism movement of these years was not, for the most part, a grassroots phenomenon like the Progressive reform movement of the 1890–1920 era. Nor was it a top-down movement like the New Deal of the 1930s. Unlike the Eisenhower administrations of the 1950s, this new movement had both liberal and conservative supporters as it worked its way up through the government. In its initial stages the deregulation wing of antistatism focused on specific governmental agencies and their programs, and during the 1970s deregulation provided a new answer to political scientist Herbert Kaufman's question, Are government organizations immortal?[44]

Insofar as antistatism emerged at the grass roots, it arose as a result of concerns about the cost of government. In California, the opposition to mounting public expenditures led to a tax revolt and the passage in 1978 of Proposition 13, which put a lid on property taxes and local expenditures. Other similar state movements arose, and such expressions of frustration put up a warning flag to legislators and signaled a widespread drift toward retrenchment.[45] A series of well-publicized governmental problems accelerated the process. The TVA, long one of the Left's leading examples of a successful SOE, encountered enormous difficulties with its forays into nuclear power. The organization's leaders, "prisoners of myth," led the institution into a "self-defeating escalation of commitment in both the power and nonpower missions."[46] State institutions such as the San Francisco Harbor Commission had long been the subjects of controversy, as were municipal urban renewal projects.[47] Confronted by an energy crisis, a high rate of inflation, and a decline in private-sector economic activity, many municipalities and states floundered into deep financial trouble. The resulting watershed was reflected

---

[44] Kaufman 1976. When the Brookings Institution published the book, the question appeared to be rhetorical.

[45] Campbell 1998. Twenty-one states adopted limits on local finances and sixteen adopted limits on state finances between 1978 and 1983.

[46] Hargrove 1994, 155–94. The leader selected (by President Jimmy Carter) in the late 1970s to lead the TVA through organizational renewal failed to achieve that goal; he explained in 1980, "The hardest job in the world is to take on an agency that's moving in one direction and turn it in another direction." Quoted in ibid., 240. The TVA was not the only institution to encounter problems with nuclear power. See Balogh 1991a; Hirsch 1989.

[47] Fox 1986, 190–220, 238–42; Nash 1964, 213–20, 233–8. As Fox points out (242), "planned shrinkage" became extremely popular in the wake of the fiscal crises.

in the figures on total state and local expenditures as a percentage of gross national product; they peaked in 1975 and steadily declined throughout the rest of the decade (Kirlin 1984, 162).

The deregulation phase of antistatism provided many examples of the Iron Law of Subsidies. Each change in public policy threatened the interests of powerful, well-organized, well-financed groups, and the result was an intense series of battles over the proper role of government in the economy.[48] The triocracies opposing change were weakened, however, by the bipartisan nature of the reform movement and by the lack of widespread support for their government-sheltered subsidies. In the context of the 1970s, it was hard for their spokespersons to develop effective arguments that countered the professional analyses mustered by the networks of market-oriented opponents. Moreover, regulated interests were not united in their defense of the existing systems.

In the 1980s, during the Reagan administrations, the reform movement became broader and the pace of change accelerated.[49] Privatization as well as deregulation became an important battlefront, and Chicago school concepts of political economy began to play a significant role in debates over the future of the administrative state.[50] At the heart of this transition was an effort to improve efficiency in providing goods and services. Most (but not all) academic studies comparing public and private operations indicated that private institutions had lower costs.[51] Municipal and state officials seeking savings in capital costs and operating expenses found it difficult to ignore those findings. Here, as at the federal level, the Iron Law was still in effect, and few changes were made without intense public controversies. By the mid-1990s, however, the drift of policy throughout the United States was away from SOEs and toward private ventures in both state and local governments. As antistatism spread through the country's 80,000 different governments, the movement focused the attention of voters on subsidies – under one name or another – and governmental inefficiency.[52]

---

[48] Derthick and Quick 1985. In addition to the three-sided alliances, coalitions of interest groups were important in the defense of subsidies.

[49] Another issue, which I have not discussed, is welfare reform. By the 1990s, the pressure to cut back and reformulate welfare programs was intense at both the national and state levels of government.

[50] See President's Private Sector Survey on Cost Control 1983.

[51] Bennett and DiLorenzo 1983; Crain and Zardkoohi 1978; Hanke and Walters 1987.

[52] The figure of approximately 80,000 is from Anton 1987, 37. This figure includes the national, state, county, municipal, township, school district, and special district governments. Consolidation had reduced the number of governments by more than 75,000 since

At the federal level, one of the initial privatization battles was waged over public lands. As late as 1981 about one-third of the land in the United States was still in the public domain. Some of it was being used for national facilities such as military bases and parks; some of it contained trees and minerals that could be economically farmed and extracted; much of it consisted of relatively poor grazing land and desert. Academic studies indicated that most of the latter two categories of land were being used uneconomically, and the White House proposed dramatic changes in the existing system of land use.[53] Those proposals brought a storm of criticism from interest groups whose members were exploiting the current system and from environmental groups dedicated to preserving the existing ratio of public to private land. The harder the executive branch pushed, the more resistance it met from this formidable coalition of self-interested and environmentally dedicated organizations. After eight years of effort the Reagan administration had lost to the Iron Law, but it had successfully introduced the subject of privatization to American political debates.[54]

As the new discourse reverberated through state and local politics, a multitude of SOEs came under increased scrutiny. The economic pressures on state and local governments aroused many of their political leaders to consider what came to be called "rightsizing," a euphemism for the public counterpart of the "reengineering" taking place throughout the private sector in the 1980s and 1990s. Water and wastewater utility operations were reexamined and sometimes privatized. The economic pressures driving policy in this direction were significant: local expenditures for wastewater facilities had increased by 50 percent between 1980 and 1987. By the early 1990s there were hundreds of contracts that turned over local wastewater treatment and other activities to private organizations.[55]

In these years, few cities and states completely ignored the trend toward privatization. By 1992 one survey indicated that 90 percent of state government agencies had adopted some type of privatization and

1942. An exception to the trend in state and local government activity was provided by the new interest in competitive encouragement of economic development. See Eisinger 1988. As Eisinger notes, the contraction of federal funding contributed to this shift in policy at the state and local levels.

[53] Hanke and Dowdle 1985, 1987; President's Private Sector Survey on Cost Control 1983.

[54] Hays 1987a, especially 491–526. See also Hays 1987b.

[55] Hartman 1993; *Privatization 1993*. See also the annual reports on privatization for 1989, 1991, and 1992.

that most anticipated increased efforts to do so during the next decade.
The privatization movement was having an important impact on public
institutions in health and social services, education, and waste management and recycling.[56] Although that process is ongoing, it is clear
that the long planning phase of SOE development that began at the end
of the nineteenth century was coming to a close in the 1990s.

CONCLUSIONS

Neither cycle of SOE development in the United States was unique. In
the twentieth century, the involvement of the federal and state governments in the business of managing public lands had some unique
aspects, as did the failure of the United States to nationalize major industries in the planning phase of SOE evolution. But during the nineteenth
century's development phase, state and municipal involvement with
SOEs closely resembled the changes taking place in the major Western
nations. When one combines state, local, and national SOEs during the
twentieth century, the gap between the United States and the rest of
the West narrows, although it does not disappear.

What was unusual about the United States in the nineteenth century
was the juxtaposition of a dynamic period of private-sector expansion
and an extremely negative experience with SOEs. For many decades the
cultural and political residue of these contrasting experiences thwarted
efforts to develop public capabilities. Public service remained a low-
status occupation, and civic values throughout the society were weak.

These deeply planted values forced Americans to compromise when
they found it useful to experiment with SOEs in the twentieth century.
As the need for public planning increased, Americans turned more often
than their counterparts in Europe to local and state governments and
to public–private and national–state programs to perform activities that
were done through national SOEs in many of the world's advanced
economies. The total mix of public SOEs in the United States was thus
different in degree but not in kind.

The fall of SOEs in the United States accompanied, was influenced
by, and influenced the changes taking place in other parts of the public
sector, both domestically and internationally. This was and still is a global
phenomenon, and the transformations in the United States closely
resembled those that have taken place throughout much of the West. In

---

[56] *Privatization 1993.*

America these transitions have already been comparable, in their impact on society, to the New Deal of the 1930s and the reorganization of American business and public life during the years 1890 to 1920. During the end of the planning cycle of SOE development, the United States dismantled some parts of its administrative state so fast that many Europeans became critical of the heartless "American Solution." But the differences were matters of degree and timing, and neither Europeans nor Americans can today lay claim to a unique political economy.

REFERENCES

Adams, S. B. 1997. *Mr. Kaiser goes to Washington: The rise of a government entrepreneur*. Chapel Hill, N.C.

Alchon, G. 1985. *The invisible hand of planning: Capitalism, social science, and the state in the 1920s*. Princeton, N.J.

Alexander, C. C. 1975. *Holding the line: The Eisenhower era, 1953-1961*. Bloomington, Ind.

Ambrose, S. E. 1984. *Eisenhower: The president*. New York.

Anderson, A. D. 1977. *The origin and resolution of an urban crisis: Baltimore, 1890-1930*. Baltimore.

Anderson, W., C. Penniman, and E. W. Weidner. 1960. *Government in the fifty states*. New York.

Anton, T. J. 1987. Intergovernmental change in the United States: An assessment of the literature. In *Public sector performance: A conceptual turning point*, ed. T. C. Miller, pp. 15-64. New York.

Baker, P. 1991. *The moral frameworks of public life: Gender, politics, and the state in rural New York, 1870-1930*. New York.

Balogh, B. 1991a. *Chain reaction: Expert debate and public participation in American commercial nuclear power, 1945-1975*. New York.

1991b. Reorganizing the organizational synthesis: Federal-professional relations in modern America. *Studies in American Political Development* 5(1): 119-72.

Bard, E. W. 1939. *The Port of New York Authority*. New York.

Bennett, J. T., and T. J. DiLorenzo. 1983. Public employee unions and the privatization of "public" services. *Journal of Labor Research* 4(1): 33-45.

Bennett, L. L. M., and S. E. Bennett. 1990. *Living with Leviathan: Americans coming to terms with big government*. Lawrence, Kans.

Black, N. M. 1956. *Water for the cities: A history of the urban water supply problem in the United States*. Syracuse, N.Y.

Blackford, M. G. 1977. *The politics of business in California, 1890-1920*. Columbus, Ohio.

Bogue, A. G. 1980. Land policies and sales. In *Encyclopedia of American economic history*, ed. G. Porter, pp. 588-600. New York.

Brock, G. W. 1981. *The telecommunications industry: The dynamics of market structure*. Cambridge, Mass.

Brock, W. R. 1984. *Investigation and responsibility: Public responsibility in the United States, 1865-1900*. New York.

Bruchey, S. 1990. *Enterprise: The dynamic economy of a free people*. Cambridge, Mass.

Buchanan, J. M. 1977. Why does government grow? In *Budgets and bureaucrats: The sources of government growth*, ed. Thomas E. Borcherding, pp. 3-18. Durham, N.C.

Bushnell, A. T. 1995. *Establishing exceptionalism: Historiography and the colonial Americas*. Aldershot, Eng.

Cameron, D. R. 1978. The expansion of the public economy: A comparative analysis. *American Political Science Review* 72: 1243-61.

Campbell, B. C. 1998. Tax revolts and political change. *Journal of Policy History* 10(1): 153-78.

Caro, R. A. 1974. *The power broker: Robert Moses and the fall of New York*. New York.

Castaneda, C. J., and J. A. Pratt. 1993. *From Texas to the East: A strategic history of Texas Eastern Corporation*. College Station, Tex.

Chapin, C. V. 1901. *Municipal sanitation in the United States*. Providence, R.I.

Cheape, C. W. 1980. *Moving the masses: Urban public transit in New York, Boston, and Philadelphia, 1880-1912*. Cambridge, Mass.

Collins, R. 1981. *The business response to Keynes, 1929-1964*. New York.

Crain, W. M., and A. Zardkoohi. 1978. A test of the property-rights theory of the firm: Water utilities in the United States. *Journal of Law and Economics* 21(2): 395-408.

Cuff, R. D. 1969. Bernard Baruch: Symbol and myth in industrial mobilization. *Business History Review* 43: 130-3.

——— 1973. *The War Industries Board: Business-government relations during World War I*. Baltimore.

Derthick, M., and P. J. Quirk. 1985. *The politics of deregulation*. Washington, D.C.

Doig, J. W. 1987. To claim the seas and the skies: Austin Tobin and the Port of New York Authority. In *Leadership and innovation: A biographical perspective on entrepreneurs in government*, ed. Jameson W. Doig and Erwin C. Hargrove, pp. 124-73. Baltimore.

Duffy, J. 1974. *A history of public health in New York City, 1866-1966*. New York.

Eisinger, P. K. 1988. *The rise of the entrepreneurial state: State and local economic development policy in the United States*. Madison, Wis.

Faulkner, H. U. 1951. *The decline of laissez faire, 1897-1917*. New York.

Feller, D. 1984. *The public lands in Jacksonian politics*. Madison, Wis.

Fogel, R. W. 1960. *The Union Pacific Railroad: A case in premature enterprise*. Baltimore.

Foster, M. S. 1981. *From streetcar to superhighway: American city planners and urban transportation, 1900-1940*. Philadelphia.

Fox, K. 1986. *Metropolitan America: Urban life and urban policy in the United States, 1940-1980*. Jackson, Miss.

Galambos, L. 1975. *The public image of big business in America, 1880-1940: A quantitative study in social change*. Baltimore.

1982. *America at middle age*. New York.

1996. Paying up: The price of the Vietnam War. In *Integrating the sixties: The origins, structures, and legitimacy of public policy in a turbulent decade*, ed. B. Balogh. *Journal of Policy History* 8(1): 166–79.

Galambos, L., D. van Ee, E. Hughes, R. Coblentz, R. Brugger, J. Seraphine, and J. Friedman, eds. 1996. *The papers of Dwight David Eisenhower*. Vol. 14–17, *The middle way*. Baltimore.

Goldman, J. A. 1997. *Building New York's sewers: Developing mechanisms of urban management*. West Lafayette, Ind.

Goodrich, C. 1960. *Government promotion of American canals and railroads, 1800–1890*. New York.

Goodrich, C., J. Rubin, H. J. Canmer, and H. H. Segal. 1961. *Canals and American economic development*. New York.

Graham, O. L., Jr. 1976. *Toward a planned society: From Roosevelt to Nixon*. New York.

Greenstein, F. I. 1982. *The hidden-hand presidency: Eisenhower as leader*. New York.

Griffith, E. S. 1974a. *A history of American city government: The conspicuous failure, 1870–1900*. New York.

1974b. *A history of American city government: The progressive years and their aftermath, 1900–1920*. New York.

Hammond, B. 1957. *Banks and politics in America: From the Revolution to the Civil War*. Princeton, N.J.

Hanke, S. H., and B. Dowdle. 1985. Public timber policy and the wood-products industry. In *Forestlands public and private*, ed. R. T. Deacon and M. B. Johnson, pp. 77–102. Cambridge, Mass.

1987. Privatizing the public domain. In *Prospects for privatization*, ed. S. H. Hanke, pp. 114–23. New York.

Hanke, S. H., and S. J. K. Walters. 1987. Privatizing waterworks. In *Prospects for privatization*, ed. S. H. Hanke, pp. 104–13. New York.

Hargrove, E. C. 1994. *Prisoners of myth: The leadership of the Tennessee Valley Authority, 1933–1990*. Princeton, N.J.

Hartman, R. 1993. *Contracting water and wastewater utility operations*. Los Angeles.

Hartz, L. 1948. *Economic policy and democratic thought: Pennsylvania, 1776–1860*. Cambridge, Mass.

Hays, S. P. 1987a. *Beauty, health, and permanence: Environmental politics in the United States, 1955–1985*. New York.

1987b. The politics of environmental administration. In *The new American state: Bureaucracies and policies since World War II*, ed. L. Galambos, pp. 21–53. Baltimore.

Heclo, H. 1978. Issue networks and the executive establishment. In *The new American political system*, ed. A. Kind, pp. 90–3. Washington, D.C.

Hellman, R. 1972. *Government competition in the electric utility industry: A theoretical and empirical study*. New York.

Hirsh, R. F. 1989. *Technology and transformation in the American electric utility industry*. New York.

Hoover Commission. 1949. *The Hoover Commission report on organization of the executive branch of the government*. New York.

Jensen, R. J. 1978. *Illinois: A bicentennial history*. New York.

John, R. R. 1990. Spreading the word: The postal system and the creation of American society – A sketch. *Business and Economic History* 19: 22–5.

1995. *Spreading the news: The American postal system from Franklin to Morse*. Cambridge, Mass.

Katznelson, I., and B. Pietrykowski. 1991. Rebuilding the American state: Evidence from the 1940s. *Studies in American Political Development* 5(Fall): 301–39.

Kaufman, H. 1976. *Are government organizations immortal?* Washington, D.C.

Keller, M. 1977. *Affairs of state: Public life in late nineteenth-century America*. Cambridge, Mass.

Kirlin, J. J. 1984. A political perspective. In *Public sector performance: A conceptual turning point*, ed. Trudi C. Miller, pp. 161–92. Baltimore.

Lessoff, A. 1994. *The nation and its city: Politics, "corruption," and progress in Washington, D.C., 1861–1902*. Baltimore.

Lipartito, K. 1989. *The Bell System and regional business: The telephone in the South, 1877–1920*. Baltimore.

Macneil, N., and H. W. Metz. 1956. *The Hoover Report, 1953–1955: What it means to you as citizen and taxpayer*. New York.

McAvoy, P. 1970. *The economic effects of regulation: Principles and institutions*. New York.

McCraw, T. K. 1971. *TVA and the power fight, 1933–1939*. Philadelphia.

1984. *Prophets of regulation: Charles Francis Adams, Louis D. Brandeis, James M. Landis, Alfred E. Kahn*. Cambridge, Mass.

McDonald, T. J. 1984. San Francisco: Socioeconomic change, political culture, and fiscal politics, 1870–1906. In *The politics of urban fiscal policy*, ed. T. J. McDonald and S. K. Ward, pp. 39–67. Beverly Hills, Calif.

McKelvey, B. 1973. *American urbanization: A comparative history*. Glenview, Ill.

Melosi, M. V. 1973. "Out of sight, out of mind": The environment and disposal of municipal refuse, 1860–1920. *The Historian* 35(August): 621–40.

Miller, N. 1962. *The enterprise of a free people: Aspects of economic development in New York State during the canal period, 1792–1838*. Ithaca, N.Y.

Mollenkopf, J. H. 1983. *The contested city*. Princeton, N.J.

Monkkonen, E. H. 1984. The politics of municipal indebtedness and default, 1850–1936. In *The politics of urban fiscal policy*, ed. T. J. McDonald and S. K. Ward, pp. 125–59. Beverly Hills, Calif.

Nash, G. D. 1964. *State government and economic development: A history of administrative policies in California, 1849–1933*. Berkeley.

1980. State and local governments. In *Encyclopedia of American economic history*, ed. G. Porter, 4, p. 520. New York.

Noll, R. G., and B. M. Owen. 1983. *The political economy of deregulation: Interest groups in the regulatory process*. Washington, D.C.

Numbers, R. L. 1984. The third party: Health insurance in America. In *Sickness and health in America: Readings in the history of medicine and public health*, ed. J. W. Leavitt and R. L. Numbers, pp. 233–47. Madison, Wis.

Posner, R. 1974. Theories of economic regulation. *Bell Journal of Economics and Management Science* 2(Autumn): 33–58.

President's Private Sector Survey on Cost Control. 1983. *Report on the Department of the Interior*. Washington, D.C.

Privatization 1993. 1993. Los Angeles.

Rockoff, H. 1984. *Drastic measures: A history of wage and price controls in the United States*. New York.

Rose, R. 1989. How exceptional is the American political economy? *Political Science Quarterly* 104(1): 91–115.

Rosenberg, C. E. 1987. *The care of strangers: The rise of America's hospital system*. New York.

Ross, D. 1991. *The origins of American social science*. New York.

——— 1993. An historian's view of American social science. *Journal of the History of the Behavioral Sciences* 29(April): 99–112.

Rourke, F. E., ed. 1972. *Bureaucratic power in national politics*. Boston.

Saunders, R. 1978. *The railroad mergers and the coming of Conrail*. Westport, Conn.

Scheiber, H. N. 1969. *Ohio Canal era: A case study of government and the economy, 1820–61*. Athens, Ohio.

Schultz, S. K., and C. McShane. 1978. To engineer the metropolis: Sewers, sanitation, and city planning in late-nineteenth-century America. *Journal of American History* 65(2): 389–411.

Selznick, P. 1966. *TVA and the grass roots: A study in the sociology of formal organization*. New York.

Sherman, R., ed. 1980. *Perspectives on postal service issues*. Washington, D.C.

Skocpol, T. 1992. *Protecting soldiers and mothers: The political origins of social policy in the United States*. Cambridge, Mass.

Skowronek, S. 1982. *Building a new American state: The expansion of national administrative capacities, 1877–1920*. New York.

Smith, W. B. 1953. *Economic aspects of the Second Bank of the United States*. Cambridge, Mass.

Starr, P. 1982. *The social transformation of American medicine*. New York.

State of New York, Conservation Department. 1945. *The Saratoga spa*. Albany.

Stein, H. 1969. *The fiscal revolution in America*. Chicago.

Stevens, R. 1989. *In sickness and in wealth: American hospitals in the twentieth century*. New York.

Stigler, G. 1971. The theory of economic regulation. *Bell Journal of Economics* 2(Spring): 3–21.

Swierenga, R. P. 1968. *Pioneers and profits: Land speculation on the Iowa frontier*. Ames, Iowa.

Sylla, R. 1971–2. American banking and growth in the nineteenth century: A partial view of the terrain. *Explorations in Economic History* 9(2): 197–227.

Tarr, J. A. 1984. The evolution of the urban infrastructure in the nineteenth and twentieth centuries. In *Perspectives on urban infrastructure*, ed. R. Hanson, pp. 4–60. Washington, D.C.

Teaford, J. C. 1984. Local government. In *Encyclopedia of American political history*, ed. J. P. Greene, 2, pp. 777–90. New York.

Temin, P. 1969. *The Jacksonian economy*. New York.

Thorelli, H. B. 1955. *The federal antitrust policy: Origination of an American tradition*. Baltimore.

Tierney, J. T. 1988. *The U.S. Postal Service: Status and prospects of a public enterprise*. New York.

Toman, J. A., and B. S. Hays. 1996. *Horse trails to regional rails: The story of public transit in greater Cleveland*. Kent, Ohio.

Vatter, H. G. 1985. *The U.S. economy in World War II*. New York.

Warner, S. B., Jr. 1968. *The private city: Philadelphia in three periods of its growth*. Philadelphia.

Whinery, S. 1903. *Municipal public works: Their inception, construction and management*. New York.

White, L. D. 1958. *The Republican era, 1869-1901: A study in administrative history*. New York.

White, R. 1991. *"It's your misfortune and none of my own": A history of the American West*. Norman, Okla.

Wiebe, R. 1967. *The search for order, 1877-1920*. New York.

Conclusion

Schumpeter Revisited

LOUIS GALAMBOS AND WILLIAM BAUMOL

In 1942 Joseph A. Schumpeter published his grand synthesis of political economy, *Capitalism, socialism, and democracy*. He demonstrated with impeccable logic that socialism would inevitably evolve out of capitalism, not because of the latter system's failures à la Marx, but because of its successes à la Schumpeter. With a literary shrug of the shoulders, he pointed out that the economic system he loved, the entrepreneurial brand of high capitalism, was gradually giving way to democratic socialism. Surprisingly, he predicted that the new state-controlled economy could continue to be efficient and could even perform the vital entrepreneurial function needed to provide greater wealth and income for the population. He concluded "that socialization means a stride beyond big business on the way that has been chalked out by it or, what amounts to the same thing, that socialist management may conceivably prove as superior to big-business capitalism as big-business capitalism has proved to be to the kind of competitive capitalism of which the English industry a hundred years ago was the prototype" (Schumpeter 1942, 195-6). He had serious reservations about bureaucratic authority, and he issued other "warnings."[1] But

---

[1] Schumpeter 1942, 200-18. "The bureaucratic method of transacting business and the moral atmosphere it spreads doubtless often exert a depressing influence on the most

asking, rhetorically, "Can socialism work?" he said, with typical assurance, "Of course it can."[2]

In this book, each of the authors has in effect returned to Schumpeter's predictions, much as Schumpeter did to Marx's predictions about the collapse of capitalism. On the basis of the previous essays, we can now evaluate three central aspects of Schumpeter's political economy: the origins of state-owned enterprises (SOEs), the central feature of any socialist system in various times and national settings; the performance of SOEs in those different settings; and the reason for their fall from grace in the recent past. Although we are less inclined than Schumpeter to use the word "inevitable," we would like to add to these conclusions our own predictions as to whether the recent turn away from SOEs is likely to be a short-term or a very long-term aspect of the national economies the authors have surveyed.

THE ORIGINS OF SOEs

Two general situations appear to have accounted for most of the experiments with SOE. One was the unsatisfactory performance of the private sector of the economy, something akin to, but broader than, the idea of market failure. The other was the desire to introduce measures of equity and security, including national security and public health, that seemed not to be forthcoming from a market-oriented capitalist system.

In addition, enterprises were operated by the public sector as a means to protect the consuming public from exploitation through the exercise of market or monopoly power. Firms that were nationalized generally included those in industries believed to be characterized by substantial scale economies, so that only large firms could be expected to survive in a competitive market or attain low production costs. Size threatened or at least appeared to threaten to confer market power on those enterprises. In at least some cases, the scale economies implied that the industries were, in fact, natural monopolies with the power to set and keep prices well above their competitive levels, thereby also introducing significant misallocation of the economy's resources. To deal

---

active minds. Mainly, this is due to the difficulty, inherent in the bureaucratic machine, of reconciling individual initiative with the mechanics of its working. Often the machine gives little scope for initiative and much scope for vicious attempts at smothering it" (207).

[2] Ibid., 167. "No doubt is possible about that once we assume, first, that the requisite stage of industrial development has been reached and, second, that transitional problems can be successfully resolved."

with this danger, regulation was the policy instrument favored in the United States. Elsewhere, public-sector operation of the firms was the preferred alternative.

Most of the nations surveyed experienced, at one time or another, a desire to achieve faster economic growth than the private sector was providing. Impatient with market processes, political and economic leaders and their organizations employed the state, at some level, to provide the undergirding for agricultural, commercial, and manufacturing enterprises. The major emphasis was on infrastructure development of the basic transportation and communications systems that required very large capital outlays. Frequently, these systems were linked in the minds of public planners with national security. In Germany, Great Britain, Austria, the Netherlands, and the United States, similar impulses led to somewhat similar institutional results. Only in the United States, however, was there a significant withdrawal of the state following unfortunate experiences with SOEs in the nineteenth century.

In all of the countries surveyed, including the United States, concerns about urban growth and public health led to a spurt in SOE development in the late nineteenth and early twentieth centuries. Municipal SOEs provided water and sewage facilities, as well as transportation services and energy supplies. In this phase of SOE expansion, planning began to be discussed aggressively as an alternative to a market-oriented system and began to provide a new, partially independent influence promoting further state investment. The ideology of planning blended with various political ideologies on the left and created an intellectual platform for discussion of market failures and state-led alternatives to capitalist development.

The third and most dramatic increase in the employment of SOEs to promote growth, equity, and security through planning came during the interwar, World War II, and immediate postwar decades, when major economic crises fostered a new enthusiasm for public alternatives to private enterprise. Now the interest was in developing public manufacturing and commercial enterprises, not just the infrastructure that would support the capitalist sector and urban life. It was in these decades that SOEs were truly tested, as were less radical innovations such as Keynesian planning, as means of accelerating the growth of national income and wealth. In economies devastated by the international downturn of the 1930s or by the war, it was not unreasonable to turn to the state in search of an engine that would improve welfare faster and more reliably than capitalism.

In both the second and third surges in experimentation with SOEs, new considerations that resonate with both the Schumpeterian and Marxian analyses became substantially more important. By the early twentieth century, a powerful left ideology that emphasized equity and security blended with the desire to promote growth. In its various permutations and national variations, this ideology favored state enterprise and regulatory systems and fostered a culture critical of capitalism. SOEs were seen as an appropriate solution to a wide variety of economic and social problems. If unemployment was a problem, SOEs would provide jobs. If the masses could not afford necessities, SOEs would provide goods and services at reasonable prices. If competition drove down the price of labor, SOEs would sustain the working class with a fair wage. Whether national or local, planning would "rationalize" the economic systems that seemed, to all but a few professional economists and the business interests, to be characterized by haphazard structures and all too frequent changes. SOEs in a planned economy would, it was hoped, eliminate the class struggles on which Marx had focused attention and attenuate the depressions that Schumpeter had seen as a natural consequence of "creative destruction," the essence of a well-functioning capitalist system.

Since the advocates of SOEs now were able to blend the promise of faster growth with the assurance of security, equity, and prevention of exploitation of the public through exercise of market power, their programs became irresistible in most of the nations surveyed in this volume. By the 1960s, the momentum of history appeared to be carrying the entire world toward a reliance on state-owned ventures, and in the United States there was concern among many national leaders that the remaining capitalist nations might soon find themselves isolated, without trading partners, in a world dominated by public systems. Even in Japan, which depended primarily on private enterprise, central controls – or at least guidance from the center – were an outstanding feature of an economy that had made an astonishing recovery following the nation's defeat in 1945.

THE SUDDEN FALL FROM GRACE OF SOEs

Then, with an alacrity unanticipated even in those circles most ardently dedicated to capitalism, SOEs throughout the world went into decline. The 1970s were a decisive turning point. In the 1980s the trend accelerated, and by the 1990s even China, one of the few remaining national societies ostensibly dedicated to Marxism, was steadily promoting the capitalist sector. This was a transformation that neither Marx nor Schumpeter anticipated, although the latter's "warnings" touched on some of the problems that SOEs and centrally planned economies had encountered.[3]

In many cases, SOEs had failed to achieve levels of efficiency in the use of labor and capital that would enable them to compete with private enterprise. Political controls in Italy, France, Spain, and elsewhere imposed constraints on SOEs that made them ultimately dependent on subsidies to remain in business. The quality of their goods and services fell short of what consumers demanded. Not all the SOEs were this unsuccessful. But even in countries like Great Britain, where they compiled "a defensible record" in some infrastructure industries, SOEs found it difficult to respond to the changing economic environment of the 1970s and 1980s.

SOEs were not alone in this regard. Many of the world's largest capitalist enterprises found that the competition and inflation of those decades made successful SOE operations impossible. But in the private sector, market discipline brought about relatively quick corrections when companies were unable to compete. SOEs found it difficult to change either their strategies or their structures quickly. The changes hurt too many interested parties too deeply to expect rapid adjustments in democratic societies.

Throughout Europe, the approach of economic unification accelerated the decline of the remaining state enterprises. The Maastricht conditions left most governments struggling to reduce their deficits and put their fiscal and monetary policies in better order. In effect, governments were sometimes compelled to sell their nationalized firms in order to raise the cash they needed to meet the Maastricht requirements. They could no longer afford to support inefficient enterprises that would shortly face stiff competition from firms in other European countries and overseas. The privatization movement swept through Western Europe.

While unfortunate experiences with SOEs and fiscal crises were the

---

[3] Here it should be recognized that Marx, unlike Schumpeter, generally avoided any detailed discussion of his vision of the future. His occasional remarks that can be interpreted as prognostication (such as those in the Critique of the Gotha Program, never intended for publication) were broad and general. Sometimes they are better read as poetry than as serious attempts to analyze future prospects.

prime movers, the ideology of planning also suffered a serious decline. The rise of Communism and the military, technological, and economic accomplishments of the Soviet Union had once lent strength to that belief system; now the collapse of the Soviet Union and of Communist regimes in Eastern Europe and elsewhere undercut this ideology. Failures in central planning had more devastating effects than market failures in particular industries, as the entire world could see in the news coming from the formerly Communist states.

GROWTH RECORD OF THE FREE ECONOMIES

Alhough one of the goals of SOE had been facilitation of growth, by the 1980s it was beginning to become clear that this is an illusory hope. The fact is that free enterprise, with all its warts and blemishes, has been able to achieve long-term growth rates not remotely paralleled in human history or in any contemporary or nearly contemporary form of economic organization. In the industrial economies it has yielded levels of productivity and per capita income that also are totally unprecedented. This observation about entire economies suggested the inference that something similar is true about individual enterprises – that there is no substitute for the profit motive and the rigors of fierce competition in eliciting growth of output, productivity, and innovation from the individual firm. Free enterprise has brought with it inequality, unemployment, business fluctuations, and a number of other unfortunate consequences, but it can be estimated to have increased per capita income in the United States more than tenfold and in other countries by an even greater multiple in the course of two centuries. And this after fifteen centuries in which, taken as a whole, per capita incomes probably grew very little – if at all.

The most extreme consequence was the upheaval in the nations that claimed to be Marxist, where the populations clamored for the living standards they identified with the capitalist economies. In economies that followed the "middle way," it is arguable that similar beliefs added to the pressures for privatization.

TRENDS AND PROSPECTS

What about the future? Will this new trend away from SOE and toward dependence on the private sector continue? If so, how long? Here we obviously proceed at our peril. Whatever forecast we venture to offer is all too likely to prove wrong in detail or even in its entirety. Yet there are trends and developments that are at least suggestive. In the short and middle terms, we believe that the rush to the private sector will continue and even accelerate. Intense global competition is putting financial pressure on firms and governments to remain flexible and innovative. There is no sign that this pressure will abate in the foreseeable future. Less sure of ourselves than either Schumpeter or Marx, we do not think any particular economic development is "inevitable." We are certain that it will not be a linear trend in democratic societies. There will be pressures again to protect the security of particular groups who are suffering the effects of economic change; there will be demands that a more equitable distribution of power, wealth, and income be instituted through SOE. These pressures may well give the privatization movement a cyclical pattern of development somewhat like the pattern that accompanied the rise of SOE and the regulatory state. Already in the former Soviet economies, resistance to continued economic reform is arising as a consequence of the transition hardships and disappointed expectations attributable in part to failure by the politicians to explain the length of time needed for free enterprise to achieve its growth miracles, as well as the blood, tears, and sweat required in the interim. Recession in Western Europe and East Asia may also lead to similar demands for increased intervention by the state, to a slowdown in privatization, and to further restriction of the freedom of action of the privatized firms.

Over the long term, however, it seems plausible that it will be difficult to resist the appeal of a private sector that has demonstrated two remarkable strengths: first, the ability to use capital and labor efficiently to produce the goods and services that people want; and second, the capacity to adjust successfully to new technologies, new sciences, new patterns of competition, and even new governmental environments. The capacity to sustain innovation over the long term is a market-oriented economy's greatest strength, which brings us full circle back to Joseph A. Schumpeter, who would applaud the fall of SOE even though he did not predict it.

REFERENCE

Schumpeter, J. A. 1942. *Capitalism, socialism, and democracy*. New York.

Index

additionality, 37n7
aerospace industry, France, 190, 202
aircraft industry: Britain, 165, 166;
  France, 187-8, 201-2
airline industry, France, 188-9, 205
Alchian, A. A., 64, 176
Amato, Giuliano, 35
Andeweg, R. B., 262-3
antistatism, United States, 292-4
Arthur, W. Brian, 89
Attlee, Clement, 18
automobile industry: Britain, 166;
  France, 188, 201, 205; Germany,
  116-17, 124-5; Italy, 130, 151;
  Spain, 224-7

Bacon, Francis, 84
Balladur, Edouard, 34, 201
Balogh, Brian, 292
banking system: Austria, 238, 241;
  France, 187, 188, 190, 192, 196-7,

205; Germany, 109; Italy, 129-30,
  141; Netherlands, 259; Spain, 233
Beneduce, Alberto, 130, 143-4, 147,
  148, 154
benefits, social, 51
best practices, national variations,
  38
Bishop, M., 178
Bismarck, Otto von, 106
Bombay Plan, India, 20
Bonelli, Franco, 140
Borcherding, T. E., 59
Bös, D., 51
Botero, Giovanni, 87
Bowles, Chester, 286
British Broadcasting Corporation
  (BBC), 168
British Electricity Authority (BEA),
  168
British Transport Commission (BTC),
  168

Brougham, Henry, 87
Buchanan, J. M., 176

Cadman Report, Britain, 165
Callaghan, John, 18
Carey, Henry, 92
Caves, D. W., 57-8
Central Electricity Board, Britain, 164, 168-9
Chadeau, E., 6
chemicals industry: France, 203; Netherlands, 259
Chirac, Jacques, 34, 201
Christiansen, L. R., 57-8
Cianci, Ernesto, 133, 139, 154
Citroën, André, 196
club goods: state as provider of, 43-4
coal industry: Britain, 158, 164-8; France, 189, 198-9, 203; Germany, 120-3; Netherlands, 255-6, 259-60
Colbert, Jean-Baptiste, 33
commonweal concept, 74, 86-7
Compagnie du Canal de Panama failure, 196
Conti, Ettore, 143

David, Paul, 89
Davies, D. G., 58-9
Defense Plant Corporation, United States, 286
De Gaulle, Charles, 188
denationalization, 43; in France (1986-7), 201-2; policies in Latin America related to, 22
deregulation: in Federal Republic of Germany, 121
developing countries: performance of SOEs in, 62
Dosi, Giovanni, 90
Dunkerley, J., 175

Economic and Monetary Union (EMU), 219
economic development: growth-inducing activities for, 87-9; obligatory passage point, 91, 94; role of Renaissance state enterprises in, 93-5; role of state in early, 84
economic growth: activity-specific, 82, 87, 91; idea of nationalization to promote, 8; Renaissance tradition, 76-81; state as promoter of, 81-4; state role during Renaissance, 89
economic theory: neoclassical theory, 90; new growth theory, 89-90, 96; new trade theory, 89-90; role of Renaissance state in light of, 89-93
efficiency: allocative and dynamic, 50-2; as criterion for performance, 50-1; x-efficiency, 51, 170; x-inefficiency, 51
Eisenhower administrations, 287, 290-1, 293
electric industry: Austria, 238; Britain, 151, 158, 159-64; France, 19, 189, 195; Germany, 107-9, 111-13, 121, 124; Italy, 130, 132, 143-4; Spain, 231-2
entrepreneurs, and state entrepreneurship; in Renaissance economics, 84
equity concept: related to French nationalization, 198-201
European Union (EU) (formerly EEC): Austria's membership in, 251; effect of Spain's membership in, 215, 233-4; influence on French public sector, 202; interest in

telecommunications and postal services, 265-6; rules related to SOEs, 26-7

European Unit Act (1986), 205

Fanfani, Amintore, 132, 146-7
financial groups, France, 190
Finsinger, J., 59
firms, private: Austria, 243; compared to SOEs, 54-62; determinants of performance, 62-7; manufacturing sector (1950-85), 171; in Spain's oil industry, 228-30
firms, x-inefficient, 51
Fokker, Antony, 257
Franco, Francisco, 210, 214
Franco regime, Spain, 216, 232-3
Freeman, Christopher, 90
Freycinet Plan, 194
Friedman, M., 176
Furet, François, 206

Galal, A., 61
Galbraith, John Kenneth, 286
Gardini, Raul, 32
gas industry: Britain, 158, 159-65; France, 189; Germany, 107-9, 113, 124; Netherlands, 259-60
gold standard, 96
government intervention: as entrepreneur, 40-2; France, 33, 185-6; during German Weimar Republic, 14; in Italian history, 133-42; Netherlands, 254-7; in nineteenth-century Britain, 159-60; Spain, 210-13; unsuccessful, 96. *See also* state entrepreneurship
government intervention, United States: antistatism movement,

292-4; factors influencing demands for, 281-3
Graham, Frank, 92
Grayson, L. E., 55
Greasley, D., 167
Grossman, Gene, 89

Hamilton, Alexander, 11, 40
Hare, P. G., 175
Helpman, Elhanan, 89
Heyworth Committee, Britain, 165
Hirschman, Albert O., x, 74, 90
holding companies: France, 189; Italy, 143-4
Homestead Act (1862), United States, 280
Hoover Commission, United States, 287-8

Iheduru, O. C., 66
import substitution, 95
income distribution, 81
industrialized countries: obligatory passage point in, 91; role of state in, 84
industrial policy: Britain, 164; importance of collective interests, 41; Italy, 32, 133-42; Netherlands, 259-62
industrial sector: industry rescue as reason for nationalization, 8-9; Italian state intervention to develop, 140-1; nationalization (1981) and denationalization (1986-7), 200-4; during Nazi regime in Germany, 115-18; regulation in Britain (1920s, 1930s), 159; Spanish post-World War II state-owned firms, 210-13; state-owned firms in Austria, 238-40. *See also* INI (Industrial

industrial sector (*cont.*)
National Agency), Spain; Institute
for Industrial Reconstruction (IRI),
Italy; *specific industries*
industrial sector, Netherlands:
post-World War II industrial policy,
259-62; technology policy, 262,
263-4
infrastructure sector: British
nationalized firms (1950-85), 171;
U.S. productivity (1938-77),
171-3
INI (Industrial National Agency),
Spain: automobile industry, 227;
creation of public sector firms
(1940-84), 210-15; under EEC
regulation, 234; electric industry,
231-2; iron and steel industry,
220-2; oil industry, 229; origin, 16;
reprivatization policy (1984),
215-16; shipbuilding sector,
222-4; transportation and
communication, 232-3
Institute for Industrial
Reconstruction (IRI), Italy, 32;
origin, 16; as permanent public
agency, 143; role in Italian
economy, 142; state shareholding
company, 128-30
Institute of Economic Affairs (IEA),
175-6
institutions: influence of privatization
on, 35-6; provision by the state,
81
interest groups: influence in
European PTT markets, 266-8;
politics of subsidies in United
States, 290-1, 294
International Monetary Fund (IMF):
effort to increase private sector

role, 68; privatization
recommendations, 49
IRI. *See* Institute for Industrial
Reconstruction (IRI), Italy
iron and steel industry: Austria, 238;
France, 189, 205; Spain, 220-2.
See also steel industry
Iron Law of Subsidies, United States,
290-1, 294-5

Jeanneney, Jean-Marcel, 203
Jefferson, Thomas, 276
Johnson, Lyndon B., 287
Jordan, W. A., 59

Kaldor, Nicholas, 80
Kennedy, John F., 287
Keynes, John Maynard, 12, 96
Kikeri, S., 59-60
Krugman, Paul, 89

Lacina, Ferdinand, 250
land, France: nationalization of
subsoil, 198-9
land industry, United States: Hoover
Commission recommendations,
288; privatization debate, 295; role
of federal government, 283-4,
288-9; sales during nineteenth
century, 276-7; as SOE, 280,
283-4
Latin America: denationalization
policies, 22; state intervention, 17
Leibenstein, H., 51
List, Friedrich, 11
Littlechild, S. C., 176
London Transport Passenger Board
(LPTB), Britain, 164, 169
Loucheur, Louis, 196
Lucas, Robert, Jr., 90
Luraghi, Giuseppe, 151

Maaastricht Agreement, *ix*, 205
McCraw, Thomas K., 285
Mcgowan Committee, Britain, 165, 166
machinery–manufacturing sector, Italy, 130–2
Madelin, Alain, 34
manufacturing sector: private firms (1950–85), 171; U.S. prouctivity growth (1950–85), 171–3
Maraffi, Marco, 143–4
market economy: failure as justification for state role, 29; failure as reason for nationalization, 7; long-term economic growth of, 308
Marshall, Alfred, 90, 92
Marshall Plan: in Austria, 245; in France, 199
Marx, Karl, 12
match industry, Spain, 208
Mattei, Enrico, 130, 132, 145–7, 149
Mauroy, Pierre, 19
Millward, R., 59
Mining Code (1811), France, 193
Ministry of International Trade and Industry (MITI), Japan, 21
Mitterrand, François, 31, 190, 201
multinational companies, France, 190
Mussolini, Benito, 142, 144

National Coal Board (NBC), Britian, 168
Nationalisation Acts (1945–9), Britain, 168
nationalism, postwar Italy, 145–6
nationalization: economic reasons for, 7–9; motives for, 5–9; in Netherlands before and after World War I, 15, 17; political and

ideological reasons for, 5–6; post–World War I Germany, 109–10
nationalization, Austria: ÖIAG (Österrichische Industrieholding Aktiengesellschaft), 245, 249-51; post–World War II, 19; rationale for post–World War II, 238–9, 241, 249
nationalization, Britain: before and after World War I, 15, 17; criticisms of, 175–6; of enterprises in postwar, 158, 163; post–World War II, 18; steel industry, 167
nationalization, France, 17; before and after World War I, 15, 17, 186–8; banks and insurance companies (1945–6), 198; of electric power (1946), 198, 199; equity concept, 198-201; as a means of protection, 200; post–World War II, 18-19, 188–9; roots in French Revolution, 191–4; third peak (1981), 189–90
nationalization, Italy: before and after World War I, 15; post–World War II, 19-20; role of state entrepreneur, 133–47
nationalization, Spain: before and after World War I, 15; post–World War II, 210-13; of transportation and communications, 232–3
Nehru, Jawaharal, 20
New York Port Authority, 289
Nitti, Francesco Saveno, 144

obligatory passage point, 91
oil industry: Austria, 238; France, 198-9, 199, 203; Germany, 120; Italy, 146, 151

oil industry, Spain, 227-31
Osti, Gian Lupo, 148

Parker, D., 178
Peacock, Alan, 176
Peirce, Charles Sanders, 80
Peltzman, S., 64
Perroux, François, 90
Plesman, Albert, 257
policy networks: in the bargaining state, 38-9; concept of, 37; in the expert state, 38; influence on policy making, 39-40; in mercantilist framework, 37-8; as policy bottlenecks, 40; in the referee state, 38
politics: of Austrian SOEs, 240-1, 243-5; of French nationalization, 190-1, 199-200; of Italian state ownership, 34-5; of nationalization, 5-6; of policy networks, 38-9; of privatization, 31; of SOEs, 52, 66-7; of state intervention in Italy, 146-7, 149-50
Pompidou, Georges, 202, 204
Porter, Michael, 90
postal services: Britain, 150; France, 194-5; Germany, 104-5, 110-11, 123. *See also* PTT (post, telegraph, and telephone)
Post Office Department, United States: Hoover Commission recommendations (1949), 287-8; as SOE, 279-80
Prest, Alan, 176
private sector: development in France (1969-74), 202; economic growth in nineteenth-century United States, 279; IMF and World Bank efforts to increase, 68; predictions for future of, 309. *See also* firms, private
privatization: Austria, 241; domestic and international causes, 26; elements in process of, 30-1; government revenues from, 65; implication for the state, 43-4; Italy, 34-5, 129, 133; neoliberal view, 27-9; opportunities for, 30-1; Spain, 220-2; variation in outcomes, 32
privatization, Britain: firms privatized (1979-91), 177; sales of public enterprises, 21, 27
privatization, France: rationale for, 34; reversal in (1980s), 31; sales of nationalized firms (1986-96), 186; sales of public enterprises, 21-2
privatization, Germany, 28; East Germany, 45; in Federal Republic, 121-3; post-World War II, 119-20, 122-3
privatization, Netherlands: interest group influence, 266-8; as part of technology policy, 262
privatization, United States: debate related to public land, 295; during Reagan era, 294-6
productivity growth, Britain, 171-2
property rights, 176; in an SOE, 63-4; in France, 191-2; incentives influenced by structure of, 63-4; private property provided by the state, 81
PTT (post, telegraph, and telephone), Netherlands: EU policy related to, 265-6; pressure to privatize, 266-8; privatization, 263, 269-71

public enterprises: at central and local levels, 4–5; decline (1963–90), 21–2; history of, 10–14; national/federal and industrial sector, 4; nationalization before and after World War I, 14–17; within and outside Europe, 13–14; in post–World War II Germany and Japan, 20–1; in post–World War II Canada and Australia, 20; post–World War II nationalization, 18–21; in Renaissance state, 93–5; in United States, 11–13

public policy: changes in ideology in economic policy (1980s), 264; in privatized economy, 35–42; related to SOEs, 51–2. *See also* industrial policy; policy networks

public sector, France: denationalization (1986–7), 201–2; enlargement by degranting, 197–8; enlargement by purchase through legislation, 198; goals for industrial part, 198; goals of reformers (1981), 200; long-term debt (1980s), 204; start-up of new public firms, 198

public sector firms: post–World War II creation, 210–12; Spanish firms in context of five European countries, 209–10

railroads: Britain, 158, 159, 164, 166; France, 187–8, 194, 200; Germany, 106–7, 110–11, 123–4; Italy, 128; Spain, 210; United States, 291n11

Railways Act (1921), Britain, 164

Ramamurti, R., 53

Rathenau, Emil, 105

Reagan administrations, 294–5

regulation: in nineteenth-century France, 192; Spain, 216

regulatory state: American model, 11–13, 36; post-privatization, 36–7; post–World War I Britain, 159–62

Reid Committee, 167–8

Renaissance economics: arguments for policy intervention, 86–9; role of public enterprises in, 93–5; the state and private sector in, 84–9; state in light of recent, 89–93

Renault, Louis, 196

resource distribution: as reason for nationalization, 9

reverse salients concept, 91

risk: state as distributor of, 81

Romeo, Rosario, 128

Roosevelt, Franklin D., 284–5

rule of law: provided by the state, 81

Sallinger, Rudolf, 245

salt industry, Netherlands, 257, 259

Samuel Commission, Britain, 165

San Francisco Harbor Commission, 293

Sankey Commission, Britain, 165

Saraceno, Pasquale, 143–4, 150–1

Schneider, Eugène, 196

Schumpeter, Joseph, 80, 303–4, 307, 309

Schurz, Carl, 280

Serra, Antonio, 76, 86, 89

shipbuilding: Netherlands, 260–1; Spain, 210, 222–4

shipping companies, France, 188

Shonfield, Andrew, 143–4

Short, R. P., 9

Sinigaglia, Oscar, 130, 145, 148–9, 151

Smith, Adam, 78, 85, 86
Sombart, Werner, 93-4
Stanbury, W. T., 58
state, the: bargaining state, 38-9;
debate in Western countries over
role of, *x*; distribution of income
and risk by, 81; economic
development role, 84; expert state,
38-9; history of direct economic
activities of, 10-14; income
distribution, 81; in industrialized
countries, 84; post-Renaissance
role, 85; with privatization, 27-9;
in a privatized economy, 35-42;
promotion of economic growth by,
81-2; as provider of club goods,
43-4; provision of institutions, 81;
referee state, 38-9; in Renaissance
economics, 74, 84-5; reshaping
with decline of SOEs, 36-7. *See
also* government intervention
state enterprises: history in France,
191-201
state enterprises, Britain: at
municipal level, 160-4; vesting
dates, 158
state entrepreneurship: categories of
activities, 9-10; in Italian history,
133-47; role of, 40-6; survival and
prospects, 42-6
state holding companies, Germany,
113-14
state ownership: decline of, 42-3;
defined, 40-1; different national
routes to reduce, 31; function of,
45-6; in global economy, 42-6;
multilevel, 45; in nineteenth- and
twentieth-century Germany, 44-5,
103-18; in postwar France, 33, 41;

process of decreasing, 30-5
state-owned enterprises (SOEs):
Britain, 158; compared to private
firms, 54-62; decline (1970s-
1990s), 306-8; determinants of
performance, 62-7; under EU
rules, 26-7; to facilitate economic
growth, 308; financial
performance, 547; during German
Nazi regime, 115-18; improved
postprivatization performance, 62;
Italy (1930s), 128; motivations for
Renaissance, 93-4; as obligatory
passage point, 94; origins of,
304-6; performance before and
after privatization, 60;
performance in developing
countries, 62; range of activities,
9-10; from Renaissance to end of
nineteenth century, 10-11; social
objectives, 51-3; subsidies through
price mechanism of, 66-7. *See
also* public enterprises; state
enterprises; state shareholding
system, Italy
state-owned enterprises (SOEs),
Austria: competition with private
firms, 243; factors influencing
reorganization of, 248-9; influence
of political parties, 240-8; losses
(1978-85), 249-50; privatization
process, 250-1; tradition and role
of, 238-43
state-owned enterprises (SOEs),
France: as investors and
borrowers, 199; oil companies,
199
state-owned enterprises (SOEs),
Germany: coal companies, 121-2;

in Federal Republic of Germany,
118–23; gas and electric utilities,
107–9; history, 103–4; liquidation
in postwar, 123–5; during Nazi
regime, 115–18; postal service,
104–5; railways, 106–7; savings
banks, 109
state-owned enterprises (SOEs),
Netherlands: post-1982
privatization, 262–3; post-World
War II, 259–61; pre-World War II,
254–8
state-owned enterprises (SOEs),
Spain: decline in number
(1963–74), 214–15; in industrial
sector, 212–13
state-owned enterprises (SOEs),
United States: history of, 273–97;
hostility toward, 280–1; of New
York Port Authority, 289; shift
away from idea of, 289–94; state-
level governments creating, 283;
Tennessee Valley Authority, 284–5,
290, 293
state shareholding system, Italy: as
conglomerate, 147–52; crisis,
138–9; formation, 128–9, 132,
146; sectors participating in,
132–3
steel industry: Britain, 167; Germany,
115–18, 120, 124; Italy, 130, 145,
150–1
Steenbergen Commission,
Netherlands, 269–70
Suanzes, J. A., 210, 212, 213, 214
subsidies: to Dutch industrial sector,
260–1; government as source in
United States of, 279–80; Iron Law
of Subsidies in United States, 290,

294–5; through SOE price
mechanism, 66–7
Swarttouw Commission, Netherlands,
269

telecommunications, Spain, 210
telephone and telegraph system,
France, 194–5
Tennessee Valley Authority (TVA),
United States, 284–5, 290, 293
Thatcher, Margaret, 27, 33, 34
Thompson, F., 58
tobacco industry, Spain, 208, 232–3
Tobin, Austin, 289
transportation sector: Britain,
159–64, 168; France, 199; Spain,
232–3; United States, 277–8
Treaty of Rome, 26–7
Truman, Harry S., 287

van Zanden, Jan, 253
Vickers, J., 59
Vico, Giambattista, 80
von Stephan, Heinrich, 105

Wagner, Adolf, 12
Wassenaar Agreement, Netherlands,
261–2
water supply, Britain, 158–65
Weimar Constitution (1919),
Germany, 110
Weir Committee, 165
welfare: activity-specific nature of
economic, 82; in cost-benefit
analysis, 51; mechanisms related to
growth and distribution of
economic, 76–81
White, Leonard D., 280, 288
Whitney, Eli, 94
Williamson Committee, Britain, 165

Wilson, Harold, 18

Wiseman, Jack, 176

World Bank: arguments for private enterprise, 62; data related to privatization, 25-6; efforts to increase private sector role, 49-50, 68; study of state firms with private management, 61

x-efficiency concept, 51, 170

x-inefficiency, 51

Yarrow, G., 59